* *Quiet Pilgrimage*

Also by Elizabeth Gray Vining

I, Roberta
Flora
Take Heed of Loving Me
Friend of Life: The Biography of Rufus M. Jones
Windows for the Crown Prince
The Virginia Exiles
Return to Japan
The World in Tune

By Elizabeth Janet Gray

Meggy MacIntosh
Jane Hope
Young Walter Scott
Beppy Marlowe
Penn
The Fair Adventure
Adam of the Road
Sandy
The Cheerful Heart
I Will Adventure

Quiet Pilgrimage

by

Elizabeth Gray Vining

J. B. LIPPINCOTT COMPANY
Philadelphia / New York

✳ *Contents*

Photographs follow page 186.

*PART *I*.

✷✷✷✷✷✷✷✷✷✷✷✷✷✷✷✷✷✷✷✷✷✷✷✷✷✷✷✷✷

1.

Parents

John

M Y STORY begins in Aberdeen, Scotland, where my father, John Gordon Gray, was born on November 27, 1850. His father, Alexander Gray, was the Aberdeen representative of Virtue and Sons, publishers and booksellers of London, a firm which had considerable standing in its day. The whole family, root and branch, was a bookish one, with whom reading was an addiction. An uncle of mine carried a book in his pocket to his brother-in-law's funeral, lest he become bored and be stranded without anything to read.

My father's mother, Janet Callam, had Highland blood, and a touch of what used to be called "second sight." My Aunt Christine told me the story of the meeting of Alexander and Janet. On Halloween Janet and some other girls, following an old custom and superstition, ate hard-boiled eggs that had been heavily salted, walked upstairs backwards and went to bed without speaking. The men who brought them water in their dreams would be the men they were to marry. In the morning they told their dreams. I know nothing about the experience of the other girls, but Janet was disconsolate. The man who offered her a cup of water was no one she had ever seen before. Months passed. The following summer she visited her aunt and uncle in the Highlands. One afternoon, as she sat on the lawn under a tree, sewing, her uncle brought a young man to her, saying, "Janet, this is a young friend of mine who has torn his coat. Could you put a stitch in for him?"

She looked up—and saw the man of her Halloween dream, "the handsomest man that walked the kirk road." She mended his coat for him, and when she had finished he said that he could not tell where it had been torn.

They were married, presumably in 1849 or early 1850, for my father was their first child, the eldest of eleven, all of whom lived to grow up. John, Alexander, James, Robert, Andrew, Isabella and Christine were born in Scotland; Georgina, William, Charles and Thomas in Philadelphia. Charles was not so bright as the rest; William was the black sheep—he ran away from home, married a Roman Catholic and was heard of no more, except in occasional whispers. The family was strongly Presbyterian, except for their father, who gloried in being an atheist, and my father, who became a lukewarm Episcopalian.

The first daughter, Isabella, was named for Isabel Braik, an adored grandmother of legendary charm and beauty who had four tall brothers, all devoted to her; whenever she went out, they accompanied her in a body. Isabel's daughter Jessie was courted by two cousins, both named Alexander Callam. When she accepted one of them, the other said, "Very well, Jessie, I'll come back for your daughter." And off he went to Canada to make his fortune. Twenty years later, a substantial citizen of Windsor, Ontario, he returned and married her daughter Margaret, who was the sister of Janet Callam, my grandmother.

There was on my grandfather's side an Uncle Duff, who had a farm in Aberdeenshire which they all loved to visit, and another relative, Alexander Duff, who went to India as a Presbyterian missionary and won considerable recognition in missionary circles in his day. There was extant in my childhood an all but unreadable book which he wrote about his spiritual ministrations to the heathen. He was evidently badly frightened by the Sepoy Rebellion of 1857–58; when the British Army suppressed it, he wrote triumphantly, "Now the wretches will know the might of the British people!"

Janet and Alexander with their growing family lived in Old Aberdeen, then quite separate from the main borough of Aberdeen, with its own provost, council, trade guilds and so on. They had a house with a garden, and the raising of flowers was a family passion second only to reading. Janet had a concern for their poorer neighbors, on whom she used to bestow baskets of food. She took John with her to carry the basket, and the expeditions were made in secret since her husband did not approve, whether from stinginess or an enlightened distrust of the Lady Bountiful complex or as part of his atheism, I do not know. They had a dog, a large collie named Duchess, who was an important member of the family. An oil portrait of Duchess carrying a basket of flowers in her mouth was one of the treasures that accompanied them to America.

Janet, who had a wide and tender heart, had also an inquiring mind. When a famous doctor came to Aberdeen and offered a series of "Health Lectures" to married women, Janet signed up for the course. He had a model of a uterus, which could be opened to show the foetus inside, and an assistant whose function was to apply restoratives to the ladies who fainted dead away at the sight of that terrifying object. The doctor was undismayed by the havoc he wrought. "A glass of water here, Richard," he would cry, "A glass of water over there!" and would go right on with his lecture. Janet stayed the course to the end, fascinated and instructed. She must have learned things other than embryology, for it was to those lectures in "Health" that she ascribed her skill in nursing.

My father and his next younger brother, Alec, were inseparable. Alec was to die in his young manhood, and my father's grief at the loss of his favorite brother was vivid to me as a child forty years later. The two as boys in Aberdeen prided themselves on their hardiness and went swimming in the North Sea throughout the winter, taking with them a crust of bread for a "shivery bit" on which to fasten their chattering teeth when they came out of the icy water. Up to his last illness, when the doctor put an end to it, my father took a cold bath every morning of his life, a practice he tried in vain to inculcate in his daughters. Violet screamed so loud that it was feared the neighbors would intervene; I was so obviously pusillanimous that he gave up on me with scarcely a struggle.

John and Alec, and probably James too, attended the Aberdeen Grammar School, a very old institution, the direct descendant of a medieval burgh school. In 1863 it acquired a handsome new building in the Scottish baronial style, with a statue in the front quadrangle of George Gordon, who attended the school from 1794 to 1798, when he inherited the title of Lord Byron and departed for England. The tradition is that my father sat at a wooden form on which young Gordon had carved his initials. As Byron had a passion all his life for carving his name on all kinds of places, including a column on the temple at Sunion, he probably did carve it more than once on convenient surfaces in the Aberdeen Grammar School. In any case Byron was a passion of my father's. Though he was usually puritanical about all forms of immorality, he turned a blind eye on Byron's irregularities of conduct and to the end of his life read and reread his hero's poetry and delighted in the romantic bravery of his death. Once, when a scheduled speaker for a St. Andrew's Society dinner defected at the last moment, my father delivered extemporaneously a lecture on Byron that was remembered by some of the members for years afterwards.

Another feature of Old Aberdeen was King's College, founded in 1494, and in 1860 united with Marischal College of the main borough to make the University of Aberdeen. My father looked forward to entering the University and to becoming ultimately a professor of Classics. This hope faded when he was fifteen and the decision was made for the family to emigrate to America.

One of his masters at the Grammar School, who had taken an interest in him, begged his father to leave John behind with him, to finish at the Grammar School and go on to the University as he longed to do. It was one of those crucial turning points in a life that sometimes pass almost without examination. To the parents, and especially to my grandmother, whose favorite child he was, it was unthinkable that the family should leave the country without their brilliant eldest son. Apparently the offer of the Grammar School master was remembered for its generosity but never seriously considered as a possibility.

Why they decided in 1865, at the end of the Civil War, to emigrate to the United States has never been clear to me. Did Virtue and Sons close their Aberdeen branch? Did my grandfather's weakness for whisky cause him to lose his job? Was his increasing deafness a factor? Or was it the lure of the land of promise?

Alexander Gray had, it is true, been there before. He was actually already an American citizen. As a very young man, before his marriage, he had spent some time in the United States, where an uncle had already settled in Georgia, and he had liked it so well that he had actually taken out citizenship papers. So that my father, as the son of an American citizen, never had to forswear allegiance to Britain, which he often declared he could never have done. The laws must have been much more lax in those days; I do not think that now anyone could carry a double allegiance so easily.

Nor do I know why they decided on Philadelphia; but to Philadelphia they came, with seven children, the eldest of whom was fifteen. They lived for a couple of years on South Thirteenth Street, and my father, his schooling over, worked as a clerk for Folwell Brothers and Company, a textile firm on Market Street. Here he laid the foundation for a knowledge of fibres that years later led to his being called to Washington to give expert advice on those scattered fibres in our paper money that make forgery difficult. His schooling was over, but not his education. All his life he read voluminously in the fields of science, government and literature, and he had a phenomenal memory; the thing that everyone spoke of after his death was his broad knowledge.

After two or three years the Grays acquired a house in what is now called Roxborough, with a garden that ran back from the Ridge toward the valley of the Wissahickon, that wonderful six-mile-long stretch of creek and wooded hills, of winding road and steep trails, that is now a cherished part of Fairmount Park. In the garden of this house there was—or was built—the greenhouse where my grandfather intended to support his family as a wholesale florist.

The business, Alexander Gray and Sons, lasted about ten years. The children had pleasant memories of the house in Roxborough. My father had a horse and used to ride in the Wissahickon, a joy that continued all his life. Within my memory, though he had long since ceased to have a horse of his own, he used to ride every Saturday in the Wissahickon with his friend Theodore Justice, who was a Park Commissioner. They used to put red tags on leaning trees along the drive that needed to be shored up with stone retaining walls. My Aunt Christine, who was born just before they left Scotland, remembered a large and shabby house full of people and of life; besides the family, increased by a new child every other year, there were always guests. The widow of the uncle who went to Georgia and died in the Civil War arrived with a trunkful of Confederate money and stayed for months until she was finally convinced that she could not convert all those lovely bills into gold or even silver. An elderly friend came for two weeks and stayed the rest of her life. Whenever my grandfather came into the house—that house boiling with offspring, guests and neighborhood children—if he did not immediately see his wife he would exclaim, "Where is everybody?"

Even before the florist business had quite petered out, my father had gone to work for James W. Queen and Company, 924 Chestnut Street, which had begun with optical instruments and went on to a variety of scientific instruments—transits, barometers, thermometers, hygrometers, pyrometers and the like. In time he was to do pioneer work in the early development of X rays, or Röntgen rays as they were called then, and he also was involved with the surveying instruments used in building the Trans-Siberian Railroad and those that Peary took with him on his expeditions to Greenland and later to the North Pole. By that time my father was president of the company.

One thing about the Gray family that has always puzzled me is that they had no Scottish accent, not one of them, not even a burred R. Nor did they pick up the Philadelphia twang, not in the first generation at any rate. My Aunt Christine had one of the most beautiful speaking voices and purest accents I have ever heard. My father's accent was distinctly English. My sister and I used often to regret that our father had not a good Scottish burr, for that is regarded in this country as lovable, whereas English broad a's and clipped syllables are "affected" in American ears and put people off. With his deep reserve and formality combined with irascibility, his accent contributed to alienating people from him.

In 1876, the year of the great Centennial Exposition, my father went with a friend of his, Philip Huebner, a young German working for Folwell Brothers, to spend a week end with the Folwell parents in South Jersey near the village of Mullica Hill, an old Quaker settlement about halfway between Camden and Salem. While the two young men were there, Philip took John to a neighboring farm to call on his fiancée, Emily Iszard. Emily was a strikingly lovely girl of seventeen with golden hair and enormous brown eyes. Her younger sister Anne, fifteen, equally beautiful, had dark hair and violet eyes of such intensity and purity of color that she was, romantically, nicknamed Violet.

John Gordon Gray and Anne Moore Iszard were engaged almost immediately but not married for another five years.

Anne

The farm on which my mother spent her childhood was an old one; the earliest part of it, the kitchen end, had been built in 1691, the "new part" in 1783. It had belonged from the beginning to the descendants of Thomas French, Quaker, of Nether Heyford, Northamptonshire, one of the original proprietors of New Jersey, who had come to Burlington in the *Kent* in 1680; but it had gone out of the family for a period when my mother's grandfather, Samuel Ellis French, who lived in Woodstown and owned several farms, lost it by going on a friend's note. The friend had not been able to pay his debt, and the farm was sold to satisfy the creditor. It was a common practice, it seems, in those days, and this was not the only farm which my amiable great-grandfather lost in that way.

His daughter, Mary Elizabeth, at sixteen fell in love with Franklin Iszard, aged twenty. Franklin was also of old South Jersey stock. His ancestor, Michael Iszard, had come from the village of Buckland in the Cotswolds and settled first in Pennsylvania, where he was Collector of the Port of Upland in 1656; but before 1700 he moved to Greenwich, New Jersey, then the port of entry for Philadelphia. A relative went to Charleston, South Carolina, and up until the Civil War there was intermittent correspondence between the two families; but whereas the Charleston Iszards married rich widows, the New Jersey Iszards lost money in glass manufacture.

Young Franklin Iszard, of Clayton, New Jersey, was educated at Lawrenceville Academy and at a small college long since absorbed in Cornell. He had intended to be a teacher until he fell in love with Mary Elizabeth French, who had lustrous black curls and beautiful velvet brown eyes. In the course of his courtship Franklin presented Mary Elizabeth with a handsome tome bound in leather and tooled in gold, entitled *The Republican Court: Or, American Society in the Days of Washington*, with twenty-nine steel engravings of portraits of the wives of the Federal leaders, including Mrs. Ralph Iszard, by Gainsborough, and Mrs. Thomas Randolph, by Sully. He said that Mary Elizabeth resembled Mrs. Thomas Randolph, and indeed, when one looks at the pictures of both, she did.

Mary Elizabeth, who was almost never spoken of by family or friends without the adjective "wonderful," was charming, capable, beautiful, confident, and not in the least intellectual. She considered teaching a very flimsy vocation for a man; to her, land was the only solid foundation. Where the two got the $10,000 to buy the old farm I don't know, but buy it they did, and at twenty and twenty-four they were married. Since she was marrying "out of meeting" they could not have a Quaker wedding, and I suspect that she did not want a Methodist one. Snobbishly speaking, Quakers occupied the top rung on the social ladder of the region; Episcopalians came next, Presbyterians next and after that Methodists. They compromised by both becoming Presbyterians, but that was later. In 1857 they went to Philadelphia and were married by Richard Vaux, who was then Mayor—a way of getting around the difficulty followed by other New Jersey Quakeresses of the same period. Richard Vaux was a well-known Friend. As a young man appointed Secretary to the United States Legation in London, he

had gone to a ball and danced with Princess Victoria; his letter
home caused his mother to shake her head and say, "I do hope
Richard won't marry out of meeting."

The farm lay on a long lane between two roads out of Mullica
Hill and was not visible from either road. It was a lonely place for
small girls, Emily born in 1859 and Anne in 1861. The two boys
did not come for ten years more. There were two tenant houses on
the place, and the Negro tenants, I gather, did much of the hard
work of the farm, which raised wheat, hops and corn, and bred
Patchen horses. My grandfather read aloud to his family in the
evenings from *Paradise Lost* and from the plays of Shakespeare. I
am quite aware that this is a cliché of American farm life in the
nineteenth century and not considered a credible one at that, but
I have still his well-worn folios of Milton and Shakespeare, and
my mother's lifelong love of books and her discerning taste attest
to influences that she could not have got from the schools she attended.

Her first school was a dame school on a farm which was two
miles away through fields and woods and across a brook, a walk
that the little girls loved. The establishment was an odd one. Three
women lived there in apparent concord: the farmer's third wife,
his daughter by his second wife, and the sister of his first wife.
What made it unique was that the first wife's sister carried on the
school for the benefit of the illegitimate daughter of the second
wife's daughter who, by reason of her shame, was a shadowy and
mysterious figure to the children. My mother learned to read at the
school by pricking out with a pin the letters in the newspaper, and
she learned the capitals of the states of the United States and the
rivers on which they were situated by chanting in singsong, "Maine,
Augusta, Kennebec River, New Hampshire, Concord, Merrimac
River," and so on to the end. When she had absorbed all that she
could from this school, she went on to the district school, of which
she never had much to say.

She loved the beauty of that flat countryside, the wide expanse of
sky, the clouds, the fields, the cedars growing along the snake
fences, the woods with their wild flowers in spring, the occasional
excursions into the pine barrens, where they wound along the
creek in a boat with a sheet spread over it in which to shake down
the huckleberries that hung over the water. She liked the farm, the
baby animals, the fragrance of ripe hop blossoms, the old brick
house with the big kitchen where once friendly Indians used to

stop in for breakfast, the mahogany chest of drawers in her room especially made by a cabinetmaker for her grandmother's sixteenth birthday in 1816. She enjoyed the farm food—rich cream, oysters brought in a barrel from Bivalve and kept in the cellar and fed on corn meal, guinea fowl, little yellow tomatoes preserved with lemon and ginger, angel food and devil's food cake, sunshine cake, homemade root beer, and on and on, a variety and a richness that caused her to look upon the Gray fare with horror when she encountered it. "They ate nothing but boiled mutton, boiled potatoes and boiled cabbage!" she was to exclaim all her life. That was what they liked. She would talk nostalgically of the farm as long as she lived, but she never wanted to go back to the country. It was too lonely.

An important personage in her girlhood was Cousin Lydia Folwell, the mother of William and Nathan of Folwell Brothers. Occasionally Anne had the joy of going to Philadelphia to visit Cousin William and his wife in their large and hospitable house on Columbia Avenue. She rejoiced in Philadelphia as the seat of unimagined cultural attractions, one of which was an art show that impressed her greatly. Some enterprising man brought oil paintings from Europe, which he displayed one by one on an easel in a lecture hall, and discoursed about them. The hall was packed, and those who sat at the back used opera glasses to see the wonders of art. At the Folwells' house Anne met Philip Huebner, and he gave her Tennyson's poems in two calfbound volumes. But she was only thirteen then, and when he visited Cousin Lydia Folwell near Mullica Hill and came to the farm, he saw and fell in love with Emily, two years older. Still the Tennyson must have been useful when, later, Anne met John and charmed him not only with her violet eyes but with her love for and knowledge of poetry.

In the same year that Anne first met John and became engaged to him, she went to Philadelphia for the great Centennial Exposition held in Fairmount Park; she stayed a week and she saw everything: Memorial Hall, where the collection of paintings belonging to a distant cousin, Mrs. Bloomfield Moore, was displayed; Machinery Hall, where the Emperor of Brazil spoke on a fabulous new instrument called a telephone; Agricultural Hall; Horticultural Hall; and many other wonders. Especially she remembered with pleasure the Japanese exhibit of lacquer, cloisonné and porcelain, where the young men who were the commissioners were so very polite and charming. They gave her a colored picture of a group of vases which she had framed and kept always. Long after my mother's death I met in Japan one of those young men, then a very old man and a famous one. It was Yokichi Mikimoto, the Pearl King, who had invented a way to grow cultured pearls and made a fortune out of the process. I was having lunch with him in his house high on the hill over the bay at Toba where the "Pearl Farm" was, and he told me that he had first seen my country when he went to Philadelphia to the Centennial in 1876.

Though they became engaged when Anne was fifteen and John twenty-five, they were not married for another five years. In spite of having a good job with a good firm, in spite of being engaged to a girl whose idea of heaven was to live in the city, my father in 1878 threw up his job with James W. Queen and Company and went to Kansas to try his fortune at sheep ranching, one of those occasional impetuous acts that his family deplored. Two of his brothers, Robert and Andrew, had already gone West and later were to prosper in Oklahoma; my father had discovered in himself a love for horses and for riding. Perhaps, tied down too young to earning money to support himself and help his family, he longed for freedom and adventure before he settled down for life.

It was not a success and within two years he was back again working for James W. Queen and Company, but he loved to remember his time in Kansas and to talk about it. As a child I heard about the beauty of those seas of grass without any trees, and about the great storms that would sweep over the prairie, how my father would dismount from his horse so as not to be the highest object anywhere about and lie down in the grass, while the lightning forked into the ground all around him. Once, thrown by his horse when it was frightened by a prairie dog popping out of its hole at its feet, he fell on his head and was knocked unconscious. He never knew how long he lay there before he was found by a German settler who picked him up, took him to his cabin and nursed him back to consciousness. All his life after that he was subject to periodic devastating headaches, which were possibly a result of that concussion. Many years later by some chance he heard again from this rescuer, who had moved away from Kansas; by that time the man was very old and was having trouble with his eyes—he could no longer read the newspaper. My father took pleasure in sending him one of Queen and Company's best and most powerful magnifying glasses.

The florist business had come to an end. James had gone to Pittsburgh, where he became a successful lawyer; the other sons were in the West. My grandfather, by now stone-deaf, retired from active life and was supported by his sons. He and my grandmother wound up on a little place outside of Vineland, New Jersey, where he divided his time between raising flowers for fun and reading the *Encyclopedia Britannica* through each year from beginning to end. By the time he reached Z, he had forgotten A and would start in again with zest. I remember him vividly, though I was only four when he died. He was tall and handsome, with deep-set fierce gray eyes and a long white beard. He looks in my mind's eye like Michelangelo's God Separating the Heavenly Bodies, a much more severe deity than his benevolent God Creating Adam or God Dividing the Waters. I recognized my grandfather instantly when I saw him on the roof of the Sistine Chapel. And like God he was all-seeing.

I remember going with him into the garden to pick strawberries. The sun was warm; the berries half-hidden under their green leaves were scarlet and glistening. I had been told to pick only the red ones, but one that was brilliant on the side towards me proved in my hand to be green underneath. Guiltily I tried to put it back on the plant again. Aware of something in the atmosphere, I looked up, and there, bending down toward me, just like God dividing the heavenly bodies, were those brilliant eyes and that accusing beard. "I saw you!" he thundered.

I know now that he was amused, but in that moment of terror I was face to face with the angry Jehovah and I expected fire and flood.

My grandmother was altogether different; little and dear and blithe, crippled with rheumatism, she sat all day in her chair, reading and sewing. If anybody did anything to annoy her, she would exclaim, "Oh, the great donkey!" seize her Bible and read it furiously until she was calm again. She had a fund of Highland stories and sayings of which I remember two. One was said of any stormy night: "Eh sirs, it's a wild night for a soul to be flitting!" The other applied when anyone was overapprehensive of disaster. "Aye," she would say scornfully, "and if the sky should fall and crush *one* laverock!" She taught me, at five, to hemstitch a piece of cheesecloth, where threads were large enough for young eyes and loose enough for small fingers. What the completed handkerchief looked like I don't know, but nobody else ever had to teach me to hemstitch. I adored her and would have sat by her side all day long if they had not driven me out of doors into the sunshine. With so many children and grandchildren, her small store of treasures was spread thin, but I still cherish six of her small silver teaspoons and a brooch with an enameled portrait of Mary Queen of Scots surrounded by silver filigree.

John and Anne were married on September 30, 1881, on the hottest day of that summer, and lived for their first five years in New Jersey, where my sister was born in 1883. They named the poor child Violet, because of my mother's eyes, and Gordon, because my father was convinced that Gordon and Gray belonged together. He signed his own name J. Gordon Gray. Violet passionately hated her name, which she considered both sentimental and tacky. From her earliest days she regarded her guileless parents with a slightly sardonic eye and weary patience for their silliness and impracticality.

When she was five they moved to Chestnut Hill, where Emily and Philip were living, and after a few more years to Germantown, where Violet went to Miss Stevens' School.

James W. Queen and Company overextended itself and was caught in the panic of 1893. When it was forced into bankruptcy, my father was named assignee, and he brought it through the liquidation with such skill that all the creditors received a hundred cents on the dollar. In delight and relief they gave him a testimonial dinner at the Manufacturers' Club, a handsome leather-bound set of the *Encyclopedia Britannica* and a gold watch. I have the report of that dinner, April 16, 1896, with a history of the company and all the speeches made on that occasion. My father's began with a touch of the ironic humor so characteristic of him that, reading it, I hear his voice again.

"When I first became aware that a movement of this kind was on foot—a movement which has developed into this reception—I supposed that a few of those more specially interested would meet together, indulge in some mutual felicitations and, as is the custom among Anglo-Saxons the world over, would put a crown upon the occasion by eating something. I had no thought—" and so on.

The company was reorganized as Queen and Company, and my father was made president. Queen and Company manufactured X-ray apparatus only a few months after Röntgen's announcement of his discovery. But my father was not really cut out for a business executive any more than my mother's father was meant to be a farmer; both were frustrated college professors. Some of the brilliant young men in the company broke away and founded a scientific instrument company of their own which became enormously successful as Leeds and Northrup Company. Queen and Company over the years to come suffered various vicissitudes in the course of which it became Queen-Gray Company and then The Gray Instrument Company, each time a little more diminished.

In 1902, however, it was still fairly prosperous. In that year, at 5536 Wayne Avenue, Germantown, I was born, a quite unintended addition to a family that had long considered itself complete. They were through with sentimental names; they called me for both grandmothers, Elizabeth Janet Gordon Gray.

2.

The First Five Years

THE FIRST five years of our lives, psychologists are now telling us, are much more important than we have realized. The things that happen in those years have a far-reaching influence on the rest of our lives; we learn faster then than at any other time and we are capable of learning much more than we actually do, because those around us fail to offer us the intellectual fare that we are able to digest.

Be this as it may, the first five years of my life were happy and rich and full of seminal memories: of my first awareness of people, my first encounter with injustice, with the principle of moderation in pleasure, with natural beauty, with intellectual discovery, with places—Bryn Mawr College and Japan—that were to be important to me later, and the first recognition of the fact that I was to be a writer.

It is always surprising to me to find that there are people whose memories do not go behind their fifth or sometimes even their sixth year. Perhaps a happy early childhood holds on to first memories with a tighter grip or perhaps the difference lies in the nature —not the quality—of the receiving apparatus. My mind is strongly visual. It is full of pictures which unroll like a motion picture reel. From time to time emotion stops the movement and a single frame remains motionless for my inspection and my permanent possession. Often the roll cuts off before the end of the experience has been reached.

My earliest memory of all is of a very simple scene in which nothing happened; there remains only a picture and an awareness. The room was flooded with sunshine. I was sitting in the middle of my mother's bed, on a wide expanse of white counterpane. Later knowledge fills in the details of the bed for me; it was a so-called sleigh bed with high mahogany head- and footboards rolling back at the top like the front of a sleigh; the counterpane, which survived for many years, was of the embossed kind called Marseilles. My mother was there, close to me but behind me. I did not feel in the least small, but everything else was very large. In the doorway stood—or towered—my father. He appeared to me enormously high. I was aware that he was angry and aware too, not with an awareness for which I had words but with a feeling that moved from her to me like a penetrating mist or through the not-so-long-ago-severed umbilical cord, that my mother was frightened. I was not myself alarmed, only interested. I knew that I could not get away, for though I had legs I did not use them and I was marooned on the vast surface of that bed. I have been told that although I began to utter distinguishable words at the age of nine months, I did not start to walk until I was nearly a year and a half old, so that I must at this time have been no more than seventeen months old. It was a scene nobody could have told me about, and I bring from it vivid impressions: the sunshine in the room, the feeling of not being able to or expecting to walk, the knowledge of my father's wrath and my mother's fear, both factors in our family life.

My first impression of my mother as a person came on my third birthday, when they gave a party for me, attended by several children and more adults. Except for Agnes and Freddy, who lived next door and with whom I daily played in my sandbox or their big nursery, the children were strangers to me. They all brought presents, which they thrust at me on entering—all but Agnes, who could not be persuaded to yield up the tissue-wrapped package in her hands. This action seemed to me reasonable and not worth the attention it attracted. The grownups cluttered up the room, and the party went on a long time. Finally Agnes said to me, "Let's go over to my house," and as this seemed a good idea I agreed. Going through the gate, she dropped the package which she was still clutching and there was a tinkling sound.

"Oh," she exclaimed, "I've broken your doll"—to my surprise, for I did not think of it as mine.

At this point our departure was discovered, and my mother, following us out onto the path, called to me to return at once to my birthday party.

"I've had enough party, Mama!" I called back. "I don't want any more party."

Here the reel stops moving and that one frame remains. I see my mother standing on the front walk, half-hidden by the shrubbery, as if I were seeing her for the first time, separate from myself, a personality in her own right. She was pretty and she was smiling. Dimly I felt a quality of elegance and of humor that, along with her beauty, marked that moment out for me—that and the permanent conviction that parties should stop while they are still fun.

"I've had enough party, Mama" became part of our family folklore and no doubt further etched the memory in my mind, but that picture of my mother was something I never told about and it was the real fruit of the experience.

There had been a gap between nurses after Irish Annie left. Annie had been particularly concerned for my accent and had trained me diligently. "Don't say tub and rug, Betty," they heard her admonishing me. "It's t-u-b, toob, and r-u-g, roog." It gave the family a certain pleasure to hear me conscientiously saying "toob" and "roog"; that was not why Annie left. She left to get married. Then one day my mother said to me while she was putting on my stockings as I sat in her lap, "How would you like to have a nurse named Leah?"

As I thought the name "Leah" offensive I said "No," and supposed that the matter ended there. Two or three days later, however, when I returned from playing next door with a discarded locomotive that Freddy had given me, I found a stranger sitting in the rocking chair in our big kitchen.

"This is Leah," my mother said.

Without so much as another look at her, I fled yelling up the back stairs.

Leah has often told me since how disconcerting it was to be thus rejected on her first frightening venture into the world. Fortunately, it did not last long. Mother pursued me and firmly brought me back. Leah observed that my locomotive ought to have a string tied to it so that I could pull it. A string was found in a cupboard drawer, Leah tied it to the battered cowcatcher and I pulled it across the kitchen linoleum. From that moment Leah entered into my heart, where she has been ever since.

She was just sixteen, a tall, thin, bony girl with curly yellow hair, wide-apart blue eyes, high cheekbones, hollow cheeks and a quality of inner simplicity, calm and love that made her irresistible to all animals and children and to discerning adults. She was the daughter of an Ulster mother and a German father. Her mother's father was a clergyman in the Church of Ireland, which was neither Roman Catholic nor Presbyterian but Anglican. For some reason never quite clear to me Leah's mother ran away to London, where she met a young German named Rau, married him and went with him to the United States. He died when their three children were still small. Too proud to let her family know of her plight, she made a brave and desperate struggle to support her children, but the odds against her were too great and she died when Leah was in her early teens. Leah, through the church which had helped the little family and through my godmother in particular, took her first job as my nurse. She was young herself, hungry for fun and gaiety; she played with me as if—so it seemed to me—we were the same age. When anyone referred to her as my nurse, I would say indignantly, "No, she's my playery."

It must have been on one of Leah's days off that I first met with the fact of injustice in the world. I had gone next door to play with Agnes and Freddy, who had a wonderful big nursery with all kinds of exciting toys in it. That morning as I stood in the swing, which was one of those with two wooden seats facing each other and a platform between them, I trustfully watched Freddy approaching me with a gleam in his eyes and a wooden block in his hands. He came straight on and without a word of warning bashed me in the face with the block. I went home howling, with blood streaming down my front. After Mother had cleaned me up and comforted me, she inquired what had happened. "Freddy," I explained, "laid a block down on my nose."

That afternoon, restored, I went back to play some more with Freddy. He was nowhere to be found. When I inquired about him, Agnes explained, "He was sent to bed for hitting you."

I felt the barb of injustice. I had suffered twice through no fault of my own, once in having my nose battered and the second time in being deprived of my playmate.

The house that we lived in then on Wayne Avenue near the corner of Chelten Avenue was, my sister used often to say, the only house she ever lived in that she really liked, until she and I came to the house in Wallingford more than fifty years later. It is gone now, and there is a bank where it used to be. A supermarket now sprawls across the street where Judge Penrose's house and garden once were; there is a used car lot where the Unitarian church was; a large public school is being built on the site of a Victorian mansion with a high wall around it; and where Balbirnie's drugstore stood, with the ruby and amethyst jars in its window, is now a flat, cluttered building where auto supplies are sold. The great trees, the smooth lawns and well-pruned shrubbery, the air of moderate wealth and good taste are gone as finally as the clip-clop of horses' hooves.

Our house was a Victorian twin, of stone covered with pebble dash, with a deep back garden where an old cherry tree foamed with beauty in April and spread shade over my sandbox. A side porch downstairs and a sun deck upstairs opening from the back bedroom looked out on the garden in the privacy provided by fences and shrubs.

In my fourth year someone made my father an offer for this house that he felt he could not afford to refuse, and so to Violet's grief the house was sold, our furniture was put into storage and we launched into more than a year of random hotel-living before another house was found into which we settled for the next twenty-one years.

The first summer we spent at Low Buildings on the campus of Bryn Mawr College. Low Buildings was a large, sprawling, brown-shingled house on Gulph Road with apartments for members of the faculty. Most of them went away during the summers, subletting their apartments to city dwellers who still considered the suburbs satisfactory summer resorts. Violet was not with us; she was spending the summer with friends in Maine.

There were no other children about, but Leah and I had the campus to play on, great stretches of green lawn with big trees, and near Low Buildings a little hill just right to roll down. The turf was so fine and soft that I could run barefoot on it. My father used to tell me to keep my eyes open for molly cottontails and tortoises and squirrels. The rabbits and the squirrels moved too swiftly to be examined, but I remember watching in absorption while a box turtle slowly made its way across a path. It was here on the Bryn Mawr campus in the green and brooding heat of summer that was first awakened the love of natural beauty which has been one of the deepest and most enduring loves of my life. "Beauty," as George Santayana said, "is a pledge of the possible conformity between the soul and nature, and consequently a ground of faith in the supremacy of the good."

We encountered, Leah and I, as we played happily under the trees, another Bryn Mawr phenomenon. A dignified and substantial female figure with a cane and a limp approached us one day over the grass, stopped at a little distance to survey us disapprovingly and then retired without speaking. In a few minutes a gardener came and told Leah that we were not to step off the paths lest we damage the grass.

My father, when this was reported to him, said to Leah, "Next time you may tell Miss Thomas that if her large, well-shod feet do not injure the grass, it's hardly likely that the baby's little bare feet will."

Fortunately, Bryn Mawr's distinguished president did not appear again and so this rude message was not delivered; a future vice-president of the Board of Trustees of Bryn Mawr continued to enjoy the soft green grass undisturbed.

The other feature of that summer was the presence of a delightful couple from New Orleans who also had sublet an apartment in Low Buildings. They gave me the first books that I remember enjoying. I had had picture books before, of course, but these were stories with characters who became lasting friends. One was *Little Black Sambo* and the other a story of Southern plantation life called *Diddie, Dumps and Tot*. It entered no one's mind at the time that Negroes could possibly object to such books, nor would it have troubled anyone if it had, so completely can the mental climate change in a little more than half a century.

Toward the end of the summer we left Low Buildings and went to Cape May Point, where in previous summers we had had a cottage, to spend two or three weeks at the old Cape House. After we had been there a few days, Violet came back from Maine to join us. I had not seen her all summer. In happy excitement at the prospect of having her at home again, I planned a suitable reception for her.

"When I see her," I announced, "I'm going to say, 'Good morning, Yiyee.' " ("Yiyee" was what I made of the name "Violet," and she liked it better.)

We took the trolley from Cape May Point to Cape May to meet her, Mother and Leah and I. The trolley ran about two and a half miles along the shore, the last part of the way over a high trestle, beneath which the tips of waves at high tide came swirling in. The trolley cars were open in those days, and the air was full of the fragrance of sea and wooden piles hung with seaweed, of sea pinks and beach plums.

The train came into the old station at the end of the trolley line beside the beach, and Violet got off and came toward us down the long platform in the sunshine. She was twenty-three, a Gibson girl, with her long linen dust coat and blue scarf blowing in the sea breeze, her blue straw hat perched on her pompadour.

She bent down and kissed me. They waited for me to say, "Good morning, Yiyee."

I couldn't. She was too beautiful, too strange. I couldn't utter a word.

I was tongue-tied all day. From time to time she would put her arm around me and say with love and laughter in her voice, "What's the matter, funny-bunny? Cat got your tongue?"

At last, near sunset, I sidled up to her, murmured, "Good morning, Yiyee," and burst into tears.

This is my first conscious memory of my sister whom, next to Morgan Vining, I have loved more than anyone else in all of my life.

It had not been easy for her when I was born. She was nineteen and a half on that day in October which began with Mother's humming a catchy popular song of the moment, "I've a terrible lot to do today, today to do," and ended late in the evening when my father went to fetch her from an uncle's house to which she had been sent to spend the day, and told her, "It's a girl." There was something embarrassing and absurd about the birth of a child at that late date and so obviously an afterthought. As time went on and Queen and Company began to falter, the presence of another member of the family to be made room for and educated was a drain upon a not-expanding income. I quite early understood the situation and sometimes felt oppressed by it, but Violet from her height always represented to me gaiety and tenderness and generosity, a model to admire and imitate, in so far as mortal could. Much later when life in many ways had disappointed her, she found a measure of compensation in me and the fulfilment of some of her unmet needs.

We spent the autumn of 1906 at Evergreen Hall in Woodbury, New Jersey, the winter and spring at the Normandie Hotel in West Philadelphia, and the following summer in Vineland with my grandparents. In the middle of the winter Leah left us. My mother saw that she had gifts which ought not to be wasted on child-tending, that she had the makings of a first-rate trained nurse. She encouraged her to go into training first in St. Christopher's Hospital for Children and from there into the Pennsylvania Hospital, which offered the best training and experience then available

in Philadelphia. When she was graduated, a fashionable doctor in
Chestnut Hill sent her to one of his patients, and from then on
until at seventy-odd she retired she was passed from one family to
another in the same circle, always in demand, always loved. She
never married; indeed, in the nunlike life of a nurse in those days of
twenty-four-hour duty, I doubt if she ever had a beau, but her sister's and brother's children were very close to her and made a focus
for her life. After her retirement she took a nephew with her and
went to Ireland to visit her mother's family there, a wonderful
and heart-warming experience.

Leah's departure that winter was the first grief in my life. Night
after night I cried for her into my pillow. Not that we lost her entirely. She used to come back to see us on her days off, and after
she began earning money she would bring me generous and glamorous presents that were landmarks in my childhood.

After Leah left I had no more nurses. Mother took care of me
herself. When she bathed me, she liked hot water for it, and I well
remember whining and protesting. "Nonsense!" Mother would say
briskly. "This isn't hot at all. If you lived in Japan, there would
be a fire *right under the tub.* Then you might have some reason to
complain."

This seemed to me a totally wrongheaded way of life. I resolved
to stay away from Japan.

The new house was bought early in September just before I was
five. It was on the edge of Queen Lane Manor, a settlement between
Germantown and East Falls of the kind which we had not yet
learned to call a development. Ours was one of four large twin
houses on small lots, built of solid stone eighteen inches thick
with a modified mansard roof of expensive slate, with porches on
two sides, and bulging with bay windows like bunions. It was a
very ugly type of architecture, which was soon superseded by the
so-called colonial style that has prevailed ever since. It was for its
day modern and rather luxurious, with two large stone fireplaces,
two bathrooms, and a butler's pantry, and with both electric and
gas fixtures in every room, since electricity was not considered entirely dependable. As ours was the corner house, with Queen
Lane across the front and Wissahickon Avenue down the side, it
had an extra ration of the double line of trees—silver maples and
pin oaks—which had been planted years earlier when the land belonged to Carlton at the other end of the block. By now the trees

had reached a good size, so that our lot was too shady to grow anything but ferns, violets and Hosta lilies, though Mother never
gave up the struggle.

The place where the two streets met was a bridge, under which
ran the railroad tracks of the Chestnut Hill Local. The so-called
railroad cutting was actually a natural rocky ravine made by an old
stream, now no more than a trickle beside the tracks. Here the
Revolutionary War soldiers encamped a little to the west had
gone to fill their canteens with water. The trains which came at
half-hour intervals during the day and oftener at rush hours were
still steam trains with locomotives and great puffs of smoke which
covered our windowsills with smuts. We got used to the noise of
the trains, but the dirt continued to bother us until at length the
line was electrified. There was dust too from the roads, which were
unpaved for many years.

Queen Lane Station was just across the street, with a driveway
where horse-drawn equipages came to pick up the masters returning
from their work in the city, and an iron bar to which cab horses
were tied. The Strawbridges' carriages were the smartest and could
always be recognized by their yellow wheels. The clop-clop of
horses' hooves in the road was a pleasant sound, much more natural
and leisurely than the screech of brakes and the roar of motors.
Besides the gentlemen's carriages there were also the delivery
wagons, the huckster's wagon, the occasional drays and, in summer, the water sprinklers that filled the air with a sudden coolness
and the smell of wet dust. There were still in those days a few street
cries: "Peanuts, five a bag?" and "Bowlegged, highly educated
Baltimore crabs!"

"Up the street" from Queen Lane Station was one of the old villages which have been strung together in the making of Germantown. This one was called Pulaski Town, and it was our shopping
center, with drugstore, grocery store, butcher store, bakery, hard-
ware, plumber, and all the rest, with small, shabby houses, a
church or two, and a public school. From the grocery store a
clerk used to come to our back door every morning and take our
order, which would be delivered by lunchtime in a wagon drawn
by a droopy-headed horse.

In the other direction, west of us, was Queen Lane Manor, where
new houses were constantly being added as time went on. Beyond the block of twin houses where we lived was a large single
house of equal ugliness inhabited by the Hutchinsons; Elizabeth

and Edward became my playmates, taking the place of Agnes and Freddy, whom I still missed. Behind the Hutchinsons' house was a field where we played. It was not an empty lot with all that the phrase implies of bareness, weeds and broken bottles; it was a real field left over from the country that not so long ago had been here. It was a place where the wild flowers that Browning called "the little children's dower"—violets, buttercups and daisies—grew in abundance for the picking. Between the daisies and the asters the Hutchinsons were away in Belmar, New Jersey, where they had a cottage, and I stayed mostly in the shade of my own yard.

Beyond the Hutchinsons' the houses became progressively larger until at the end of the long block was Carlton, the beautiful eighteenth-century mansion to which all this land and more had once belonged. It stood there still in my childhood, with a field in front of it where cows grazed and on the other side of it the big stone barn and a wall with a plaque saying, "This wall destroyed in 1777 by the British army was rebuilt in 1792 by the trusty Isaac Tustin Company." As I grew older and went into my Revolutionary War phase, this place was a source of great romantic and patriotic feeling to me.

The best rooms in our house were the very large ones on the front with the southern exposure. In those days people had parlors and sitting rooms, as today we have living rooms and family rooms. We had none of those. The "hall"—as in Scottish castle or English manor house—was the room where we entertained our visitors; above it was the library. Both hall and library had large stone fireplaces where we had wood fires on all but the hottest days. We never ran out of wood, and my father kept the wood boxes filled and usually the fires lit.

The house was cold. Through all of my childhood before the second furnace was put in, winter meant a constant struggle with drafts and a penetrating chill. The furnace was shaken down vigorously night and morning and well stoked with the best anthracite coal, but the water in the radiators was seldom really hot and the radiators in any case were too small for the big rooms. We supplemented the furnace with portable oilstoves. To keep the air moist, we had open pans on top of all the stoves with water simmering in them. The water would evaporate, the pans go dry, and then there would be a popping sound, metallic, like tiny pistol shots, as the pans spat bits of enamel into the room. When one ran to refill them with water, there would be a hot, sizzling sound. When we went to bed the beds were cold. We warmed them with flatirons heated on the kitchen stove and wrapped in pieces of old blanket.

Two blocks north on Wissahickon Avenue was School House Lane, where the houses were mansions, set far back from the road, with grounds running down the hill to the woods of the Wissahickon Valley. There were beautiful walks through all this region, and my father loved to walk. Not infrequently he walked all the way home from his office in town, a matter of more than eight miles at the end of a day. I was often his companion on the shorter walks. As I had gone out in Bryn Mawr looking for molly cottontails and tortoises, here, that first fall, I sallied forth on the quest for wild flowers. There were still edges of fields where asters and goldenrod and eupatorium might be picked and carried home drooping in small hands.

I enjoyed these walks with my father, but it was through them that I, just turned five, learned one of the most bitter lessons a woman can learn, that it is possible to bore the man you love. I overheard, one day, an exchange that went on over my head between my mother and father.

"Why don't you take Betty?"

"She keeps harping on finding wild flowers," he said ruefully. "I just can't stand it today."

I had never heard the word *bore*, but at that moment I knew its meaning. With it I tasted chagrin. I had been happy about the search for wild flowers, and it had never occurred to me that my father's pleasure had not been equal to mine. It was possible, I realized further, to be tiresome without being naughty, to be on one's best behavior and still to be unacceptable. The female, I knew in my bones, existed to charm the male, and I had failed.

The walks went on again on later days and in later years. My father forgot his boredom if I did not. I stopped harping on wild flowers and tried to think of pleasing things to say.

Before I was able to make contact with the Hutchinson children, whom I used to see sometimes passing in their carriage, I spent a good deal of time playing alone in our yard, scrambling up the little hill that separated our back yard from the one behind and running down again, inventing games with twigs and stones. One gray afternoon the air was suddenly full of snowflakes. Exhilarated, I thought of a poem, and after I had got it to suit myself I went indoors to tell it to Mother, who listened kindly but without excitement.

Snowflakes flying,
Flowers dying,
Children glad,
Now are clad
In warmer clothing.

It rhymed, it scanned—though I did not then know either word
—but the content was of only minor interest even to a mother. It
was characteristic of my efforts for many a year; I had a technique
long before I had anything to say. Nevertheless, I had tasted the
heady wine of composition.

Winter drew on. I made friends with "E. Hutch" and Edward.
Talk of Christmas began to fill the air. I examined the story of
Santa Claus and found it, to my regret, incredible.

To the left of the stone fireplace in the hall was a built-in settee
upholstered in brown velvet, and hanging over it a large steel en-
graving of Landseer's *Monarch of the Glen*. I used to study this
great stag with his spreading antlers; I thought he was a reindeer.

One day, after looking at him for a long time, I pictured eight
of him hitched to a sleigh and the sleigh coming to rest on the
sloping roof beside the top of our chimney. How could it balance
there? It was a large chimney, but how could a stout man with a
pack manage to squeeze down it without getting stuck? Furthermore, it would take time. How could he visit every house in every
neighborhood in the city in one night, let alone the whole country?
Obviously it was all nonsense. It could not be done.

My sister was sitting reading by the table.

"I don't believe all that stuff about Santa Claus," I told her.

She laid aside her book and took me in her lap, to clear the
whole subject up for me.

"It's a beautiful story. It stands for the love parents feel for their
children. So parents fill the stockings and trim the tree and put the
presents under it."

This was clear enough, though I did not yet see why they had
invented Santa Claus to account for it. She went on to tell me about
the baby Jesus, who seemed still further removed from Christmas
than Santa Claus did. While I was pondering this, I lost the thread
of the story. The next thing that caught my attention was, "So
those wicked men put a crown of thorns on his head and they
mocked him and then they crucified him."

The autumn dusk had drawn in and my sister had not turned on the light; we were sitting now in a twilight dimness that suddenly became darker. She explained to me what it meant to crucify someone.

"They nailed him to a big wooden cross. They drove nails into his hands and feet and left him hanging there till he died."

Now it was totally dark. I felt those nails in my own hands. I was stricken with a pain and terror that I could in no way express.

"So that's why we celebrate Christmas," finished my sister triumphantly. "But you mustn't tell the other children. They still believe in Santa Claus. You mustn't spoil it for them. Get down now, dear. You're getting powerful heavy."

I did not tell the other children. I had no wish to talk about this terrible thing I had learned. As Christmas came closer, my contemporaries were full of happy talk of presents hoped for, of opening the stocking, of finding toys under the Christmas tree; I felt that I had lost something very nice and got something very dubious in return. I decided to *pretend* that I still believed in Santa Claus. It was a happy game that I could still play, even though I knew it was only a game. Besides, I wanted that stocking. I wanted a Christmas tree and presents under it. So I too babbled about Santa Claus and what he would bring.

One evening, while they were putting me to bed together, I overheard my sister say to my mother with amusement in her voice, "I notice now that Christmas is closer she does believe in Santa Claus after all."

I can still feel the surge of helpless rage that went through me. I hated being laughed at, but still more I felt frustrated by their failure of understanding. Of course I did not believe in Santa Claus. How could I when I knew what they knew, what really happened? But I could enjoy pretending, and still know that it was pretending. I did not want to be shut out so soon from the carefree circle of the other children. Unconsciously I felt entitled to preserve the illusions proper to my age. I had unwittingly discovered the peril of pursuing truth.

Though I had made one intellectual discovery that led to sorrow, I made another that winter that was an opening into fields of joy and freedom. I learned to read. I already knew my letters from my blocks. As I played with them on the floor near Mother, who sat sewing, she had said to me, "Bring me big girl A. That's it. Now bring me little girl *b*," and I would find the capitals or the lower-case letters with no idea that I was learning anything or that Mother was following out the long-ago directions of Saint Jerome. That crusty saint, whom one would scarcely expect to be an expert on the education of little girls, however good he might be with lions, wrote, in his famous letter to Laeta about the education of little Paula, that the child, who was to start with Greek at an early age and learn Scripture by heart in both Latin and Greek, should begin by playing with ivory blocks on which letters had been carved.

Among my books were a primer telling the adventures of a little girl named Nancy and a Robert Louis Stevenson primer with bits from *A Child's Garden of Verses*. Suddenly, in a flash like that which struck Archimedes in the bathtub, I realized that letters made words—and words made stories. All one had to do was to read out the letters to some adult to find out what the words were and then remember them. I accumulated words that winter as if they had been marbles or beads.

"What does b-r-o-w-n spell? Oh. What does r-i-v-e-r spell? Oh."

I lay on my stomach on the floor in front of the fire and "worded" my reading relatives. I tracked them down in their pursuits. "Can I word you now?" Sometimes they patiently consented to be interrupted, sometimes they shooed me away promising, "Some other time. I'm busy now." I learned to guess words from the context; I invented my own pronunciation. It made no difference to me whether it was correct or not; what I was after was the story.

Now I could read. I had even composed a poem myself. I knew what I wanted to do with my life. We were in the library together one afternoon, Mother darning stockings, Violet talking to her, I sitting in the Morris chair, thinking.

"When I grow up," I announced, flinging one leg over the arm of the chair for emphasis, "I'm going to write the best book in the world."

3.

The School Years I

Not long after we moved to Queen Lane Manor, our life rather drastically closed in. My father's business suffered in the depression of 1907; first my mother's younger brother and then one of my father's brothers became involved in it, not to its benefit. Quarrels and estrangements followed; other members of the families took sides, or were thought to do so. There was no more of the normal coming and going of relatives, and I grew up scarcely knowing that I had aunts, uncles, cousins.

"The Bank," to my childish mind a mysterious and menacing entity akin to the Devil, was always threatening to call in its loan. For many years financial disaster hung over our heads, never quite falling, perhaps never as near to falling as my mother and sister feared, but still near enough to put strain into our lives and to impose strict economy on us. Our neighbors sold their horses and got a Pierce-Arrow; their coachman, Michael, became the chauffeur; they used to pass me as I walked to school. We stayed home in the summers instead of going away to the mountains or the sea. We had a maid only intermittently; usually they were "green" when they came and after they had been trained left to get better wages elsewhere. Sylvia, our laundress and cleaning woman, was permanent and much loved. She was a black woman of great presence and dignity who lived with her son in a little court in Pulaski Town, in a three-storied, three-roomed brick house. She walked like a queen and, though she never hurried, with great rapidity; we would see her approaching in the distance and then suddenly she was there.

Mother made most of our clothes—Violet's, mine, her own—and very skilfully. She was a beautiful, charming, capable woman, able to do anything well that she turned her hand to; she had other talents besides cooking and sewing; she had enjoyed studying

French and German; she liked social life, but she found it difficult to invite people to her home unless she could do it "properly," with the right kind of service and appointments; she had loved her family, especially her sister Emily, and she felt the estrangement deeply. She must have been lonely and often frustrated. Grown-ups sometimes asked me pointed questions about my Aunt Emily and her family which made me very uncomfortable, for I did not know how to answer them. I drew the conclusion that we were in some way different from other people; but I was unable to ask about this at home, for I felt dimly that it would only increase the unhappiness in the atmosphere.

Violet, who had taken a kindergarten course, longed to go out into the world and get a job, but my father forbade her to on the grounds that "The Bank" would see and draw unfortunate conclusions. Two attractive and hitherto devoted suitors faded discreetly away; her school friends married and became absorbed in their families. It was a muted, lonely, withdrawn time for her too, until at length she was offered a position at the Friends Library, where well-bred daughters who lived at home worked for salaries that would not alarm even the most skittish of banks.

Throughout all the retrenchment, no one ever doubted for a moment that I must have the best education available, which meant private school and later college; nor did anyone entertain the idea that the scholarship offered by the Stevens School, which Violet had attended, could be accepted. My father's fierce Scottish pride would not allow it. He paid my full tuition throughout all of the years of my education.

The school was then on Chelten Avenue, around the corner from our old Wayne Avenue house, a little less than a mile from our new home. With three other little girls—my old friend Agnes, Frances and Lucinda—I entered Miss Lyons's first grade just before my sixth birthday. The whole school gathered in the gymnasium for morning prayers, at the end of which the classes were dismissed one by one, the youngest on the kindergarten chairs in front first.

"Class A may leave," said the principal.

No one stirred. Miss Lyons rose from the back of the room. "They don't know their name yet, Miss Bentley."

"Oh. Well then, Miss Lyons's babies."

We four stood up without hesitation and trotted down the narrow aisle between the rows and rows and rows of Big Girls.

School was to me a joy from the first. Lessons presented no difficulties and sometimes offered the excitement of genuine intellectual discovery. I had mastered the two-table ahead of the others and sat dreaming. Miss Lyons said to me, "Why don't you go on to the three-table? I haven't got time to show you now, but you can make it up for yourself. You just add three every time." With a mounting exhilaration I put together a multiplication table of my own.

Most of all I rejoiced in the companionship of the other children. No doubt because of the good start that Leah had given me, I had none of the difficulties in adjusting to my contemporaries that only children sometimes suffer—and with Violet completely grown up I was to all intents and purposes an only child. I made friends easily; I enjoyed my friends enormously. I felt fulfilled both when I was in school and in the play hours afterwards among my own kind. School in those days lasted from 8:40 to 1:15. We went home for lunch, and after that the whole afternoon was free for play until dark fell and we were called in for homework and for dinner.

With "E. Hutch," who lived only four doors away, I played dolls sedately in a continued game that we called "Real–O," or made playhouses in the field behind her house. It was in this field that one of the uncomfortable, never-told incidents of my childhood took place, no more than a conversation but a scarring one. We must have been still quite small, for I remember that we stood waist-deep in daisies. There was another little girl in the neighborhood whose behavior irked us, and "E. Hutch" brought a word from her mother intended, no doubt, to make us more tolerant.

"Her parents didn't want her," she explained to me. "That's why she's queer."

I was startled. "*My* parents didn't want *me!*"

Elizabeth looked at me aghast. "That *always* makes people queer," she pronounced.

But though I was troubled and did not want to be "queer," I think it did not weigh too heavily on me. I knew that I was loved.

My playmates were not all in my own neighborhood, though all were within walking distance, which in those days, when we still had the use of our legs, meant a range of a mile or so. They represented a range of interests. With one I stalked hostile Indians and ran screaming war whoops all over her large old-fashioned garden. With others I roller-skated in an ecstasy of motion over smooth cement walks that sent my long hair flying out behind me in the breeze of speed, and over uneven flagstones that rattled the teeth in my head and made me wave my arms to keep my balance. I went hunting for birds and wild flowers with another, wrote and acted plays with still others, and with a yellow-haired little girl named Helen Alexander invented imaginative games that were continued day after day and month after month. We had a deck of Mythology cards, which were like Authors but with pictures of the Greek and Roman gods and goddesses instead of the respectable bearded countenance of Henry Wadsworth Longfellow or the sausage curls of Elizabeth Barrett Browning. We disregarded the rules of the game and, using the cards as if they had been paper dolls, played out absorbing dramas of our own invention, in which Cupid and Psyche were the *enfants terribles,* always in hot water because of being impudent to Mars and playing tricks on Juno. Because Helen's father was attorney for the Wideners, he had great volumes of beautiful colored reproductions of the Widener Collection of the English portraitists and landscape painters of the eighteenth and nineteenth centuries. From the moment I looked at them, I saw that each picture had a story in it. By the hour, we sat on the floor in the Alexanders' living room, slowly turning the pages and alternately recounting the stories we found there. We maintained a consistent point of view; I was a belted earl. "This was my first wife when she was young," I would begin. "She adored that little dog. I couldn't stand him. Perhaps I was jealous. I—" Or a Constable village scene would provide a wealth of material connected with my family, my dependents, my enemies, my estates. The hours that today's children spend passive before a television set seem to me vacuous in comparison with the rich, creative play that I and my friends enjoyed.

Along with these exuberant and satisfying social activities, my secret life continued. I was a writer. Though I got a story into the *School Review* in first grade and contributed regularly to school magazines thereafter, I never considered what I wrote for school part of my "real writing." That was done on my own time and to my own demands: poems, short stories, novels. As I look at what survives of all these efforts today, I marvel at their banality. Occasionally a vivid phrase leaps out of the page or there is some understanding of the use of dialogue, but most of it is jejune to a depressing degree. The only significant part of it is that I did it at all—that I had already learned that essential lesson of the serious writer, to set apart a definite time for writing and to stick to it.

"Well," I would say after lunch, "I guess I'll go write something." And for half an hour or so I would sit down at the shabby oak roll-top desk that had been turned over to me in the library and add another chapter to the novel of the Revolution or the improving tale of two children, one rich and the other poor, who exchanged places and learned to value anew their own unsatisfactory families.

The contrast between my winter life and the summers when everybody else went off to summer cottages and we stayed home was acute: no school, no playmates. Even my writing languished; it seemed that too much time, too little outside stimulation dried up the springs. Germantown is hot and humid in the summer. Our house with its thick stone walls was usually cool even on the worst days, but outside the windows hung the leaves of those eleven trees, motionless and limp, giving off green effluvia of their own, growing bigger and bigger as the summer dragged on, until in August they hung large as salad plates, lush, heavy, still.

Then the library, which had been a resource for rainy days and snowstorms, became the center of my life. The bookshelves occupied nearly three sides of the large room, with space out for fireplace and east window and the portiered doorway. The fourth side was a large southern bay window filled with Mother's plants. To the left of the fireplace was the section set aside for me, with battered treasures from Violet's childhood—*Lady Jane, Little Women, Little Lord Fauntleroy, The Story of England, Child Life, The Dog of Flanders, The Blue Fairy Book, The Three Vassar* (which I pronounced with the accent on the last syllable) *Girls on the Rhine.* To those were added the books I got for Christmas and birthdays and the school textbooks that I liked, such as *Poems Every Child Should Know* and *The King of the Golden River.* Books were considered expensive, and those that I owned I read over and over again. *At the Back of the North Wind,* with colored plates by Jessie Wilcox Smith, was the gift of one of Violet's beaux; it both puzzled me and satisfied something deep in me that reached out for the mysteries it seemed to hint at. *The Secret Garden, Rebecca of Sunnybrook Farm,* the Alcott books, I read and reread till they fell apart. I was allowed to take from the Public Library only the books that were clean—clean in the strictly physical sense of fresh bindings and unstained pages—which made the long walk to the library practically useless, for all the good books were worn and grimy. I was early driven into the grown-up regions of the shelves. The *Encyclopedia Britannica* which had been presented to my father offered, as well as information useful for school papers, color plates of great fascination. I pored over the pictures of foreign orders with no faintest inkling that the enameled cherry blossoms and phoenix-crested gold crown of the Japanese Sacred Crown would some day be mine. The *Last Essays of Elia,* for some reason that I cannot now fathom, exerted a strong charm when I was barely ten. It was not even the collection which contained the "A Dissertation upon Roast Pig." I think it must have been the gentle, humorous, childlike spirit of Charles Lamb himself that held me. At any rate I went back to it again and again, and I owe to it my first experiment in the use of quotation.

My father was an inveterate punster; the family response was the conventional groan. One evening at the dinner table when he got off one of his puns, I remarked loftily, "A pun is a pistol let off at the ear; not a feather to tickle the intellect."

There was a moment's stunned silence before with one voice all three of the grownups turned on me: "*Where did you get that?*"

The real treasure in the library was the long row of the novels of Sir Walter Scott, bound in dark red cloth, printed in small type and illustrated with steel engravings of improbable-looking castles, cottages, ruined abbeys and craggy mountains. I discovered *The Abbot* first, and after I had followed Roland Graeme when he left the Canongate and dived into a wynd, whatever that was, I was off. *The Monastery, Rob Roy, Peveril of the Peak, The Fortunes of Nigel* (which I pronounced "Niggle") followed. I devoured them all, having learned from the first to skip the descriptions and get on with the story. At this point my father discovered what I was up to. Not that he objected. On the contrary he was entirely too pleased. He wanted to tell me at length what he enjoyed in Scott; he was thrusting another novel at me before I had finished the one I was on; he demanded in season and out to know my response to this character and that. Soon I was reading his choices instead of my own, and all the discovery and adventure had gone out of it. I stuck in the middle of *Anne of Geierstein,* and Scott was finished for me.

I went on to Cooper and *The Last of the Mohicans* and the Natty Bumppo stories, which lasted until I was thirteen, when in my English class at school, Lawrence Burgess read us Mark Twain's parody of Cooper, in which Chingachgook brought down the enemy on his party by stepping on a twig which snapped loudly—"If there was a twig anywhere within miles, Chingachgook stepped on it"—and the stories became forever ridiculous, just as the *Little Colonel* stories lost their charm when Violet pointed out that though all the characters in the book were Kentuckians, it was only the Little Colonel whom the author granted the glamor of a Southern accent. I was not able to perceive these absurdities for myself, but once they were pointed out to me I could see nothing else.

Nothing in the library was forbidden, though *The Wide, Wide World* and *The Heavenly Twins* were stigmatized as trash. I enjoyed both. It would be gratifying to be able to say that I read instead the oatmeal-colored volumes of Balzac, but I did not. I looked into them, as I looked into everything in the library, but, finding nothing to attract me, I put them back on the shelf.

The things one teaches oneself are perhaps the most important of all that one learns. I had been scolded one day, for what I do not now remember, and, I felt, scolded unjustly. Hot with resentment and humiliation, I went out into the yard, my kitten in my arms. No doubt, in the grip of my emotions, I held her too tightly; she struggled to escape, digging her claws into me. My anger flared. I slapped my kitten on the head. She laid back her ears and cowered in my arms. The next instant, overwhelmed with remorse, I cried over her, kissed her again and again and at last succeeded in soothing her. I saw quite clearly what I had done: I had passed on to a small helpless creature that I loved an injury done to me. I was bitterly ashamed; for years I could not think of the incident without wincing inwardly.

Most of the important experiences of my childhood I was unable to talk about with my family and, indeed, as I write them now I am telling them for the first time. They are only what everybody learns in one way or another, but they cut deep into my heart then. I hardly know why it was so difficult for me to speak of them; it was not that the adults in my family were unreceptive; perhaps I vaguely felt that they were too receptive, too ready to take what I said, to interpret it, to return it to me explained, ordered, made over into something subtly different with overtones of admonishment or approval. Perhaps most children feel that it is safest to keep to themselves experiences that are frightening or puzzling.

Through Helen Alexander's father, a group of children were taken one day to see one of the Widener model farms; it was to have been a great experience for us suburban young, and I suppose it was. All that is left in my memory of it is an impression of rolling green fields, whitewashed fences, large stone buildings, and the Horror.

A prize sow had littered, and we were taken as a special treat to see the baby pigs. The sty was large and clean; the sow was enormous and clean; the piglets were small, pink and white, with big ears and crinkly tails. The sow was eating something, which turned out to be—incredibly, horribly—one of her own babies. She had gone at it quite methodically, beginning with the tail end. When we surprised her at her meal and she looked up at us, we saw the front half intact, the large, pink ears, small, open eyes, snout, front legs and half a torso, with red and white entrails oozing out. The farmer who was showing us around was annoyed. "They *will* do it sometimes," he said, as he scooped the little half-corpse away with a hoe.

The moment for me was a blaze of shock and terror. The sunlight, the little corpse—so complete and natural-looking at one end, so appalling at the other—the great, grunting, heaving sow, the barnyard smell imprinted themselves indelibly on my mind. Here was something in the world I had not guessed at: a mother, even a pig mother, eating its own child, a man with a hoe sweeping away the results but admitting casually that it often happened. The adult with us seemed not even to have noticed. We were swept on to something else; nothing was said.

I carried the sight and smell with me like a weight in the pit of my stomach. It was unbearable to think about, and yet I could not keep away from it. I came back to it again and again in the days and years that followed; there was a small, dark pool of evil in my mind that I had to look at from time to time to see if it was still there and to shudder away from with a stab of grief that seemed never to lose its edge.

I did not see the other children again, except for Helen, and we never spoke of it to each other. I told my family nothing. It was a secret knowledge that I had, that there was in the world a mindless greed and cruelty that contradicted everything I had been told about mother love, that grown-up people knew it and swept it away with a hoe, saying it was too bad but it sometimes happened.

When I was a little older, my father and I on one of our walks passed through an old settlement called Bluebell Hill on the way to the Wissahickon Woods near Walnut Lane Bridge. The houses were old and small and close to the street, of a kind that day laborers used to live in and that now are expensively remodeled and prized by the prosperous. In the window of one of them, separated from us as we passed only by the pane of glass, sat a girl of about my own age, with strange, tilted eyes that looked at once vacant and excited, set far apart in a wide, flat face. She was eating something and slobbering it down her chin. The movements of her hands were jerky. I had never heard the term *Mongolian idiot*, but I felt at once that here was something abnormal, both pitiful and sinister. I looked at my father. His glance had swept the window without apparently seeing anything to surprise or disturb him into comment. Perhaps he thought that I had not noticed and that he would not call to my attention something I might find painful or difficult to understand. We went on, but now I had a new, secret knowledge. There were in the world children who were not like the rest of us, who sat in windows and slobbered, who seemed to have a blank, irrational joy in their strange eyes. The grownups knew it but did not talk about it.

Without ever reasoning it out, I felt that the grownups either did not realize the implications of what they saw and passed over or could not bear them. Why else should they have invented a Santa Claus to gloss over the Crucifixion? I fell into the way of withholding from my family anything that might be too dreadful for them. I was as ready as any child, perhaps more so, to show my own hurts and be comforted, but these dark, impersonal evils in the world I could not talk about. Gradually I became less open, more reserved, more silent about what touched me most closely. When in college English I read the Old English poem *The Wanderer*, and came on the words, "The way of the high-born fast in his heart his feelings to fetter," I fastened on them happily as a rationalization of what had been my practice since childhood.

My father was a formal man. No one took any liberties with him. I never heard anyone call him John. My mother called him "Dear"; others, Mr. Gray. He was not a man whom a child would ever climb over. Occasionally he would invite me to sit on his knee and I would perch there uncomfortably, trying to support my own weight by a foot on the floor, an elbow on the arm of the chair. His characteristic caress was a light pat on my cheek with two cool, dry fingers. I could not conceivably have told him that I had to go to the bathroom. My sister had been taught to call him Papá, with the accent on the second syllable, and so of course I imitated her, though it was a trial to me, for the other children found it both funny and affected, which was almost the most opprobrious term in their vocabulary. I am sure now that if I had changed to Daddy —Poppa he would not have tolerated—he would have made no objection; but obscurely I felt it to be a test of family loyalty, and stubbornly I would not yield to ridicule.

I was not afraid of him, but I was in awe of him and usually on my best behavior with him, as if he had been an important guest in our house. I always carefully thanked him whenever he took me out with him, and the necessity of composing suitable phrases to be delivered on the doorstep on our return occupied my mind during the last quarter of the walk.

He expected decorum and modesty of me. Once when I was small enough to be playing with my paper dolls under the library table beside which he sat deep in a book, my mother called me from another room. As I scrambled out to obey, I murmured to myself, "Now what does *she* want?" Immediately the heavens opened and the sky fell on me. My father had heard me refer to my mother as *she*, and he demanded in a voice of thunder to know what I meant by such vulgar disrespect. At about the same time Mother had made me a plaid gingham dress with the glorious, freeing innovation of bloomers to match. I went into the library to show off my new costume and, sitting down in the chair opposite my father, carefully arranged my skirt so that a little bit of the bloomer underneath showed. He glanced up over his pince-nez.

"Pull down your skirt, Betty," he said. "Your drawers are showing."

On the other hand he could be understanding and comforting. When I tore a new dress climbing over a fence the first time I wore it and Mother's justifiable exasperation issued in a scolding that made me feel an outcast from the human race, it was my father who dried my tears and restored to me a sense of proportion. "That was too bad," he said in a voice regretful but not condemning, kind but not solicitous. "But never mind now. It's done. Wash your face and come to dinner." Subdued but not abject, I was able to rejoin my family.

For the most part there was no discussion of controversial issues at our dinner table. My father pronounced his opinions at length, and the rest of us either agreed or stayed quiet. But during my Revolutionary War phase, which lasted from the time I was eight until I was past twelve, he and I had frequent and frank exchanges on a subject on which we were in fundamental disagreement. He considered Lincoln a greater man than Washington and Napoleon a greater general. I cried when he said Lincoln was a greater man, but I was only eight then; by the time I was eleven I could point out triumphantly that Washington had been able to defeat the British whereas Napoleon had not. My father never wavered in his conviction that the American Revolution was a huge mistake and that our country and the world as well would have been far better off if we had remained a colony of Great Britain. Passionately patriotic, I found this view shocking and grievous, but I realize now, looking back, that it was good to know at an early age that there might be another view of one's country than one's own.

Perhaps it was living in Germantown that made me so aware of the Revolution. There was Carlton, at the end of our block, with its stone wall that had been knocked down by the Redcoats; at the other end of Queen Lane was Grumblethorpe, where the British general Agnew had been killed in the Battle of Germantown. Farther up Germantown Avenue were Cliveden, which had been a veritable fort, with Americans inside and British soldiers outside and the bullet holes still there in the fabric of the house, and Wyck, which became a hospital for wounded soldiers on both sides in the Battle. In the Morris House Washington had lived when he was President of the newly born United States and the yellow fever epidemic had driven him out of Philadelphia; its stately portico and front door were directly on the street, but beside and behind it was a large old-fashioned garden, with tulips and cherry blossoms in spring, which you could see through a little grill in the door in the high brown-painted wooden fence. On Mondays when Miss Bessie Morris's underwear was hanging on the clothesline to dry, the grill was closed. And there was the Germantown Academy, so old that it still had the British crown on its weathervane, where Washington's step-grandson, George Washington Custis, had been a pupil and Washington, it was said, had sometimes walked to school with him.

I read all of the Peggy Owen books and the Lucky Sixpence series, and then I went on to *Pemberton* and *Hugh Wynne*. My father took me with him when he made a business trip to Washington, and we went to the church at Alexandria, where Washington worshiped, and Mount Vernon, where I saw running on the green lawn in the spring rain my first cardinal. Cardinals have since become common in Pennsylvania, but at that time they were still a

Southern bird, and the sight of the brilliant, crested little creature in that beautiful place was a symbol to me of all the color and romance of the long-ago struggle for freedom. My father took me too to Valley Forge, where the sufferings of the common soldiers, the bleeding tracks in the snow, the cold and hunger in the little huts over that long winter of 1777–78 gave me my first understanding of the part that faith and endurance and fortitude and defeat must play in the life of a country, as of an individual.

But the most golden of all my Revolutionary War pilgrimages, because it was a rare family expedition as well, was the Sunday in May when we went, all four of us, to an afternoon service at old St. David's Church in Radnor, where the Revolutionary general known as Mad Anthony Wayne is buried. The occasion was a garden party which Dr. Lamb, the rector of old St. David's, gave to the members of the St. Andrew's Society and their wives. Dr. Lamb, whose wife was a distant cousin of Mother's, was then chaplain of the St. Andrew's Society, the society of Scotsmen established before the Revolution primarily to give assistance to poor Scottish immigrants in Philadelphia and secondarily to eat dinner together at the Bellevue-Stratford twice a year, and my father was its president, succeeding Dr. S. Weir Mitchell, his friend and the author of *Hugh Wynne*.

We set out on the train, taking the Chestnut Hill Local to West Philadelphia and the Paoli Local from there to Devon Station, where horse-drawn omnibuses met us and took us through the blossoming countryside of big estates to the small old stone church under its great trees. I saw the grave of the dashing general who, next to Washington, was my hero, and my father recited for me part of Longfellow's poem about old St. David's. After a brief service in the church, which was crowded with affluent and benevolent Scots, we all walked across the road to the rectory, where we had ice cream and strawberries in the garden.

Mother had made an enchanting dress for me, of pussy willow taffeta of the shade of blue sometimes called madonna, and had smocked it by hand. As I had fallen through shyness into a bad habit of ducking my head and looking down at the ground when a grownup spoke to me, Mother had put it up to me beforehand as a condition of my being included in the party that I was to look everyone whom I met squarely in the eyes, curtsey and say clearly, "How do you do?" Conscientiously, over and over again that afternoon, I went through this routine, looking at blue eyes, gray eyes, brown eyes, hats piled high with flowers and fruit, gentlemanly bald heads and chins propped up by stiff white collars with points. The consciousness of being supremely well-dressed was a great support to me and, as I was the only child there, I received an amount of attention that made me feel the occasion was as successful socially as it was historically. Best of all was the deep, rich, nourishing sense of being a family out together, enjoying the party and one another.

Those three or four years of immersion in the period of the American Revolution gave me something invaluable to a writer. The techniques of research in a period of history I was to learn much later, but the faculty of putting myself back into another age, so that I lived in it, thought in it, saw and heard and smelled and tasted in it, so that it was as real to me as the world of my daily life, came to me before I had any way of knowing what a useful—and rare—gift it was.

Despite the withdrawal of those years, a few people of unusual interest did penetrate the walls we had erected about ourselves.

In my class at the Stevens School was a little girl named Lucinda Iliff, a quiet child with two tight pigtails and a quaint way of speaking. Her father was English, her mother Pennsylvania Dutch. The English father was a shadowy figure seldom seen, but the mother was an enthusiast, an original. At a time when few were aware of the treasures to be found in New Mexico, Mrs. Iliff had visited, studied, made friends with the Pueblo Indians of Taos, and with the Navahoes of Albuquerque. Her house was full of Indian treasures—feathered headdresses, buckskin tunics fringed and beaded, silver and turquoise jewelry, pottery, woven rugs. They were not arranged; they were simply there. Nor were they explained. One looked at them, handled them and wondered. When there was a May Day pageant at school, all our class was fitted out with Indian costumes.

The Iliff house was also full of moths, not clothes moths but beautiful, mounted Cecropias and lunas and others. Mrs. Iliff was a naturalist. Her knowledge of moths was extensive and accurate. Gene Stratton Porter's *Girl of the Limberlost* was a best seller at that time, and part of its attraction for people was the picture it gave of the great swamp called the Limberlost and the wildlife that flourished there. Inspired by questions from readers, the publishers conceived the idea of a factual book called *Moths of the Lim-*

berlost, and for this Mrs. Iliff was asked to supply the plates from her own collections.

A lanky, loping, plain woman with a long, pointed nose, mousy hair and a flat, singsong Pennsylvania Dutch voice, Mrs. Iliff was Pied Piper to a small group of Lucinda's classmates. Nearly every Saturday, spring and fall, she led us out into the fields and woods in search of birds and wild flowers, moths, butterflies, rabbits, chipmunks, frogs' eggs, tadpoles. The Wissahickon Valley, the strip of woodland along the railroad cut below Queen Lane Station, where now are factories, the open fields still remaining on the fringes of Germantown, offered us long days of tramping and discovery. While we ate our picnic lunch—and if one wanted to make a meal entirely of sticky cinnamon buns Mrs. Iliff, who seemed to be entirely without fussy grown-up notions, accepted that as natural—we showed our trophies wilting in our baskets and Mrs. Iliff explained to us what they were. She listened to what we said, laughed at our jokes without condescension, talked to us without moralizing, taught us without pressure.

Dr. Charles Johnston was a distant cousin of my father's, of the branch of the family that had included the missionary Duff. As a young man he himself had gone to Africa as a missionary, realized that he could do little for the people with the Bible alone, and had returned to Edinburgh to study medicine. When he went back to Central Africa with his skills and his medical supplies, he had a wide success. He was said to have been—by whom? by himself, I must assume—the first white man to cross Africa without a shot fired in anger. After years there, during which he developed a love of the African people that was evident years later in his voice as well as his words, he contracted tuberculosis and retired to live in Jamaica. Having married a well-to-do Englishwoman, he lived there in some state, and from time to time came to Philadelphia and spent a week or so with us. Very fat by that time, he wanted no other entertainment than to sit and talk and be listened to. He brought us, besides his exotic tales of jungles and of tropical beaches, fruit from his own trees: grapefruit; bananas; alligator pears, then a rarity even in the sophisticated fruit stores; and mangoes. He sat always in the same chair, and after he left we sent it to have the bottom put back again in readiness for his next visit.

His daughter Gertrude, a very smart and striking young woman —"dashing" was the word then—of Violet's age, came to New York and got a job as Mistress of Deportment at the fashionable Miss Spence's School. In time she married Dr. Rolfe Kingsley, who was to step into a crisis of my own life many years later.

Another of my father's friends was Theodore Justice, a well-to-do, worldly Quaker with snowy white hair and beard, who had a passion for horses. He lived three or four blocks away from us in a Victorian house with a stable, where he kept always two or three beautiful horses. He rode, he drove a pair in summer with a carriage, in winter with a sleigh. Every Saturday he and my father rode together along the Wissahickon, my father on a local riding stable's one thoroughbred. Mr. Justice often offered to mount him, but his pride demanded his own horse, as the McNeil had his ain boat. Mr. Justice was a member of various hunt clubs around the city and attended all the horsy events: the Devon horse show, the point-to-point races, the hunts, the drag hunts, the beagle hunts, the polo games. From time to time he took us with him to one or another of these affairs, and often we went driving with him along the Wissahickon. Best of all were the sleigh rides in winter, under a furry rug, with the sleigh bells jingling, the horses trotting along briskly, now and then blowing or tossing their heads, the sun on their round, shiny chestnut rumps, and Mr. Justice telling stories about his experiences hunting in England, about the Civil War campaign in which he, a boy of fifteen, had fought, and about how the local hunt clubs brought in foxes from the South, buried them in the ground and let them dig their way out, thus providing them with a burrow to return to, and how a farmer once said to him, "It must be true what they say, that foxes enjoy being hunted, for we never used to have any hereabouts before the hunt club came." Often in the late afternoon Mr. Justice would stop at our house for a cup of tea in front of the open fire in our hall.

Cousin Emma Acton was a distant cousin on Mother's side, of the variety described in the country phrase, "Her grandmother's cat ran through my grandmother's garret." She lived in Salem, New Jersey, in a frame house that she and her husband, an insurance broker, had designed and built when they were first married in the 1870's. The house had an odd bulge on one side, owing to the fact that when it was almost finished, the builder had come to them with the announcement, "You forgot the stairs!" and a narrow flight of steps with murderous twists top and bottom had been stuck on.

Cousin Emma, who came frequently to the city, used sometimes to stay overnight with us. She was a beautiful woman with a cameo profile, fine, dark brown eyes, rich chestnut hair and a commanding presence. Well-dressed, kind and generous, with a connoisseur's knowledge of antique furniture, gourmet food, old silver, and Oriental rugs, she brought with her an aura of a world beyond our ken, but she had a—to me—startling disregard for the niceties of English grammar; to be explicit, she said "he come" and "she don't." When she was overcome with laughter, she would bend forward, pick up her skirt by the hem with both hands and throw it up over her face.

Once a year or so I was invited to visit her in Salem, sometimes with Mother, sometimes by myself. Salem was only thirty miles away, but the trip involved the train to Broad Street Station, the trolley car down Market Street to the river, the ferry boat across the wide Delaware, with the great piles creaking and smelling of seaweed at the far side, then the Camden terminal and the walk out the long platform to the train.

"If you go to the left you're right," Cousin Emma would say and I found it exquisitely funny; "if you go to the right you'll be left."

Salem was at the end of the line. There was a walk to Seventh Street, where Cousin Emma's house was, with a porch across the front and another at the side opening off the kitchen. There was a formal parlor to the right of the front door and a sitting room behind it, with curtains made of strings of beads between it and the dining room. In the kitchen there was a pump, besides the running water, and the side porch faced on a narrow, deep, old-fashioned garden with a grape arbor and roses and a stable on the back alley. Upstairs I slept in the spare room, where the beautiful old mahogany furniture included a washstand with a Canton china ewer and basin, and the blinds were kept drawn when the sun was on that side of the house, lest the flowered carpet be faded.

Two of Cousin Emma's sons lived in Salem with their families and were often in and out of the house. They were big, jolly young men with a warm, teasing way with children that was enchanting to me. Cousin Emma's husband was a kind, quiet man who made little impression on me. It was his brother's widow and her children who were the big attraction in Salem for me. "Mrs. Jon," who lived on the other side of town in a large, shabby old house, also filled with priceless antiques, was like Cousin Emma, a beauty, but softer, gentler, gayer. Her English was impeccable, her voice low and rich, she was a great reader of books which would

now be called avant-garde. I was aware, though I did not understand them, of tensions between Cousin Emma and her sister-in-
law, Mrs. Jon Acton. Mrs. Jon's three older children were out of my
ken except as they made a pleasant bustle in the house, but Con,
who was exactly a month older than I, and Margaret, who was a
year younger, were my especial friends.

Playing at Con-and-Margaret's house, roaming the town in
search of adventure, driving with some complaisant grownup to
the Country Club on the river, which was still clean enough to
swim in: the pleasures in Salem were simple ones but rare and
wonderful to me. Like my mother, I came to love the wide, flat
countryside with its limitless sky, the reed-grown bird-haunted
marshes, the old farmhouses at the ends of long lanes, the cedars
along the fences, the straight, white roads made of ground oyster
shells.

Once I was there in June before the Salem school was out, and
Margaret took me to visit her class. When she introduced me to the
teacher, I looked her straight in the eye, curtseyed and said clearly,
"How do you do?" It was a mistake. Wherever I went for the rest
of that visit, little boys and even big boys who had only heard
about it curtseyed to me as they passed in the street and little girls
giggled and called out, "How do you do?" Fortunately, and probably with Violet's help, I thought it was funny and was greatly
pleased when Violet later used the incident in her first book.

Con taught me to ride his bicycle, as later he was to teach me
to drive a car. I was not allowed to have a bicycle at home because
of the increasing number of cars on the streets. For a brief period
each year I had the illusion of having a brother and a sister of my
own age, of being part of a big family the doors of whose house
were always open, and it was a heady, joyous experience.

As automobiles replaced horse-drawn vehicles, our corner became a dangerous one, with cars rushing from both directions,
meeting and often crashing at the intersection. My father, who
liked to read his Sunday *Times* in peace on the porch, was disgusted
by the proliferation of Fords.

"Workmen and people like that these days," he complained, "all
think they have to have cars."

Have cars, I thought. Why shouldn't they? Was there any reason
they should not if they could pay for them? Because they crowded
the roads and were noisy? But why should some people be allowed
to go out for rides and others not? Perhaps there were not enough

cars to go round. But the car manufacturers could make more; that was their business. I turned the problem over and over in my mind. I could never find a reason why people like that should not have cars.

4.

The School Years II

THREE THINGS happened at the end of my twelfth and beginning of my thirteenth year that changed the whole color and tempo of my life: going to the Germantown Friends School, the outbreak of the first World War, and an injury to my back in a scuffle with another child which gave me trouble for the next seven years.

The injury was diagnosed as sacroiliac strain, and I had to wear a surgical brace made of canvas and whalebone, with steel clasps, which I was careful to conceal. The pain in my back and right thigh was not acute, but it was steady, nagging and grinding. It cut me out of athletics and made me feel different from the other children, increased the sensitivity natural to adolescence and the shyness that was innate. Quite possibly it had a psychosomatic origin, although in those days we had no such respectable term; one was always under the suspicion of succumbing to nerves and imagination. My sister became my fiercely protective champion and so deepened the already developing rift between her and my mother. I was troubled by the tension between them and the stress of my own position in the middle. After a series of doctors had tried and failed to find the real source of my pain, a well-known diagnostician discovered a lack of hydrochloric acid in my system, which, he said, caused poisoning that sought out the old injury and expressed itself through that. A stringent diet and perhaps also the new environment of college finally cleared it up completely, but during the five years that I was at the Germantown Friends School and for two years after that I seldom felt really well physically.

The "Great War," which struck much of the world with astonishment in the summer of 1914, was no surprise to us. I am always a little incredulous when I read memoirs and novels of that period to find that many—perhaps most—people then saw nothing especially significant in the assassination of the Austrian archduke on June 28 and had no inkling that it would result in the ultimatums of July and August and the march of the German armies into Belgium. My father for two years or more previously had been watching the expansion of the German military power and the preparations for war; he had talked a great deal about it at the dinner table, with that especial emotional shrillness of the Cassandra whose warnings create nothing but tedium. On Dr. Johnston's last visit to us before his death, my father had said to him so often, "You British must open your eyes. You are blind to what is going on," that Dr. Johnston had taken Mother aside and said, "I am a little worried about your husband. He has the Germans on the brain. You must be very wise. Don't oppose him, but don't encourage him either."

Mother herself, who had enjoyed studying German, speaking it whenever she had an opportunity and reading Goethe and Schiller with pleasure, had considered Germany, as so many did, the font of civilization; she was troubled and divided in mind.

So from the moment when the headlines first appeared on June 29, 1914, my family was on the alert. They followed each development with foreboding and alarm. There was no radio to bring us the news. The daily papers, of which Philadelphia then had five, issued numerous extras, which were brought by train to Queen Lane Station and there sold on the newsstand. Many times a day during that summer I was jerked out of whatever I was doing and sent to fetch the latest extra.

From that June on through to the false and then the real armistice in November, 1918, little else was talked of at our dinner table but the War. It dominated our lives. It made no difference that for nearly three years the United States was not in it or that President Woodrow Wilson, whom my father could not abide, was urging the country to be neutral in thought. We as a family were in it from the moment when Sir Edward Grey said, "The lamps are going out all over Europe" and Britain declared war.

We had *The Public Ledger* and *The Evening Bulletin* daily and *The New York Times* on Sundays. My father read the British papers, two weeks late of course, every day when he went to the Union League for lunch. We had the German atrocities for dinner, the horrors of the march through Belgium, Edith Cavell, the shelling of Rheims Cathedral, the taxicabs of Paris, the angels of Mons,

the *Lusitania*, the U-boats, and, most distressing of all, the slaugh-
ter of the beautiful young men from Oxford and Cambridge, whose
photographs we saw in page after page of *The Illustrated London
News*. We had the poems of Rupert Brooke, Alan Seeger, John
McCrae and other "war poets" but not those of Siegfried Sassoon
and Wilfred Owen, whom I did not discover till long after the war
was over.

English officers appeared in Philadelphia to make purchases for
the British Army and Navy, and my father entertained them at the
Union League. One of them was a very tall, thin young man
named John Reith, later to become the head of the BBC—"that
wuthering height," in Winston Churchill's phrase. One day my
father told us at dinner that officers from the Japanese Navy had
come to him that day to see about some orders. He was high in
his praise of their style and bearing, their intelligence and the perfection of their manners. For the second time, I became dimly
aware of Japan, and I used the incident in a composition for
school.

Queen-Gray Company, as it had become by that time, was making gun sights, chronometers and other instruments for the armies
but was scarcely more prosperous than it had been, for there were
losses on the gun sights and when the war came to an end the company was left with unfinished orders that were immediately canceled. Still, my father was able to put aside Liberty Bonds enough
to ensure my college education. I can see to this day the light in his
eyes when he told me about it.

At school I heard the Quaker point of view on war, but I learned
not to report it at home. To my father it was treason and folly.
That the United States did not immediately go to the rescue of
Britain was a daily source of anger and grief to him until at last, in
April, 1917, the United States declared war. The arguments and
assumptions of both points of view fell on the blank pages of my
mind. At the time I accepted almost without question my father's
ideas, but in the end Quaker thought and the mental climate of
the early thirties prevailed; I was already a pacifist when I joined
the Society of Friends.

It was at the end of sixth grade that, for reasons which they did
not disclose to me, my parents decided to transfer me to the Germantown Friends School. My mother went and talked to the headmaster, Stanley R. Yarnall, who expressed a sympathetic interest
but explained that although there were openings in the eighth

grade the seventh grade, for which I was ready, was full to capacity.

"Put her in the eighth grade then," said Mother, undaunted.

Two teachers gave me an oral examination to determine whether this was possible. Irvin C. Poley, then a very young man, now in his late seventies and still a cherished friend, and Teacher Emma Roberts, one of the best loved of the older teachers, both asked me a few questions so gently that I was scarcely aware that it was an examination and, surely on faith or else on my mother's confidence, declared me capable of skipping a grade. So at not quite twelve, abandoning a whole year of arithmetic, which I really needed, American history, geography, general science and large chunks of English grammar, I went into eighth grade. After the first month I was on the Honor Roll again and Mother was vindicated. So easily, almost casually, I was brought to one of the few decisive changes of my life, reached a fork in the road and was shoved down the path that "has made all the difference."

On Thursday mornings all of the school except the four primary grades went to Meeting. The school, like the Friends Free Library, where Violet was now an assistant librarian, was situated on the grounds of Germantown Monthly Meeting. The Meeting itself, though not the meetinghouse, went back to the 1680's when German Quakers accepted William Penn's invitation to join his holy experiment and founded the settlement near Philadelphia which was soon called Germantown.

At quarter to ten we all filed decorously into the large, unadorned room, whose beauty lay in its perfect proportions and in the view from the high windows of trees against the sky, and sat down on the old wooden benches, then uncushioned, girls on one side, boys on the other, a teacher and a senior to each row. The school was small enough at that time to fill only three-quarters of the room; the fourth quarter was left for the members of the Meeting, who came in their sober clothes for the regular midweek worship. On the high "facing benches" sat the elders of the Meeting, men on the right, women on the left. Though the strict Quaker garb had for the most part disappeared and been succeeded by a general dowdiness, there were still on the facing bench one or two elderly women Friends who wore the traditional Quaker bonnet and gray dress, and one man, ruddy-faced and white-haired, whose gray coat had no lapels.

There was a general rustling and stir while the school entered and sat down, then a silence of a particular kind, not merely an absence of noise, spread over the room, telling us that Meeting had begun. Sitting still, for me at twelve, without a book to read was sheer punishment. I sighed. I yawned. I squirmed. I caught a classmate's eye and tried not to giggle. Each week I thought of my father's story of the time he went to Friends Meeting and, sitting in the corner of the bench on the center aisle, wondered what he would do if the Spirit moved him to get up and dance a Highland fling in the aisle. Over and over again I pondered this question. What would you do? How would you know if it really was the Spirit? If you were certain it was, *shouldn't* you get up and dance in the aisle? What would I do if a prompting to so conspicuous and embarrassing an act should come to me? I thought I was getting nothing at all from the tiresome forty-five minutes and wasting time that could be better spent in a hundred ways, but actually I was engaged in meditating on a fundamental Quaker question.

Sometime during the Meeting someone, usually on the facing bench, rose and spoke. I seldom noticed very much what they said, except that there was one man who always talked about making our practice consistent with our profession. What really impressed me, as I came to know them better, was that busy men, men with offices in the city, left their work on a weekday morning in order to come to Meeting. It was that important to them.

Occasionally the mother of my new and dear friend, Betty Warren, spoke from the facing bench, a gentle, deeply spiritual, tender person, whom I knew and loved in daily life. This too was impressive, a woman preaching, a woman who could make jokes and laugh and receive confidences and understand exactly how one felt.

Once one of the older boys, the president of the senior class, spoke, and this was awe-inspiring. Once the school daredevil hid an alarm clock in the register: it went off with a metallic shriek when Meeting was about three-fourths over, and the room shook with suppressed laughter. The crime must have been handled with firmness and humor; we all knew who had done it, but he became neither a martyr nor a hero.

By the time I had reached senior year and myself sat with a row of younger girls to weigh my composure against their restlessness, I had learned to accept Meeting, not only to accept it but to welcome it for what it gave me of release from outside pressures, of serenity, of inner exploration.

The school had at that time, as it still has, a remarkable body of teachers. I was never in the classes of the two I had already met, but I had Teacher Jennie Jones in arithmetic and algebra, Miss Edith Knight in French, Miss Helen Zebley in Latin, three women of great integrity, high standards of behavior and a detached, humorous, sympathetic understanding of youth. Of the men, those who most deeply impressed me were D. Lawrence Burgess, shy, austere, keen, witty, kind, who taught me English during the first two or three years, and Harry A. Domincovich, known as Domi, who had a Russian warmth and fervor combined with a latent sadness that conveyed to us wordlessly something of that European sense of the tragedy of life foreign to our young and confident American thought. Domi awakened in me a love of poetry that has been a lifetime resource; he carried on the Latin which I started with Miss Zebley, and which also I loved. Though I had missed a crucial year of English grammar, I got from Latin something that more than compensated: an understanding of the fundamental structure of language itself, a sense of the beauty of its bones.

Two real, live poets visited the school while I was there; they both came twice and read their poems to us. Vachel Lindsay was in his mid-thirties at that time; he had already written the poems for which he is best known: "General William Booth Enters into Heaven," "A Negro Sermon:—Simon Legree," "The Congo," "The Santa Fé Trail"; and he had developed a way of chanting them and of drawing his audience into the performance that was irresistible.

"Daniel in the li-on's den," he would intone, his blue eyes blazing, his hand waving to us to come in.

"We *are* the li-ons!" we would roar in response.

Or, "I've been to Palestine" he would sing, and we responded, "What did you see in Palestine?"

I remember shouting "Down, down to the dev-ool" in the Simon Legree poem, and shivering over the "Fat black bucks" in the Congo poem; the contrasts of the Santa Fé Trail with the thunder of the rolling wheels, the tramp of feet, the hooves of the buffaloes, and then the sweet, sweet, quiet song of the Rachel-Jane transported me to the spaces and the romance of the West.

The other poet who came to us was Robert Frost, just back from England, where *North of Boston* had been published and well received. He seemed young, even to us, though actually he was five years older than Vachel Lindsay. Curly-haired, slender, diffident, he read his poems in quiet, conversational tones, as if they were not poetry at all. "Mending Wall" was the one that found the most lasting place in my mind. "Something there is that doesn't love a wall." Not walls of any kind, I thought, especially not the inner ones we build, even between ourselves and those closest to us.

Senior Bible was taught by the school's famous headmaster, Stanley R. Yarnall, known in those days as Master Stanley. He was a tall, fine-looking man with thick, wavy hair which turned prematurely white and a commanding presence. Violet, musing one time upon that impressive crown of white hair, wondered what difference it might have made in his reign over children and parents if Master Stanley had been bald, but I felt sure that he would have surmounted even that; he had a fine, authoritative nose too. That he was also a famous raconteur and mimic I did not discover until many years later, after I had joined the Meeting and he and his very much younger wife, Sue, moved from the realm of authority into that of friendship.

Going from a girls' school to a coeducational school was not the drastic change then that it might have been later. The boys and girls at Germantown Friends School in those days merely tolerated each other as brothers and sisters might. Right through senior year we had no "dates" among our classmates; indeed, I think the term had not yet come into general use. My boyfriends, a term then used but not approved, were outside of school altogether. During senior year there was a sudden blossoming of parties, but the fact that there were seventeen girls in my class and only ten boys dimmed their glamor.

After Betty Warren left to go to Westtown, the Quaker boarding school, Elizabeth Sheble came into the class to be my most congenial friend. Three months younger than I, she replaced me as youngest member of the class. A vibrant, eager, talented girl, she too wanted to write; she cared even more about the drama and was the moving spirit in our plays, which at that time we were not permitted to put on in the school. There had been, it is true, an ambitious and successful Shakespearean Festival on the three hundredth anniversary of Shakespeare's death, with a great procession singing "Gaudeamus igitur" in which all the school marched in Elizabethan costume, and with parts of the plays acted by different classes. I was Titania in A *Midsummer Night's Dream*, and Helen Thomas, who played Puck, did it with a verve, a hilarious, malicious joy, that I have seen in no subsequent Puck. But

an ordinary, secular, extracurricular play was another thing altogether, and not to be permitted in a Quaker auditorium.

Accordingly, with what I now see as considerable enterprise, we
put on *A Twig of Thorn,* a folk play by two sisters named Warren, reminiscent of Yeats's *Cathleen ni Houlihan,* at the Germantown Boys' Club, with Elizabeth Sheble playing Aileel, my cousin
Clara Iszard the feminine lead and I the priest. It was, oddly as it
seems now, the girls of the class who put on the play. Whether because the boys were not interested or because the school would
have balked altogether at a mixed performance, I do not remember.
Irvin Poley coached us unofficially. Much later in more liberal times
he was to come into his own when he instituted at the school his
brilliant Malvern Festival, a whole week given over each year to the
production of plays.

Elizabeth Sheble was to accompany me to Bryn Mawr and to
die of meningitis in her freshman year, my first serious grief and my
first realization that a person of my own generation could die.

Clara Iszard was the daughter of my mother's younger brother
Charles; she entered Germantown Friends two or three years after
I did, an enchantingly pretty, curly-haired little creature with big
brown eyes and a darting wit. There were still no relations between
our families and it would be pleasant to record that a warm
friendship between us two brought the feud to an end and reconciled the families, but this was not the case. I did her Latin preparation for her and was often the butt of her wit, but otherwise we
had little in common beyond a certain respect on the part of each
for the other's strengths and, as years went on, a slowly growing
affection.

I went sometimes to the theater with my father or Violet during
those years. My father took me to see DeWolf Hopper in *The Mikado* and Sarah Bernhardt on the Keith circuit in a short piece
called *The Field of Honour,* in which she played the part, at
seventy-two, of a young French soldier-poet lying wounded in a
horizon-blue uniform on the ground under a tree. She spoke passionately in French to someone who tried to take a flag away
from her; in spite of Miss Knight and Chardenal's *French Grammar* I had no idea of what she was saying except that it was obviously of a patriotic nature. Still, I had seen the great Bernhardt,
and while the comedies and dramas that Violet and I saw together
have gone out of my mind, except for Maude Adams in *A Kiss for*

Cinderella, that huddled horizon-blue figure and the strangely compelling voice are still fresh.

In the summers Violet usually took me to Cape May for a couple of weeks. It was there, late one August afternoon, that I saw my first airplane and had my first experience of that sudden joyous, intense lift of the heart in response to beauty that I came to call a "minor ecstasy" and to collect, as children used to collect the birthday pearl each year on a slim gold chain. I was twelve and we were walking on the boardwalk at sunset. At Cape May, because of its position at the mouth of the wide Delaware Bay, one can see the sun set over the water in one direction and the moon rise in the other. As we watched, the plane, like a great silver bird, flew out of the golden heart of the sunset and disappeared into the eastern sky silvered by the moon. I felt as if I had at the same moment touched history and stepped outside of time, and my young heart was stretched by a wonder that I have never forgotten.

Though we had the War at dinner and though my father in his library was buried in the newspapers and the tide of war books, the women of the house in their own quarters—my mother's bedroom at the other end of the second story from the library, Violet's third-story front and my third-story back bedroom—were absorbed in something quite different. We were all writing.

Mother was at work on a novel based on her own childhood on the farm and some of the odd characters in the neighborhood: a mad, poetic girl who called herself "Teaberry Wings," a mysterious couple from the city who lived in some formality of style without the formality of marriage. Unfortunately, Mother became deeply interested in the history and philosophy of Quakerism and prefaced each chapter of the novel with long quotations from Penn, Fox, Penington and Rufus Jones. Mother's novel went the rounds of the Philadelphia publishers, and was turned down by all but one which offered to publish it if she would put up a sizeable sum of money. In a fit of despondency she burned it in the kitchen range. Many years later, on my urging, she wrote some notes on her memories of the farm which have a charm and beauty that indicate what she might have done if she had had competent advice and more time to work at it.

Violet wrote a story for children, called *Margery Morris,* about a girl who came from California to visit her grandfather in Salem,

New Jersey, called Renwickstown in the book, and who through a series of coincidences and misunderstandings got into the wrong house, where her experiences wrought a salutary change in her fundamentally sound but superficially spoiled character. The book had freshness, interest and humor, and children have loved it. After it had been rejected by two or three publishers in New York, she sent it to the Penn Publishing Company in Philadelphia, which accepted it, but on the condition that she make it the first of a series of four, to be called *The Margery Morris Books*. She fell into the trap. The necessity of producing a book a year for four years sapped her enthusiasm and her creative energy. For the third, *Margery Morris and Plain Jane*, she used a plot and character of real substance that ought to have stood alone; in the series it was lost. The last one, *Margery Morris in the Pine Woods*, was written with gritted teeth and loathing. It was her last book until many years later she wrote two novels which were delightful but too slight for the taste of the day.

I was the willing guinea pig for Violet's stories for children but shut out of the long and sometimes vehement discussions of Mother's novel. No matter, I was deep in work of my own. Every month the incomparable *St. Nicholas Magazine* came to the house, with its rich treasure of stories, articles, serials and above all the original St. Nicholas League, which offered each month a graded series of awards for stories and poems by readers under sixteen: roll of honor, special mention, silver badge, gold badge, cash prize. Regularly I sent in my offering and waited eagerly for the magazine to arrive. I never got into the money, but the silver and then the gold badge provided my favorite jewelry.

Writing for the St. Nicholas League was midway, in my mind, between writing for school and my "real writing," since a subject was assigned. My real writing, on the other hand, was done at my own will and prompting. Like my elders I aspired to publication, and I selected—or perhaps Violet suggested—*The Young Churchman* as a target. It was a small Episcopal weekly, which always had one story between the sermonlike main article and the Sunday School lessons. I wrote a story called "The Boys' Revenge," which was just about what one would expect from the title, Violet typed it for me, and I sent it off to the editor with a stamped and addressed envelope for its return. For a while I watched the mail daily, but after two or three weeks gave it up and forgot about it.

One day, running out into the schoolyard during recess, I met Violet coming from the library in search of me with a letter in her hand.

"This came for you," she said, "after you left this morning. It was in your return-address envelope and I thought they were sending it back, so I opened it. But look!"

The editor of *The Young Churchman* began her letter, "Dear Mrs. Gray." She liked the story. She was enclosing a check for two dollars in payment. She hoped I would send her more stories. "Dear MRS. Gray." She had no idea that I was only thirteen!

I had long known the deep pull of the impulse to write, the self-transcendence of total absorption in the act of writing, the muted joy of release when the work is finished—muted because the expression so seldom rightly clothes the vision—but now for the first time I tasted the heady delight of acceptance. Later came the solid satisfaction of seeing what I had written in actual print, with my name and illustrations. *St. Nicholas* baptized me as a writer; by *The Young Churchman* I was confirmed.

Two years later I wrote another story which *The Young Churchman* accepted and for which they paid me three dollars.

When I was fourteen, it was decided by my parents and Mr. Yarnall that I was destined for Bryn Mawr. New England was what I had set my heart on, and any of the women's colleges there would have done, though on the whole I preferred Mount Holyoke because Betty Warren was going there. New England had nurtured Longfellow, Hawthorne, Emerson, Lowell, Louisa May Alcott and Robert Frost. Boston had been almost as important to the Revolution as Philadelphia. The stone walls, the apple trees and stony pastures, the mountains, the white villages under wine-glass elms, the rocks and bayberry bushes of the seacoast had entered my imagination and I longed to go there. I longed, in fact, to travel anywhere, to Scotland, to London, to Rome, but especially, since it was nearer and within the bounds of possibility, to New England. And when I went to college I wanted to go a long distance from home. But in those days no one asked a daughter what she wanted or took her to inspect several colleges so that she might choose among them. I did not even see Bryn Mawr until I went there to take the entrance examinations, and then I saw only Taylor Hall, an awkward, bastard-Gothic stone building with a clock tower, and inside, a tiled corridor with enormous busts of Zeus,

Athene and company looming on posts and a large, grim room with blue examination books on small battered desks.

Violet knew how I felt and she pled my cause with tears, but they brushed her aside. I was very young, they said, totally ignorant of the ways of the world, thin as a colt from growing so tall so fast, and I had that pain in my back. It was better for me to be where they could keep an eye on me. And anyhow Bryn Mawr was the best. So once again I was shoved along the road that I came to recognize as my own.

Among the festivities attendant on graduating from school was a party given the class by the teachers. Teacher Emma Roberts, the same one who had examined me so gently five years earlier, a Bryn Mawr graduate herself, wrote me a poem in the meter of Kipling's "Philadelphia," which began,

So you're off to Bryn Mawr College in the morning,

and ended,

> Don't forget that Aphrodite
> Is so many times more mighty
> Than Athene, patron goddess of Bryn Mawr.

5.

Higher Education

M Y CLASS at Bryn Mawr was the only one ever to be in college under three presidents. In my freshman year Miss Thomas was abroad on leave, and Dean Helen Taft was acting president. Miss Thomas returned for two more years before she retired, and in the fall of my senior year Miss Marion Edwards Park was inaugurated. The administration was to me a lofty but transient body whose attention on the whole I preferred not to attract. Of the existence of the Board of Directors I was blandly unaware; only later did I learn that Rufus Jones was its president. Members of the faculty I knew through my courses, but I seldom encountered them away from the lecture room. Communication was a word never used in that connection.

Beyond a battery of required courses, one was obliged to take two majors in certain prescribed groups: I was not permitted to combine English and History, as I wished, quite reasonably, to do, and so I took Spanish as my second major. English literature came to an end with Matthew Arnold and Thomas Hardy; American literature did not exist. Our way of life on campus was circumscribed. Our dances and the plays we put on were strictly without men. As I was tall, men's parts fell to me, which did not suit me at all. We could not go unchaperoned to the theater with a man or ride in a taxi with one after dark. Men could come to Bryn Mawr and sit in stiff parlors known as Show Cases or walk on campus paths under weeping cherry trees.

It was a rigid system, but we accepted it for the most part without question. To most of the private school graduates who then formed 80 per cent of the student body, the college years were a golden time when one made friends and cultivated one's mind and tastes; for those of us who looked forward to earning our living, it was also the prerequisite for a job. In that connection the Bryn Mawr degree, especially in the Philadelphia region, had unquestioned prestige.

We were not burdened by the wrongs and sorrows of the world. The war was over; the terrible bloodbaths of the Bolshevik Revolution were past; hunger in Germany and famine in Russia were being taken care of by Herbert Hoover and the American Friends Service Committee. Warren G. Harding, a handsome man though unfortunately a nonentity, was elected president. Prosperity was at hand. Skirts were knee high, youth was flaming, everybody was dancing. A few "worthy" people were concerned about labor relations and social justice, but almost nobody was aware of the racial tensions beneath the surface or of the forces preparing to push the Oriental Exclusion Act through the Congress. In the best of Dorothy Canfield Fisher's novels, *The Deepening Stream,* published in 1930, the well-intentioned, likable heroine reflected that when she and her family had what they needed, it was enough. Shameful though it is to remember, that was how we felt, most of us, in the early 1920's. The most difficult and painful thing to understand is the assumptions of earlier periods, not what we thought but what we assumed without examination.

Sometimes, rather superficially, I like to try to sum up in a few words what Bryn Mawr gave me, apart from the essential tools of study: the knowledge of how to do research, where to go for sources, how to examine one's material for bias, for objectivity, for omissions, for distortions, how to organize it for reports. Three nuggets come to mind: (1) Always define your terms. (Whole wars might be prevented if terms of treaties were accurately understood.) (2) Question everything. (3) A statement of biological theory that has parallels in the psychological and social history of man: "The life history of the individual recapitulates the life history of the race." More fundamental than these was the motto on the college seal, *Veritatem dilexi,* which did indeed in an unspoken but recognizable way pervade the intellectual atmosphere of the college in my day.

I have forgotten most of the lectures I heard, the books I read, the reports I wrote, but deep within me remains the conviction that the purpose, the basis, the reason for it all was the search for truth, the conviction that here is an eternal value, not ever fully attainable but forever worth reaching for, that the search in itself is rewarding and in some measure ennobling. Truth to me at first was a crystal, hard and clear and graspable. It later became a light, susceptible of being colored or dimmed by the lens through which it passes; but it was at college that this basic, often overlaid or neglected, principle became part of my underlying thought: that the search for truth is fundamental to education, to writing, to life itself.

Bryn Mawr, to a degree then unusual among women's colleges, had as many men as women on its faculty. I found that except for Mrs. Frederick de Laguna, the small, austere, lucid professor of Philosophy, and Miss Mary Swindler, the luminous, humorous scholar who then taught Required Latin but later had a brilliant career in Classical Archaeology, the men on the faculty were more stimulating and large-minded than the women. There were several women who were very well known at the time, considered stars in Bryn Mawr's crown, who seemed to me to belong to a Victorian world of "emancipated women," self-conscious, precious, surrounded by little coteries of devoted disciples.

Of the men, I remember five with especial affection. Howard J. Savage was a burly, red-faced, thick-necked man whom we nicknamed "The Brute," brusque, blunt, impatient of fuzzy thinking, easily bored, whose test for a composition was the question, "Does it *go?*" and whose occasional *good* in a small, stabbing hand at the bottom of a paper was worth working for. David Tennent, whose course in Minor Biology I took as my required science, was a quiet, illuminating teacher who gave me a glimpse into the mystery of evolving life; later he taught for a year at Keio University in Tokyo, where he is still remembered. Fonger de Haan, a thin, tall, bony, blue-eyed Dutchman, a world authority on the picaresque novel, taught me Spanish for three years; he poured out his extraordinary knowledge of Spanish idiom upon us in a glittering stream but preferred that we not offend his ears by attempting to speak the language. Samuel Chew, a suave, charming, elegant Baltimorean, author of books on Byron, Swinburne and Hardy, expounded the glories of the Elizabethan and Jacobean dramatists in Major English; and Carleton Brown put the key to Chaucer into my hand.

Dr. Brown was one of the best-known Chaucerian scholars of his day. A short, stocky, white-haired man with a squarish face full of good humor, he cut through grammatical and linguistic barbed wire to make a path for us straight into the literature itself. "We

are going to start with something that will seem to you difficult,"
he said, "and after that Chaucer will be easy." Without further pre-
liminaries he plunged us into the Middle English poem, *The Owl
and the Nightingale*. We had a dictionary; we had a text with a
minimum of notes; we had Dr. Brown, who read parts aloud to
show us how it was pronounced, to bring out the music and the
humor. After that came *The Pearl*, after which Chaucer, as he had
promised, was easy. Five hours a week for two semesters we read
The Parlement of Foules, *The Hous of Fame*, *The Boke of the
Duchesse*, *Troilus and Criseyde* and *The Canterbury Tales*. At the
end of the year I had a delight in Chaucer that sent me back to reread him ten years later, when I had a great need for books that
would help me to understand life and love and death. Out of my
work with Carleton Brown was to come, too, the one of my children's books that has been most widely read and praised, *Adam
of the Road*, a story of a thirteenth-century minstrel boy.

Perhaps there was also in Adam a faint reminiscence of Big
May Day, which occurred at the end of my freshman year, a vast,
elaborate medieval English May fair invented by Miss Thomas and
Miss Lucy Martin Donnelly, of the English Department, for which
we worked and prepared all year. It lasted two days, during which
the whole campus was turned into a medieval English village, with
flags flying from Gothic towers, maypoles with fluttering ribbons,
and a May Queen crowned on the green, jugglers, maidens, towns-
folk swarming everywhere, morris dancing, and plays performed
simultaneously in the library cloisters, in a leafy hollow on the
campus and on Radnor Green. The climax of it all was a great procession led by a pair of white oxen garlanded with (paper) flowers,
the May Queen on horseback with Robin Hood beside her, and
everybody else in costume, prancing along singing lustily, "It was a
lover and his lass, With a hey, and a ho, and a hey nonino."

Throughout the year we had made thousands of paper flowers,
practiced dances and songs and rehearsed plays. I had the part of
Demetrius in *A Midsummer Night's Dream* and strove to say, "It
is the wittiest partition that ever I heard discourse, my lord," in a
manner acceptable to Samuel Arthur King, the Englishman who
controlled our diction and produced the so-called Bryn Mawr accent. I wore a Greek tunic and long white cotton stockings dyed
flesh color. When we got caught in a shower the first day, the dye,
which had been inexpertly applied by me, ran in streaks, and my

legs looked as if they had been clawed by a cat. I look at young women now with skirts almost to the waist and remember with awe what decency required in 1920.

Miss Thomas, Bryn Mawr's first great president, whom I am grateful to have known even a little, lived in the Deanery, a large brown-shingled house of no architectural distinction, which had been cobbled together out of two old houses left over from the original farm purchased for the College in 1885, plus such additions as occurred to Miss Thomas and her friend Miss Garrett who lived with her. The two ladies traveled extensively in the summers and came home primed with ideas which found expression in the Deanery: a green garden in the Japanese style which, lit with lanterns on spring evenings, had magical beauty, and the Dorothy Vernon room, inspired by Haddon Hall and furnished with cabinets inlaid with mother-of-pearl, brassbound chests from Korea, brass tray tables from India, Oriental rugs, American sofas and tables of the Federal period, and a swing from Siam hung from the great beamed ceiling.

Here Miss Thomas gave each year four receptions for the seniors. Dressed in their best clothes, they sat in a circle around the open fire with Miss Thomas in the center. When silence had fallen, she would say, slowly, "Now, what shall we talk about?" And some brave soul would venture a topic thought up beforehand. After the ordeal was over, she sent them into the dining room, where a feast had been prepared, including all the favorite delicacies but of the highest quality and in the greatest abundance, crowned with *marrons glacés*. Tactfully she left them to it and did not reappear herself until time to stand at the door and receive their thanks as they left. Though she retired before my senior year, she gave one reception for my class as juniors, so that we might have this unique Bryn Mawr experience. But I enjoyed even more a smaller party that she gave for Amy Lowell, to which she invited a few students who were known to be interested in writing.

After being introduced seriatim to Miss Lowell, we sat in the usual circle facing the fire and the poet rose to read to us. She was all in gray, and she was shaped like a truncated cone. At the top of her head was a neat little pat of gray hair, from which her forehead sloped downward and outward, her nose projected a little farther, her chin beyond her nose, her bosom, upholstered in gray silk, beyond her chin, her waistline beyond her bosom, her stomach beyond her waistline, her skirt swelling bell-shaped to the floor. She prefaced her reading with a brisk admonition,

"If you like my things, clap, if you don't like them, hiss, but for God's sake do something."

We clapped enthusiastically at once.

Her poem "Patterns" had made a good bit of stir, partly because of that then-shocking last line, "Christ! What are patterns for?" She read that to us and she read "Lilacs," which was still in manuscript. In spite of S. Foster Damon's large and respectful biography, nobody reads Amy Lowell very much these days. Her rebellions are commonplace now, and perhaps there was not really very much behind them but the desire to rebel. At that time, however, she had a firm position, and to be in the room with her, to shake her hand, to hear her read something that had not yet seen print, was a memorable experience.

Other luminaries came to Bryn Mawr while I was there, but Amy Lowell and Siegfried Sassoon, who was remarkable to us chiefly for his slim figure and his total inaudibility, were the ones I remember.

I was given in those days, as indeed I still am, to filling notebooks with quotations that speak to my condition. A small black leather notebook survives from my college days, full of Edna St. Vincent Millay and John Donne, Walter Pater and Oscar Wilde, Sir Walter Raleigh and Masefield, Amy Lowell and George Moore, Shakespeare and Kipling, Webster and Barrie, Heine and Walt Whitman, Emerson and Epictetus. More of the quotations, rather surprisingly, are ironic than inspirational; one bit of anonymous doggerel perhaps summed up the longing of my heart more accurately than any of the more literarily respectable:

> Wide world, tried world,
> Give me of your best;
> Give me savor of the sea
> And the sea's unrest;
> Bitter bread if need be
> But courage for the quest.

In the fall of 1921 Violet went to New York to take a course in Library Science at the New York Public Library. The course has since been absorbed in the Department of Library Service at Columbia University, but at that time it was held in the Main Library at 42nd Street and Fifth Avenue. An A.B. was announced as prerequisite, but a few students who could pass a stiff examination in general knowledge were also admitted. Violet, whose school days were twenty years behind her but whose reading had been vast and whose mind was clear, vigorous and retentive, sailed through the examination with ease.

She shared an apartment on Claremont Avenue with our cousin Muriel Iszard, who was studying to be an opera singer, and a younger girl who was a kindergarten teacher. Our family feuds had worn themselves out by this time, and cautious relations were resumed with some of the cousins and aunts.

Violet's going to New York was an act of great daring. She had some help from our father, but she had saved most of the money for the venture from her small salary and the proceeds of the Margery Morris books. In a further act of courage and faith she took some of her hoard and carried me off with her to New England for three weeks in September before she left for New York and I for Bryn Mawr.

We stopped in New York coming and going; we visited Boston, walking as directed on "Winter Street until it turned into Summer and Milk Street till it turned into Water"; we went to Annisquam, where we stayed at a rambling summer hotel called the Bywater Inn, perched on the rocks above the Bay of St. Ann. From there we walked all over the charming old village of Annisquam, were rowed across the narrow inlet to Wingaersheek Beach, then lonely and inaccessible, went to Gloucester and Rockport by open trolley, had tea and cinnamon toast in every quaint teahouse on all of Cape Ann, and sat on the porch of Aunt Emily's friends the Damons giggling at the witticisms of the youngest member of the family, now well known as Harvard's S. Foster Damon.

It was a time of ecstasy for me. I was not quite nineteen, Violet thirty-eight; the years between us seemed to have folded together like an accordion. We both were students, we enjoyed the same books, the same jokes, we had an elliptic language out of shared family understanding. There grew between us a friendship that was independent of years and sisterhood.

After that memorable trip to New England, I made more forays out into the world beyond Bryn Mawr and Germantown, Salem and Cape May. That fall I went for the first time to West Point for a week end complete with football game, hop, Sunday morning service at the Chapel and afternoon stroll on Flirtation

Walk—and, of course, trim cadet in 1812 uniform. The beauty of the Hudson in October, brilliantly blue between its gold and scarlet enclosing hills, the marching, the military band, the dance programs, the view from the balcony of Cullum Hall of the black river below and the lights of the night boat signaling to West Point as it passed were even more thrilling to me than the attentive but somewhat stereotyped young man who made it all possible.

During that winter of 1921–22 I spent many a week end in New York with Violet and Muriel, sleeping on a cot in their living room, exploring New York, going to Gray's Drug Store for cut-price tickets to plays. We saw Tallulah Bankhead in *Nice People* when she was more famous as the daughter of the Congressman from Alabama than as herself, and a number of other popular plays of the moment: *Kiki, Blossom Time, The Dover Road, Chauve Souris, To the Ladies, The Bat* and half a dozen others.

The following summer I went to New Hampshire. A close friend of mine at Bryn Mawr was Elizabeth Child, daughter of Clarence Griffin Child, one of the stars of the English Department at the University of Pennsylvania. The Childs had a cottage at Wonalancet, New Hampshire, and in the summer of 1922 I went for the first time to visit them.

Wonalancet lay in an "intervale," a flat valley remaining from a glacial lake, eight miles from the nearest village over a narrow, steep and winding road. The Childs' cottage was encircled by a swift ice-cold brook which made music at night; ferns and columbines grew up to the windows, the fire in the big fireplace in the living room never went out. Across the narrow road was a long, flat field, from which the mountains, Whiteface, Wonalancet, Hibberd, Hedgehog and Paugus, with Chocorua hidden behind Paugus, rose into the sky.

The Child family, like their mountains, were a delight: Bill, the youngest, friendly, eager, full of projects; Elizabeth, my friend, interested, like me, in writing—she wrote a short story with a beginning I have seldom seen bettered: "I killed my next door neighbor, no matter why"—Mrs. Child, of Boston heritage, white-haired, aquiline, discriminating; and Mr. Child, tall, homely and fascinating, a raconteur, an enthusiast, a man of almost unlimited knowledge in many fields besides English literature, an immensely popular teacher. The story was told at the University one year that when he entered his lecture room at the beginning of the term, it was crowded to more than twice its capacity, with students standing in the aisles. Nonplused, he announced that he would leave the room for a few minutes, and when he came back, all who had not found seats would have to form a second section, to be taught by an assistant. On his return, all two hundred were seated, on window sills and on the floor.

In the cottage economy he washed the dishes and I dried them; he talked and I listened—to such a flow of wisdom, commentary, humor, anecdote as I have never in all the years since heard equaled. My delight in Chaucer reached out to his vast and perceptive knowledge of him, and we talked about Chaucer's people as if we had been gossiping about contemporary friends and neighbors.

I was graduated from Bryn Mawr College at twenty, in 1923, and came home to write. I wrote short stories and sent them to the *Saturday Evening Post, Redbook, The Cosmopolitan* and the women's magazines, of which there were then six. All the stories came back, some with rejection slips, some with personal notes from the editor, all of which, without originality, I pasted on the wall behind my desk. I wrote a book for children, and that too came back several times. In a discouraged moment I sent it to the Penn Publishing Company, which promptly accepted it; but when they insisted on a contract for a series of four books about the same characters, I wrote them a stiff letter and took back my manuscript. The only thing that I had accepted was an essay on the Scots called "A Guid Conceit," which was published in the Contributors' Club of the *Atlantic Monthly*, but without my name, as their custom was. To supply myself with funds during this unremunerative period, I tutored children in any subject but mathematics or science at two and a half dollars an hour, which was good pay in those days.

After Violet returned home from New York with her library degree in her pocket, she was offered the position of librarian at Starr Center, a neighborhood house in Philadelphia on Lombard Street between Seventh and Eighth. The area at that time was a foreign quarter with a population of Russian and Polish Jews, Italians, an occasional Chinese, a few Negroes. The neighborhood house itself consisted of two eighteenth-century houses which had been thrown together; the library was on the second floor. Violet succeeded an elderly woman who had been much loved for her kindness but who had held the old-fashioned view that a successful library was full of books in neat rows to be looked at by a few

well-mannered children with clean hands. Violet had had no training in social work, but she had a clear vision of what books could
bring to eager minds. She went into that dead library and made
it into a living one. The physical changes she wrought were simple and inexpensive; walls painted yellow, woodwork gray, fresh
white dotted-swiss curtains at the windows, a few bright prints,
some handmade pottery from our own supply, window boxes in
summer foaming with petunias. She spent most of the funds on
new books: books to read for pleasure, books for schoolwork, light
novels to take home to mothers. Every afternoon and every evening
the two rooms of the library were crowded with eager, thrusting
children. "Teacher! I need a book about Physics!" "Teacher! I want
a good book for a lady that sews pants at home!" All of the books
but the reference collection went out again as soon as they were
returned; the shelves at the end of the day were swept bare.

They were bright, those children of foreign immigrants, hungry
for knowledge, for life. They wanted all she had to give; more even
than the books, they wanted a friend, a listener. They crowded
around her to tell of their experiences in the old country, their
hopes in the new, their troubles, their successes. It was an hour's
trip for her each way commuting by train and two streetcars; the
work drained both body and heart; she was often exhausted; but
she knew during the thirteen years that she was there a constant
giving and receiving, a loving and being loved, a rich, turbulent, rewarding life. When she left, in 1936, to return to the Friends Library as its head librarian, it was because the neighborhood
around Starr Center had changed. Many of her friends had moved
away to more prosperous neighborhoods, to mount the next rung
on the ladder of American life; the Negroes who came to take their
place were not readers; tenements were torn down and warehouses
built; nearby public schools began to get libraries of their own;
the neighborhood house changed its emphasis, the library was dis-
continued.

In the spring of my first year out of college Bill Child outgrew his
strength, and his family decided to take him out of school for the
last six weeks of the year and send him to Wonalancet for fresh
air and relief from tension. Elizabeth, then engaged to Dick
McKey, who was staying that spring with his mother and sister at
the other end of the intervale, was to go with Bill to take care of
him and run the cottage; I was invited to join them.

We got there early in May, when there were still snowdrifts on the tops of the mountains and a veil of heather-colored buds covered the trees on the lower slopes. It was cold. We piled on blankets at night and filled hot-water bottles; we had great fires in the fireplaces, and we used the wood range in the kitchen instead of the oilstove. Most of the days we were out in the sun and wind watching spring come with a rush.

I was there for seven weeks with Elizabeth and Bill, until the apple trees and lilacs bloomed in June, when, reluctantly, I went home. Alone, with Bill or Elizabeth, or with the son of the farmer from whom we got our milk, I walked, fished, climbed, wielded a machete on the overgrown trails, looked for birds and wild flowers, ran to a forest fire, collected the stories and legends of the region. For the first time in my life I was long enough in the real country to feel immersed in it, and some deep holes in my being were filled. Without taking a note, I stored up impressions, scenes, incidents that emerged a year later in a book.

That summer I took a large step toward freedom. I bought a Ford of the type we had not yet learned to call a Model T. A two-seater without the self-starter and the speedometer, which were extra, it cost a little over three hundred dollars, the smallest and cheapest car available, and I paid for it out of my savings and a loan from my father, to be repaid at the rate of ten dollars a month. (He gave me the rest of it as a Christmas present when he thought I had paid enough installments to get the idea.)

For several years my father had been inveighing against the Ford. Cheap, ugly, noisy, smelly, ubiquitous, available to the lower orders, or, in his euphemism, "people like that," it was changing, he maintained, the whole tenor of our lives, destroying our peace, our settled habits, our untroubled countryside. Now the viper entered his own family, and he accepted it with a rueful amusement.

No one who has not possessed a Model T Ford can have any idea of the fun it was. Snub-nosed, high on spindly wheels, it rattled and squeaked in every joint as it struggled to a top speed of thirty-five miles an hour and threatened to leave the road altogether on the curves. The door on the driver's side was painted on, for economy: it did not open; the gas tank was under the seat, and there was no gauge. You descended, lifted off the seat, unscrewed the cap and measured the contents of the tank with a ruler; when it was full it held five gallons. There was no accelerator; you increased the gas with a hand-throttle. It had two forward gears, low and high. In high gear the clutch pedal was altogether released; in low it was halfway down; all the way down was reverse. When the brake linings wore out, as they frequently did, you braked by stepping hard on reverse. When the engine got so hot that your feet were in danger of igniting, the person sitting next to the driver would open the door and hold it open till the breeze brought some relief. But these were minor flaws. The car went and it kept going; it positively liked hills.

There was considerable hilarity in the family over my car. Mother, who saw it before anyone else, came to my defense. "I thought it was a very *handsome* Ford," she declared, and The Handsome Ford became its name. After four driving lessons I passed the test and got my license. Violet and I started off together for New Hampshire before I had driven as much as fifty miles at any one time. She quoted a popular song as we left, "Put your feet in the Ford/And trust in the Lord." We went all the way to Wonalancet (taking the ferry at Tarrytown in order to avoid New York) without benefit of route numbers or road maps; Violet kept the *Automobile Blue Book* open on her lap and read out the instructions: "At 75.9 miles turn left at church; 80.6 bear right past horse trough," etc. It was fairly unusual in 1924 to see a car driven by a young woman at any great distance from home. On the New Hampshire roads owners of other cars with Pennsylvania licenses would wave a salute, as if we were ships meeting on remote seas.

It was the beginning of a pattern that lasted with but few exceptions until Violet's first stroke forty years later, that I should take the responsibility for planning and carrying through her summer vacations, and my marriage made no difference. Usually we went by car and usually to New England, though sometimes to the mountains of North Carolina, or of Britain, or of Japan. She never wanted to learn to drive, herself, though when I married I offered to give her my car, the successor to the Handsome Ford, a Model A.

It was clear by the beginning of 1925 that I was not going to be able to make my living by writing. Walking up Walnut Street one day late in January, I saw large letters painted on the side of a building: Bryant Teachers Agency. On an impulse I walked in and signed up. Three days later I had a job at fourteen hundred dollars, and four days after that I was driving to Asbury Park, to begin work.

The high school in that North Jersey shore resort had discovered that when the second term started on February 1, they would need another teacher to catch up some loose threads. I was to teach freshmen: two classes in Ancient History, two classes in Community Civics, one in English Literature and Composition. In the sixth period I proctored Study Hall, which was sheer torture.

For my courses the principal gave me three textbooks and turned me loose. Occasionally someone from the office would come into one of my classrooms, on an obviously manufactured excuse, to see if the roof was still on, but no department head ever troubled to interview me, let alone give me advice, and there was never a teachers' meeting to attend. I soon knew two or three of my fellow teachers but only in the most casual way. There was no teachers' room where we congregated, no lunchroom. School began at nine and stopped at one-thirty, after which we scattered, unless we returned to discipline some errant pupils, which meant sitting with them in whatever empty classroom we could commandeer. I soon discovered that that was more punishment for me than for them and gave up the practice.

Of course I had trouble with discipline. This was my first job. I was twenty-two. I had never had a course in "Education." I made the mistake of laughing at the boys when they were funny, as they frequently were. But it was a good-natured tussle on both sides, and we ended as friends. There were Negro boys and girls in all my classes, but no discernible tensions. They fitted in as individuals, and I did not even hear the word *integration* until years later.

My English class went like a breeze; it consisted of twenty girls; we understood each other at once and I was on home ground. Community Civics was another matter. I had never, either in school or college, encountered anything of that nature. The textbook had to do with local government, playgrounds, police, voting, fire departments and the like. I learned on the first class and taught the second, in which there were sixty pupils. The history textbook was Myers's *Ancient History*, which I had had myself in my first year at Germantown Friends School. It was a good textbook, and I remembered it well. What made it difficult to teach was that most of my pupils were repeating the subject, some of them for the third time. Several of the boys were sixteen and had had "concessions" on the boardwalk the previous summer—weighing machines and the like—where they had made more money in three months than I made in a year. They knew exactly what my salary was, for my check was brought to me each month from the office naked in the hand of a secretary, and anyone who craned his neck could see the amount on it. In the light of their experience they asked me pointed questions about the value of the study of Ancient History.

I liked Myers's *Ancient History* myself, especially the part about Greece. It seemed to me to be full of valid insights about life. People weary of hearing anyone continually praised; they will vote to exile an Aristides simply because they are tired of hearing him called "The Just." Allies who fight loyally shoulder to shoulder in a war become enemies when the war is over. Governments follow a depressing cycle: the people revolt against a tyrant and establish a democracy; the democracy suffers internal divisions because of unreconcilable minorities and disintegrates in anarchy and chaos; unable to endure disorder, the people turn thankfully to a benevolent dictator, who is succeeded by a tyrant, against whom the people revolt. . . .

Asbury Park that winter and spring was seething with indignation because someone in a newspaper had called it a "shoddy, shop-girl's paradise." So it was, no doubt, in summer. In winter the stores along the boardwalk were boarded up; the boardwalk itself was empty; there was seldom anyone at all on the narrow beach, and the ocean stretched away to the horizon, blue and green and lavender and gray, ever changing. Along the ocean side of the boardwalk there were at intervals little kiosks with glass on three sides and the fourth open to the sea; inside there was room for a large rocking chair or two. Each afternoon when school was out I hastened to one of these kiosks, wrapped myself up in a steamer rug and, facing the sea and the salt air, got on with the book I was writing.

It was a story for children based on the spring I had spent in Wonalancet, with a mystery thrown in; three of the characters were disguised versions of Elizabeth and Bill and myself, and the heroine was a little girl whom I had seen in Whiteface Intervale, one summer evening, driving a dogcart, a golden-haired, brown-eyed child with a merry little face who had caught my imagination and developed a life of her own within it. I set the story in Whiteface Intervale instead of Wonalancet because there was a fine old farmhouse there—a manor house, Mr. Child called it—and an old mountain family of character and substance, who became the Merediths of the book.

During the four and a half months that I spent in Asbury Park I boarded with a Catholic family named Deerin, of whom the father was Irish and the mother German. As they had just recently bought the large, white be-porched house near the ocean which was to be their new venture, I was the only boarder, and was soon a member of the family, which besides the parents consisted of five children, all in school but none in any of my classes. Mrs. Deerin, warmhearted, capable, loving, a wonderful cook and an understanding mother, was my favorite. I used to help her with the dishes and we would talk long. Her philosophy of life was a simple one of prospering through industry and honesty and kindness, her religion true and deep. "I like to go into a church when there aren't many people there," she told me once, "and kneel down and say, 'I haven't come to ask for anything; I've just come to visit.' "

Those months were a time of growth for me, through the long hours of writing on the boardwalk, the learning to teach and control my pupils, the being for the first time really on my own in a place where, except for busy Mrs. Deerin, I found no friends. In June, however, when the school offered me a raise if I would return the following year, I decided that I had had enough of teaching and applied for admission to the Graduate School of Library Science at Drexel Institute.

When Violet and I came home in September from New Hampshire, where we had a cottage for three weeks, we returned to a house in which the whole atmosphere had changed; as palpable as fog or thunder was the heavy foreboding of illness and death. Mother told us that our father had had a lump which he had at last admitted. He had gone to the family doctor, who had sent him on to a specialist. The verdict was cancer of the liver, and he was given three months to live.

He was not told that it was cancer, and he never gave any sign that he knew it, though once he said to Mother, "It is a long journey to take alone." He lived for a few days over the three months, not suffering pain but enduring increasing discomfort, sliding down from short walks to long hours in his easy chair, to the library couch, and at last to his bed. Mother took care of him herself with the help of a trained nurse who came in for a few hours each morning. And now those two, who had so often seemed to us to be to each other almost strangers, were bound together in a world of their own, a world of weakness and selfless devotion, a world where all was understood and nothing said, from which sometimes, incongruously, came laughter, and always courage. Violet and I were both out all day, she at Starr library, I at Drexel. We came home to do what little we could to help, getting meals, carrying trays, sitting with our father in the evenings until he tired, telling him the small events of the day. His seventy-fifth birthday passed; Chrismas came and went; on January 3 we were all with him when he slipped into a coma and then stopped breathing.

It was not my first experience of death; Elizabeth Sheble had died during our first year at Bryn Mawr. I knew the shock of seeing the familiar body, its spirit gone, turned clay; I knew the taste of finality, of unfathomable mystery; the irreplaceable and final loss of the person to whom one turns to say something and finds emptiness. But the death of a father is a fundamental shift of the platform on which one stands, an exposure to winds and currents from a larger world. Mingled with my sorrow was regret that I had not been closer to him, had not opened my mind more freely to him or expressed more generously my gratitude for the sacrifices he had made for my education.

It has taken me many years to get to know him and to love him better and more deeply than I did when he was living. The dead, someone has said, come back and tell their story. I was touched when, going through his desk at the office and clearing out the masses of unsorted papers, I came on a pocket diary with pages on which as a baby I had scribbled and he had noted in his fine, distinguished handwriting, "Elizabeth Janet Gordon Gray, August 7, 1904." Long after his death there came back to me a letter which he had written to a niece in Oklahoma when I was twelve, describing me with an affection and pride which I had not dreamed he felt. He was locked in a reserve which held us all prisoners and of which I felt the danger in myself. I think I could not have broken through my own barriers without the help of Morgan Vining. My father's friends at the St. Andrew's Society saw him at his most genial and perhaps his truest self. A memoir of him written by one of the members and spread upon their minutes was inscribed beautifully on vellum and given to my mother. It said in part:

"He was a man of profound learning and versatile talent, quick of comprehension, logical in conclusions, a ready speaker, noted for his fine diction, skilful in debate, and possessing in high degree the art of imparting his knowledge to others with lucidity. He took delight in doing people 'a good turn' and was always glad to help others along life's path especially when that path led to the acquisition of knowledge and education."

During the summer of 1925 I had typed my book for girls, which I called *Merediths' Ann*, and sent it off to Macmillan, whence it returned with a polite and rather encouraging note. Next it went to Doubleday (then Doubleday, Page & Company), where May Massee was in charge of the newly established children's book department and making a name both for herself and for it, although I, ignorant and inexperienced, had at that time never heard it. My father read the manuscript and expressed faith in it; I was longing to have it accepted while he still could know about it, but it was not until two or three weeks after his death that a very short letter came from Miss Massee. It said,

"Do you ever come to New York? I'd like to talk to you about your book."

If I had known then what I know now about publishers, I would have dropped everything and taken the next train to New York. Then, however, I thought it a most unsatisfactory letter, and I wrote back rather loftily that I was exceedingly busy in library school but hoped to get to New York during the spring holiday.

Nearly two months later, on a sunny, windy day in late March, I went to New York and had lunch with Miss Massee at Maillard's on Madison Avenue—shad roe, asparagus and strawberry tartlets, the very apotheosis of a spring luncheon. I was twenty-three, she was forty-three. She was beautiful, with clear, composed features, fair hair, blue eyes, a quiet, infinitely assured manner, a degree of sophisticated simplicity that both attracted and awed me. Years later she told me that I had frightened her—I looked so young, so sure. She kept the reins of the conversation firmly in her own hands, and it seemed to me hours before I could bring her to talk about my book. First she made a good many discouraging comments on being a librarian, which she said was the worst possible thing for a writer to be. Too many books, too little life. It would be far better for me to work for a newspaper or even to sell corsets, anything but immure myself in a library. Teaching would be just as bad, especially in a college, for there I would be smothered in academic dry rot.

We came at last to my book. This year's list, she said, was already filled. Furthermore, my book was not ready to be published; it needed working on. I had doubled up on my plot, repeating similar patterns of incidents; it needed "more invention." If I was willing to make changes along these lines and to wait a year and a half for publication, Doubleday would accept the book and give me a contract later.

I walked down Fifth Avenue afterwards in alternate states of elation and despair: I was going to have my book published; I was about to enter upon a profession fatal to a writer.

My report of May Massee's views on librarianship and my own agonized question as to whether I should drop the library school and get a job on a newspaper forthwith filled my mother and sister with disgust and perhaps panic.

"You couldn't support yourself on a newspaper," they said. "Go and find out how much you would make. Just find out before you burn your bridges."

So I went to *The Philadelphia Inquirer* and asked to see the City Editor. I saw someone, I don't know who he was. He sat at a desk at the end of a long room full of men at desks all pounding away at typewriters, some of whom looked up at me with curiosity as I passed. I asked the astounded, busy man how much I would make if I decided to take a job on his newspaper. I have no memory of what he said, but it was very clear that it would not be enough. I returned to Drexel.

In the spring, at library schools, the job opportunities come in, and the Dean, executing a power which has been throughout the year not only implied but held as a threat, summons the students one by one to distribute the plums and the lemons. One of the plums was offered to me: the post of first assistant in the Cataloguing Department of the Library of the University of North Carolina in Chapel Hill.

It was not easy for my mother and sister to let me accept it. They had expected that I would find a job in Philadelphia, live at home and contribute to the family economy. My father had left a small estate with a very complicated will which fell heavily on Violet, who was made executor. To fit hours of waiting in lawyers' offices into her already full schedule was a heavy drain on her strength and spirits. I felt guilty as I took the night express to Durham at the end of August, but my whole being cried out for experience, for freedom.

*PART II.

✻✻✻✻✻✻✻✻✻✻✻✻✻✻✻✻✻✻✻✻✻✻✻✻✻✻✻✻

1.

Chapel Hill I

CHAPEL HILL, as I saw it first on August 31, 1926, is clear and vivid in my mind still, but it is another place entirely than the Chapel Hill I came to know as I lived in it, a colored poster without details or depth, a stage backdrop to look at but not to walk in. All the places where I have lived or sojourned over months have in the same way two aspects: the sharply outlined first view and the vaguer, deeper, changing contours of later experience.

Two kind young women sent by the library met Mary Gocher and me with a car at the railroad station in Durham, drove us through the heavy, sweet tobacco fumes of the commonplace little town past the castellated dingy brick cigarette factories and shoddy shops, and across the twelve miles of sad, red-clay fields stretching away to dark horizon woods, with here and there a gray, sagging cabin bulging with Negro children or a billboard on which a pretty girl in a flowing pink dress urged a handsome, dark-jacketed, white-trousered young man smoking a Camel cigarette to "blow some my way."

Chapel Hill did in fact crown a hill. The road wound up through woods to the plateau on which the village lay stretched underneath its trees: white oaks, red oaks, black oaks, willow oaks, a few elms, poplars, pines, glossy-leaved magnolias. The street on which we entered was wide, with grass verges burned brown by the August drought, red graveled walks and low stone walls, wide brown lawns and, behind the trees and shrubs, large old-fashioned white frame houses with porches. Motes danced in shafts of sunshine, the air under the trees was still and dry and dim, over everything brooded the high, hot blue sky and a pervading atmosphere of somnolence. The occasional person along the street walked slowly, dreamily. This, then, I thought, is the South, and here I am.

Turning off Franklin Street before we reached the churches, post office and shops, we entered a shady lane and came to the angular brown-shingled house where were the rooms already engaged for us by the Reference Librarian. Mrs. Julia Graves, descendant of a Signer, widow of a well-liked University professor, mother of Louis Graves, whose *Chapel Hill Weekly* was known over the country for its salty flavor, came out on the porch to greet us. White-haired, spare, with a slightly rasping voice and strong North Carolina accent, she had become through the years of letting out rooms a little guarded, more than a little reserved, critical, conscientiously kind. With her lived her daughter, Mary Rees, an artist whose marriage had been unhappy, and her grandson, an engaging five-year-old with enormous brown eyes.

Across the lane was a grove of great oaks with mistletoe clotting the high branches like big, untidy nests and little paths running underneath; one went to the street beyond and the Arboretum, another ran down a slope to a brook beyond which new dormitories were being built.

It was the dead time of the year. Summer School was over, the autumn term had not begun, most people were away on vacation. Offices were closed, shops were taking inventory, only a handful of people gathered around the dinner table at Mrs. Bain's boarding house whither, again by the motherly Library, we were directed, and where, for thirty-five dollars a month, we were to encounter brains and eggs and grits, light biscuits, fried chicken, turnip greens, black-eyed peas, sweet potato pie and other Southern dishes over the months to come, at two long tables filled with librarians, secretaries, and unmarried instructors and presided over by Dr. H. W. Wilson, the distinguished biologist known as Dr. Froggy, and Miss Lily Hamilton, a white-haired, large-bosomed maiden lady almost visibly draped in the traditions of the Old South. Every evening after dinner we were all expected to gather in the living room or on the porch behind the wistarias and silver moon roses for half an hour or so of general conversation, joined by Mrs. Bain and her lively and entertaining daughter Beppy, a famous "college widow" then in her thirties who worked in the University as the secretary of a department.

"Chapel Hill's gotten spoiled," Beppy told us, "now that it's so big. There are twenty-six hundred students this year. Before the war when you went down Franklin Street you never saw anybody you didn't know. Everybody knew everybody else and all the girls had a grand time."

The next day, my first whole day in Chapel Hill, I met Morgan Vining. I saw him first in the morning when Mary and I walked from Franklin Street to the library by a short cut through the Methodist churchyard. He came walking toward us, a tall, slender man with the careless, loose-limbed, graceful coordination of the athlete, a long, oval face with fine, dark eyes, long upper lip, sensitive, humorous mouth, a smile that began in his eyes and illuminated his whole face. We passed. In that moment recognition had taken place.

At lunchtime Mary and I walked across the campus under the big trees to the Inn Cafeteria. Crape myrtles were in bloom, the first that I had ever seen—fountains of color, deep rose, pale rose, lavender. When we came out on the cafeteria porch after lunch, I saw them shining through a sweep of slanting rain. One of those sudden deluges had come up; rain poured down in sheets and we had no umbrellas. We stood with others on the porch, wondering uneasily how long it would last and what the library would think if we were late back from lunch on our first day.

The handsome man whom I had seen earlier had a black Ford parked near the cafeteria, lettered in gold with the name of the Extension Division. He dashed back and forth more than once through the rain between the car and the Inn. I knew from the way that he looked at me as he passed that he was going to offer us a ride, and I wished that he would get on with it. He told me later that he was trying to muster courage, not sure if a Northern girl would consider it an impertinence from a man who had not been introduced.

On the third trip he mustered courage to say that he was going to the library anyhow (he wasn't) and could give us a lift, and we thankfully climbed into the Extension Ford. On the way I found that he already knew my name, where I was working and where I had come from.

A day or two later he appeared at Mrs. Graves's when we sat on the porch in the twilight. He had a *Saturday Evening Post* cover by Norman Rockwell in his hands; he had come, he said gravely, to consult Mrs. Rees about the suitable framing of the picture for his office. Advice about the color and size of a mat was given with equal solemnity, but nobody at all was fooled. He had come to be properly introduced and after that to make a date.

He lived diagonally across the lane, in a suite with a sleeping porch in the house of Professor Hickerson of the Engineering School.

"Beware of propinquity," wrote my mother half humorously, half seriously, in answer to my letter describing in detail my first week in Chapel Hill.

Propinquity was oddly selective; Hick's other lodger, a secretary in the School of Economics, I practically never saw, but Morgan I ran across daily, in our lane, in the grove, at the post office, on the campus, in the cafeteria, in the library. The catalog department of a university library might seem to be a dead end and the ultimate in dry routine and fusty detail, but this was not actually the case. There are many reasons why a cataloger has to leave her desk and repair to the reference room or the main hall where the catalog itself stands near the circulation desk. Morgan was not, that fall, the only one who found me there before the catalog, filing cards or checking subject headings; Chapel Hill was full of young instructors, known as "the scrub faculty," and I was a novelty in the village. My evenings were soon nicely filled.

One of my earliest—and firmest—friends in Chapel Hill was a professor in the English Department, George McKie, warm, kindly, humorous, a widower in his fifties who was a beloved figure on the campus. He belonged to Old Chapel Hill by virtue of having taught there a quarter of a century, though he was New York State born. He was also a friend of Morgan's, and quite early in the fall he said to him, "Morgan, there's a girl here whom you ought to meet. I think you'd like her."

To which Morgan replied, "I've already done something about that, Mr. Mac."

Mr. Mac, who was a cherished friend until his death in 1941, watched with interest the course of our romance, always feeling that he had abetted it, if not aided it.

We had had several dates by the time my twenty-fourth birthday came and Morgan took me to the Inn itself, not the cafeteria, for dinner. Afterwards we walked about the village in the mild October evening and came at length to sit in the lawn swing in Mrs. Graves's side yard. I felt myself tasting the very essence of the South—the moonlight, the bland evening air, the mockingbird singing his autumn song in the dark, the handsome, magnetic man sitting opposite me keeping the swing creaking slowly. If we were not in love that evening, or not admitting it to ourselves, we were aware of the possibility of falling in love, of the danger of being hurt. Southern men, I had been warned by my southern friends at college, were given to "sweet talk" which Northern girls must never take seriously; Morgan had seen me enjoying the attentions of other men. We made a pact that night, sitting under the trees in the gently moving swing while the mockingbird sang, that whatever else happened, there would be truth between us two.

Our backgrounds were poles apart yet oddly similar. He was the grandson of an Englishman, Reuben Vining, who had eloped with a young girl from a village in Kent before the Civil War, bringing among his hasty baggage bound volumes of *Punch*; they had settled in New Orleans in 1860, and he had named his only son, who was Morgan's father, Lincoln, with a fine independent disregard for what was politically tactful. Morgan's mother was of an old American family, the Morgans of Kentucky. His mother's father had been "the youngest colonel in the Confederate Army" (there must have been dozens of them); surviving the war, he had moved to Texas, where his daughter Lulu met and married Lincoln Vining, who had gone to Austin to seek his fortune. The fortune was never achieved, though Lincoln Vining was a capable lawyer and his sisters had made good marriages. An option in oil lands, held not quite long enough, had just missed bringing millions to the young family, which included two children, Morgan Fisher and Beatrice. Our differences were obvious: Morgan was a Southerner, a Democrat and a Presbyterian, I a Northerner, a Republican and an Episcopalian, yet we were alike in our half-British, half-old-American heritage, our understanding of genteel poverty, of wealth just missed; we both had sisters with whom the bond was unusually close.

Morgan, who was twelve years older than I, had grown up in Austin, gone to the University of Texas, where he won his letters in football, basketball and track and left his photograph in the gymnasium among the aristocracy of "three-letter men," had added LL.B. to his A.B. and after a brief, boring period as an attorney had gone to teaching in the University. In April, 1917, two weeks after the United States declared war on Germany, he volunteered in the infantry and after three months at training camp was commissioned captain in the 40th, or Sunshine, Division.

Most of the next year he spent at Camp Kearney, San Diego, as aide-de-camp to Major General Frederick Smith Strong and Division censor. It was evidently a very good year. Not from anything that Morgan told me but from papers and albums that I found much later, I learned how able and popular the young aide had been.

"He is diplomat, athlete, friend to newspaper correspondents and society man," wrote the *Los Angeles Graphic*. "Above all else he is a soldier. . . . In his double capacity of aide and censor Captain Vining has made an enviable record for himself at Camp Kearney. He has been extremely popular both with the military men and civilians."

Late in July, 1918, the Sunshine Division was sent overseas. In the four days he spent in London, quartered at the Ritz, Morgan lost his heart to London as he never did to Paris in the longer stay there. In October, finding his pleasant life behind the lines too tame, he applied for more active duty and was sent to the Army School of the Line at Langres for a three-month course. Before it was completed the Armistice had been signed, but even before that Morgan had been stricken with a baffling and long-lasting form of gastritis. He was in army hospitals at Langres, Bordeaux, Cannes and Hyères, and after he returned to the United States with the 40th Division in February, 1919, he was in the hospital at Camp Kearney, from which he was discharged in May. He went home to Texas barely in time for the death of his beautiful and tender mother, whom he adored. During the following years his search for health and congenial work in a mild climate brought him to Chapel Hill in 1925 as Associate Director of the Extension Division of the University. Though when I first met him on September 1, 1926, he was just back from a siege at the Walter Reed Hospital, he was in better condition than he had been for a long time and his spirits were high. His disability, rated by the army doctors as 66 percent, was a direct result of his war experience, but because it came not from a wound or from being gassed but from the lowly stomach, he found no compensating satisfaction in it, and if he spoke about his part in the war at all, it was usually just to talk with enthusiasm about London, to which he looked forward to returning.

I saw him with increasing frequency that year in Chapel Hill. Amusements for courting couples were simple: dinner at the Inn, movies, football games, followed by basketball and baseball, endless, slow, conversational walks, couples playing bridge together, a crowd going on a possum hunt in the moonlight with a Negro and his hound dog, dances at the Country Club, an occasional concert or lecture sponsored by the University, and the performances of the Carolina Playmakers.

Dr. L. R. Wilson was the head of the library, an amiable, slow, kind, scholarly man of great originality and prodigious energy. The creation of the University of North Carolina Press was just one of the things he did with his left hand while his right was running the library. My immediate superior, Miss Elizabeth Thompson, was a spare, active little New England woman who never learned, as the rest of us Yankees quickly did, to saunter along the gravel walks under the trees, but who fairly ran to and from the library and sprinted from room to room within it. She came to work in the mornings fifteen minutes early in order to read the newspaper; at 8:30 on the dot she put the paper aside and bent to her desk. I was very fond of her and found her easy to work with, fair and generous in her dealings with subordinates and very understanding about the need sometimes to shift hours around.

Very early I attached myself to the Carolina Playmakers, the creation of Frederick Koch, affectionately known as "Prof" Koch, who had come from Colorado several years earlier to start the drama department at Chapel Hill. By the time I got there it was already famous for the one-act plays, written and produced by students in his course and published in a series of volumes entitled *Carolina Plays*. Its most famous product was Paul Green, who had come from a tenant farm in the eastern part of the state to write plays at the University, and whose *In Abraham's Bosom*, which was to win a Pulitzer Prize, was at that very moment running in New York.

I arranged to get off from the library for an hour three mornings a week and make up the time in the evenings so that I could attend the course. As I passed Old South Building, where the Extension Division offices were, on my way to class, Morgan would just happen down the steps and would walk with me to the door of the building where the class met. My play, about which I cannot now remember a single thing, was considered good enough for me to read one Sunday evening in the Playmaker Theater to a small audience in which Morgan loomed large, but it got no further than that. Later in the year I had a small part in a three-act play put on by the Playmakers—I was, not very convincingly, Thalia, Muse of Comedy. Shepherd Strudwick, who became known in the movies later, had a much bigger part, and the play was directed by P. L. Elmore, who also made a home in New York and who now lives in Rensselaerville, New York, which was in the thirties and forties to be one of my favorite summer resorts.

During the winter Morgan's part in all this was to wait for me and take me home from rehearsals, but in the spring he was immensely involved with another phase of the Playmaker movement. In high schools from one end of the state to the other, drama groups were putting on one-act plays from the Carolina books and engaging in contests, first local and then regional; the winners from each region came up to Chapel Hill for the finals, a week-long series of plays. All of this being done under the auspices of the Extension Division, Morgan had his hands full making arrangements of all kinds, lining up judges, settling disputes, providing comfort, encouragement and properties and coping with last-minute crises. His enthusiasm, which was genuine and infectious, was not so much for the plays, which were apt to be grim little tragedies of the mountain coves, with much tobacco-spitting and pipe-smoking by old crones and hollow coughing by doomed young girls, full of homespun reflections beginning with "Hit air," but for the young actors themselves, especially those fresh, innocent, wondering young things who were away from their mountains for the first time.

Living in Chapel Hill was enchanting to me as I came to penetrate deeper into the village and to know it in all its aspects and moods. The "old campus" occupied the center of the town, as opposed to the newer one stretching out into the hills and woods to the south; the original buildings, plain and dignified, were shaded by trees and surrounded by wide lawns crisscrossed with paths which swarmed with students at the turn of the hour, to empty again for another fifty minutes of somnolence. In the streets along the perimeter moved the stripped-down Fords of the period, with names painted on their sides: "Passion," "Opportunity—Hear it Knock," "No One Dead in this Wreck," "Bored of Education." Kay Kyser, whose orchestra later became famous throughout the country, had a bright blue Ford reputedly without brakes; when he parked, he threw out an anchor. Around the campus nucleus were the wide and shady streets with the faculty homes, hospitable houses whose doors were never locked, surrounded by low stone walls introduced a century earlier by a president from New England. Beauty passed over them as the seasons changed, from the autumn chrysanthemums in tangled rows through the winter jasmine and pallid but fragrant sweet breath of spring, the first chilly daffodils of February, to the dazzling bridal wreath foaming in every garden, the peach and pear and apple blossoms, the redbud and dogwood, the American pillar roses over trellises, the silver moons over porches, the sun-warmed honeysuckle inexpressibly fragrant in the moonlit evenings, the great waxy magnolias, and at last the crape myrtle—oh the crape myrtle. "If you can smell the fragrance of the crape myrtle," said Beppy Bain, "you're in love." And all of it under a sky of a deeper blue than any I had seen before. At night there were the stars close enough to prick your fingers on, and fireflies winking in the grass, the mockingbirds singing like nightingales, the whippoorwills crying in the distance.

The country around Chapel Hill also, I learned, had a charm quite different from that first sun-baked impression that I had of it, as Morgan and I together explored it in the Chrysler roadster which he bought in the spring. Saturday or Sunday afternoons usually found us driving on the red clay roads to Hillsboro in one direction, where the columned brick courthouse, the double-balconied frame houses hidden behind box bushes, the small, square church with its graveyard and cypress trees, had scarcely changed from the days of the Revolutionary War, or in the other direction, past peach trees marching in brilliant rows over the sandy earth and forests of longleaf pines where the air was indescribably pure and pungent, to the golf courses and hotels of Pinehurst and Southern Pines. I saw Negro cabins, some of chinked logs, with chickens scratching about on well-swept earth under chinaberry trees, crossroads hamlets with wooden chapels and general stores with sagging porches; an occasional unpainted wooden house of some pretensions, with big brick chimneys and a box-bordered path to the front door. For the first time I saw cotton growing and tobacco; I saw Negroes plowing with mules.

I took notes on all of it for stories I was sure I would want to write later, notes on expressions new to me, on comments I heard made, on characters that touched my imagination, on the stories people told of their childhood or of the Negro servants, of whom all spoke with affection and condescension and without the slightest realization of the storm of rebellion that was gathering behind the smiling faces. During the winter the slightly revised version of my book was formally accepted and I received a contract, which

I handed over to Morgan as a lawyer to examine for me. His half-serious report assessing it and recommending "that same be signed and returned at your convenience" has survived among my notes, headed "Memorandum in Re Author's Contract and signed Fisher, Morgan and Vining, Barristers to Her Highness, Princess of Gordon."

One day in June I met a real writer and devoted pages in my notebook to recounting every detail of the occasion and exactly what he said. James Boyd came to the library from Southern Pines to do a bit of research, and someone directed him to the cataloguing room, where he might find a girl who was to have a book published in the fall. I had read and enjoyed his *Drums* and *Marching On*, popular historical novels about the Revolution in North Carolina, and I was awed to meet the author. I found attractive his sandy hair and tortoise-shell goggles, blunt nose, scrubby moustache and wide smile, and when he invited me to go with him to Hillsboro that afternoon while he looked up some old houses there, I hastened to arrange with Miss Thompson to make up the time on Saturday. I had already been to Hillsboro with Morgan; it was not Hillsboro that I was interested in, but garnering whatever pearls about writing that this rare creature might let fall.

He had been, he told me, in the publishing business before the war. After the war, when his doctors told him he must live in the South and he came to Southern Pines, he remembered that when he was in the business he had noticed that publishers often paid a great deal of money for things that were very poor and he decided that he might as well get some of the money. This, he said, was how he came to be a writer. While he liked the life and the rewards, he loathed the actual writing. I pondered within myself—but did not dare ask him—whether he was joking, or whether he was simply expressing the chic literary attitude at the time, but decided that he was too sincere a person to do anything but speak the simple truth. I felt a little sorry for him. He went on to tell me that writers and artists were deadly when they got together. He said that writers were either afraid of each other or trying to impress each other or stealing each other's ideas; more than two of them in one place were impossible. "So if a third one came along now," he said, "we'd throw him out of the car."

It was titillating to hear him bracket himself and me as writers, but beyond that I was caught by his idea that writers were uneasy when they were together in numbers, and I thought it might well be true. It has been one of those chance suggestions that find a lodging in one's mind and perhaps exert an unacknowledged influence. At any rate I have never sought to be a part of a circle of writers, though New York, where so many congregate, is within easy reach, and though in many ways it would be comforting and strengthening to be surrounded by others working in one's own field and basing their lives upon the same assumptions. On the other hand I have found that two writers together, whether casual acquaintances or a veteran and a tyro or, best of all, two who are friends in depth, provide one of the heady and fulfilling joys of writing as a profession.

For the most part, on the way to and from Hillsboro we talked about North Carolina and its history and the tradition of aristocracy in the South, which, he said, was largely myth. "It wasn't the war, it was the slaves that made the South poor. A few people had them, but the great numbers did not. They couldn't afford them, and they couldn't afford to hire labor. Then the war came. They lost their money, they lost their slaves, they lost their homes, their land was ravaged. They were *beaten*. How could they face that? They couldn't. Nobody could. So they said they were fighting for a civilization, the best that the world had ever known, and they've built that civilization out of their defeat." But he was himself, I remembered, a Pennsylvanian.

The trip that day was important for me. It reminded me of my own long ago Revolutionary War phase, turned my mind to North Carolina's early history, set me to thinking about the Scots Highlanders who came there after Culloden, about Flora MacDonald.

The notes that I so carefully wrote down in my copybook during that year were all of details that I might some day want for stories, only indirectly about the people who were becoming so central a part of my life. There was very little about Morgan, though the initial M was often there incidentally: "M and I to walk in the woods"—and then a description of the pines and the wild flowers; or after some notes on waking up in Chapel Hill, the morning air, the sounds, the peach blossoms that I saw from the window by my bed, I added, "Across the street a door slams and a sound of whistling is heard. I draw back and look around the edges of the curtain to watch M as he goes down the lane." Reading it now, I feel again the surge of happiness that I then accepted as part of the wonderful beauty and excitement of living in the South.

In the summer I moved over to Mrs. Bullitt's house next door to Mrs. Bain's boarding house. It was more convenient, and it was also much pleasanter. The house was big and cool, the Bullitts were delightful people who took me at once into their family, which consisted of Dr. James Bullitt, a Kentuckian with Philadelphia connections who taught in the University Medical School; Mrs. Bullitt, one of five Bryan sisters of Virginia, warm, charming, altogether lovable; Jimbo the son and Margaret the daughter, both then students. All of the family were great talkers; they never interrupted each other, but courteously took turns; I was a listener, not above writing home a description of how Mrs. Bullitt gave me a recipe for egg sauce.

"Her mother would say, 'Oh you just take some butter and sugar and an egg and a cup of brandy' but she never wrote it down, and so Mrs. Bullitt never made it. Then she switched to the Wheelers' Christmas party, with a description of who was there and what they did and who wrote the verses to go with the presents in the Jack Horner pie, and what they had for dinner and how the plum pudding was brought in blazing. 'Did you ever play snap dragon? Well, raisins are brought in on a big platter, blazing, and you try to pull them out with your fingers. The one that gets the most wins. It isn't very hard, the point about it is that you look perfectly ghastly in that blue light. You cyahn't imagine how ghastly people look. You dream about it afterwards. Well, we didn't play snap dragon at the Wheelers'.' But they had egg sauce with the plum pudding. And Mrs. Bullitt said. . . . And Mrs. Wheeler said. . . . And *then* Mrs. Bullitt told me how to make egg sauce."

In July my ten author's copies of *Merediths' Ann* arrived. The seeing of one's first book in actual type with cloth covers and a bright jacket is an unrepeatable experience; nothing again ever quite touches it. I sat down and read the book through from cover to cover as if for the first time. It was a world I had created and lived in; now it was whole, finished, and I was shut out of it. Oh, I took delight in inscribing copies for my friends, I watched for and collected reviews and notices, but the book itself I never looked into again. It was over. I began to plan the next one.

Morgan, as it happened, was away when the box of books arrived, and so it was a very nice young instructor in the History Department who took me out to dinner to celebrate the book. Morgan and I had been engaged, but at that time we were not engaged. When I had written my mother and sister of Morgan and our love, our decision to marry, I had met with a burst of grief that shook me to my foundations. Violet had struggled with the executing of our father's will and the overseeing of the Gray Instrument Company, which had fallen upon her; she was tired and discouraged, and she felt that I had abandoned her and with consummate selfishness was disappearing into the hinterland, leaving her with unendurable burdens. "The waters are cold and deep," she wrote, "and the swimmer is exhausted. The waters are closing over her head." Stricken with pity and with guilt, I impetuously resigned from the library and accepted an offer of a job teaching English in a private girls' school outside of Philadelphia. Denying Morgan's pleas to wait and see, on the grounds that a clean break was fairer and more honest, I broke off our engagement.

It is difficult now to understand why I did it, what was the mixture of emotion that drove me: pity, guilt, an urge to self-sacrifice, fear of the unknown, a craven desire to be free of the torment of conflicting loves? At all events I went home at the end of July.

The first thing I did when I got there was to buy another car—I had sold the Handsome Ford the previous summer. This was a Model A Ford, a sedan. Violet and I went to New Hampshire in August, where we rented a cottage beside the brook, and Mother, who did not like the chill of the mountains, went to Salem to visit Cousin Emma.

I found, when I got home, that the financial situation was less bleak than I had thought. Violet's salary was good, for the times; Mother was getting something from the "estate." In a burst of youthful energy I put through the sale of the house in which we had lived for twenty years; it was too big, too inconvenient, too much in need of expensive repairs and improvements, and the money that it brought would provide further income for Mother. I found an apartment which was attractive and livable, organized the sale of the furniture we could not take with us, and accomplished the moving while Violet was at work and Mother visited Cousin Emma. When Mother came back she remembered that she had left a chamber pot in the closet of her bedroom, and she insisted upon going back to hide it. If I would not go with her, she declared, she would go alone. By that time I had started teaching, and so we returned to the empty house in the blue October twilight. The electricity had been turned off. Mother fumbled long in her bag to find the key which she had kept, and I snapped at her impatiently. Settlement had been made and the house was no longer ours; I felt that we were housebreakers; I was sure that someone would see our flashlight wavering through the dark up the front stairs, along the hall to Mother's bedroom, down the back stairs, through the kitchen to the cellar stairs, and would come to investigate. The cellar itself was pitch dark and cavernous and the flash made only a small pool of light as Mother led the way to the most remote corner behind the furnace, where she directed me to place the pot and cover it with a newspaper. "Now," she said, "we can go."

That chamber pot, a handsome one decorated with roses, may be there still in the corner of the cellar, or perhaps a tenant of one of the apartments into which the house has been converted has found it and elevated it into a genuine antique flower container. At the time it seemed to me a symbol of all that I disliked most about my life.

The Ogontz School in Rydal, of which Miss Abby Southerland was headmistress and, I think, owner, was an expensive and pretentious boarding and day school for girls. A classmate of mine at Bryn Mawr was teaching History there, a sister of Norman Thomas's taught Mathematics briefly before she went on to the more congenial Quaker boarding school, Westtown, and my cousin Nanette McDonald had taught Art there the previous year. Abby, they all told me, was a terror but all right if she liked you. A distinguishing feature of the school was the cadet corps; all of the girls were required to put on expensive blue broadcloth uniforms twice a week and go through a military drill with wooden guns; once a year in the spring they had a grand parade presided over by a retired colonel and attended by admiring parents. A few girls were prepared for college, more for social life. Every day after lunch, while the whole school stood in the main hall and watched, the seniors one by one descended the impressive stairway without looking down at their feet and practiced entering a drawing room and shaking hands with Miss Southerland. During meals, if anyone left the dining room, teachers included, she turned at the door to face Miss Southerland and curtseyed. I was spared this, having been assigned to preside over the separate dining room for day pupils.

My job was to teach all of the English composition in the school, and I read and corrected sheaves of themes weekly, the best of which, I soon learned, had previously appeared in the *Cosmopoli-*

tan magazine. My main function, it developed, was to make sure that certain seniors produced essays good enough to be read at Commencement. "So-and-so's father," Miss Southerland told me, "is very anxious for her to have an important part in the graduation ceremony, and he gives a great deal to the school. She must be on the program. You are to see that she writes something presentable."

So-and-so was a lovable girl, graceful, willing to do her part but sweetly, invincibly dull. I sat beside her in the sunshine on the terrace, looking out on tulips and mock orange, while she wrote her essay. When she flagged, I would suggest, "Why don't you say something like this," and she would scribble on thankfully. When Commencement day came, she read an essay and her father was pleased; she never knew that it was not all her own accomplishment; some remnant of her integrity, if not of mine, had, I felt, been preserved. Weeks before that time I had declined reappointment for the next year.

All through that winter I worked on my second book, which was, actually, the first, rejected book, rewritten. I would get up at five-thirty, put on my dressing gown and repair to the kitchen, where I wrote in longhand on the metal counter of the cabinet until seven. In the evenings when I wasn't correcting papers, I typed what I had written. It was a story of a large and united family, the first but not the only book in which I fulfilled my lonely childhood dreams, and I called it *Tangle Garden*. It was accepted that spring and published in the fall. It is the least good of my thirteen books for children, and I think might better have been allowed to perish unseen, even though occasionally I have encountered a little girl who declares it is her favorite of the lot. Unlike *Merediths' Ann*, which was kept in print until 1962, it died away early in the 1940's.

I started a new book at once, a story for younger children in which I drew on my mother's memories of her childhood on the farm.

During spring vacation I took my car, and Violet and I went to Chapel Hill. We stayed with the Bullitts, who at once took Violet to their hearts, and Chapel Hill was at its most beautiful. Morgan was on hand, and Violet was charmed with him, as I might have known she would be. In May he came to Germantown and made a conquest of Mother. In the summer he followed me to Wonalancet, where I was sharing a cottage with Elizabeth and

Dick McKey and their two babies, and there we became engaged again. By this time I had my values straight. "I'll go with you anywhere, any time," I told him. We had lost a year, and I had no inkling of how few years there were to be; but I had learned a good deal, and knowledge is bought at a price. I had progressed a little further on the long, slow road to maturity. A little, not very much.

There was one more crisis before my mother and sister finally and permanently and wholeheartedly accepted my marriage. Though they liked Morgan at this point and conceded his charm and good looks, he was not what they wanted for me. He was twelve years older than I; he still suffered from the gastritis he had contracted during the war; he was in a poorly paid profession and, what was worse, in a Southern university. They wanted me to marry, of course, but they had hoped for a Philadelphian of the kind that a girl of my "looks, education and upbringing" might be expected to fall happily and naturally in love with. This crisis, however, we met and survived together.

We were married on January 31, 1929, in the Episcopal Church of the Good Shepherd in Queen Lane Manor, with Morgan's cousin, Joe Gazzam, as best man and only a very few intimate friends present. Neither of us wanted a large wedding; we wanted to get on with our life together.

2.

Chapel Hill II

A BOOK OF reminiscences of Chapel Hill life by William Meade Prince is entitled *The Southern Part of Heaven*, and so it seems to me to be as I look back on those brief, crowded, happy years—little more than three in all—that Morgan and I had there together. Heaven it seemed to me at the time, too, and later it was to be a source of consolation that at any rate I had known what it was when I had it, that I had savored and loved and been thankful for each irreplaceable moment.

After our return from our honeymoon, which began in Washington in the apartment which my college roommate and her husband, Nell and Mitchell Owens, recent bride and groom themselves, had vacated for us, and ended in Daytona, with stops at Charleston, where we saw Al Jolson in our first "talkie," and Savannah, we set about the building of our house at once. Morgan already had a lot, an acre of woodland on North Street fringed on the sunny edge with mimosas. He had named it Tangle Garden, for my second book, and our letters during the previous summer had been full of the house we were going to build there.

"I quite agree about the edifice to be erected at Tangle Garden," wrote Morgan. "I think it would be especially nice to have twelve window boxes with a very small house attached thereto."

"I found a pamphlet today entitled 'Forty Ways to Lower Building Costs,'" I replied. "The first way I fell upon was, 'Omit a clothes chute. That will save you $50.' That sounded great, especially as we would have had to climb up on the roof to shoot the clothes down it anyhow."

We had decided on a one-story gray shingled house with an unroofed terrace instead of a porch (saving four to five hundred dollars) and I worked out on graph paper a plan for the interior.

Somewhere I had read that the classical Greek proportion was five to eight, and so I designed a living room fifteen feet by twenty-four with a fireplace at one end and at the other built-in bookcases with a shallow arch above and cupboards below. The dining room was an alcove off the living room, just big enough to take the mahogany sideboard and round dining table from the house in which I had grown up. The two small bedrooms and bath were to be reached by a hall off the living room, and from the kitchen a staircase would go up to the attic, where we would have our studies.

The kindly architect to whom we presented these plans not only approved them but said he would like to have a house like that himself; he provided an exterior with a beautiful roofline and an outside brick chimney with squash joints to catch the shadows. Between the living room and the dining alcove he put an arch with conjugate foci like the one over the bookshelves. After World War II the country was flooded with Cape Cod and ranch-style houses, but ours was a pioneer among one-story dwellings, and it had an individual and satisfying charm. It was placed on the big lot with the gable end to the street and the long terrace, part flagged and part grass, facing south. We had kept the tall trees at the corners for shade in summer, but in winter the house was flooded with sunshine.

During the five months while it was being built, we lived first in Morgan's suite at Mr. Hickerson's and later in a house on Cobb Terrace which we rented from a professor on leave. When we left Hick's, our friend "Mr. Mac" moved in, and there his daughter Elizabeth, who was teaching in Boston, came to join him for vacations and to become a loved part of our circle.

Building a house is a deep emotional experience. As the house we had created in our minds and hearts took physical shape—the sturdy foundations, the first outlines of stud and beam, the roof-tree—as the chimney rose and rooms with windows declared themselves, so our marriage defined its foundations, took form and substance. Every afternoon we went to see how much the house had grown and to work on the lot, clearing out the undergrowth beneath the elms and oaks and persimmons, marking saplings to cut so as to free the larger trees, planning, planning. We would have a grassy plot around the house wide enough to let in the sunshine, would plant crape myrtles to shield the kitchen door, build a rock garden on the slope at the back. The rest of the lot we would keep in a sort of controlled wildness, with ground cover of periwinkle (when we could root out the honeysuckle) and thousands of bulbs in spring. And of course there must be a low stone wall across the front of it.

During this time I was also doing research for a new book, a teen-age historical novel with the scene laid first in Edinburgh and later in North Carolina, with Flora MacDonald as a character in it and the Battle of Moore's Creek Bridge, 1776, as the climax. The heroine, Meggy MacIntosh, was a Scottish girl of fifteen, who had come into my mind, homely, courageous and salty, and demanded that I tell her story. I knew the resources of the University Library well, and my friend in the History Department, Christopher Crittenden, later to become the State Archivist, directed me to the State Library in Raleigh and the Loyalty Commission Papers there.

When the Scots Highlanders who had emigrated from Scotland after the tragic diaster of Culloden were faced with the prospect of fighting a second time against a Hanoverian King, they felt the risk to be too great and they raised an army in North Carolina to oppose the Revolutionaries. Once again they were on the losing side, defeated in a battle as decisive in its area as the better known battles of Bunker Hill and Concord, and many of them abandoned their farms and mills and stores and returned to Scotland via Nova Scotia. After the war was over, they put in claims in London for the property they had lost through their loyalty to the King. Photostat copies of these documents were in the State Library in Raleigh, with inventories of their possessions and descriptions of their sufferings, a wealth of detail for anyone trying to reconstruct the life of the period.

Flora MacDonald had been one of them, though she with her family had come so soon before the war that she had had no time to develop either love or loyalty for the new land. There were, I found, accounts of her life in North Carolina and many legends; there were other accounts of her rescue of Prince Charles Edward Stuart when he was being pursued through the Highlands with a price of thirty thousand pounds on his head, but no complete, balanced, documented biography of her. I resolved some day to write such a life of Flora MacDonald.

For the Edinburgh part of my research also I found much material in the University Library: maps and pictures of eighteenth-century Edinburgh, letters, bound volumes of the *Edinburgh Re-*

view. Lord Cockburn's *Memorials of His Time* and Graham's *Literary History of Scotland* were already familiar to me from my father's library. I made maps of my own and traced every move of Meggy's until in White Horse Close, dressed as her cousin Veronica, she took coach on the first lap of her long journey to North Carolina to find Flora MacDonald. The places in North Carolina that I needed to see—Cape Fear, Wilmington and Fay-etteville and the country in between—I saw when I went on trips with Morgan on Extension Division business—"extending," we called it. Even before we moved into our house and I had my desk and bookcases at one end of the attic, I had written the first sentence of my book:

> "It is Melancholy," wrote Meggy MacIntosh, "to be fifteen and poor and homely in close proximity to a cousin who is eighteen and rich and beautiful."

Besides the house and the book to occupy my mind, I had two courses in the summer school first to prepare and then to teach. The University at that time did not have a School of Library Science, but it was paving the way for one by summer courses. Dr. Wilson asked me if I would teach both Cataloging and Reference, and I accepted with alacrity.

Chapel Hill in summer was a different place altogether from Chapel Hill in winter. What had been entirely a man's town became overnight predominantly female. Pretty young schoolteachers, well-groomed and well-dressed in a fluffy, feminine sort of way, poured in from all over the state, earnestly pursuing knowledge— or a higher certificate—and incidentally keeping an eye out for a man. The easygoing, deep-voiced male sloppiness gave way to an intense, chattering femininity, which seemed forever on the move, filling buildings and paths and restaurants, swarming in and out of drugstore and movie, exclaiming, "Hi y'awl!" and "Be seein' ya." Over it all settled down a blanket of heat, intense and unrelieved. The July flies (locusts to a Northerner) rasped shrilly all day, growing sleepy and slow by midnight and finally dying away to silence; crape myrtle succeeded magnolia, mockingbirds sang at night, the very shade was a hot dimness. On Saturday nights in the bleak gymnasium, dances were held with no glamor but the music of a student orchestra and the trooping of young feet eager to dance.

I taught my classes, which were large ones, and Morgan came

to pick me up afterwards. ("Who is that handsome man I saw you with?" "Too late. He's my husband.") We went every afternoon to the house. In the evenings it cooled off a little; after a bath and clean clothes we revived, and went for a ride in the moonlight. "I love these lonely fields with the trees black against the sky," I wrote to Mother, "and an occasional dim light in a cabin window." Or we had dinner with friends on somebody's terrace or in a restaurant cooled by electric fans and tall glasses of iced tea. Air conditioning was still in the future.

We moved into the house on August 10. The dining-room furniture came from Germantown; we went to High Point, where fine reproductions were being made in the furniture factories, and bought a wing chair, a love seat, twin four-posters for our bedroom. Morgan gave me a dressing table that I still think is the prettiest one I have ever seen. Bits and pieces for the spare room we found in antique shops in the mountains and secondhand shops in Durham. The terrace was still to be made after we moved in, and for what seemed an endless time we lived surrounded by a sea of mud and approached our front door by a plank over a gaping hole. One day a large white sow escaped from its Negro owner in the woods behind us and came to wallow in our terrace. But it was finished at last, and we had our first party there. The house was all that we had hoped and dreamed it would be. The living room was a beautiful room with tree shadows on the floor and the old brass andirons on the hearth—and before long two black cocker spaniels sprawled on the rug before it. We loved it in every season —in May, when the wood thrushes sang with ineffable sweetness in the early mornings; on summer evenings, when friends came to join us for dinner on the terrace under the high canopy of the trees; in September, when the orange spider lilies bloomed beyond the kitchen windows; and in February, when the first daffodils opened chilly fragrant trumpets and the winter jasmine along the wall was starred with blossom.

To rest and recover from the summer and the moving in, we went for ten days in September, the blank days after second summer school and before the autumn semester began, to Valle Crucis, a hamlet in the shadow of Grandfather Mountain about eighteen miles from Boone and perhaps twenty miles from the fashionable Blowing Rock. The name, Valley of the Cross, came from the meeting of two creeks which appeared to cross, and it was given its Latin form by the Episcopal bishop who established a mission school in the valley in the 1840's. It was the first of several visits there, some with Morgan, some with Violet, none more than two weeks long. When I think of the place, I see them all rolled into one, a composite picture of June and September.

We used to board with the Masts: Mr. Will; Aunt Josie, his wife; Aunt Leona, his sister; and Joe, his blind son, who were the manor folk of their community. The family was of Swiss origin; with the migration of Germans and Scotch-Irish in the late eighteenth century the pioneer Masts had made their way from Pennsylvania down the Shenandoah Valley into western North Carolina and bought all of what is now Valle Crucis for a rifle, a pair of leggings and a dog. Aunt Josie was a remarkable woman in any time or place. A slender, vigorous, gray-haired little figure filled with energy and warmth, she ran her part of the farm—the vegetable garden, the dairy and the house, with its dozen or so paying guests —with almost careless competence; she mothered the people of the countryside, who were forever coming to her with their troubles, which ranged from ailments which she treated with herb remedies and hunger which she fed with baskets of food to questions about the direction of their lives or the resolution of family conflicts; in her spare time she relaxed by going into the loom house and weaving several inches of bedspread, rug or bag.

Though we went to Valle Crucis by car and though we found in the old house modern plumbing and electric lights, nevertheless going there was like stepping back into another era, a time when the Jeffersonian ideal of American life prevailed. Almost everything that we ate was grown on the place. Every day there appeared on the long, white-clothed table at which we all sat fried chicken, ham, homemade sausage, hot biscuits and spoon bread, home-churned butter, thick cream, cottage cheese, vegetables just out of the garden, ever-bearing strawberries, applesauce, peaches. Once I counted twenty different dishes. Only coffee and tea, sugar and salt came from the store. Soap was made on the place in big iron cauldrons and bacon and ham cured in the smokehouse. Every bed had a hand-woven spread, in the old patterns—Cherokee rose, pine bur, continental—dyed with vegetable dyes—madder, indigo, black walnut—some of them a hundred years old but still bright. In the loom house, which was the first cabin built on the place, Aunt Josie and Aunt Leona had woven bedspreads and curtains for Mrs. Coolidge's "Appalachian mountain room" in the White House.

The Mast Farm had been discovered as a pleasant and inexpensive place to stay by university people long before we began to go there. There were always friends from Chapel Hill on hand; and usually a judge from Washington somehow involved with the Treasury Department; two sisters came every summer from New Orleans and a humorous and vivacious widow from Charlotte, North Carolina, who professed to be given to "spells" brought on by any revolutionary thought or slightly risqué joke. These three ladies, whom we met each year, had a glorious time with Morgan, who treated them with a mixture of deference and teasing that delighted them. I know now, a widow in my sixties myself, how delightful it is when a handsome young man puts himself out for one; at the time it was all just a part of the glow and gaiety that Morgan spread around him, in which I basked even while taking it for granted.

The conversation around that table was good; there were keen minds, aware of the questions of the day, people who had traveled, people interested in folklore and the changing customs of the mountain life. Good, except when the Mule Trader was there.

The modern antiromantic Southern novel had started to appear on the scene. Ellen Glasgow, in *Barren Ground* in 1925, had already revolted against what Stephen Vincent Benét called "the sick magnolias of a false romance"; William Faulkner, having published in 1929 *Sartoris* and *The Sound and the Fury*, was getting into his stride; Paul Green was writing with honesty and compassion about Negro tenant farmers; and *Tobacco Road*, published in 1932, had not yet been made into a play. These, however, were only beginnings; I was not prepared for the Mule Trader.

We always referred to him as the Mule Trader, though he bore one of the good Highland Scottish names and was said to be well-to-do, living in a Southern mansion with white pillars and a long tree-lined drive. He bought mules in Missouri, brought them to North Carolina and sold them to small farmers, mostly Negroes, who used mules for plowing and for pulling the wagons that took their cotton or tobacco to market. He was gross in appearance, squat, thick-shouldered, bull-necked, with a jutting square chin, monstrously thick lips and small, hard, brown eyes like marbles. Loud and coarse in his speech, he dominated the conversation at the table, scornful of anything that he considered highbrow or impractical; he held forth on his triumphs in making deals, the things he bought for his family and his contempt for "niggers."

Once he brought with him his son, his son's wife and his grandson. The son was a tall, fine-looking, university-bred young man, and the little boy was brown-eyed, rosy-cheeked, silent and hungry with a ten-year-old's appetite. The son's wife was beautiful and disdainful, dark with the traditional creamy complexion, slender, elegant, hostile and unsmiling. Obviously there against her will, she sat at the table with her husband and her son between herself and her father-in-law, to whom she ostentatiously said not one word. If the old man baited her beyond her endurance, she would say to her husband in a low voice, "Tell your father . . ." She appeared not to notice her father-in-law's efforts to ingratiate himself with her son, addressing the boy in a voice dripping with adulation, offering promises of future benefits, to which the child, embarrassed, made reluctant, jerky response.

The rest of us, fascinated and repelled, tried not to watch the drama being played out before us, but our attempts at general conversation dwindled to murmured remarks to immediate neighbors. Once the lady from Charlotte said to me, "He's not all bad, you know. He has his points." But I could not see them.

One summer the Mule Trader had the bedroom next to ours. The wall between the rooms was thin and the beds must have been placed head to head, for we were awakened by his nightmares. "Lucy!" he cried out, "Lucy, you black bitch!"

There was the raw stuff of a novel there, I used to think, and I would turn it this way and that in my mind, but it never developed a life of its own in my imagination or plucked at me in moments when I was thinking of something else, as an idea that is really meant for one invariably does. It was not, I realized, for a Northerner fresh from Bryn Mawr and suburban Philadelphia to write; I was too foreign, too ignorant, too immature, too intolerant.

Another person in whom I saw material for a novel, from which again I was held back by ignorance, was Mrs. Hartley, a fragile little old woman who lived with her wisp of a husband in a three-roomed cabin on a ledge halfway up the mountain on the other side of the creek. In June wild azaleas flamed against the cobalt sky as we walked the high meadows to visit her.

She had reared eleven children, all of whom were out in the world and one of whom had gone as far as China, from whence he sent her a black satin dress banded with bright embroidery which she wore when she went calling. She had provided each of the nine children who had married with a quilt, a feather bed, blankets and a hand-woven bedspread, all of her own making. We went several times to see her and were shown her immaculate little house with the parlor organ which she was learning to play by correspondence, her loom house, and the storehouse cave where sausage and berries and vegetables were preserved in rows of large Mason jars made about 1850, and shaped like squat milk bottles without shoulders.

Passing through the garden on the way to the storehouse, I marveled at the wealth of flowers—snapdragons, lady's-slippers, bachelor's buttons, nicotiana and the like. "Where do you get the seeds?" I asked.

"Look in a catalog and write for 'em," she answered tartly.

Before we left she gathered some seeds from her flowers and gave them to me in a little twist of paper. When I thanked her, she said quickly, "You must never thank anybody for flower seeds. It's bad luck."

"What do you say then, when you are grateful and want to show it?"

"You say, 'I'll think of you when they bloom.' "

Many a summer since then, seeing the bright annuals in a garden, my own or another's, I have thought of Mrs. Hartley standing there, a small, gnarled, sunny figure with her cabin and her parlor organ behind her and, towering over her, Morgan, his face alight with interest, and have been for that fleeting instant carried back into the wholeness of that sunny moment and felt myself part of it again, as if time had become circular instead of linear.

In 1968, in May, on the way home from a trip to the Great Smokies with my Irish friend, I made a detour and went back to Valle Crucis for the first time in thirty-six years. All along the road as we approached it, I saw evidences of prosperity in trim little brick houses, filling stations, small businesses. Valle Crucis itself had a fine new school, and there were summer houses on the hillsides. We came on the Mast Farm sooner than I expected, almost hidden by the hemlocks that had grown up between it and the road.

The house was closed and wore a dejected, unlived-in look. Bedraggled white curtains in the windows suggested that someone had gone out and shut the door on it just as it was when the old people died. The springhouse and woodshed were empty, the washhouse crumbling, the loom house filled with old wheelbarrows and rusty tools; a half-finished bedspread on the loom was gray with age and dust and festooned with cobwebs. At some time a flood must have changed the course of the brook and the forget-me-nots were gone.

Up on the hill beyond the brook, well fenced, well cared for, in contrast, was the family burial ground. Here under handsome stones slept the family whom I had known—Mr. Will, Aunt Josie, Aunt Leona—and there were other graves going back through a century and a half of Masts. The sun shone, the May breeze stirred the trees, the way to Mrs. Hartley's lay high on the hill beyond the creek.

We parked the car on the edge of the lawn, which someone had roughly mown, and ate our picnic beside the ravished brook. It was not everyone whom I would have taken to visit the place that Morgan and I had once enjoyed together. You cannot expect another's eyes to see through present neglect and decay to the charm, elusive in its simplicity, of a day long past, but my Irish friend, perhaps because she found many aspects of American culture overglossy, perhaps because she was accustomed to crumbling remains of past glories, perhaps just because she was in herself sensitive and generous, was able to understand what it was that I had loved in the place, to taste with me something of the flavor of an unrecapturable innocence and beauty.

In the fall of 1929 my third book, *Tilly-Tod*, was published. It was a story for young children evoked by my mother's memories of her childhood on the farm. I turned my mother and her elder sister Emily into Quaker twins; the small events of the farm made up the story, with the distant Civil War hanging over the family and the news of its ending providing the climax and the much-hoped-for flags which the children longed to wave. I had had to soften the original episode, which was touching but too sad. Emily and Anne, like Tilly-Tod, had longed to own a flag, and their parents had promised to bring them each one from the Sanitary Fair in Philadelphia. When at last the carriage rolled up the long lane, my grandparents put the furled flags into the small hands and said, "You may have the flags, but you may not wave them. Abraham Lincoln has been assassinated."

The book was illustrated by a competent New England artist

who did not know Quakers. The children in the pictures were angular, stylized little Puritans, and the background bore no resemblance to the flat, luxuriant South Jersey countryside or the ample Quaker farm. Years later when Marguerite de Angeli wrote and illustrated her own Quaker tale of a slightly earlier period, *Thee, Hannah!*, she got into it the very body and spirit of Quaker Philadelphia. I have often thought that if she could have illustrated *Tilly-Tod*, it might have sold better. It was the first of my books to go out of print and for many years the only one. Those who liked it liked it very much; it marked a growth in my writing, and for the first time Mr. Child in his letter of congratulation ceased to be indulgent and gave me instead a serious analysis, and praised it as being "in a true sense, poetry."

When *Meggy MacIntosh* came out the following year, Marguerite de Angeli did illustrate it, and the Scottish girl in the North Carolina pines looked exactly as I had hoped she would. It was to be several years more before I was to meet Mrs. de Angeli at a book fair in Camden and so begin the friendship that has been a deep and abiding joy to me ever since.

The fall of 1929 marked also the beginning of the great depression. Morgan and I were in Wanamaker's in Philadelphia buying Numdah rugs for our bedroom on the twenty-fourth of October; suddenly no one was interested in waiting on us. Ashen-faced salesmen clustered around a radio which was issuing the news of the plunging prices on the Stock Exchange.

We had no stocks ourselves, and Mother's few were of a sound, conservative variety that reduced dividends but never passed them. My Uncle Charles, Mother's younger brother, who had been speculating, was wiped out. For days after the blow fell no one talked of anything else. The depressions of 1893 and 1907, which had loomed so large in the history of my family, had been comfortably forgotten by most people, and many a convincing article had been written to prove that the United States had learned the secret of prosperity and that financial panic would never come again. Nobody was prepared; there were no cushions to break the fall.

The market rallied a little before it fell again, and kept falling. The President assured the country that prosperity was just around the corner. The real agony did not come for another year or two.

All that autumn—and indeed all the time that we lived in Chapel Hill—Morgan worked hard on our lot, cutting out dead and unnecessary trees and grubbing up stumps, making cement strips along the driveway to the garage. If I was out when he came home from the University, he would not go into the house alone, except to change into his work clothes in the basement where there was a shower.

His health steadily improved. I pinned my faith on regular, simple, appetizing and well-balanced meals in an atmosphere of serenity, and it worked. Before long his digestion was normal and his resilient energy matched his splendid physique.

Our first Christmas was celebrated in our house. Mother and Violet came to spend the holidays with us. All their doubts and reservations about my marriage had vanished, and they had taken Morgan wholly to their hearts. He gave Mother deference and tenderness and Violet a younger brother's warm and teasing affection. His laughter, his gaiety, his gift of making a celebration out of a small event delighted them, and they leaned on his masculine strength and clarity. For his part, after the years of illness and loneliness he found deep satisfaction in being once again in the center of a close family life.

So our first anniversary came round and our marriage, like our house, was an edifice in which we lived and grew, were sheltered and nourished. It was an old-fashioned marriage, reticent, passionate, faithful and joyous. Morgan was gay, full of jokes and quips, teasing in a boyish way enchanting to me who had grown up without brothers. He could tell a preposterous story with a perfectly straight face, and if you believed him would say "Oh?" politely puzzled. He would report to me conversations he had had with the dogs, the disrespectful things they said about me and how he had rebuked them for it. He called me "Janet" because he liked the name, but he allowed no one else to use it. When we were alone together, he was apt to call me "Mouse." I called him "M" or "Angel-baby," and once forgot myself and said it in front of a group of students. To their credit—and his—not one of them cracked a smile, and there were no echoes of it afterwards. Morgan laughed at me often about it.

Our minds, though quite different—for his was keen, analytical, rational, practical, while mine was intuitive, flexible, literary and somewhat flighty—moved at the same rate of speed, which was, I think, rather quicker than the average. We saw jokes and laughed at the same moment, we understood each other's line of reasoning and came to decisions swiftly and without a maze of argument and explanation. Once when Mother was visiting us, she was astonished at the speed with which we reversed a decision firmly made some time earlier. The conversation went like this:

"You know, I've been thinking about so-and-so."

"Yes, so have I. I've meant to say something about it."

"I wonder if we really want to do it."

"Let's not."

So we didn't. "It would have taken us hours of discussion to come to that conclusion," said Mother.

Aside from the great gift of his love and the love he awakened in me, Morgan set me free. Not free to be myself—for I had as yet no self to be, immature as I was, pliant, overconscientious, sensitive to every current that touched me—but free to seek myself, to establish my own values. He released me from the pressure of money worries, which had so cramped and hindered my own family, not by providing financial security, for no one had that in those days, but by being himself never under the blight of anxiety about money. He left me free to form my own opinions even when they differed from his. In the 1932 election he, a Democrat, voted for Hoover because he thought Roosevelt lacked principle and was vindictive; I, a Republican, voted for Norman Thomas because I admired him as a man and I thought he was concerned to spread the wealth more widely. Morgan's only comment was,

"Thomas is all right himself, Janet, but I don't trust the crowd he would bring in with him."

He left me entirely free to do my writing without criticism and usually without comment. He was openly relieved when he first read something I had written, a story in *St. Nicholas*, because it was not sentimental and would not embarrass him. He was pleased about my books because they were something I enjoyed doing that brought me in some money of my own, and proud of me in the same way that he would have been had I been good at golf or playing the piano, but children's books were not his interest and he did not pretend that they were. Every writer needs one person he can trust to whom he can read his first drafts, and for this I had Violet, who was ever receptive and encouraging and occasionally critical. I sent manuscripts to her to read or saved them for when we were together, and Morgan found our absorption and the time we spent on them no threat to him.

Most fundamentally, he set me free from the fear of love, released the shackles of taboo and inhibition in which I had been reared, and taught me through passion and tenderness—"rich as the earth and wide as heaven is wide"—and joy, to lose myself in love.

I do not want to give the impression that he was perfect, that he had not the normal human flaws. He was hot-tempered, proud and sensitive, as of course I was myself. We quarreled sometimes, usually over trivial misunderstandings and wounded feelings, but in our quarrels we never said barbed things that left scars and we never quarreled about money.

We were both reasonably responsible about money; we had a joint bank account and we did not overdraw it; we believed in saving for a family, for education, books and travel, but we also believed in spending for present joys. Our tastes were simple and similar. Once on an impulse we went off for a spring week end to Myrtle Beach, where we did nothing but walk the long, empty sands skipping shells at sea gulls, and sit talking or being silent together in a beached rowboat among the dunes. On the Sunday evening Morgan said, "I suppose more sensible people would use the money we have spent on this week end to buy furniture they need for the house." I replied without hesitation, "I'd rather have the memories."

He had to a degree that I have never known in anyone else a clarity and sweetness of spirit that I can only call purity of heart. There was no residue of resentment when his anger passed, no nursing of wounded pride, no pocket where unaired emotion soured and curdled; his spirit cleared as a mountain spring after the stirring has settled. The things he wanted were free of greed; he recognized ugly realities and raged against them but remained essentially untouched by them. I used to think, but never told him, that the beatitude, "Blessed are the pure in heart: for they shall see God," was especially his.

✳✳✳✳✳✳✳✳✳✳✳✳✳✳✳✳✳✳✳✳✳✳✳✳✳✳✳✳✳✳✳✳✳✳✳

3.

The Depression

In the summer of 1930 the University decided to conduct a "Trans-Continental Study Tour (Coeducational)" in which for eight weeks, from June 8 to August 2, two caravans of buses would cross the country to the West Coast and back, camping and studying along the way, with university professors to lecture and the country itself for laboratory. Courses for credit were offered in Geology, Geography, Botany, General Science, Sociology, and Economics. The tour was divided into two sections, with Russell Grumman, director of the Extension Division, as educational director of the first and Morgan in charge of the second. A travel bureau in Charlotte provided the "business management," which was a mistake; when the tour was repeated the following year, the Extension Division was in entire charge. Vida Grumman and I and some of the instructors' wives went along for the ride.

In our section Lee Brooks taught Sociology. There were also courses in Geography and Economics. We left on June 7—a staff car, in which Morgan and I, a young man from the travel bureau and the dietician rode, a cook and a baggage truck, and five or six small buses holding eight passengers each. Our itinerary led across Tennessee, through Arkansas and Texas, across New Mexico and Arizona to California, and back via Nevada, Utah, the Yellowstone, Wyoming, Colorado, Kansas, Missouri, Illinois, Indiana and Kentucky.

At night we camped in fairgrounds, school gymnasiums, university stadiums, open deserts and tourist camps of every degree. Early in the mornings we would get up and have breakfast, the students would gather round their instructors for classes, and the wives would pack the lunches: three sandwiches, a cookie and a piece of fruit in paper bags soon stained with mayonnaise oozing from the sandwiches. It was years before I could bear to eat mayonnaise again. By ten-thirty we were off, stopping along the way for the Sociology class to visit a penitentiary, an Indian reservation, a foreign quarter, a juvenile court; for the Geography class to inspect a marble quarry, a diamond mine, a meteor crater and of course the Painted Desert, the Petrified Forest, and the Grand Canyon. The Economics class, I remember, visited the Cotton Market in Memphis, and I with it, fascinated by the board, the brokers, the telegrams coming in from New York, New Orleans, Chicago and Liverpool, the shirt sleeves, the general stir of the romance of the South's own business. Meanwhile, the baggage and the cook trucks would have gone ahead to the next camping place, to have the tents and cots unpacked and a hot dinner ready for us. Sometimes they had car trouble, sometimes they stopped to sight-see, sometimes they got lost; often we all arrived at the same time and then we ate dinner, tired and cross, at eleven-thirty at night.

But with all the inconveniences—once we had fourteen punctures in a single day and another time two broken axles and a burnt-out bearing—it was a gay and stimulating experience. I who had never been west of Harrisburg was thrilled to see the whole vast and beautiful sweep of the country, its resources and problems, its accomplishments and failures interpreted by skilled teachers as we went along.

Morgan and I were fortunate in having Lee and Evelyn Brooks in our section. New Englanders, a little older than I, a little younger than Morgan, they had both majored in English and minored in music in their undergraduate days, and Lee had taken his doctorate in Sociology, specializing in isolated communities. Lee and Morgan were already friends; they played tennis together in Chapel Hill; both big and boyish, they had the same irrepressible humor and they teased each other unmercifully. Evelyn, not very long over a serious illness, was fragile physically, and almost poignantly gentle, but her spirit and her interest in new ideas and fresh experiences were indomitable. I was none too strong at that time myself—the following year I underwent a serious operation—and it was a great comfort to me to be able from time to time to slip off with Evelyn to rest. Whenever we had more than a single night in a place and there was free time, we made a regular foursome.

Highlights of the trip remain fresh in my mind: Beale Street in Memphis, home of the Beale Street Blues; the vast, flat cotton fields of Arkansas, gray with dust; the tiny boxes of houses with Negroes and hogs asleep together on the sagging porches; dreary little towns with no evidence of schools, churches or libraries; the wild flowers of Texas and the oil derricks and the rows of storage tanks. At Texarkana Morgan and I left the group and went ahead to Dallas by night train, to meet cousins of his and drive with them to Coleman and Ballinger, where I met two of his aunts and more cousins. It was delightful to rest in cool, perfectly kept houses with awnings and lawns and beds of bright phlox, overwhelmed by affection and laughter and every attention that generous hospitality could devise.

We rejoined the caravan two days later at Abilene with no idea that the dull, dusty little frontier town would one day be famous as the home of a great general and President of the United States. Days in the desert followed. We were too late for the wild flowers, though a few cacti bloomed, but I felt the fascination and the mystery of it, the beauty of those bare, jagged red-violet mountains, the long-legged road runners dashing across the road ahead into the sagebrush, the mesquite trees and tumbleweed, the colonies of prairie dogs, the jack rabbits, the sudden rains in purple sheets, the arroyos full of water and the swift freshness in the air. For the first time I realized that the Spaniards had indeed preceded us to this part of the new world, I felt their presence in Juarez, where in the mission church of Our Lady of the Guadalupe, under the great beams carved in 1659 by primitive Indians, an aristocratic Virgin in a black satin gown held a lace handkerchief by its exact center in her right hand; in the little sleepy town of Socorro, known to Spanish explorers in the sixteenth century, where priests established a mission in 1626.

It was the time of the dust bowl, and even Chapel Hill had experienced a dust storm blown more than a thousand miles over forests and mountains, but we were not aware of the wave of migrants making their difficult way into California. Once or twice a filling-station owner would tell us of a jalopy that had broken down, and next to us in a cabin in a tourist camp in Los Angeles was a pathetic little family on its way from Houston, Texas, to Portland, Oregon, where the unemployed father had heard of work, but otherwise we saw little of the suffering that was gripping the country. That there were not many tourists on the roads and the camps were not crowded only made our own trip easier.

We fell in love with San Francisco, Morgan and I, and as we stood on the back of the ferry for the last time returning to Oakland where the caravan was camped, and saw the dark water widen between us and the lights of the city, like strings of beads festooning the dark hills, we told each other, "We'll come back. We'll come back some day and stay long enough to really see it."

At the Yosemite the young ranger who greeted us told us that he had lived in New York City until he was twenty and had never seen a Broadway show, that he had studied forestry in Montana, and that he found the ranger's life in the mountains less lonely, winter and summer, than the city. One night we camped at Lake Tenaya, eight thousand feet up, shut in by granite cliffs eleven thousand feet high. After dark when we sat around the campfires in the icy air, suddenly the moon rose and threw the shadow of one cliff sharp upon the other.

The Great Salt Lake Desert was a waste of white with violet hills against the sky and mirages of islands in between; sea gulls appeared to tell us we were nearing the Great Salt Lake and to remind us of the sea gulls that saved the Mormons from the plague of locusts. In Salt Lake City Morgan and I ran away from the tour to have a civilized dinner on the roof of the Hotel Utah and see the statue of Moroni on top of the Temple gilded in the sunset.

Pocatello, Idaho, followed Ogden, Utah, and there the money that the Travel Bureau was to send us failed to arrive. The faculty advanced money, and we went on to the Yellowstone, to Laramie, to Denver, where no one had any more money to advance. Morgan wired the University on Friday, and we spent the week end on the outskirts of the city in a cheap tourist camp between a railroad and a deserted factory, beset by mosquitoes, noise and boredom. Morale nevertheless remained high. It was amazing how girls with only a crumpled suitcase and the most meagre of bathing facilities could turn themselves out fresh, well-groomed, modish; amazing how men without money, food or rest could console themselves by tossing a baseball about.

Funds came from the University on Monday morning, and we headed for home over the hot plains. In St. Louis we met Morgan's cousin Betty Gibson and her husband George, minister of a Congregational church there, and had a cheerful time with them. From Columbia, Missouri, to Vincennes, Indiana, where we camped on the grounds of the Harmony Society (a German musical club), was a very long way. The cook truck was pinched for speeding and their fine cut deep into our purse; dinner was not ready till after eleven, when everyone was dead tired and fighting cross. Next morning final exams were written on the Harmony Society picnic tables.

At Louisville Morgan put me on the train at midnight so that I could get back to Chapel Hill in time for the opening of second summer school in which I was again to teach. The upper berth, which we were lucky by that time to be able to afford, seemed unutterably cool, comfortable and luxurious.

Morgan's younger sister, Beatrice Hurt, whose husband had died earlier in the year after a long and courageous fight against tuberculosis, had come to Chapel Hill before we set off on our trip, stayed in the house while we were gone, taking library courses in the first summer school, and stayed on through August with us, returning to Texas in the early fall to take up the post of librarian in a boys' school in Kerrville. She was small and plump and pretty with bright brown eyes and an affectionate, lively manner; she adored her big brother and was full of stories of their childhood, to which I listened eagerly. It had been a warm, close family, just the four of them with a devoted Swedish maid, centering around the brilliant, handsome boy but able too to laugh at him. One of the stories she loved to tell involved a plate of tamales, a Mexican delicacy which both children loved. There had been an even number on the plate when they began, but Bee ate faster. Morgan, looking at the single one left, struggled to be polite. "You take it, Sis," he said generously; "you started first."

As associate director of the Extension Division, Morgan had charge of short courses and institutes. His work began in January with the Press Institute, a three-day gathering of editors of North Carolina newspapers, with lectures, conferences and a banquet. He was popular with the newsmen, and he enjoyed the contact with them thoroughly.

The Drama Festival in the spring I have already written about. More demanding were the refresher courses for doctors, dentists and lawyers which he arranged each year. An authority on pellagra, for instance, which, next to tuberculosis, was the most killing disease in the South, would be brought from the North to lecture one night a week in five different centers for six weeks;

local doctors would come in from neighboring villages for the lectures and for conferences. Morgan's part of it, after enlisting the visiting authority, was to arouse the interest of the local doctors, get them registered, plan the schedule, make arrangements for housing and transportation, be on hand to start the courses off and stand ready throughout the six weeks to meet any emergency that might arise. Each year the courses were held in a different part of the state. Negro doctors and lawyers were included. At that time it was a shibboleth among white Southerners never to call a black man by anything but a first name, either his own or a generic one like Jim; Morgan drew down some criticism upon himself by punctiliously giving the Negro doctors the same respect that he paid to the white ones.

One summer he began a new venture, a two-week school for policemen, who came to the University, stayed on the campus, and attended lectures on government, police methods and so forth. It was tentative, but it was groundbreaking. Later Albert Coates of the Law School created the now famous Institute of Government, which has a fine building of its own and a national reputation.

Morgan was the first to conceive a university radio program. It is hard to remember now that at that time there was no television and that radio itself was fairly new. Less than ten years earlier the first broadcasts had come in on crystal sets grounded to bedsprings. Morgan had no budget for it, and even the shoestring on which he operated had to be squeezed from other things. With the cooperation of the Raleigh station and the generosity of faculty members he put on a weekly University Hour, of which the crowning achievement was a course in French given by Leon Wiley of the French Department, with mimeographed lesson sheets for which a very respectable number of serious listeners wrote to ask.

To prepare for all these and other courses, Morgan had to make many trips over the state, and often I went "extending" with him. So it was I got to know the state fairly well in a short time, from Edenton, Washington, New Bern and Wilmington in the east, those lovely old coastal towns full of colonial history, to Asheville and Boone in the western mountains, as well as the less glamorous stretches in between. I remember once driving with him over lonely roads through the pines west of Carthage, where old women in sunbonnets drew water from wells and swarms of children came to cabin doors to watch us pass. At Jugtown we met and talked to the Buzbys, who did so much to revive the old crafts in North Carolina. Mr. Buzby told us much about the people in their region, who still cooked over open fires and had wooden shutters over their windows instead of glass and who spoke an English that was old when they had brought it with them from England two centuries earlier.

Chapel Hill at that time was full of interesting and creative people. Howard Washington Odum, author of the best-selling *Rainbow Round My Shoulder,* was bringing the Sociology Department into national prominence with his battery of research workers who were making pioneer studies on the Negro and the sharecropper. Paul Green was writing plays and short stories. His *House of Connelly* was running in New York; in 1931 he read one Sunday evening at the Playmaker Theater his *Tread the Green Grass,* a fantasy with a metaphysical horse to indicate to the audience in moments of doubt what their emotions should be. He had not yet embarked on the "symphonic dramas" given at Manteo, Williamsburg and Berea for which he has since become famous—*The Lost Colony, The Common Glory, The Wilderness Road.* In the early 1930's he was teaching Philosophy in the University and with his wife Elizabeth bringing new breath and spirit into the social life of Chapel Hill. They were the first to entertain talented Negroes socially in their home. Lynn Riggs came back to Chapel Hill one week end to read at the Playmaker Theater his play *Green Grow the Lilacs,* then playing at the Theatre Guild in New York, later to become a musical named *Oklahoma.* Archibald Henderson, "official biographer" of Shaw, was writing his *Bernard Shaw, Playboy and Prophet,* Raymond Adams making a name for his solid, scholarly work on Thoreau. Howard Mumford Jones, the critic, was about to leave Chapel Hill for the University of Michigan and later for Harvard.

Social life was presided over by a hierarchy of matrons of "the Old Village," of whom my dear Mrs. Bullitt was one. Bridge parties which began at eleven A.M. with "bridge breakfasts" and went on all day and into the night, luncheons, dinners, vast candlelit afternoon teas at which the younger women in full evening dress circulated about "receiving," could keep anyone fully occupied who had time for it.

I very soon cut out bridge altogether, for I had no time for daytime bridge and Morgan had no liking for the game. We had a circle of young couples whom we enjoyed being with: Frances and Lewis Patton of Duke—Fanny has since become famous as the creator of Miss Dove; Freddie B. McCall, of the Law School, and Adeline, his wife, a musician; Lee and Evelyn Brooks; Manson and Ruth Valentine, of the Biology Department; Christopher and Janet Crittenden of the History Department; Felix Grisette, who was a fundraiser for the University, and his wife, Genevieve, who had beautiful red-gold hair and a rare skill in homemaking; Gladys and Albert Coates, of the Law Department; Richmond and Marjorie Bond, of the English Department; Elizabeth Chesley and H. G. Baity, of the Engineering Department. Elizabeth, usually known as Chesley, came to Chapel Hill as a bride shortly after I did. Original, charming, and gifted in many fields, she was at that time pursuing music and modern art; later she wrote poetry and still later took up anthropology and wrote scholarly and absorbing books for young people such as *Man Is a Weaver* and *Americans Before Columbus*. H. G., after making a wide reputation for himself throughout North Carolina as a sanitary engineer, was called in the early 1950's to the World Health Organization, and they lived for some years in Geneva.

I had a part-time maid named Nelly Morgan, the only white maid in Chapel Hill. Her father had been of "good stock," a farmer whose forebears had given their name to Morgan's Creek, which flowed under the Pittsboro Road at the bottom of the Hill; an old man, he had married his housekeeper, who was known for moral flightiness. Nelly herself had had a somewhat checkered life; when I knew her she was living in a rickety wooden house on Windy Hill, not far from us, with her ramshackle mother and her two little boys, her husband having deserted her some time earlier. She was just my age, slender, fair-haired, awkwardly graceful, her teeth ruined by dipping snuff. She came every morning to clean the house, get lunch for us and do anything I asked her to do in preparation for dinner. She was honest, generous, hard-working and loyal, with an unusually sensitive feeling for people and situations, and I loved her. She interested me too, as representing a life hitherto entirely outside my experience, and I enjoyed her conversation and her turns of phrase. Of a neighbor with two small children she said, "She has an arm-baby and a knee-baby," and once, when she had made some coffee cakes that did not turn out as they were expected to, she said, "They look awful ornery but they eat elegant."

The Depression, which had begun with widespread unemployment in North Carolina even before the crash of October, 1929, was shaking the University seriously by 1931. Student registration was falling off, salaries were cut by 10 per cent and it was openly questioned how long certain departments could maintain their numbers. A mood of anxiety prevailed.

Even earlier Morgan had begun to feel that if he was going to remain in university work he should have the union card, a Ph.D. He began work on a master's degree in English Literature at Duke University, twelve miles away in Durham. The little Methodist college, Trinity, had only recently come into the Duke money and changed its name. It was in the process of building a great new campus in the pine forest to the west of the town, with traditional Tudor Gothic buildings with steep roofs and small windows appropriate to a cold climate and most unsuitable for the burning heat of North Carolina. The first course Morgan took was Middle English, and I went with him to audit it and to renew my pleasure in the metrical romances. The stories of King Horn, Sir Beves, Havelok the Dane, Floris and Blanchefleur and others, long and repetitious though they were, seemed to me full of vitality and interest, and I conceived the idea of making my own translations and retelling them for children. I would have, I thought, a collection of tales in the frame of a medieval minstrel and his son, who would wander over the roads of England, going into all kinds of English life—the castle, the manor house, the inn, the fair, the village—and telling in each place the kind of story appropriate to it.

Morgan took his master's degree in June, 1932, but by then I had put the medieval tales aside for the time being; my imagination had been captured by a fair-haired, tempestuous little girl who was to grow up in Chapel Hill in what were called the "lotus-eating" years before the Civil War, and I was doing research for the book that I was to call *Jane Hope* in the University Library.

Since my days in the Cataloguing Room, the University had built a great new library on the southern edge of the campus and moved into it. Dr. de Roulhac Hamilton, who lived near us on North Street, had been for years collecting material for the North Carolina Room; he had traveled all over the state, visiting people who lived in old houses, persuading them that the papers in their attics, the diaries, letters, account books and bills stuffed into old trunks, had historical value and should be given or sold to the University. Mary Thornton, head of the North Carolina Room, had not yet had time to organize these masses of assorted papers, which had been thrust into steel boxes and stored in a windowless room in the stacks. She allowed me to rummage among them to find whatever I could, and day after day in the hot summer of 1932 I pored over those papers, discovering almost at random things that would come to life in my book when I wrote it. I knew, for instance, that in the spring after Fort Sumter was fired on, the students had petitioned the Governor of the State to close the University for the ensuing term so that students might join the Confederate Army. In a box among all kinds of (to me) useless bits and pieces, I found the petition itself, with the original corrections and interpolations and the signatures of the students. By this time I knew that anything I wanted about Chapel Hill in the 1850's I must get now or not at all. We were going to leave Chapel Hill.

The Depression still had the country in a vise; if anything, it was growing more acute. Unemployment was widespread. Prices had tumbled frighteningly; you could get a steak dinner for fifty cents, buy a three-pound pork loin for thirty cents. Banks were closing their doors. We read of bread lines in the cities. The University too was feeling the pinch; the Extension Division was considered a luxury, its very existence was in question. Would this not be, we wondered, a good time for Morgan to stop trying to get his Ph.D. piecemeal but to take a leave from the University and concentrate on his degree?

President Harry Woodburn Chase had been succeeded in 1930 by Frank Graham, once an associate professor in the History Department and our friend. It was easy to talk the situation over with him. He strongly advised Morgan to get all the academic preparation that he could; the University was in serious straits; if the Extension Division survived, there would always be a place in it for Morgan; if it did not, with a Ph.D. he would be in a better position to go elsewhere. Morgan decided on Teachers College, Columbia, where he would work not in English but in university administration. We had enough money in the bank to take us, with careful management, through at least one year.

We made our preparations. Bee came from Texas to be with us most of the summer. Morgan took another course at Duke, I was doing research in the library and also beginning the packing up of the house, which we had arranged to rent to Frank and Jennie Hanft of the Law School. It was a busy summer, the hottest of all those that I spent in Chapel Hill. After Bee left, in the last two weeks when the final packing was done, the temperature went over the hundred mark every day.

On one of those last days I went to a luncheon, one of those summer affairs which the Chapel Hill women did so well, with rooms polished, cool and a little dim, tall glasses of minted iced tea, crisp salad, fresh summer dresses and an air of gaiety and nonchalance. The talk turned to the closing of the banks. "I hear," someone said, "that the First National Bank in Durham is in trouble."

The First National was where we had our money for New York. I left early to find Morgan and tell him, but it was too late to do anything that day and the next day the bank closed its doors.

We still had eight hundred dollars in a savings bank. I was getting a dribble from my children's books. There would be tuition to pay, rent of fifty dollars a month for the apartment already engaged in Bancroft Hall, the apartment house for married graduate students, and all the other expenses of a year—or more—of study in New York. We decided that we could manage.

We left Chapel Hill in the car for which we already had a purchaser on the morning of September 1, 1932. The last thing we did was to go and say good-by to the Bullitts. Morgan shook hands with Dr. Bullitt; I kissed Mrs. Bullitt. My eyes filled up with tears.

"Never mind," she said. "You'll be back next year."

"That's just it," I said. "I'm afraid we won't."

4.

New York

THE DEPRESSION in North Carolina had been distressing, but in New York it was terrifying. Without the reassurance of the land all around, the comfort of belonging to a network of known and knowing human beings, the people of New York were inconsiderable nuts and bolts of a huge machine that had broken down and was flying apart. Countless numbers of men had lost their jobs and could not get new ones; often their wives, adaptable and ill-paid, could find some work to tide them over, but that in itself was a reversal of the proper order of things and added to their loss of confidence. There were long lines of drooping, shabby men waiting for handouts of soup; war veterans sold apples for five cents apiece on street corners; unkempt and sometimes menacing men stopped one on the street demanding five cents for a cup of coffee, and, even more frighteningly, respectable middle-aged men in well-cut but worn suits would say in low voices with averted eyes, "Could you possibly help me? I am— hungry."

On the flats along the Hudson at 72nd Street, below the corner of Riverside Drive where stood the "Chateau Schwab," was a squatters' community of huts made of corrugated iron, waste lumber and cardboard, which had been dubbed the Bonus Camp, because veterans lived there hoping that the government would pay them a lump sum for their services in the war. In Washington General Douglas MacArthur dealt harshly with the straggling army of Bonus Marchers who had come to present their case to the Congress.

Faces of passers-by in the streets of New York, even on Fifth Avenue, where people still went well dressed in an atmosphere of elegance that has long since vanished, looked anxious and depressed, often despairing. Ten years later, after Pearl Harbor, when the war was still going badly both in the Pacific and in Europe, I looked at the faces of people in the streets and saw them in contrast alive, keen, purposeful. The loss of livelihood and of work or even the threat of it apparently cuts into the very basis of personality in a way that the loss of loved ones or the fear of it does not.

In that year when the Depression hit bottom, even people who had been wholly successful and secure were suddenly unemployed. May Massee, one of three great pioneers in the field of children's literature, the creator of Doubleday Doran's first children's book department, moved to the Viking Press, then a new firm, in which she was brilliantly successful.

At Columbia there were many others like us who were using this time to prepare themselves to take advantage of the upswing when it should come; most of them were doing it on very slim resources. Rumors flew about, of students living in warehouse rooms without furniture, stories of illness and desperation. Twice during the winter graduate students, losing hope altogether, committed suicide, and a shudder went through the entire student body.

Morgan and I had an apartment in Bancroft Hall on 120th Street across from the dark red walls and battlements of Teachers College. We had a living room, bedroom, bath (enormous fixtures, dark woodwork and cracked tiles) and tiny kitchen. I made a dressing table out of orange crates covered with chintz, and we bought a large easy chair on 125th Street for sixteen dollars, to supplement the scanty college-mission fumed-oak furniture. The kitchen had some shelves, a small sink and an old-fashioned icebox underneath a two-burner gas stove. In the mornings a block of ice came up on the dumb-waiter; one clasped it to one's bosom, knelt and shoved it into the icebox. Roaches came up the dumb-waiter at night.

It was enough; it was all we needed; we were completely happy. All that fall and into the winter I worked on *Jane Hope*, which was to be one of the twelve books on May Massee's first list for Viking the following autumn. Morgan plunged with zest into his courses. Among the students living at Bancroft Hall we found two congenial couples—Merle and Edna Ward, Leslie and Rachel Patton—who became our friends.

We threw ourselves with joy into the savoring of New York

itself. Morgan was fascinated with the life of the streets; he used to take long walks and come back to tell me of the people he had seen and talked to: the old men playing odd games in the street in the Italian quarter on the Upper East Side, the bums on Riverside Drive who advised him always to swallow some olive oil before drinking whiskey on an empty stomach, the policemen on the beat who found time to talk with someone intelligently interested in their problems and experiences.

We went to the Automobile Show in the new Waldorf-Astoria; we attended night court, where a kindly judge gave vagrants the sentence they wanted, thirty days of a bed at night and regular meals; we were in the enormous crowd on Times Square the night that Roosevelt was elected, watching the electric lights run around the Times Building with election returns, and there again on New Year's Eve. Both nights the streets were packed so tight with rejoicing people that no cars could get through.

Like everybody else we lived anxiously through the four months of the interregnum between the election on November 9 and the inauguration on March 4, while the country sank deeper and deeper into slump because Hoover was helpless alone and Roosevelt would not meet with him or make any move until he had all the power in his own hands. In the world beyond New York events were moving toward a dark and hidden future.

On January 31, 1933, the fourth anniversary of our wedding, Morgan came into our living room, where I was typing away at *Jane Hope*, with a *New York Times* in his hand and a look of distress and excitement on his face.

"What's happened?" I asked in alarm.

"That madman has got into power in Germany! It will mean war."

"What madman?"

"Hitler. Von Hindenburg has made him Chancellor."

"Let me see the paper."

There was a three-column headline on the first page: "Hitler Made Chancellor of Germany but Coalition Cabinet Limits Power. Centrists Hold Balance in Reichstag."

"That doesn't look so serious," I said. "He only represents a minority."

But Morgan was sure of his ground. He had been following the growth of the Nazi movement; he knew about the meeting in Potsdam three months earlier when Hitler had addressed 30,000

German young people who had acclaimed him wildly. Hindenburg, he pointed out, was eighty-five and would not long withstand Hitler's declared determination to seize dictator's powers.

"It will take a few years, no doubt," Morgan reiterated. "But there will be war. In the next war I shall go into the Air Force."

It is interesting now to read that *New York Times* of January 31, 1933. Other headlines on other pages read: "Hitler News Fails to Stir Wall Street. Reaction of Markets Is Mild." "Italians Acclaim Hitler Regime." "Poland Sees Reich Showing True Face." A report from the *Times* of London said that Britain would watch the German attitude towards armaments "with some misgivings." The first editorial in *The New York Times* that day was on the subject of the state budget; the second, entitled "Germany Ventures," said, "It would be useless to try to disguise the qualms which the news from Berlin must cause to all friends of Germany. . . . Hitler has boasted that he will destroy the Republic and set up a personal dictatorship . . . but President Hindenburg will retain supreme command, prepared to unmake Hitler as quickly as he has made him. . . . There is thus no warrant for immediate alarm." The final editorial that day was called "Energy from Atoms" and was based on a speech made by Dr. A. H. Compton. "In a future that may be less than a century away," it prophesied daringly, "we even see a world transformed by the atomic engineer, even though we have scarcely a glimmering of the processes that he will apply."

There were in *The New York Times* qualms, misgivings and watchfulness about Hitler's chancellorship, but the word *war* was not spoken that day as Morgan had spoken it. For my part I tried not to hear him. I wanted no talk of war. Pacifism was in the air of the time, but even if it had not been, my memories of the 1914 World War and my father's excitement and bitterness, and the conviction of war's horrors and futility which my Quaker schooling had given me, had made a pacifist of me. I had now, moreover, a deep personal reason for fearing war: a husband who was talking of going into the Air Force. It made me shudder to hear him speaking of war as a certainty. He did not welcome it; he saw it as a disaster but one into which the United States would inevitably be drawn. He saw France once again in the path of German armies and England threatened, and he had no question in his mind that the United States would—and should—go to the aid of Britain.

Although it was widely said and believed that labor, like the Communists, stood strongly for peace, the only people whom I heard speak in favor of war that year were two workingmen in overalls and caps who sat in front of us on the top of a Fifth Avenue bus one spring evening. They were talking of the Depression, of unemployment, of hard times.

"Things will never be better," said one, "until we have a war."

The other nodded agreement.

We blame now the rich men, the military-industrial complex, but the labor unions also have a stake in "defense" contracts. War and preparations for war are built so fundamentally into the structure of our world that it will take a total revolution of thought and feeling, of imagination and will if ever we are to get rid of it.

During February and March of that year things happened fast. The Reichstag Fire occurred and was blamed on the Jews; in the elections the Nazis got a majority in the Reichstag; they began a drive against pacifists, Socialists, Communists and Jews. On March 17 Albert Einstein appealed for the moral intervention of the world against Hitlerism and soon afterwards renounced his Prussian citizenship. On the 21st it was reported that concentration camps were to be established in Bavaria; on the 24th Hitler achieved power to rule as a dictator. On April 4 we went to a Forum at Columbia in which three of the speakers—Reinhold Niebuhr, Isador Ginsberg and Rabbi Sidney Goldstein—spoke against Hitler, and the fourth, a young German, hotly defended him, branding as "contemptible propaganda" the reports of anti-Semitism in Germany. Though the audience applauded the first three and laughed at the last one, the discussion in itself was disturbing. Already in two months the subject had become important.

Some time in March I delivered my book to the Viking Press and received a small advance. It was not enough to meet the financial crisis that faced us. I went to the Teachers College Library and asked Miss Eleanor Witmer, the librarian, for a job. She looked over my credentials.

"But I have nothing commensurate with the sort of thing you have been doing," she said.

"That doesn't matter," I replied. "I'll do anything."

So a small job in the cataloguing department came my way, and soon after that there was need for someone to do a special piece of work on college documents; I was put in charge of that with two assistants under me. In the summer I was offered the job of running the School Library Laboratory, which was a model school library maintained for the benefit of students in Teachers College.

It was good to be in a library again. I felt at home with the smell of books, the shop talk behind the scenes, the kind of public that comes into a library. Librarians I have always found to be reasonable, relaxed, interesting people, as why shouldn't they be, for they deal with two of the most interesting and rewarding things in the world, people and books.

The School Library Laboratory drew me a little deeper into the world of children's books, which was made up even more of editors, librarians and booksellers than of writers, who are necessary and tolerated but not really members of the club. It was a warm world, chiefly of dedicated women who had a vision of what children's books might be, who had respect for the child as well as for the book and who wanted to bring the best of writing, illustrating and bookmaking to the young readers. May Massee I already knew, and charming Peggy Lesser, formerly May's assistant, who became head of Doubleday's children's book department; others I met were Alice Dalgleish, then teaching at Teachers College, later to edit children's books for Scribner's; Frederic Melcher, editor of *Publishers' Weekly*, who had established the John Newbery award for the most distinguished book for children published each year; Anne Carroll Moore, lovable, brilliant director of children's work in the New York Public Library and author of the "Three Owls Notebook," a page in *The New York Herald Tribune* in which she reviewed children's books with respect and discrimination; and—though she lived in Boston and it was not till later that we really became friends—Bertha Miller of the Children's Book Shop, who had created the *Horn Book*, a first-rate magazine devoted to children's books.

It was a warm world, if somewhat ingrown. I was glad to be admitted into it, even while I found it subtly confining. I was disappointed that it was so little regarded by the literary world at large, where no one seemed to take children's books seriously or seemed even to have any idea that there were differences among them, everyone lumping the well-written and the potboilers together as an inferior form of writing unimportant to all except those whose business they were. For that reason and also because I felt that I had something to say to adults as well as children, I began to look forward to writing novels and short stories. I had tried once and failed, it was true, but I was ready to try again. I began to realize that the publication of four or five books for children was not a first step into the world of adult fiction; that there was no door between the two worlds, or at any rate, May Massee either could not or would not open one; that it meant starting again from the beginning in a new field.

Very soon after I first went to work in the Teachers College Library, Morgan came home one day and announced that he too had got a job: washing dishes in the T. C. Cafeteria, in return for which we could both have all our meals there. It took him about two hours in the early afternoon, working in the heat and steam of the basement, stacking the thick white crockery, lifting the heavy metal baskets in and out of the great vats of boiling water. His fellow workers were husky Italians; sceptical at first of the Ph.D. candidate, they began by putting the heaviest jobs on him and waiting with unconcealed smiles to see him crumple under them. But he had not been a three-letter man for nothing, and his muscles were still in good trim. His physical strength and his good humor won them over, and he used to tell me zestfully of the talks he had with them. I have been proud of Morgan Vining many times and for many reasons, but never, I think, was I quite so proud as I was of Morgan the dishwasher.

It did not, actually, last very long; three months at most, then some clerical work for Teachers College opened up for him, he relinquished the dishwashing and we returned to my cooking.

During the summer months we moved to an apartment on 107th Street, nearer the river and cooler, with a roof terrace to give it a more elegant name than it deserved. We had our cocker spaniel to take care of, and we could not have him at Bancroft. When we left Chapel Hill, we had sold Dinah the pup to Chesley Baity, who loved her, and we had lent Rastus to Nell and Mitchell Owens, who by then had a house in Chevy Chase, and two small children, Niki and Betty, my namesake. It seemed an ideal arrangement: a gentle and gay playmate for them, a home for our dog until we could claim him again. By spring, however, it was evident that it was not working out as we had hoped; Rastus developed a bad case of eczema and took to running away. So Morgan went to Washington and brought him back, and for six weeks we had him at a veterinarian's near us on Broadway, where he was cured of his eczema and where we could visit him.

It was too expensive, however, as a permanent solution. We had to find another place to live, where we could have Rastus with us.

Morgan undertook the search. How he got in touch with Thomas Dixon I do not now remember, but we were invited to his house to have tea and to inspect an apartment which he proposed to make out of his garage. The author of those once notorious books, *The Leopard's Spots* and *The Clansman*, was living then with his wife at 867 Riverside Drive. Just under seventy, he was still a handsome man. Born in North Carolina, the son of the man who was credited with starting the Ku Klux Klan, he had been a Baptist minister before he became a novelist. The bookcases on one whole side of his living room, which quite dramatically overhung the Hudson, were filled with morocco-bound copies of his own books, of which the latest were *The Love Complex* and *The Sun Virgin*. He had made vast sums, it was said, out of *The Clansman*, for which he had himself written the movie script, called *The Birth of a Nation*, but the depression had made a poor man of him. He was then writing prolifically, he told us, for the pulp magazines. The apartment venture seemed rather an impractical one, and furthermore it was not ready.

Morgan next produced a young adagio dancer who with his wife, also a dancer, lived in an apartment on the top floor of a house on 107th Street. The young pair, it seemed, wished to go to Europe that summer; they were looking for someone to sublet their apartment and take care of their things; they would rent it to us for what we paid at Bancroft Hall, and we could have Rastus there. In September we would have to return to Bancroft, but we would face that, we decided, when the time came.

We moved in mid-June. The apartment, which was reached by seventy-one narrow, winding carpeted steps, consisted of a long narrow living room furnished with a piano, some Turkish taborets, a couch with one leg propped on bricks and covered with an Oriental rug, a fifteenth-century wooden madonna in faded blue and gold paint, whom we loved at once, a shaky chair or two and numerous photographs of our landlord and lady in dynamic poses. From the bedroom window we stepped out—after climbing up on some wooden boxes in order to reach the sill—onto the flat roof of the apartment below us; here were window boxes with petunias and geraniums, some deck chairs and a table on which every fine evening we ate our dinner, looking down a narrow passageway past backs of houses to a segment of the Hudson River.

We were situated between Riverside Drive, where we walked Rastus and saw the river in all its moods—flecked sometimes with whitecaps and the wings of sea gulls—smelled the change of the tide, and watched the night boat pass, looped with lights; and Broadway, where were the little shops in which we bought whipping cream for thirteen cents a half-pint, strawberries and cherries, hamburger for Rastus and steak or sweetbreads for ourselves.

I was enjoying my work at Columbia, but I was also thinking about writing. I had an idea for a book which teased my mind, and I brought home Lockhart's *Life of Scott* from the library and put in any spare hours I had in the stacks where were the books on eighteenth-century Scotland. In the boyhood of Sir Walter Scott I saw a story for young people, the story of a boy handicapped by what they did not then know to call polio, who made his place among the lads of his school and neighborhood without asking for special treatment, who grew and learned in the atmosphere of eighteenth-century Edinburgh, then so full of brilliant minds and personalities that it earned for itself the sobriquet of the "Athens of the North," who fed his imagination on ballads and tales and poetry, who at nineteen, when my story should end, fell in love with a girl as he walked her home from church in the rain: a courageous, large-hearted, human, exuberant boy whose early life foreshadowed and explained the drama and greatness of his later years.

Our summer pleasures were similar to our winter ones, except that we added boat rides, to Bear Mountain in the daytime and down to the Narrows on hot, breathless evenings, and trolley rides in the open trolleys that still swayed and bounded the length of Broadway. Saturdays were our days for celebrating together. Morgan was fascinated with the subway system; I loved the buses, which were still double-deckers, many of them open on the top deck. Often we would stop for lunch at a narrow restaurant off Times Square, just wide enough for a counter and stools, where for fifteen cents we got a delicious hot ham sandwich, cut before our eyes from a great sizzling baked ham, a cup of coffee for five cents and a saucer of mixed fruit for another five cents. Then we would take the subway to the Battery and after walking about and looking in on the penguins in the Aquarium, we would take the ferry to Staten Island, a leisurely and colorful ride (for five cents) across the harbor among boats of all sizes

and ports of origin. Coming back, we loved to see the great
flying wedge of skyscrapers looming toward us across the water,
their windows golden in the setting sun, the shadows blue around
their feet.

"We can have more fun on a dollar," we used to exult, "than
any other two people in New York."

There were three New Yorks that we saw that year: the region
around Columbia, which was like a village in itself, where we saw
the same faces again and again, shopped in the same stores, met
friends and acquaintances in the streets; the center of the city,
where were the publishing houses, the big hotels, the elegant shops,
the theaters, the luxurious apartment houses; and then those other
parts of the city where people lived and worked and suffered,
crowded together in high, shabby buildings whose windows looked
into each other, or sat on the steps in swarms on hot nights; little
shops where men paid tribute to gangs for protection from other
gangs. It was another world, always there and infinitely depressing
to me. In the South people were often poor, but at least they had
air and sunlight; their cabin doors opened onto the good ground,
with grass and trees and sometimes a view; the air was clean.
They lived close to the earth and to living creatures that shared
it with them, birds, mules, chickens, hogs; they knew their neighbors; friends gathered on Sunday afternoons on their porches or
in the dooryards under the chinaberry trees.

For us—for Morgan and me—it was the best year of all. Our
world had contracted around us, enfolding us; all that was threatening bound us more tightly together. We worked at the same
table in our living room, our heads nearly touching across it; sat
and read in the same big chair; met after the separation of our
work with the excitement of lovers reunited; went off on our
excursions with joy.

"Imagine our being this way about each other after four years!"
Morgan exclaimed one day. And once, as we sat together I looked
at his hand beside mine, and saw with surprise that the impulse
from my brain that moved my fingers had not stirred his, and my
surprise told me that Jesus' words were true for us, "Wherefore
they are no more twain but one flesh."

In September we moved back to Bancroft and, by a special dis-
pensation, were allowed to take Rastus with us. He was the dearest of coal-black cocker spaniels, with the long, silky ears, floppy
paws, vibratory tail of his breed, and his own gay, affectionate,

eager nature, his whole little life geared to giving and receiving love.

We looked forward to our second year in New York with confidence. Morgan had finished, with distinction, the courses for his degree, and the subject of his dissertation had been approved. I was happy in my work at the School Library Laboratory, I had a book coming out in October and another one taking shape in my mind. We had our apartment and our dog.

There was much talk at Teachers College the last week in September about the seven new residence colleges which had just opened at Yale, a new venture in American university education designed to keep open personal channels and prevent the loss of communication (a word which had not yet become a cliché) in the vastness of large student bodies. We thought it would be interesting to go and see for ourselves what was happening. The Pattons had brought their car from Georgia; they proposed that the four of us drive to New Haven together.

October 1 was a Sunday, the kind of gold and blue sparkling morning that belongs especially to October. Rachel Patton and I packed a lunch, the men consulted knowledgeable friends about the route. The Merritt Parkway had not been built, but there were some fine new roads that were much talked about. We were advised to go north on the extension of the Sawmill River Parkway to U.S. Route 6, which went past Lake Mahopac, and then cut across into Connecticut and down through Danbury to New Haven.

Pat drove and Morgan rode on the front seat beside him; Rachel and I sat on the back seat. The river sparkled, and here and there amid the green of the woods after we turned eastward a branch of a tree was a bright flame. The day that I first saw Morgan is associated in my mind with crape myrtle in bloom, the last day with a scarlet branch of maple overhanging a road. We had passed Lake Mahopac gleaming among the trees. Morgan in the front seat turned around and smiled at me, his wonderful smile that began in his brown eyes.

I never saw him again.

I did not see the car, containing two boys, that shot out of a side lane into the highway, I did not hear the crash or know that our car, struck broadside, was flung across the road and turned upside down. I had been looking at Morgan.

5.

Awakening

Several hours later I returned to consciousness in a small emergency hospital at Lake Mahopac. By the evasive answers which the nurses gave to my anguished questions about Morgan I felt the truth begin to press in upon me, but it was the coroner bending over me to put under my pillow a summons to appear at the inquest next day who put it into words. Morgan had died instantly of a fractured skull.

Pat and Rachel had been injured also but not seriously. In the late afternoon we were taken, the three of us, in an ambulance to the Columbia Presbyterian Medical Center at 168th Street, whose tall buildings I had so often seen against the sky beyond the George Washington Bridge. Throughout the confused hours of pain and nausea I clung to the one comforting word, "instantly." If I had not known when the collision came, then neither had Morgan, who had turned to smile at me. He had not suffered either physically or mentally. He had simply, in an instant of time, been translated. I wished passionately that he had taken me with him. At the Presbyterian Hospital the resident, Dr. Bruner, diagnosed my case as concussion and shock, and I was transferred to the Neurological Institute. A telegram was sent to Mother, and the swift reply was given me to hold in my hand: "Coming. Violet."

Sometime after midnight she was there, the sister who from my early childhood had been a light to look up to, a rock to depend upon. She had me moved at once from the four-bed ward into a private room, and then she disappeared. The slow hours of that interminable black night crawled past. Actually Violet was in a room down the corridor, sleepless herself, longing to come to me but afraid to disturb me, for she had been told that I was in shock and that my life lay in the balance. Every hour a nurse came in to take my blood pressure, which had fallen to 60 over something even lower.

That I had been taken to the Presbyterian Medical Center rather than to another of New York's many hospitals was one of those fortuitous circumstances that seem to fit into some prearranged plan. Dr. Rolfe Kingsley, the husband of our distant Scottish cousin, Gertrude Johnston, was a consulting surgeon there. Violet got in touch with him immediately, and he in turn called upon his friend Dr. Byron Stookey, the distinguished neurosurgeon in attendance at the Neurological Institute. Dr. Stookey, who later I was to discover was the husband of one of my classmates at Bryn Mawr, came at once from his summer home in Connecticut. Of all this, of course, I knew nothing at the time.

I heard a voice say, "Early American heritage," and opened my eyes to find three doctors around my bed. The dominant one reminded me instantly of Morgan; he was tall, athletic in build, brown-eyed, with some faint trace of English accent in his rich voice. His hands were large and gentle, his face mobile, expressive. He asked me questions and I answered them. I tried, I remember, to describe Morgan to him. I may have said I wished to die.

Of his sympathy I was immediately aware; I was surprised and touched to see tears in his eyes. But he said:

"I am not so sorry for you as I am for a little Italian girl who like you has lost her husband suddenly in an automobile accident. You have the intelligence to meet this, and you will, for the sake of your husband. There is nothing you could do that would distress him more than to collapse under this. You must go on with your life—for him."

The reminder that I was not alone in suffering loss and grief, the assumption that I must and could rebuild my shattered life, the suggestion that I might still do something for Morgan, were a life-giving injection of—not hope, not even courage, but staying power. I have never ceased to be grateful for the chance, if it was chance, that brought to me this man of insight and of heart.

His medical prescription was rigorous and nearly took from me the stiffening which his words had imparted: six weeks flat on my back in bed. Six weeks alone at the Neurological Institute would have been even more expensive emotionally than financially; everybody was relieved when Violet proposed to take me home, to the second bed in her room that had once been mine, and to get the excellent nurse who had cared for her when she had had pneumonia four years earlier to look after me.

During the week which elapsed before they thought it safe to move me, Morgan's funeral was held in Germantown. Mother was present as the sole representative of our immediate families; it was too far for his sister to come from Texas and Violet was with me. On Dr. Stookey's suggestion it was arranged that at the hour of the service in Germantown the chaplain of Columbia should read to me the burial service from the Book of Common Prayer. He sat by the window, old and gray, and read the beautiful words which seemed to me then like a splendid curtain that hung motionless and revealed nothing. After he had finished, I asked him to read the marriage service and he did. I thanked him. He sighed, seemed to try to speak, found nothing to say, and left.

On the day after my thirty-first birthday they took me by ambulance down Riverside Drive, past the end of 107th Street, where we had so happily spent the summer months, to the Pennsylvania Station. A family friend had arranged with the railroad for my stretcher to be carried on the baggage car with Violet and the nurse sitting on folding chairs beside me. The train was nearly twenty minutes late because the engineer took extra time to make the stopping and starting at stations as smooth as possible for my sake, one of countless acts of kindness of people whose hearts were touched by my plight. At the apartment in Germantown Mother was waiting to enfold me in her love and grief; our family doctor, who had been in touch with Dr. Stookey, was on hand.

The slow passage toward recovery began, lifted on a flood of love and sympathy. The apartment revolved around me and my nurse; Mother and Violet put aside their own grief for a son and a brother whom they had come to love deeply in order to minister to mine; letters and flowers and thoughtful gifts came pouring in from friends. The generosity of their love and concern brought some warmth to my inner chill, but for the most part I was isolated by preoccupation with my primary task as I lay in bed day after day and night after sleepless night: the realization and acceptance of my loss.

It is not easy, even now after more than thirty-five years, to write about those days of which I have seldom been able to speak, even to close friends; I do it because it is inseparable from the story of my life and because it may help others in similar situations to read of my passage through darkness to light, as it helped me then to read books of personal history in which the author had come to terms with disaster.

As I look back over the weeks in bed and the months that followed, I can see certain landmarks on the journey upwards. There was the moment when I realized finally that there was to be no escape. I was aware, one day soon after my return to Germantown, of reaching physically the lowest point that I had yet experienced. My life seemed to be sliding away as surely and as easily as the tide, and I felt a thrust of joy as I said to myself, "I am going to be let off after all," and turned on my side to wait peacefully for unconsciousness. It came, but in the form of a brief and strengthening sleep. When I awoke, I knew that a door had closed behind me. Dr. Stookey's words returned to me, and I rejected, finally, the temptation to defeat.

The rector of the church in which Morgan and I had been married came often to see me. He did his best to bring me solace, but his hands were empty. He was himself going through a courageous but unavailing struggle against the drug habit, and he had no resources from which to help me. I did not know at the time what his difficulties were; I only knew that his Church had nothing for me.

The real difficulty was that my Episcopalianism had never gone very deep; it had been a matter of conformity, of pleasant associations, of an ancient and beautiful ritual. Morgan had in effect been my god; when I had him I had needed nothing more. Love and beauty and courage had seemed to me adequate foundation stones for life. Now that my deepest human love had been suddenly removed, I found that beauty and courage were not enough. I began, blindly, fumblingly, the search for a meaning in life, for a philosophy in which I might find reality and strength by which to live.

Each week a package of books came to me from May Massee, first *Jane Hope* with its dedication "To Himself" and its jacket depicting in bright colors the campus at Chapel Hill with a crape myrtle in bloom, then all the other books in her new Viking catalog, by ones and twos as they appeared. I did not read them— they were too simple and cheerful for my need—but their message was clear, as she intended it to be: "You too are a writer. Your life is not over. You will write again."

Books had always been my resource in time of need; now, as

soon as I was allowed to read, I turned again to books, not for escape but to try to find meaning in what had happened. I read Whitehead's *Adventures of Ideas* and *Religion in the Making,* Maeterlinck's *Wisdom and Destiny,* Vida Scudder's *On Journey,* Vera Brittain's *Testament of Youth,* Sarah Cleghorn's *Threescore,* the poems of Yeats and Santayana, and the Bible, especially Isaiah, Ecclesiastes and Ruth. Among the books which my father used to keep on a shelf close to his hand for rereading was Edmund Gosse's two-volume *Life and Letters of Doctor John Donne.* Donne's romantic and ill-fated love for his young wife, Anne, and his overwhelming grief at her death spoke directly to me. In college I had read and enjoyed Donne's gay and cynical young poems—"I am two fools, I know,/ For loving, and for saying so." "I can love her, and her, and you, and you;/ I can love any, so she be not true." And others. Now I found and read his serious poems on love and death. "But think that we/ Are but turned aside to sleep./ They who one another keep/ Alive, ne'er parted be."

"The event itself is pure water," I read in *Wisdom and Destiny,* "that flows from the pitcher of fate, and seldom has it either savor or perfume or color. But even as the soul may be wherein it seeks shelter so will the event become joyous or sad, become tender or hateful, become deadly or quick with life."

I could not accept the idea that the event which had snatched Morgan away from me was anything but the blackest evil, but I began to understand that for me the important thing now was what I did with what had happened to me, so that it might become quick with life.

Again and again I asked Why? Why should Morgan, who had so much to give the world, have been taken away in the very prime of his life, when he stood on the threshold of new and greater opportunities? Why was it that so often the young, the talented, the good, died in the flower of their promise, while so many old, broken, sick, tired, lonely old people, who longed for release, lived on in pain and weariness? But though I battered my head against the question Why Morgan? I was never under the temptation of asking Why *me*? Why should this tragedy have happened to *me*? I knew always that through it all I had been one of the most fortunate of people. In the four years and eight months of our marriage I had had more blazing happiness than most people have in a lifetime. I was unspeakably grateful that this joy beyond anything that I deserved had been granted to me, thankful too that I had been fully aware of it when I had it. I did not have to torment myself with the regret, "Oh, if only I had known!" Now I felt that it was up to me somehow to find some way of passing on to the world some bit of what Morgan had given me.

Christmas approached, in what I remember as a particularly dark and stormy December. I was again up and about, trying to summon up energy out of the physical weakness attendant on very low blood pressure, anemia, insomnia and headaches. I went one rainy afternoon to the movies to see *Berkeley Square*, in the course of which Leslie Howard, wearing an overcoat, with his hat pulled down over his face, walked through the rain on a London street, looking for an instant so much like Morgan that I was nearly suffocated with longing. I left the theater and came to walk up and down, back and forth, in the rain myself, along the street in front of our apartment house, trying to tire the pain within me into numbness. Violet saw me from the window, came out and without a word linked her arm through mine and walked with me back and forth, up and down, until at last I said, "Let's go in." As I had already turned the corner physically, now the knowledge seeped into my mind, drop by bitter drop, that this aching loss was not going to come to an end; that it was a life sentence. All that could be done to help me had been done; now I was to get down to the daily task of learning "how existence could be cherished,/ Strengthened, and fed without the aid of joy."

Just about this time, though I did not know it, something happened on the other side of the world that was, years later, to have a profound effect on my own life. In Tokyo at 6:39 on the morning of December 23, the sirens rang once and then loudly a second time, and all Japan awoke to a burst of vast rejoicing. The long-awaited son had been born to the Emperor and Empress. A few days later his name was given to him, Akihito; he was to become almost as dear to me as if he had been my own son.

Most of that winter I spent away from Germantown: in Washington visiting Nell and Mitchell Owens and their adorable small daughters in their big, old-fashioned house in Chevy Chase; in Chapel Hill and in Florida. I knew that if I did not go back to Chapel Hill then, I would never be able to go, and I was not willing to close the door on a place so delightful in itself and so integral a part of my life. I stayed part of the time with the Grisettes and the rest with the Bullitts, those dear and warm friends who also had loved Morgan and who shared my sorrow. They welcomed Rastus, too, who went with me everywhere. Often I saw Mr. Mac, who was living in Morgan's old apartment. The physician who had been our friend gave me the passage from Tennyson's *Ulysses* beginning "Come, my friends. 'Tis not too late to seek a newer world" to keep in my wallet and advised me to take the persistent low fever I was running to Florida to the beach and the sunshine.

Several of my friends, Marjorie Stewart, her sister and brother-in-law, Gilbert and Mildred Tucker, and Elizabeth and Dick McKey with their children, Betsy and Dick, were spending the winter in Sarasota, in El Patio, a small, two-storied apartment house all cream-colored stucco and red tiles around a sandy garden with rustling palmettos, oleander, bougainvillea and a big pool with goldfish. Marjorie was the daughter of Dr. Francis E. Stewart who, with my father, had headed a committee to raise money among Americans of Scottish descent for a war memorial in Edinburgh. The original idea had been my father's; he had taken it to his friend Tait McKenzie, the well-known sculptor and head of the Department of Physical Education at the University of Pennsylvania, who had caught fire at once and had conceived and created the sculptures. When the money had been raised and only a few months before the statue and frieze had been set in place in Princes Street Gardens, my father had died, so that he had not seen the fulfilment of his dream. Through the close association of our fathers, Marjorie and I had become friends. Dark-haired, dark-eyed, slender, gay and warmhearted, she had been graduated from Vassar several years before I was from Bryn Mawr; she had flitted about alternating traveling and working; she had been in Wonalancet the summer that Morgan and I became engaged there. Steadily all the past months she had written to me of El Patio and our friends there, urging me to join her in her apartment.

Early in March, with Rastus at my heels, I went. Sarasota, in that year of the continuing Depression, was almost deserted, though a baseball team—was it the Yankees?—was training there and Ringling Brothers Circus wintered there. We could go with our bathing suits and picnic baskets to Long Boat Key or Siesta Key and spend the whole day on the beach, seeing scarcely another soul. I spent long hours lying in the sunshine, my little dog pressed close against me, the palms rustling at my back, the sea in front in all its shades of blue and green and purple—ultramarine, cobalt, sapphire, aquamarine, emerald, amethyst—with the exotic birds flying over, pelicans, ibis, cormorants. Congenial companionship was at hand, there were expeditions by car and on foot, boat rides, picnics, visits to the art museum and the circus camp, all the activities that made up the easy life of a group of friends, but there was also understanding acceptance of withdrawal. Marjorie and I talked in the evenings in the living room of her apartment or on the beach under the moon, went out to buy grapefruit at a penny apiece, or drifted in her car along white sand roads through jungles of pine and live oak hung with moss and airplants, shot through with bright flame-colored blossoms or darting yellow butterflies.

It was all good; perhaps most restorative of all were the hours in the sun on the empty beach which gave me space and quiet that I needed to "find/ Something lying on the ground/ In the bottom of my mind."

I thought of life and death and wondered as every bereaved soul must wonder about life after death and whether there is any possible chance of meeting again the beloved dead. If I could only be reasonably confident of that, I thought, I could endure a lifetime of waiting and preparation.

Once and only once, Morgan and I had discussed the question.

"I expect to go out like a candle," I had asserted lightheartedly. "I'm not afraid of that. The candle is burning brightly now. The important thing is to enjoy the warmth and the brightness while it lasts."

"Oh, no, Janet," he had answered. "There is more."

It had not occurred to me that his candle might go out before mine, nor had I asked him what he meant when he said, "There is more." It was our life, not our death, that I was interested in then; what happened afterward was remote, unreal. I assumed that there was plenty of time to think about such a morbid subject.

The nurse whom I had had during the weeks in bed was a spiritualist; she was a member of a group in Germantown which had been seriously exploring the question for years; she knew a medium whose integrity she was convinced was beyond question. She had been eager to arrange a séance for me as soon as I was out of bed, but my college training as well as my own deepest instincts had led me away from that avenue. Not only was I intellectually a sceptic about the possibility of communication with departed spirits, but all my love told me that even if it were possible I must not cling to Morgan, must not keep him subject to my needs for comfort and reassurance. I must set him free to go on joyously to whatever might come next. If he could reach me, I reasoned, he would. If not, I did not want to be deceived or to deceive myself through the strength of my desire to be in touch with him.

At Columbia on the first Sunday in January a commemorative service had been held for the members of the university family who had died during the previous year. Violet had gone with me to it on a dark, cold day when New York looked dreary, swarming with dim people in drab raincoats, both sky and river lead-colored. Twenty-seven names—seventeen faculty members, ten students—had been read, Morgan's near the end, and a visiting divine preached the sermon. Courageously he met the question head-on; Is there a life after death? Can we look forward to being reunited with those whom we have loved who have died? We cannot know, he answered; it must remain a mystery.

My whole being gave assent to this ineluctable fact. We cannot know. The mystery remains. It is, as Wordsworth said, a burden to be accepted. Like others of my generation, which was the one that invented the shabby term "wishful thinking," I feared more than anything else that I would believe something to be true just because I so much wanted it to be true. So I rejected any hope of meeting Morgan again, leaving the door open only by that crack which the recognition of the presence of a mystery made possible. And yet—to go far beyond that winter of 1934—there have been times when I have known, deep below the level of the irritable intellect or the longing heart, that what Morgan said is true. There is more. The beautiful words of William Penn bear the uncounterfeited impact of truth:

"They that love beyond the world cannot be separated by it. Death cannot kill what never dies. Death is but crossing the world as friends do the seas. They live in one another still."

There have been occasional unsought but deeply felt moments

in my life when I have experienced a strong sense of Morgan's presence: once in England when I was walking alone in the Chiltern Hills on the way to Ewelme, once on Cranbrook Mountain in New Hampshire, and once on a road in the Helderberg Hills southwest of Albany. Each time, in a scene of natural beauty surrounded by hills, I felt him to be near. That was all, but my heart lifted and sang.

In a small, cheap, paper-bound edition of Emerson's Essays that came my way that winter in Sarasota, I found a passage in "Spiritual Laws" that leapt out of the page to speak to me.

"Each man has his own vocation. The talent is the call. There is one direction in which all space is open to him. He has faculties silently inviting him thither to endless exertion. He is like a ship in a river; he runs against obstructions on every side but one; on that side all obstruction is taken away and he sweeps serenely over God's depths into an infinite sea."

My talent, I knew, was a small one, but not to be dismissed for that reason. In my early childhood I had confidently launched my little boat upon that river; now I must disentangle it from the reeds along the bank and try to reach the current once more. I began to think again about the book on young Walter Scott, which I had planned when Morgan was still there, and for which I had done some of the reading. It was part of my past happiness, a bridge between life as it had been and life as it must be. When I returned to Washington, to my studio apartment in the Owenses' house, I spent my days in the Library of Congress, reading and planning a trip to Scotland.

On Sundays I went to the Friends Meeting on Florida Avenue. My search for meaning had taken me that winter into many lanes and some blind alleys; in the end I returned to the Quaker meeting of my childhood and of my New Jersey ancestors.

It was the silence that drew me, that deep, healing silence of the meeting at its best, when the search of each is intensified by the search of all, when the "gentle motions," the "breathings and stirrings" of the Spirit which is within each and beyond all, are expectantly awaited and often experienced. In the plain room with proportion for its only beauty, where men and women sat motionless, suspended between time and eternity, I found each Sunday just enough of acceptance, of strength, of inner serenity to carry me through the week until the next Sunday. My searching, restless, arid heart was like a stranded boat which was lifted for a time on buoyant waters from an ocean beyond the boundaries of my selfhood.

Sometimes the silence was broken by a Friend who rose to deliver a "message," some thought that had come to him (or to her, for women have preached in Quaker meetings from the beginning) which he felt was intended not for himself alone but for the whole group. I was always apprehensive lest the precious silence be scattered by something alien or pedestrian, for I was in those days hypersensitive and critical. Anything that sounded as if it had been prepared beforehand instead of arising out of the gathered silence; anything that sounded contrived or perfunctory, as if the speaker thought the silence had gone on long enough and had searched his mind for something to say; anything couched in outworn theological terms or equally in hackneyed modern jargon, anything that was a routine restatement of what the same Friend had said the previous week, set my teeth on edge and broke for me the delicate web of the silence. But sometimes the message grew directly out of the silence, seeming to gather up and articulate thoughts shared by all or to carry further an idea that was struggling toward birth in my own mind; sometimes an unpracticed speaker would out of deeply felt experience say a few simple words that would reverberate through the corridors of my heart; then, when the speaker's voice died away, the silence would settle down even more deeply than before and the members would be bound together in a fresh and living unity.

The Quaker stand on peace and race relations attracted me also, the feeding of starving German children after the war and the help which was at that time being given to unemployed miners in West Virginia. It seemed to me a religion which was not kept in a pigeonhole labeled "Sunday" but which infused every aspect of daily life.

While I was making up my mind to apply for membership, I went to see the mother of my school friend, Betty Warren, to talk it over with her. Caroline C. Warren embodied my ideal of a Quaker saint, not just because she looked the part with her gray dress, white-collared, her dark hair parted in the middle and drawn down smoothly over her ears, her eyes bright behind gold-rimmed spectacles, or even because of her immaculate life and deep wisdom, but because of the love and peace that she radiated and her realistic, spontaneous humor that was as refreshing as spring water.

I was not theologically respectable, I tried to make clear to her. I really believed very little. It was a comfort to me that Quakerism had no creed. I had been deeply impressed by the statement of the Elders of Balby Meeting in 1653, reaffirmed in the latest edition of *Faith and Practice*:

"Dearly beloved Friends, these things we do not lay upon you as a rule or form to walk by but that all, with the measure of light which is pure and holy man be guided; and so in the light walking and abiding these may be fulfilled in the Spirit not the letter, for the letter killeth but the Spirit giveth light."

For me, religion was, in Fosdick's phrase, "a total response to life's meaning." I felt a firm conviction of the unity of all life, a kinship with all living things, even to the invisible busy atom, a sense that we all were made of the same stuff and moved to the same patterns, from the atoms to the universes, the macrocosm repeating the microcosm, that love and truth and goodness in a single life were interpenetrated by the infinite love and truth and goodness which we might call God.

Mrs. Warren told me what George Fox had said of Cromwell's daughter, that she was a seeker and that being a seeker was next to being a finder. She thought the Meeting would accept me on that basis.

I went next to Stanley Yarnall, the beloved principal of my old school, to whom I turned as naturally as if I were still a child, and he told me how to go about applying for membership. I wrote a letter explaining my position and telling why I sought membership. I was visited by two overseers, accepted by the Monthly Meeting and welcomed by a committee of two more. It all took a little over two months, but I now had a spiritual home. I had no idea how much I had still to learn about this faith which I had not so much embraced as caught at, as if it were a floating spar, and which so generously, so tolerantly, so undemandingly received me. I was to find in it depths and reaches which became available to me only as I grew in it.

Early in July I made another move toward understanding it. Mother went with me to the Friends General Conference at Cape May, a week-long series of interesting and illuminating meetings held within the sound of the waves. I had joined the Orthodox Branch of the Society of Friends; I did not know that these were Hicksites. No matter. They welcomed me and I learned much.

Twenty years later the century-and-a-half-long rift was healed and the two branches became one.

Earlier in the spring, in April, I had passed another of the small, inner milestones that marked my way back to life. Early one morning I was awakened by what sounded like rain falling on the porch roof outside my window. I opened my eyes and smelled the fragrance of honey locust, and realized that it was not rain drops I had heard but the white blossoms of the locust, gently plopping onto the roof. My heart lifted on a wave of pure joy to this slight, fleeting beauty and, reaching for the notebook by my bed, I recorded for the first time in many months a minor ecstasy, "The day cannot be wholly sad that starts with locust blossoms pattering on the roof."

I was now on my way again. The way was not to be smooth; I would slip back many times. For years to come, at any moment—reading, meditating, working, writing—my mind would be subject to the sudden, stabbing thought, hot with pain and incredulous as if it were the first time, Morgan is *gone*; but I was no longer a wounded, half-alive, shattered, grief-stricken creature. I had rich resources on which to draw: the devoted, understanding love of family and friends, the call of my work, the communion with the Beyond Within which came to me through the Meeting, the joy in the beauty of nature which had always fed me.

Gradually I learned one more thing, quite simple and obvious to many but hidden from me at first: that grief is something not to overcome or to escape but to live with. It is always there, as perceptible as a person who will not go away in spite of hints or plain speaking, but one can make room for it, recognize it as a companion instead of an intruder, be aware of it but not possessed by it; one can continue one's work, one's occupations, even one's joys, in its presence. A year or two later I tried to put this knowledge into words:

> I shall no longer run from sorrow
> nor seek to avoid him
> by going down another street of thoughts.
> I shall not try to overcome him with my strength.
> I shall open the door of my heart
> to his knock and let him come in.
> Whether he be sorrow for my own loss
> or for the world's pain

I will learn to live with him,
steadfast and tender.

And some day the child, happiness,
will play in the sunshine
on the floor of my house.

6.

Scotland

Going abroad—"Abroad," says a German friend of mine scornfully, "they always talk about Abroad. Where is Abroad? What is Abroad?"—is the classic prescription for wounded hearts, the widowed, the jilted, the girl unacceptably in love. Always going abroad does something for the sufferer, perhaps not what is intended but something. One comes back changed. One's first trip abroad, furthermore, is a watershed in one's life; no later one ever recaptures the delight, the wonder, the interest of the first one.

My trip in the summer of 1934 had a twofold purpose, the alleviation of sorrow and the preparation for writing my book about the boyhood of Sir Walter Scott. Much of the necessary reading I had already done; I knew the shape that the book was to take; I had written a draft of the first chapter. Now I wanted to see the places that young Walter knew, to walk from his home in George Square to the High School, to Greyfriars Church, to the Meadows, to Holyroodhouse, to the Castle, to the University. I wanted to climb Arthur's Seat and to walk the Pentland Hills, to see Kelso, where he used to make long visits to his Aunt Jenny. I also had a secret, almost unacknowledged hope that I might find somewhere, perhaps in some forgotten book, a portrait of him at the age of twelve or thirteen. It was a quite irrational hope, for which I had no basis at all, because in a book entitled *The Portraits of Sir Walter Scott* it was definitely stated that there were none at all between the six-year-old boy painted on a visit to Oxford and Raeburn's portrait of the young man of nineteen.

Violet and I set forth together on the *Manhattan* on July 18. She would be with me during the month of her vacation; I would stay on alone after she left. It was her first trip abroad since

1900, when she and Mother, our Aunt Emily and her daughter Nanette had all spent a summer and autumn in England and Scotland and Paris. We planned to be a week or so in London, with excursions to Canterbury and Cambridge, to go on to Skye, where Flora MacDonald had lived, take the Caledonian Canal to Inverness, stop over in Aberdeen and wind up in Edinburgh, where Violet would spend a few days with me before taking the night express to London and the boat train to Southampton.

The crossing reminded me of *Outward Bound*, for it was foggy all the way, the foghorn mooing night and day and the signal between the bridge and the engine room, which ran down the wall behind our beds, ringing incessantly. One night we went miles out of course to pick up a sick man from an Italian freighter; the poor man subsequently died and the combination of fog and a corpse on board gave our steward, so he said, "the creeps." He told us the story of his life, which had been destroyed by the World War. First to go was the ten thousand pounds, which he had saved by "working like blazes" so as to retire and start a business of his own. While he was away fighting in the trenches, a Zeppelin raid killed his children, his wife went to pieces and died insane. "What 'urts me," he said, "it was all for nothing." He was a good man, thin, high-strung, hard-working, with a look of tragedy lurking in his small, bright eyes.

The ride in the boat train from Plymouth to London scattered before us a series of illustrations to English literature: hedgerows and haycocks and roses, church spires rising out of clumps of trees, thatched cottages, baronial towers, and a park where deer were roaming. From Paddington to Berkeley Square the small, square taxi hurtled through streets familiar in pictures, and at Dartmouth House we ran into Mrs. McKey and Nell, Dick's mother and sister, and had our first tea in England. ("They are so possessive about their tea," said Nell. "They're always saying, 'I haven't had *my* tea' or 'Have you had *your* tea yet?'") Late in the afternoon we walked down to Piccadilly and through the Green Park to watch people coming away from a royal garden party at Buckingham Palace, carriages and taxis and Rolls-Royces, gaitered churchmen, gentlemen with high silk hats and lovely ladies with big hats and fluttering chiffons walking across the park on foot, all bathed in sunshine and followed by long shadows. For a week the season continued and Mayfair was full of gay, handsome creatures coming and going to their parties, and then suddenly it was over and they all disappeared.

One morning out of that week we spent planning our trip to Skye. To Cook's office in Berkeley Street it was as if we contemplated a safari to darkest Africa; apparently nobody they knew went to Skye. At length they produced an elaborate itinerary by which we would reach Mallaig by train at six P.M. on the third day, would spend the night there and go on to Portree by boat at noon the next day. There were two hotels in Portree, they told us; we could decide which we preferred when we got there.

After a day of rain in Oban and part of another in Fort William, our spirits soared when we stepped out of the train onto the pier at Mallaig in a glory of late afternoon sunshine. Before us lay the blue, island-dotted Sound of Sleat, with the blue mountains of Skye, layer on layer beyond, all bathed in opalescent light. Behind us was a Victorian hotel on a hill. The red-haired boy carrying our bags said, "Why don't you go on to Armadale now? The *Dolly Graham* is waiting to sail, and the sea is like glass."

Was there an inn in Armadale where we might stay? No, but the bus was meeting the *Dolly Graham*; the bus would take us on to Portree.

We had not the least idea of distances in Skye; we thought Portree might be ten miles or so from Armadale. The scene before us, so unearthly in its beauty, hypnotized us; without consciously making a decision, we followed the boy to the *Dolly Graham*.

It was a small boat, barely large enough to support its smokestack. The boy put our bags on the deck. We found something to sit on not intended as benches. The two boatmen, lean, tall, dark-haired, blue-eyed men, disappeared down the hatch. The only other passengers, two middle-aged Englishwomen, sat down beside us as if we were not there. The engines choked and coughed, the smokestack belched, the little boat chugged away from the pier.

The sea was indeed like glass. There was not a ripple on its blue surface except the wake that we made ourselves. We moved through a world of iridescent blue, like a great, glistening bubble, the sky above us, the blue hills behind, the deep grape-blue mountains of Skye ahead all reflected in the silent water. Slowly, so slowly as scarcely to disturb the surface, three porpoises rose and dived again, turning as they went.

Halfway across, one of the boatmen stuck his head out of the companionway and asked if we would like a cup of tea. Our fellow passengers declined, but Violet and I accepted gratefully. It was hours since we had had lunch, and we had been too busy looking out at the highland scenery to bother with tea on the train. He brought us large mugs of hot, strong tea, milky and sweet. "Fancy having tea with the boatmen," said one English-woman to the other. "How veddy homely."

At Armadale we found the bus waiting, a high, shaky, working bus not intended for tourists, laden with baskets of fish and large bundles brought from the boat. The few riders waiting on it spoke Gaelic with the driver. The two Englishwomen were dropped at Knock's Farm after a few miles, and we went on al-most alone in the bus for a ride of more than forty miles through the sunset and the long northern twilight. The trees and rhodo-dendrons of Armadale, the shoulder-high fuschia hedges in full bloom, the rosy foxgloves beside the road, gave way to bare moors dotted with black-faced sheep or Highland cattle, shaggy and small with wide horns and their hair down over their eyes. Mountains rose high and jagged on our left, the hills of the main-land across the water on our right. Now and then we passed peo-ple cutting peat or a small, low house of whitewashed stone al-most buried under its thatched roof. We came to a narrow sea loch (later we found it on the map, Loch Ainort) and saw our road on the other side, looking near enough to toss a stone into; there being no bridge, we drove deep into the moor under the mountains before at last we reached the place we had seen and rounded a headland into a wide expanse of moor and water starred with white bog cotton. At one place where our narrow dirt road met another even narrower, we saw a woman in a chiffon evening dress standing at the crossroad, and farther on a postman plod-ding along in the empty landscape. Still farther on we crossed an arched stone bridge over a rushing, brown stream and passed the inn of Sligachan, huddled into a fold in the ground under the dramatically beautiful, jagged, soaring Sgurr-nan-Gillean.

It was a little before ten when at length, the only remaining passengers, we saw Portree ahead, curled around its harbor, and at last climbed stiffly down into the little cobbled square. Going into the nearest hotel, the Portree, we asked confidently for a room with twin beds.

"Have ye buked?" said a reproving voice.

No.

"The boat was in almost four hours ago. However did ye get here?"

We told her about the bus, but she shook her head incredulously. "We haven't a corner," she said.

We went next to the Royal Hotel overlooking the harbor, where Flora and Prince Charles had had a meal together before they parted, after she had spirited him away from the Long Island, disguised as her maid, under the very noses of the Redcoats. The Royal Hotel hadn't a corner. Could they suggest a place for us to go? Indifferently they mentioned the Caledonian on the main street.

It was a small place with two doors directly on the narrow street. The first door opened into the bar, which was crowded with what seemed to be fishermen, all waving their arms and singing loudly. We hastily backed out. The second door landed us in a small, stuffy lobby with a musty carpet and a general red gloom. Nobody was to be seen. I went up the narrow stairs and found a maid at the top. She swayed tipsily as she repeated the now familiar rubric, "We haven't a corner."

Out on the street again we perhaps looked desperate. A kindly woman, passing, guessed our plight and recommended a nearby lodging house. It too was devoid of corners, and once again out on the street we looked at each other. It was nearly half-past ten. The bus had disappeared. There was no bus or railroad station in Portree in which to sit up all night.

From somewhere—we did not see her come—a young Highland girl appeared at our side. She was about eighteen, with dark, wavy hair, deep blue eyes, very white skin and pink cheeks, the very image of a Highland lass.

"If you'll follow me," she said in a soft voice and the precise English of one translating from the Gaelic, "I'll show you a place."

We retrieved our bags from the Portree Hotel where we had left them and followed her up the hill on a winding road that looked down on the harbor, until we came to a two-storied whitewashed stone house in a row of such houses but distinguished by the brightness of its brass doorknob and knocker. The woman who came to the door was solid and motherly, calmly welcoming. Yes, she had a room and a bath which we could have to ourselves; there was no one else in the house. Come away in.

We turned to thank our rescuer, but she was gone.

The bedroom on the second floor, which was immaculate, had two beds and windows overlooking the harbor; the bathroom had a deep, long tub and the thick towels were warmed on a heated rack. In the little parlor downstairs we were given cold ham and tomato salad, tea and scones, before a fragrant peat fire.

There was plenty of water for baths, the beds were comfortable, there was better than usual coffee for breakfast and bannocks and porridge. Our hostess told us she had been "in service" in London; she knew what ladies liked. We asked her about the girl who had brought us to her door, but she said she had not seen anyone with us; she had wondered how we had found her house. She could not think of any girl in Portree who answered our description.

All that morning we looked for her as we walked up and down the streets, in and out of the shops, and out onto the moors, beyond the town, in a fine, misty rain, but we did not see her. In the afternoon we went up to our room for a nap. The white curtains moved gently in the open windows; the air off the water and the surrounding moors was clean, aromatic, chilly. I fell into a sleep unlike any other that I have ever had: deep but not heavy, relaxing but buoyant, refreshing and restoring. It was like a wave from the sea, sweeping me off the arid rocks of sleeplessness on which I had been stranded back into the ebb and flow of the tide.

On our last day in Portree we kept asking for our Highland girl, in the shops where we bought lengths of tweed and hand-knit sweaters, on the bus that took us to Dunvegan Castle, wherever we fell into conversation with others. It is a small place, Portree; you see the same faces over and over. It seemed impossible that so pretty a girl and one who knew the place so well should not be known, or that we ourselves, constantly on the watch for her, should not run across her. She had simply vanished. Skye is an island where fairies are not strangers. In Dunvegan Castle there is a fairy flag that, unfurled in battle, has twice saved the Macleods from disaster; the bus driver on the way to Dunvegan pointed out a clear pool where, he said, the fairies did their laundry. Perhaps our little friend was not, after all, mortal.

Aberdeen was the cleanest city I had ever seen. When we woke in the morning and looked out between the green taffeta curtains that swathed our windows, we saw men hosing the granite pavement below in the pouring rain. We took a bus to the Old Town and found it gray with granite houses, green with leafy gardens; now and then there was a glimpse of the North Sea. We could not remember the name of the street where the Grays had lived; we passed Marischal College, but did not go in to see the chimney where the familiar words were carved; "They saye. Quhat say they? Let them saye." Nor did we see the Grammar School where, surely, there was a desk with Byron's name carved on it and perhaps the initials JGG as well. We had not allowed enough time for Aberdeen. It was a dignified, clean, self-respecting city, we told each other, catching the 11:30 train for Edinburgh, with a beauty of its own, and we were proud to have it in our background.

I had gone to England as a lover of English literature seeking the places on which my imagination had been feeding for years, but I went to Scotland as one goes home. To leave the sharp, nervous politeness of English service, "Yes, Moddom, Thank you, Moddom, Oh, no, Moddom," and find instead the natural friendliness or the equally natural grumpiness of the Scottish taxi driver or waitress—the frequent answer, "I couldna tell you thot"—was a relief. Scotland, I felt, was a land of sorrow, a land of poverty, a land of austere and wild beauty; the sound of pipes skirling, the swing of a kilt, the slope of a heather-purpled hill, the rich, warm voices burring with r's, the blitheness of the Scottish women lilting and fresh, the tenderness beneath the crusty surface of the men: all spoke directly to something deep within me.

In Edinburgh Violet and I went first to see the Scottish American War Memorial. Entitled "The Call," it was perhaps the best thing that Tait McKenzie ever did: a young, kilted Scot seated, with his gun across his knees and his head lifted as if he were hearing distant music; behind him a long stone seat and a frieze depicting all the types of Scotsmen who had gone to fight in the 1914 war; miners, shepherds, farmers, fishermen, students, office workers. It was situated in the gardens below Princes Street, and across the valley the great castle towered on its rock. Passers-by tired from walking stopped to rest on the stone bench and got into conversation with one another: Scots, Americans, Australians, New Zealanders. My heart ached because my father had not lived to see it. Some years later when Tait McKenzie died, he directed in his will that his heart was to be buried in front of the memorial, the act of a true romantic. Since there was no precedent that made room for such eccentricity, his heart was buried in the churchyard of nearby Saint Cuthbert's, within sight of the memorial and even closer to the castle.

When Violet left to return to her library, I settled down contentedly in a little hotel in Great Stuart Street, where I had a large room on the third floor at the back, looking out over the Water of Leith below to the Ochil Hills beyond the Firth of Forth. I sent out the letters of introduction that I had from Tait McKenzie and other friends and got myself a reader's ticket for the Edinburgh Public Library.

Though I was much alone, it was not a lonely time. On days when the weather was good, I walked the streets of the Old Town, from one end of the Royal Mile to the other, many times, and south of it to George Square and beyond to Heriot's Hospital. In White Horse Close I came on the very inn from which Meggy had taken her departure for North Carolina and recognized it from my own description; in the Edinburgh Room of the Public Library I found the book itself, among novels about Edinburgh. On the days of what Scott called "bitchiferous weather," when rain came down in sheets and the wind blew, I worked in the library, and sometimes returned to Great Stuart Street via the castle, for there was something wild and exciting about standing up so high with the rain beating against my face and seeing the west wind blowing all the banners of chimney smoke below into fluttering tails.

To Scott as a boy, lame but determined to keep up with his fellows, climbing Arthur's Seat by the Gutted Haddie was a challenge that he had to meet. Arthur's Seat is the pointed hill that rises like a small mountain behind Holyroodhouse; the Gutted Haddie a steep cleft in the rocks like a haddock that has been slit open with a knife. With the aid of his friend John and by grasping at the top for the final pull a nettle, he actually made it. If a lame boy could do it, I thought, I ought to be able to, and one day I tried it. For the first part of the way there was grass, cropped smooth by the sheep; soon the slope was so steep that it seemed but inches from my face, and then the rocks began, offering only shallow handholds. I turned to look back to see how far I had come. Below me, over Holyroodhouse and the ruins of the chapel, the city lay spread out. If I fell, I thought, there was nothing to keep me from bouncing from roof to roof all over Edinburgh. I eased myself cautiously down again, feeling rather craven, while a sheep on a ledge above baaed contemptuously. Two or three years later, after I had told this story to a group of young librarians, one of them came up to me and said,

"I climbed Arthur's Seat by the Gutted Haddie."

I offered suitable congratulations and she hesitated. "Well," she admitted, "actually I fell and I had a month in the hospital afterwards."

Another day, with a Scottish acquaintance, I did climb Arthur's Seat but by the path on the eastern side of it. It was a beautiful sunny day, and from the top we saw the Firth of Forth all the way to the Bass Rock and the Berwick Law. There was a wind that almost swept us off our feet but only set the little harebells in the crannies of the rocks to nodding. Swallows swooped over the slopes, and far below on the parade ground behind Holyroodhouse a flock of sheep ran before a dog.

I went by train to Kelso, which Scott described as "the most beautiful if not the most romantic village in Scotland," perhaps at least partly because he had had happy times there visiting his Aunt Jenny and because there he discovered the ballads that so fired his imagination. As you come down the hill from the station, you see Rennie's bridge over the Tweed and the village with its ruined abbey beyond. On the other side of the abbey was the Knowes, the commons, on which faced the Grammar School which the boy attended during a six-month visit after an illness, the parish church, and the gate into Aunt Jenny's garden, which ran down to the river. I walked along the path beside the Tweed, looking for the summer house where young Walter had read all day, forgetting dinner, lost in Percy's *Reliques of Ancient English Poetry*, but like Aunt Jenny's cottage it was gone. But I saw herons rising from the reeds across the river as he used to do, heard rooks in the trees, saw the house martins swooping and skimming and sea gulls squawking over the water. Before I went back to Edinburgh I walked in the other direction to where I could see the meeting of the waters, Tweed and Teviot, the meadows on the other side, and set far back on its lawns, Floors Castle, which was built in 1718.

With Sally Brooks, who had been my classmate at Library School and Ethel Feagley from Teachers College Library, and later with Dick McKey's small, piquant mother and his tall, fair-haired sister Nell, I walked the Pentland Hills. We would take a tram to Colinton on the west, and follow the footpaths over the hills to Glencorse on the east, where we would get a tram back again.

My letters of introduction brought me Scottish friends. Mrs. Allan, the shy, elegant Scottish widow of a Writer to the Signet, who lived with her neat maids in a house gleaming with silver and mahogany in a garden with a locked gate and a bell, gave me glimpses of a formal upper middle class life that was already disappearing. Mr. and Mrs. J. K. Stewart, who had a bright, modern house on the Firth of Forth, welcomed me for Marjorie's sake. Mr. Stewart met me at the bus stop in full regalia—kilts, bonnet and dirk in stocking—and they feasted me on crab and on grouse shot on August 12 on the Duke of Argyll's lands. "What better end for a Campbell grouse," said my host triumphantly, "than to feed a Stewart?" I was surprised to learn that the Stewarts had feuded as bitterly with the Campbells as the MacDonalds. "Dairty devils every one of them," said Mr. Stewart over his grouse.

Dr. McKenzie's letter to the Earl and Countess of Cassilis (pronounced Castles) brought me an invitation to New Hailes, the beautiful house built in 1730 on an earlier foundation where the Cassilises were then living because Lord Cassilis's ninety-three-year-old father, the Marquis of Ailsa, was still occupying Culjean (pronounced Cullayne) Castle. I went one afternoon by train, got off at New Hailes, which had its own station, where I was met by Lord Cassilis, with his Sealyham at his heels, and we walked through a wood thick with hollies to the house.

He was about seventy then, though he looked older; he had a small, screwed-up, little face like a wise monkey's, with bright, kind eyes and an abrupt manner that unnerved some Americans. Dr. McKenzie had warned me that he was "difficult," but I found him always easy and warm. He was an ardent Mason and had, I think, achieved all the degrees possible: he had visited the United States for some sort of Masonic gathering and was well disposed toward Americans.

The house was of stone, with no trace of Scottish baronial, beautiful in its balance and proportion; curving stairs from right and left led to the front door, and on the balustrade three peacocks perched. There was an accent of scarlet geraniums. As we entered the hall, Lady Cassilis came down the stairs wearing a brown straw hat in coils like the Red Queen's in *Through the Looking Glass*, a chiffon scarf wound around her throat and floating over her shoulder. She was small, vivacious, enthusiastic, loving. General Sir Alwynne and Lady Haldane were also coming for tea, she told me, but before they arrived she must show me the gardens behind the house, where between the green boles of tall beeches we saw the Firth of Forth and Edinburgh Castle hanging in the air, faint and distant. When the Haldanes came, we were all taken upstairs to see the famous embroideries that had been got out for the visit of Queen Mary the week before; they were spread out on modern brass bedsteads. The old beds had been sold, Lady Cassilis said casually. The library, for which New Hailes was famous, was full of incunabula and Burns first editions, of Allan Ramsay portraits, Ming vases, needlework chairs, tapestries and teakwood cabinets. After tea—a sit-down tea in the dining room in the Scottish way— and after the Haldanes had gone, Lady Cassilis kept me on for a heartwarming talk, after which she presented me with a large bunch of red carnations, walked me to the station for the train and kissed me good-by.

"You must go to Abbotsford," she said. "I'll ring up Sir Walter Maxwell-Scott. But don't get your hopes up because he's away a great deal."

A week or so later I had an invitation to lunch at Abbotsford from Lady Maxwell-Scott and a letter from Lady Cassilis warning me that my hostess would be an hour late but not to mind that.

I reached Melrose at one o'clock and was met by a car and chauffeur from Abbotsford. We passed the entrance where the tourists were waiting in line and went on to the private gate beyond. After a walk down a passage hung with portraits, I was announced by the butler in the drawing room, a cheerful, modern room full of chintz and roses with a fire blazing on the hearth. Sir Walter Maxwell-Scott rose to greet me.

He was Scott's great-grandson, son of a granddaughter who had married a man named Maxwell and added her name to his. He was a tall, lean, sandy-haired man who had been wounded in the war and like his great-grandfather walked with a limp. A smart-looking woman in tweeds standing by the fire turned out to be a visiting Italian countess.

"My wife is always late," said Sir Walter. "We never think of waiting for her."

Lunch was in Sir Walter Scott's own dining room, a room not shown to tourists, with three great windows looking out on the

Tweed, which flowed at the foot of the terrace, and paneled walls on which hung portraits of people whom Scott had loved: Beardie, his grandfather; Tom, his younger brother; and Charlotte Carpentier, his wife. We had finished the first course when Lady Maxwell-Scott came in, wearing checked tweeds and large gold-loop earrings. She was an American, Lady Cassilis had already told me, born in Youngstown, Ohio, the granddaughter of a General Logan, but somewhere along the way she had acquired a pronounced French accent. Inclined to plumpness, with pretty, small features, she was warm and cordial and a lover of books; she read omnivorously and liked to talk about what she read.

After lunch Sir Walter took me through Scott's library and his study. The relics that Scott had collected with so much pride, Montrose's sword, the pocketbook worked by Flora MacDonald, Mary Stuart's crucifix, did not interest me greatly, being isolated objects out of context, but I was fascinated by the little staircase by which he came down from his bedroom above early in the morning to write—write himself to death, indeed, trying to pay his publisher's debts. I was aware, too, of the tourists who with one accord turned away from their informative guide to stare at Sir Walter. Afterwards we all had a walk in the garden and through the woods on the path which Scott himself laid out, along the Tweed. Lady Maxwell-Scott's cairn terrier took off after rabbits, and while we were walking there the sun came out, first on a distant hill, then nearer, then all around us, gleaming on the swift, brown river, where a fisherman up to his waist in water was fishing for salmon. We went in to tea in the drawing room (in her letter to me Lady Maxwell-Scott had told me just what trains to take going and coming, so that I had no uneasiness about overstaying my welcome), and Sir Walter's two daughters by his first wife, Patricia and Jean, thirteen and eleven, came in with their governess: such nice, stiff, fair-haired, curtseying, yes-Mummy, no-Mummy children.

The high point of the day came when Lady Maxwell-Scott took me into her bookroom, a small room lined with books to the ceiling, all of which she had had rebound in leather of delectable shades of green, rose and blue. Over the fireplace hung a large watercolor portrait, in soft greens and tawny browns, of a boy with dreaming eyes holding a pitcher in long-fingered, sensitive hands. This, she told me, was Scott at the age of twelve. It had turned up only two or three years earlier in an attic; the unknown artist was undoubtedly an itinerant painter who had made the portrait in Kelso when Scott had been visiting his Aunt Jenny there. It was authentic; it had not yet been reproduced anywhere; if I would like to have it for my book, I might send a photographer down from Edinburgh to make some prints.

The generosity of it! The dream come true in so wholly unexpected, so beautiful a way! I was driven to the five o'clock train at Galashiels in a daze of happiness.

On September 7 a commemoration service was held at the Scottish American War Memorial, as had been done each of the seven years since its dedication, a matter of laying wreaths, of speeches, and of music. I had dreaded it beforehand, for such affairs seemed to me artificial and strained, but when the time came, after I had successfully laid my wreath in memory of my father, I was moved by it. The day was gray and soft, the speeches dwelt on peace, Dr. Hugh Black, a Presbyterian minister known and loved in America as well as Scotland, pronounced the benediction and then two pipers, coming from a distance, played the great pibroch, "The Flowers of the Forest," the music, faint at first, swelling as it approached and passed us, and then dying away in the distance. Dr. Black, in tears beside me, muttered, "I can't stand this thing; it breaks my heart." It was the Lament for Flodden, that tragic battle of 1513, when the finest of Scotland's young men and her king, James IV, were slaughtered; and by extension for Culloden, too, and for all the other losses suffered by Scots down the years. Lord Cassilis was there that day, and the McKeys, the J. K. Stewarts, and Mrs. Allan. Lady Cassilis had a toothache, but sent a message to me to come to tea again at New Hailes.

My final day at New Hailes was almost the last thing I did in Scotland. "We're all going to the Fishermen's Walk at Musselburgh," Lady Cassilis told me over the telephone. "Come for lunch first."

It was a gay party around the lunch table: Lady Cassilis in her hat; Lord Cassilis, a little deaf in the crowd and silent; Lady Cecilia Fitz-Roy, an exuberant child of eleven; Lady Blake; the Honorable Mrs. Cooper, who had large, dark eyes, a memorable sense of humor and the romantic name of Isolde; the Honorable Miss Cockburn, Sir Mark Dalrymple, nineteen, the actual owner of New Hailes, and Lieutenant Alan MacNicoll of the Australian Navy. The talk was lively and somewhat confusing. Sir Mark was pointing out the portrait of his ancestor, Sir John Dalrymple, who had interrupted a game of cards to sign the order for the Massacre of Glencoe on the back of a nine of diamonds; Lady Cassilis was telling me that Alan MacNicoll had gone to school in Scotland and had made New Hailes his second home during the holidays, that he had been in love and that the girl had died, that he wrote poetry; everybody else was explaining to me the festival that we were to attend.

I had often seen in the streets of Edinburgh the fisherwomen from Musselburgh in their distinctive costumes, skirts looped up over full red-and-white-striped petticoats, their creels between their shoulders held in place by a strip of webbing over their foreheads. In the thirteenth century fisherfolk had come from the Netherlands and had lived ever since in the same settlement in Musselburgh on the Firth of Forth. Once a year they put on their best clothes and marched in procession past the Town Hall to Pinkie House, where the gardens were thrown open for tea and dancing.

We watched the parade from the Town Hall: a kilted band first, naturally, then the fishermen in dark blue slacks and jerseys, followed by the women in striped skirts with dark blue aprons, flowered silk blouses and bright shawls which were heirlooms. When they saw Lady Cassilis, whom they all knew and loved, they burst into cheers and waved. The children wore the same costumes as the grownups, and each contingent had an emblem, a wooden ship or a pole or a doll in costume, which they raised high. After the procession passed, we followed it into the grounds of Pinkie House, the site of the Battle of Pinkie, where Prince Charles Edward was defeated by the English. Tea was set forth on long tables; there were races—potato races, obstacle races, relay races—in which young girls and men took part and afterwards dancing in three or four great circles, in which old and young, including Lady Cecilia Fitz-Roy and Sir Mark Dalrymple, joined. He was a little shy about it, but Lady Cassilis prodded him. "They'll be disappointed if he doesn't," she said to me. "He's the owner of New Hailes. They're his people really."

It was a charming sight, the fair-haired, handsome boy and the fisherfolk in their bright costumes, all looking as shining clean as if they had been washed by waves and dried by wind until they glistened in the sun. The dance required that a person in the center of the great circle call out another; they performed some elaborate steps opposite each other, then the first one returned to the circle and the last one called out another. It was a merry-faced young girl who crooked her finger at Sir Mark, but when he in his turn chose an old woman with white hair and flying feet a shout of approval went up.

Late in the afternoon Lieutenant MacNicoll and Sir Mark took me back to Great Stuart Street in Sir Mark's red sports car. I looked, Mr. MacNicoll told me, like a girl whom he had loved and lost. He sent me later the volume of his poems, *Sea Voices*, which had been printed on a hand press on the battleship *Hood*. They were elegant, exquisite verses, formal in structure, full of classical allusions. Every Christmas for the next six years I had a Christmas card from an Australian battleship, and then silence. I have often wondered if he survived the war, that young poet.

I heard from the Cassilises for more than ten years. The old father died in 1938; the Earl of Cassilis became Marquis of Ailsa, and they moved to Culjean Castle. In 1943, he died. Lady Ailsa lived to see the end of the war; I last heard from her in 1945. When I think of them the word *genuine* comes always to my mind; they were warm, direct, tender, simple, real.

During the winter that followed that summer in Scotland I worked hard and happily, writing the book that I called *Young Walter Scott*, first in Washington and later in Germantown, where I had taken a small apartment about a mile away from my mother's. The book, published under the name Elizabeth Janet Gray, came out in the fall of 1935 with the Scott portrait as frontispiece and delightful end papers by Kate Seredy of the Scott family walking to church under the shadow of the castle.

Two or three years later it was published in London by Nelson and favorably reviewed in the *Times Literary Supplement* as an adult novel. There was one thorn in this review that has pricked me ever since. I had had a bitter battle with the Viking copy editor (not, of course, May Massee) defending my manuscript from the improvements he wished to make in the style, all of which I felt substituted conventionality for freshness; when he corrected my legal terms, wearied by the struggle I let it pass, even though I had taken them from Scott's own novels. The *Times* reviewer commented, "The American author obviously is not aware that there is a difference between Scottish and English legal terms." I was not, of course, but if I had stuck to my guns I should have had the right ones in my book.

Early in the 1950's *Young Walter Scott* was brought out as a Puffin paperback. Morgan's cousins, Betty and George Gibson, wrote me of their trip to Scotland and of visiting Abbotsford, where at a stand at the tourist entrance books and maps and pamphlets were sold. They bought a copy of *Young Walter Scott* from Miss Maxwell-Scott herself. Whether it was Jean or Patricia they did not know.

7.

Germantown

During the years that followed I read widely and deeply, filling notebook after notebook with passages that impressed me. I read for amusement, for information, for background for books that I was writing, but most of all to find, if I could, the meaning of my life. The green girl who had skated over the surface of Bryn Mawr taking subjects in which she could easily get good grades, the young wife who had taken happiness as her due and expected it to go on forever, the writer who had given but half of herself to her vocation, the Friend who, in the words of William Penn, was "convinced" but not yet "converted," had things to learn that could be learned only through searching, through quietness, through meditation.

I read not only the history and the literature of Quakerism, some of the psychologists, especially Jung, Horney, Wickes and May, but the great mystics as well from Plotinus to Evelyn Underhill. They came wholly new to me, and I plunged into them eagerly, *The Theologia Germanica*, Thomas à Kempis, Meister Eckhart, *The Cloud of Unknowing*, by an anonymous English monk of the fourteenth century, *The Little Flowers of St. Francis*, St. Theresa of Avila and St. John of the Cross, Dean Inge, Baron von Hugel, Gerald Heard. My favorite of them all was *The Cloud of Unknowing*, partly because it was written as Chaucer might have written if he had been a mystic, with tolerant insight into human nature and a homely, realistic humor. I noted his caution: "Abide courteously and meekly the will of our Lord and snatch not overhastily as it were a greedy greyhound, hunger thee never so sore," advice which I thought sound even if I did not always follow it. Reminded by *The Cloud of Unknowing* of Chaucer, I read again

Troilus and Crisevde, that poignant story of a young widow which Shakespeare vulgarized.

Beppy Marlowe, which followed *Young Walter Scott,* was a story of London and Charleston, South Carolina, in 1715. London I had recently seen; to Charleston I went for six weeks at the end of 1935 and beginning of 1936. Having been impeccably introduced, I was able to stay as a paying guest in the Miles Brewton House in King Street, where Miss Mary and Miss Susan Frost gave their lives to preserving the great mansion of their ancestors. Miss Susan, small and plump and extrovert, ran a real estate office in order to subsidize the house; Miss Mary, small and thin and introvert, kept it in order and showed it to tourists, who paid a dollar at the door to the old Negro butler. She never saw the money change hands, and when I paid my weekly board I put the check in an envelope and left it on her desk.

I had the "garden room" on the ground floor at the back, with a small, unheated bathroom of its own, a fireplace, a big four-poster bed, and besides the usual chest of drawers and dressing table, a desk at which to work. Early in the morning the butler came in and built up a fire for me to dress by, and the last thing I saw at night was the bright reflection of its flames on the ceiling between the tall bedposts.

Besides the man there was his wife, old Sarah the cook. They lived in the former slave quarters on the edge of the garden. The kitchen in the Miles Brewton House, like my bedroom, was on the ground floor; food was sent up a dumb-waiter to the dining room above, but old Sarah had many steps to take as well. One evening as I sat reading by my fire, I heard her saying as she toiled up the stairs outside my door, "Thank the Lawd dis day's work is done. Thank ye, Jesus."

The French windows in my room opened directly onto the garden, which was large and surrounded by a high brick wall. It had once been formal and beautiful; now it was beautiful. Sandy paths edged with brick wound among box bushes higher than one's head, great magnolia trees, fragrant sweet olives, poinsettias, and narcissi like white stars. Miss Susan worked there early in the mornings, weeding and transplanting, but inevitably it had become overgrown, a little shabby, a little sad. In the center, not far from a Civil War cannon ball still half imbedded in the ground where it had landed, was the garden house, cloaked by trees, and built of brick with white woodwork as formal, as elegant in miniature as the mansion itself, the very apotheosis of a privy. For many years now it had been a tool house, but it was interesting to see how such a necessity was handled in the great days of the place.

I had my breakfast on a tray in my room, and whatever supper I had I got at some restaurant in the town or brought a sandwich and fruit in to eat beside my fire, but dinner at two-thirty I ate in the great dining room with Miss Mary and Miss Susan and any other guest who might be there. The food was always delicious and there were the Southern things; spoon bread, crabs, shrimps, black-eyed peas, Lady Baltimore cake. On special occasions there was homemade orange wine, and the bottle went around the table withershins, opposite to the course of the sun. They had hot biscuits, I suppose, but I remember more vividly the crusty loaf of homemade bread that always stood on the table beside Miss Mary, and how she would cut it one piece at a time as it was wanted; there was something elemental about her seriousness as she divided the loaf.

On the first floor, besides the dining room, there was a very ceremonious bedroom and two parlors, one on each side of the front door, which was reached by high, curving steps outside. The furniture was original and so were many of the draperies, which were faded and carefully mended. Across the front of the house on the second floor were the ballroom and withdrawing room. To see the enormous chandelier with more than a hundred prisms throwing rainbows at sunset into every corner of the big room and on every upturned face was a sight to remember but not equal in poignancy to the sight of Miss Mary, small and erect with a blue tulle bow tied under her chin, reading aloud to the tourists, with her eyes closed, the framed letter from Washington to her ancestor.

During my six weeks there I saw all the plantations, the islands, the beaches, the churches, Catfish Row of *Porgy and Bess*, the Battery. I met people who were kind and hospitable, went to two parties on my third Christmas without Morgan. When I returned home to write my book, I felt I had tasted the flavor of the South in a beaker of unexpectedly sweet and fragrant orange wine.

While I was in the midst of writing *Beppy Marlowe*, my black cocker spaniel, Rastus, died. I had been in Washington, staying with the Owenses while Nell was in the hospital having her third baby. Their family was now complete, three delightful little girls,

Niki, Betty and Sally, who grew up with surprising speed into a charming, gay and feminine trio surrounded by hosts of admiring young men. I was attempting out of my love and inexperience to run the house and take care of the other children while Nell was away, but I was a poor hand at it, for Niki developed a light case of mumps without my detecting it—I had not supposed that a Christian Science child would get mumps—and exposed her mother and the new baby returning from the hospital. Rastus was, of course, there with me. He went out one evening for his bedtime run and did not come back. It was two days before advertisements and telephone calls tracked him down in the hospital to which he had been brought with a broken pelvis. Black in the dark, he had run out into the road in front of a taxi, and the taxi driver had picked him up and taken him to the vet.

When I drove back to my apartment in Germantown at the end of my visit on a drizzling day in early April, I had Rastus, carefully propped with pillows on the seat beside me, to take him to his own doctor. I drove slowly and carefully so as not to jar him. At a traffic light in a town in Maryland, he raised his head to give me a long, loving look, wagged—with what pain?—his bit of a tail, and died.

He had been part of our life together, Morgan's and mine, and a comforting companion to me when I was alone; his physical presence, the warm, soft, wriggling body, the long, silky ears, the melting, brown eyes, the pink tongue, the vibratory tail, had been dear. A dog's love is given without reserve and without fear of being hurt, uncritical, inexhaustible, joyous. To have a dog breathing eagerly or yipping with joy on the other side of the door as one fumbles for one's key, and then, when the door is open, to be leapt upon or presented with a battered toy or hailed with frenzied runs around and around the room, is to have a sharp edge taken off living alone. Living alone is not such a bad thing, if one can surmount the silence and the emptiness when one first comes in after being out. After that, there are books, there is music, there is the bolstering discipline of routine, of the house to be kept, of one's work to do; there are guests to prepare for and letters to write, telephone calls to make, all the threads that keep one tied to other people. To have a little dog to welcome one and to coax one out to walk, to snuggle by one's side, is to be blessed with a precious companionship.

Though I knew I could never have another Rastus, I wanted a

dog, and I leaned toward a Sealyham, both for difference from Rastus and for a lovable quality that I discerned in the breed. A kennel in a suburb of Philadelphia advertised Sealyham puppies, and Violet went with me to see them.

The owner of the kennel led us into the Victorian sitting room of her large Victorian house and had a four-month-old Sealyham brought in to us. His points, I am sure, were good; he was calm and amiable, he accepted petting complacently, but was he a little —I looked at Violet—lethargic?

At that moment from under the long embroidered cloth on the center table a small white whirlwind darted out, untied the laces of both my oxfords and bolted back again. That was, Mrs. Thomas explained, a West Highland white terrier that she had got on a trade from a kennel in Aiken, South Carolina; she did not raise them. He reappeared, every white hair standing erect, his eyes black and bright, his black nose gleaming, his long pink tongue hanging out, wearing an expression youthful, exuberant and humorous. I picked him up, feeling the small bones under the fluff of hair, the taut muscles, the warmth, the vibrancy of the little creature; he raised his head and gave as much of my face as he could reach a swash of his warm, wet tongue.

We did not look at the Sealyham again. The West Highlander was seven months old; he had a long and honorable pedigree containing several champions; the kennel owner had not intended to sell him, but she would. I took him home.

I named him Hamish M'Connachie, the M'Connachie for the writing half of J. M. Barrie. Rastus had belonged to me, but I belonged to Hamish. It is not my intention to write a panegyric about my West Highland white terrier; everybody's dog is unique. But Hamish had more individuality, more sparkle than any other dog I have ever encountered. Blitheness is a characteristic of the breed; Hamish had it in full measure. He was gay, he was playful, he had indisputably a sense of humor, he had imagination; he had esthetic tastes: he enjoyed music and like Ferdinand the Bull he liked to smell the flowers. Many a time have I come into the living room and found him standing on a chair in order to plunge his nose into a bowl of roses on the table beside it, or walking in my cousin's garden at sunset smelling each nicotiana in turn. He had consuming energy. He lived on love as an air plant lives on air. As I was in the midst of a book when I got him, he learned from the first not to disturb me during working hours. As long as I sat at my kneehole desk, he lay at my feet. The minute I got up he was dancing around me demanding a walk and play. "Arrah!" he would say imperatively, his head on one side.

Hamish, of course, went with me when a few months later I gave up my apartment and joined forces with my mother and sister. They needed me, and I needed to be needed. Violet was fifty-three, Mother seventy-five, neither one was in good health. Violet's library at Starr Center, where she had spent thirteen rewarding and useful years among foreign-born children, was breaking up because of changes in the neighborhood, where warehouses were replacing tenements. She and Mother were rubbing on each other; the depression had reduced their income so that the usual alleviations of diversions were less easily had. I managed to find a large and attractive apartment with a view over Wissahickon Drive to a hillside that was part of the park, and we moved in the summer of 1936. I took over the housekeeping and the cooking and later, when my mother's health deteriorated still further, the care of the invalid and the supplementing of nurses when they became necessary.

In that same summer Violet went back as head librarian to the Friends Library where she had had her first job as an assistant. It was a relief to her to be free of the long and exhausting commuting and she found herself among congenial people, but she missed the boys and girls of Starr Center, to whose lives she had brought so much stimulation and encouragement and whose warm response had given so much color and interest to her life. She underwent during the next few years a series of operations and she struggled besides with high blood pressure and a painful injury to her knee. We were fortunate at that time to be introduced to a brilliant young woman doctor, Emma Boyd Bevan, who became the cherished friend of us all as well as our physician. She was on hand in all crises, but her main purpose was to build up our strength and resistance. Though Violet's blood pressure stayed high and mine for a good many years hovered between ninety and a hundred, she was able to carry on a full schedule at the library and for the most part to enjoy it, while anemia, asthma and insomnia all but disappeared from my life.

Early in January of 1937 I went to a conference at Pendle Hill with Sue Yarnall, Stanley Yarnall's wife, very much younger than he and a good deal older than I but a most companionable per-

son for any age. It is almost impossible to describe Pendle Hill
to anyone who has not been there and difficult even to those who
have. Anna Brinton said once it was like the Tao: if you could
describe it, it would not be Tao. According to the sign at the entrance, it is A Quaker Study Center—"for the benefit," the catalog says, "of men and women of all faiths, races and nationalities."
Situated on twenty-two attractively landscaped acres in Wallingford, southwest of Philadelphia, it was founded in 1930 by Friends
from several yearly meetings. The first director was Henry Hodg-
kin, well-known and beloved English Quaker; after his early death
John Hughes and Richard Gregg led it in turn until in the fall
of 1936 Howard and Anna Cox Brinton came to be codirectors
from Mills College, where Howard had been head of the Department of Religion and Anna dean of students and professor of Latin
and Greek. They had studied Oriental art and the religions
of China, Japan and India; they brought extraordinary gifts of
mind and spirit to the development of Pendle Hill.

The conference, which has since become an annual affair with
the title of Mid-Winter Institute, dealt with Quakerism and for
me was one of those experiences that Rufus Jones has called equi-
noxes of the spirit. There for the first time I came into contact
with some of the leaders of modern Quakerism. Rufus Jones came
one day to lecture and to stay for dinner with the group. His
name was already familiar to me, for Mother was a devotee of his
books and she had taken every opportunity to hear him speak; he
had been for years chairman of the Board of Directors of Bryn
Mawr, though when I was an undergraduate the members of the
Board had been no more to me than flies on the ceiling. Now I
met him for the first time, a large, sandy-haired, sandy-moustached,
homely man glowing with life and love, vitality and humor, who
spoke of God in such a way as to make him real to his hearers,
whose appeal was to mind, spirit and feeling all at once, so that
his message was received whole by the whole person. There was
no fragmented part of one to come back, after the contagion of
his personality was removed, to say, "Yes, but . . ."

Howard Brinton, physically slight by contrast, with even then
a halo of white hair, with keen blue eyes, clear-cut features and
an aura of radiance, gave a series of talks on "The Origins of
Quaker Thought" in which he traced the inward type of religion
through Hinduism, Buddhism and Taoism, the Prophets of the
Old Testament and the Gospels of the New, and the mystical

sects in European Christianity. He told also of his recent experiences in Japan when, introduced as the Abbot of Pendle Hill, he had meditated with the Zen Buddhist monks in a famous old temple in Kyoto. I felt awed at being able actually to know and talk with one who had had such an extraordinary experience, never imagining that eleven years later I would myself spend an evening meditating with Zen Buddhists in an ancient temple. Anna Brinton, his wife, whose serene beauty was the model for Sylvia Judson's statue of Mary Dyer in Boston Common, was a rare combination of brilliant intellect, practical ability, humor, and a genius for the apt and illuminating word.

One afternoon the entire group went to tea with the Whitneys in Westtown, Janet Whitney had written part of her biography of John Woolman, which was then in press, at Pendle Hill; George was an artist, a portraitist, who was head of the Art Department at Westtown School. The following year George Whitney was to illustrate delightfully my book on William Penn.

The conference was a turning point in my life, as Sue Yarnall has told me that it was for her. Up to then my membership in the Society of Friends had meant going to meeting and from it receiving strength; and the reading that I had done showed me why this was so. Now I was to enter more fully into its life. For Friends the meeting for worship is not an isolated event; one takes the insights obtained in meeting out into the world, to make whatever contribution that one can to peace, to social justice, to better race relations.

I was a writer; whatever contribution that I made must be made through my one talent. Yet I did not propose in any way to write propaganda, to sell my soul, my writing soul, for as someone has wittily said, "a pot of message." Writing stories for children and young people, I must keep the story itself the main focus, must write it as well as I was capable of doing, and if any residue of influence came out of it, it must be incidental, because the book was written with integrity, because the author's own love of life, or of truth, was contagious.

Out of my reading in Quaker history, the figure of William Penn came forth and tapped me on the shoulder. It was the story of his imprisonment in the Tower of London that did it. Here was a young man, the son of England's most popular admiral and the friend of King Charles II, given the best possible education— Chigwell Grammar School, Christ Church, Oxford, Lincoln's Inn, a tour of the continent of Europe—intended by his father to be some day an ambassador or something even more: this gilded young man had the world in his hands, and laid it aside to become a Quaker in the days when being a Quaker meant fines, loss of social standing, imprisonment and sometimes even, in the prisons of those days, loss of life itself. He had written an enthusiastic book called *The Sandy Foundation Shaken* about his new religion and as a result found himself in the Tower of London on an indeterminate sentence. Word was brought to him that he could be released if he recanted; otherwise, he could look forward to being there the rest of his life. Magnificently, he sent back word, "My prison shall be my grave before I will budge a jot, for I owe my conscience to no mortal man." On the suggestion of the Bishop of London, however, he wrote another book explaining his first one, *Innocency with Her Open Face*, and was after nine months freed. It seemed to me that he suffered from the statue of the stout middle-aged man on the top of the Philadelphia City Hall, and I wanted to show him as the handsome, lively, courageous, vigorous, brilliant man that he really was.

The reading for Penn was more exacting than anything I had yet done. Since I intended the book to be not only a biography for young people but an introduction to Penn for adults who knew little or nothing about him, I went to source material: all of Penn's own writings, and they were voluminous, often involved in language and wordy, but studded with passages of great beauty and power; the early history of Quakerism, the records of Pennsylvania, writings of Penn's contemporaries. In addition, of course, I read a number of biographies of Penn, from the earliest account by the eighteenth-century Quaker, Besse, to the latest rather acidulous one by Bonamy Dobrée.

Another trip to England was also, I felt, necessary, to get what I could from libraries there, and to see the places where he had lived and studied and worked and been imprisoned. Eleanor Wistar, the daughter of Violet's lifelong and beloved friend Beatrice Wistar, and I traveled together in the spring and early summer of 1937, parting from time to time, she to visit friends of her own and I to pursue my hero.

In England I found material about the school at Chigwell which Penn attended, saw some rare manuscripts in the Friends House Library in London, was shown the records of his second wife's family in Bristol, visited the old manor house at Chorley

Wood in which his first marriage to the exquisite Gulielma Spring-ett was celebrated, and to crown it all, spent a week end with Sylvia and William Hanbery Aggs at their manor house in Sussex. One of their farms was Worminghurst, which had been Penn's home at the time when he departed on his first voyage to Pennsylvania in 1680. There was nothing left of the house, but the great barn was still there and the view which he had had over the wide spaces of the Sussex Weald. We went to Meeting at the Blue Idol, that strangely named little meetinghouse which had been old in Penn's day, and heard stories about him that had been handed down in the neighborhood over the centuries; how Gulielma and the children had gone to meeting by oxcart and Penn had ridden over on horseback; how he walked in the orchard before meeting and, already full of his message, started to speak the moment he passed through the door.

The ghosts of two other books accompanied me on that trip in 1937. Eleanor and I went to Skye for Flora MacDonald. Violet's and my landlady in Portree was away and so we could not return to that place of happy memory, but I spent several days at Slig-achan Inn under the Black Cuillin beside the river which was in spate, and saw the fishermen come in late with their fish, which they displayed on big white platters by the front door. The collection of minstrels' tales which I had begun in Chapel Hill turned my mind to medieval England, and I made excursions that had nothing to do with Penn: to see a small twelfth-century tavern at a forgotten crossroads, to walk over the Chiltern Hills from Wat-lington to Ewelme, where Chaucer's son once lived, and to look for an Oxford older than Penn's.

I wrote part of Penn at Pendle Hill, working in an ideal atmosphere: undisturbed hours for writing in the morning and early afternoon, stimulating lectures and discussions after tea and in the evening. The results of Hitler's seizure of power in Germany were by then evident; a stream of refugees was beginning to appear in the United States. A number of them stayed at Pendle Hill until they could find employment and a home elsewhere; Wilhelm Sollman was the only one who became a permanent resident of Pendle Hill until his death ten years or so later. He had been Minister of the Interior in Stresemann's Cabinet, had been imprisoned and tortured by the Nazis, and had escaped via Lux-embourg. One afternoon each week he would give an hour's interpretation of the news, which with his knowledge and background was so illuminating that people came from considerable distances to hear him. As time went on, it was a darkening, saddening, frightening story that he had to tell. He was a slight, nervous, intense man with a broad knowledge and compassion. His love of Pendle Hill, his mingled admiration for Quakers and irritation with what he felt to be their naïve trust in human nature, his deep feeling for the freedom he found in the United States as well as his recognition of weaknesses and stupidities in our policy and the crudity of some of our culture, were broadening and balancing to all who came in contact with him.

In the summer of 1938 I acted as "head resident" in the four-week summer school, at which the lecturers were Gerald Heard, the English writer and philosopher, then at the height of his influence; Walter Kotschnigg, professor of International Affairs at Smith College; and Georgia Harkness, the poet and religious leader. It was a strenuous time for me but a rewarding one. I worked closely with Anna Brinton, helped plan meals and the work schedule by which students helped with the daily chores, did all the marketing (buying and bringing home twenty-five pounds of meat at a time almost made a vegetarian of me); made beds for unexpected visitors at ten P.M. and listened to all of Gerald Heard's lectures on "The Sense of Spirit." After I went back to Germantown, Violet took her turn at going away, and spent four weeks in England, returning just before the Munich Crisis.

The summers of 1939 and 1940 we all three spent in a cottage on Burpee Hill outside of New London, New Hampshire. Although it was there that I wrote most of *The Fair Adventure*, a modern story for girls with the scene laid in a disguised Chapel Hill, and there the following summer received the first copies of the book, it is war, not writing, that I think of when I think of those summers. We were there when the news of the Russo-German Non-Aggression Pact burst upon us, followed by the Nazi invasion of Poland and Britain's Declaration of War. I remembered Morgan's forebodings on January 31, 1933, when Hitler was made chancellor; it had taken less than ten years for him to be proved right. The following summer we lived through the Battle of Britain. Each morning I came downstairs to turn on the radio to find out if London had survived the night; each noon when I returned from the upper pasture, where I had been writing propped against a rock with my feet in a clump of ferns, I turned on the news. In the evenings we listened to Edward R. Murrow, H. V. Kaltenborn, William L. Shirer, Raymond Gram Swing, and Mother listened to the tearfully encouraging Gabriel Heatter.

I was torn. I had utterly rejected war as a method of settling international conflicts. I was a Quaker at least partly because of the three-century-old Quaker stand on peace. I wanted to live, as George Fox said when offered a commission in Cromwell's army, "in the life and power of that spirit that takes away the occasion for all wars." And yet I recognized the evil of Nazism. More than many people of the time I knew what was happening to Jews—and half-Jews and quarter-Jews—in Germany, for in the spring of 1938 I had done volunteer work for the American Friends Service Committee in the Refugee Section, which was helping to bring Jewish refugees to the United States. My work had been to read their dossiers and make notes on the skills that they had, so that work might be found for them to do. To read those brief, poignant accounts of suffering, fear and hope was a moving and an illuminating experience. I felt that the Nazis must be opposed, and yet I kept hoping that some way of negotiation might be found.

The war, of course, put an end to trips abroad, but I wrote *Adam of the Road* out of memories, out of nostalgia for a simpler time. The boy Adam had come to me late one night in the Bryn Mawr Hospital, when I was there for a week or so, not seriously ill but uncomfortable. Elizabeth McKie, by then a teacher in the Baldwin School in Bryn Mawr, had been to visit me in the daytime and had mentioned in passing how little good material there was for children on the Middle Ages. My mind had gone back to my book of tales from the metrical romances and the frame in which I had planned to put them. In the dark of the restless hospital night, the nurses coming on rubber soles with flashlight and pills, the boy Adam walked into my mind, redheaded, wide-mouthed and freckled, dressed in a striped surcoat, a small harp on his arm and a spaniel at his heels. I saw too his father, Roger, a minstrel; I saw them go with their tales into all kinds of English life, the highroad, the inn, the manor house, the castle, the fair, the churchyard. Adventures began to cluster around them. Adam lost his dog and, searching for the dog, became separated from his father. As he went hunting for his father, people along the way tried to help him; helping him, they sought to make him into something that he was not, a farmer boy, a parish clerk, a scholar. The theme of the story, I thought, should be that each of us must follow his own talent; Adam, discovering that he was a minstrel and nothing else, found his dog again and was reunited with his father. It did not come all at once, of course, but I left the hospital with a living boy and outlines of his story in my mind. The original collection of medieval tales fell away.

The research for Adam was pure joy. Back to Chaucer I went, to reread *The Canterbury Tales* and some of the shorter poems, seeking in them not only details of life and customs and ways of speech but, more important than either, climates of thought. I read too collections of manor house rolls, in which records of cases which came before the lord of the manor for decision showed what people quarreled over, how they lived, what was the pattern of their relationships. I decided that the scene should be laid in the thirteenth century, for writing at the time of the Battle of Britain, when the free world was in danger, I thought much of democracy and its meaning, its history. It seemed to me that the thirteenth century in England displayed many of the values that we cherished and that were being threatened. It began with Magna Carta in 1215 and ended in 1296 with the first parliament in which the common people were represented; it was the time of the growth and development of the universities, a time of faith and of expanding thought.

Much of the book I wrote during the summer of 1941, when Elizabeth McKie and I shared an apartment in North Conway, New Hampshire. Since my return to Germantown in 1933, my acquaintance with Mr. Mac's daughter had deepened into friendship. She was teaching in Bryn Mawr, ten miles away; she had a red cocker spaniel, Reddy, I had had a black one (the dog Nick in Adam was a combination of the two); we found ourselves congenial in many things: our love of Chapel Hill, of England and Scotland, of books, dogs, birds, wild flowers, mountains. In June of 1941 Elizabeth's father, and Morgan's and my old friend, Mr. Mac, had died as a result of what had promised to be a minor operation, and the summer was a sad and difficult one for Elizabeth. I wrote in the mornings while she answered the hundreds of letters which she had received from devoted friends and former students of her father's; in the afternoons we roamed New Hampshire by car and on foot. For three weeks of her vacation Violet joined us, having stopped to visit in the Berkshires on the way, while Aunt Georgina, my father's youngest sister, stayed with Mother.

After *Adam* was finished but before it was published, the thing that I so much dreaded happened: the United States was in the war.

✳✳✳✳✳✳✳✳✳✳✳✳✳✳✳✳✳✳✳✳✳✳✳✳✳✳✳✳✳✳✳✳✳✳

8.

The War Years

SOME EVENTS in life so shock or frighten us that we remember ever afterwards what, no matter how trivial it was, we were doing at the time of the occurrence. Everyone whom I met in Japan who had lived through the Great Earthquake of 1923 had some story to tell about where they were and what they were doing at the moment, and similarly on that day in 1945 when they heard for the first time their Emperor's voice on the radio proclaiming surrender and telling them they must bear the unbearable. Pearl Harbor Day is in the same way imprinted on our minds in the United States.

On that Sunday afternoon Violet and I were preparing to drive to Westtown to have supper with the Whitneys when Elizabeth McKie, who was coming to stay with Mother while we were gone, called me on the telephone.

"Is your mother where she can hear you talk to me?"

"Yes, she is."

"Has she heard the news?"

"No."

"Then I won't say anything about it to her. You've heard, haven't you?"

"No, I haven't."

"Japan has bombed Pearl Harbor and sunk American ships."

"Oh. Well, it's good you're coming."

All the way to Westtown through the russet and violet Pennsylvania countryside, where bare trees were etched against a saffron sky and brown fields rolled away in swells and hollows, Violet and I talked about what I had heard. Could it be true? Had Japan actually bombed us without a declaration of war?

At the Whitneys' house we found also Laura Benét, the poet,

and Louise Kennedy Brown, the playwright. Nobody mentioned the news, and as if under a spell we said nothing ourselves to disturb the pleasant and stimulating talk of books and plays. About half-past seven the telephone rang and George Whitney went to answer it. He came back white-faced and told us that Pearl Harbor had been bombed by the Japanese. From then until we left, no one talked of anything else.

The next day we had more news, and the declarations of war followed fast. I had no idea, of course, that on November 25 Secretary of War Henry L. Stimson had written in his diary, "Since the Japanese are notorious for making an attack without warning, how, when negotiation fails, can we manoeuver them into the position of firing the first shot without allowing too much danger to ourselves?"* The "danger to ourselves" turned out to be considerably greater than the heads of our government had anticipated, but the desired effect was achieved. The country had been divided; now with one brilliant but suicidal stroke the Japanese militarists had united us, galvanized us into action, as nothing else could have done.

" 'In the moment of action no one is free,' " I wrote in my journal, quoting from, I think, Gerald Heard; " 'it is then that what we have been preparing is fulfilled.' Who am I to stand out [against the war] now? What have I done to prepare anything different? But I am sorry for the Japanese people in their matchbox, crowded houses, betrayed by the war party in their government. . . . I think that our [i.e., peace-lovers'] task is now, without anxiety and without despair, to prepare for the next moment of action, for the coming of peace. We can only do it by, as individuals, building reflexes and patterns in our relationships with our fellow beings, by handling our small conflicts creatively and peacefully, by making our own word in the smallest things utterly trustworthy; by keeping all hate, bitterness and intolerance out of our thoughts; by being as well informed and as intelligent as our individual limitations allow us to be."

I then recorded, wryly, that I had begun this ambitious program by being in such a state over the war that I had entirely forgotten the meeting of the Pendle Hill Publications Committee that morning!

---

* Elting Elmore Morison, *Turmoil and Tradition: A Study in the Life and Times of Henry Lee Stimson*. Boston: Houghton Mifflin Co., 1960, p. 525.

The war, though it pervaded our thoughts and filled us with distress, did not radically change our personal lives. We had no young men of our own to go into it. Violet went on at the library as usual. I was at home cooking and taking care of Mother; coping with the ration books, which were an inconvenience but represented no real curtailment of food; and trying to write.

New friends had come into my life about this time, Francenia and Sam Fox, whose two children were in the Germantown Friends School. They had moved several years earlier from Sam's ancestral home on the Delaware near Andalusia to the Cambridge Apartments in Alden Park, and Fran and I were both members of a group of women who met twice a month to read and write poetry together. This group, informally known as The Poets, cannot be burdened with the title of Club or Society, for though we have continued to meet for thirty years without interruption, we have never had officers, minutes, dues or bylaws. "The formula for stability" in any institution, according to Marshall McLuhan, is low organization and high participation, and The Poets bear him out. Several of the group—Mary Hoxie Jones, Edith Johnson, Millicent Pettit, Margaret Cary—have published one or more very respectable "slim volumes" of verse; others have had poems in magazines. The rest of us write enough to maintain a footing in this group of imaginative, highly individual, delightful and exuberant women.

Fran Fox, a vivid, warm, outgoing personality, a loyal and devoted friend, fond of sailing, riding, walking, was also an amateur painter and endlessly clever with her hands in many ways. Early in our friendship she came and helped me to reupholster our wing chair and two others. "Helped" is a misnomer. She did most of the work and I helped with it under her direction. Her sense of humor was as refreshing as her energy and as inexhaustible. During the years when I was much confined by Mother's ill health, Fran and I and Hamish walked in the Wissahickon two or three times a week, returning to one house or the other for tea. One summer we had a victory garden on a plot provided by a neighbor of the Cambridge, where in a small space we raised beans, tomatoes, spinach, radishes, parsley and okra; I kept my tools in the kitchen and carried them on the trolley car when I went to cultivate my farm. Sam Fox was a handsome, charming and lovable man of "old Philadelphia" stock and conservative ideas, something of a recluse; they were a very close-knit family with not many intimates, but they opened their circle enough to take me in.

Adam of the Road was published in the spring of 1942 in a beautiful edition illustrated by Robert Lawson, whose knowledge of medieval England and of small boys and whose mastery of his art made him the ideal interpreter of my story. In 1943 it received the Newbery Medal, the honor which writers of books for children most value. Violet and I went to New York in June for the award dinner, which, as it was wartime, was smaller than usual but still significant. May Massee, who had a delightful way of making celebrations gay and memorable, kept us over an extra night to see *Rosalinda*, the popular musical made out of *Die Fledermaus*. It was a happy break in the midst of war and the darkening shadow that hung over our mother. Later that summer, on August 23, after several years of increasing weakness and confusion, she died at the age of eighty-two.

She had been a beautiful woman, my mother, growing up in the day of the "great beauties," the time of "the orchid woman," whose beauty was cherished, who was shielded and protected from the harsh world. The little girl on the New Jersey farm had in some sense identified herself with a kind of life not only utterly beyond her reach but essentially unreal in itself, a life in which beauty entitled one to special consideration, to admiration and ease, to an "indulgent" husband. Cousin Emma once said to me, sentimentally, about a year before Mother's death, "She was always like a lily that should be sheltered from the trials and tribulations of life." She had many trials and tribulations in her life, and she met them courageously. Though there was a certain fragility in her beauty, she had as well a robust intelligence and practical gifts. She had a flair for cooking, she sewed beautifully. For years she studied French and German and spoke them whenever she had an opportunity. She had a mystical streak that found a congenial home in the Episcopal Church, and she drew to her in sympathy and companionship the young minister of her church. She had devoted friends to whom she was a "blessing," an inspiration.

To Mother the quality of "esprit" was very important. It was one of the marks by which she rated people. "He is a man of *esprit*," she would say approvingly, or, "She is a heavy person—no *esprit*." She never explained what she meant by the word but that was not necessary; a person who had it would understand, those who did not did not matter. Not long ago I found a definition in Sanche de Gramont's book, *The French.* "The quality of *esprit* is a peculiarly French one. . . . It is not wit, not humor, nor intelligence nor anything spiritual. It is in fact defined by what it is not: not coarse, heavy-handed, obvious or insistent. *Esprit* is a verbal spark, bright and ephemeral. It serves, like courtesy, to deflect the thrust of all that is unpleasant in life."

Mother, dressed, hatted and veiled to go out one day, was told by Violet, "Mother, your slip shows," and she who never swore or allowed anyone to swear in her presence, responded swiftly, "Those are the most hellish words you can say to a woman." In a hatshop one day, trying on a hat, she was urged by the saleswoman to "Take it, dearie. It makes you look so refined." "Oh, but I'd so much rather look vulgar," replied Mother serenely. I don't know if Sanche de Gramont would consider these examples of *esprit* or not, but I believe that Mother would.

If she had not married a Scot of irascible temperament, a romantic, a businessman who ought to have been a professor of the Classics, but instead a genial, calm, money-making, admiring Philistine. . . . Or if our father had married a downright, self-confident, easygoing woman who could have opened her house to all his friends not caring whether or not she had the right appointments. . . . We used to discuss it again and again, Violet and I: what might have been if those two who had each one such real gifts and who to some degree diminished each other had only married someone else.

Violet remembered them when they were young; even as a small child she had looked on them with a critical eye which discerned in them a certain silliness that she deplored. There is extant a tintype of the three of them taken on an expedition to the seashore supposed to be for the benefit of the six-year-old daughter. It shows a smart young couple of the late 1880's, Mother half turned so as to display her elegant bustle, our father moustached, with boater and blazer, both of them candidly and blissfully posing while between them, slumped on the back of her neck in a chair, her legs dangling, sat their small, bored, sardonic child.

"I remember that day well," she used to say. "They were so silly."

But I, who knew them only when they were old, was glad to

have the evidence of a time when they had youth and hope and enjoyed posing in their smart clothes for a tintype.

During the war years I wrote a novel which did not find a publisher and entertained ideas for three other adult books. Flora MacDonald, though I had made two visits to Skye and had done work on the Carolina part of her life in the University Library in 1941 when I went back to Chapel Hill to sell my little house there, would have to be postponed until the war was over and I could go back to Scotland.

The life of John Donne had also taken hold of my imagination: the gay young poet called by some a libertine, the ambitious courtier eager for "weighty employment in the state" who regarded his position as secretary to the Lord Keeper of the Privy Seal as a springboard to higher things, the ardent lover who secretly married lovely Anne More and was imprisoned and lost his post in consequence, the hack writer of theological disputations who became dean of St. Paul's and England's most famous preacher, accounted a saint, the divine whose sermons were poetry and whose poems lived to influence profoundly unbelieving modern poets: this paradoxical man was fascinating to me, and I thought I saw the springs of the great change in his life in his love for his wife and his desolation over her death at thirty-three. I wanted to deal only with the first part of his life and especially with the thread of this love, and so I thought that it would be best to treat it fictionally, to cleave to all the facts that it was possible to uncover and to fill in the gaps with imagination. Though for several years I read poems, sermons, biographies and critiques, I was in the end impelled to put my notes away for two reasons: I wanted to go to England again before writing it, and I felt that I was in myself not yet ready, not mature enough. I had still too much unassimilated experience of my own.

The third book too I put aside, a book about a little-known episode in the American Revolution involving conscientious objectors to war, and I wrote instead a teen-age novel called *Sandy. Sandy* was a success. It won a Herald Tribune Spring Festival Award, it sold well and I had many enthusiastic letters about it; I saw it, much worn, on the adult fiction shelves in the Ernie Pyle Library in Tokyo; it was translated into several languages including Japanese; but for some reason not clear to me now I took a scunner against it. "How I loathe that book," I wrote in my diary.

On the first of March, 1945, I went to work for the American Friends Service Committee, thinking that I might be able to make some contribution to peace and reconciliation as the end of the war approached, secretly nourishing the hope that I might be sent on one of their projects overseas. Instead I became assistant to John Rich in the Publicity Department and spent fifteen months writing reports, articles, informative folders, appeals and occasionally letters. It was interesting and useful work and I enjoyed it, and enjoyed very much the people with whom I was in contact there: Rufus Jones, the Honorary Chairman; Henry J. Cadbury, the Chairman of the Committee; Clarence E. Pickett, the Executive Secretary; Mary Hoxie Jones, who was also one of the "Poets"; Frances Sandmel, a young Bryn Mawr graduate who worked with me in the Publicity Department, whose husband, Rabbi Samuel Sandmel, then a chaplain in the Pacific, has later written a number of fine books, *We Jews and Jesus* and others.

One of my early assignments was to write a pamphlet on the Service Committee's efforts to improve relations between Negroes and whites and to increase the opportunities open to Negroes. I called it *Some Quaker Approaches to the Race Problem,* and it dealt with two kinds of approaches. The Service Committee staff itself included a variety of races—Caucasians, Jews, Japanese, Negroes, Chinese—who worked together in harmony. The Work Camps, Summer Institutes and other projects also included as many members of other races as could be recruited. The Committee believed that the best climate for mutual understanding and friendship was not a conference on race relations as such but some enterprise in which all worked together for a common purpose. The other approach was the work that the Committee was actively engaged in to better the conditions of Negro life. One effort in this direction was to engage Negro professors who were eminent in their fields and send them to cooperating colleges to give a series of lectures on their own subjects, not on the race problem. In this way whites who had hitherto encountered Negroes only in menial positions could meet them as equals and receive what they had to give. One of several such lecturers was Ira Reid, the sociologist, who was so popular with the students at Haverford that he was offered a permanent professorship in the Sociology Department and thus became one of the first Negro faculty members in a white college in the Philadelphia area. The other work in which the Committee was involved at that time was done in connection with the Fair Employment Practice movement. A law barring discrimination was only a beginning; the Committee approached businessmen in Philadelphia, persuaded them to hire Negroes in stores, banks and offices where they had never worked before, and then found Negroes whose training and background were equal to the jobs. It all seems very simple, "token" and inadequate now, but it was actually a pioneering movement twenty-five years ago.

Another day of shock comparable to Pearl Harbor was August 6, 1945. That morning on my way to work I stopped to pick up a newspaper as usual to read on the train. Headlines all across the front of *The New York Times* shouted: FIRST ATOMIC BOMB DROPPED ON JAPAN. MISSILE IS EQUAL TO 20,000 TONS OF TNT. TRUMAN WARNS FOE OF A TRAIL OF RUIN. The utterly sick feeling that smote me like an actual blow in the stomach is with me still.

I knew immediately what it meant. In May, 1940, I had read William Lawrence's article in *The New York Times* in which he said, "A chunk of five to ten pounds of the new substance, a close relative of uranium and known as U-235, would drive an ocean liner or an ocean-going submarine for an indefinite period around the world without refuelling, for such a chunk would possess the power output of 25,000,000 to 50,000,000 pounds of coal or 15,000,000 to 30,000,000 pounds of gasoline." I had been dreading that the knowledge, so near at hand, of how to split the uranium atom would be reached and the weapon for which I knew that England, Germany, Russia and the United States were all frantically striving would be produced. I had expected it to come from Germany and to fall on England. Only the Nazis, I thought, would actually use it. And now the United States, my own country, which I loved, had dropped this appalling destruction without warning on a crowded Japanese city.

All day at the AFSC headquarters the wires were busy and people gathered in offices to talk. Clarence Pickett was away on vacation; John Rich was away. Board members were telephoning in. A letter was to be written to President Truman protesting the use of the bomb. I remember working on it; others improved and finished it.

In those first days after the use of the bomb all those whom I saw and talked with—not only my co-workers and friends but strangers on the trains—were sobered by the magnitude and the portent of the force that had been released. Norman Cousins's powerful article in the *Saturday Review* of August 18, "Modern Man Is Obsolete," expressed what most people were feeling. We had moved into an entirely new age. Modern man "must take the step from competitive man to cooperative man." He must make "the jump to world government." This mood of awe and of new purpose prevailed, however, for only a short time with many, perhaps most, people; they began to slip back into old ways of thinking, to say "they" would have used it if they had had it, to be openly thankful that we got it first. Six months later Elmer Davis wrote a review of a book called *One World or None* by a number of atomic scientists and titled his review "No World if Necessary."

A second bomb fell on Nagasaki, and after that the end of the war came quickly. Violet and I were having dinner with a friend at the Acorn Club. We were expecting every moment the final word that would end the war. The dining room was about half-full, the atmosphere was restless. There was no radio in the room, but whenever the door opened from the kitchen I could hear one going there, though no words could be heard. Then I saw the headwaiter come through the door looking excited; he walked purposefully to the closed piano that stood on one side of the room, put his hand on it, cleared his throat and seemed about to speak. I waited to hear him say, "Ladies and gentlemen, Japan has surrendered." But then, perceptibly, he lost his nerve. He opened his mouth and no words came. The next moment it was too late. The outburst of bells, horns and sirens beyond the windows told us what he had not been able to utter.

On September 2 the surrender document was signed on the *Missouri*; General MacArthur took up headquarters in Tokyo; the occupation of Japan began. Clarence Pickett asked me to write an open letter to President Truman and General MacArthur to go out over his name and to be released in the newspapers, urging that the occupation of Japan be undertaken in a spirit of reconciliation rather than revenge. I wrote:

"In your statement of the broad policies of occupation you have expressed a high-minded intention to develop a relationship between victor and vanquished based on justice and productive of a new and democratic life in the conquered nation. Upon the behavior of the rank and file of the occupying forces, however, hangs the success or failure of this great purpose. Though Japan stands today at the bar of judgment, in a deeper sense it is America that is on trial. We are the victors. We are a Christian nation. We are the exponents of a democratic way of life and we have set before the world the ideal of the Four Freedoms. Not only Japan, a nation sensitive to national humiliation to an extreme degree, but all the countries of the Eastern world will watch us now to see whether we manifest in our conduct those principles of justice, humanity and respect for the individual for which we have fought and sacrificed. We cannot afford to fail. . . . We of the American Friends Service Committee urge upon you a steadfast reiteration of the high principles which you have already set forth, a careful selection of emotionally mature and self-disciplined men to carry out the occupation and a determined insistence upon the exercise of courtesy and consideration, instead of ridicule and recrimination, in dealing with the defeated people."

Clarence Pickett signed the letter, and it went out at once. I haven't the least idea that the President or the General ever saw it, and certainly General MacArthur needed no advice along that line from me. Only three of the newspapers to which it was sent printed it, and it evoked from the public only a handful of replies, one of which, addressed to Clarence Pickett, began: "You skunk, you. . . ." Still, in view of my later relationship with Japan, I take satisfaction in having written that letter. It may also, for the fine threads of destiny are woven in strange patterns, have been a factor in Clarence Pickett's later feeling that I might be a suitable person to send to Japan to tutor the Crown Prince.

nne Moore Iszard at age three (1864)

Anne Iszard Gray in 1901,
the year before EGV was born

John Gordon Gray, c. 1918

The author aged five, at Cape May

Elizabeth Janet Gordon Gray at fourteen

Violet Gordon Gray
about the time of EGV's birth

Violet Gordon Gray in 1916

Morgan Vining, aged five

*Morgan Vining and the cockers
at Chapel Hill*

*Morgan Vining in 1933,
a few weeks before his death*

(Admiral)
Mr. Kotsunoshin
Yamanashi

A cold day in the classroom, Tokyo, 1946

The Crown Prince
and Princess Michiko
on their wedding day,
April 10, 1959

The Crown Prince's
boat the day of the
picnic at Hayama,
September, 1957
(left to right:
EGV, Prince Masahito,
Crown Prince, boatman)

The Crown Prince and EGV at 333 Mt. Airy Avenue, hiladelphia, September, 1953

Mrs. Shinzo Koizumi and her daughters Tae and Kayo in the room which she designed, March, 1956

Shinzo Koizumi

EGV and Tane Takahashi in the study of the Tokyo House, 1948

Hamish

EGV in the sitting room in Tokyo House, looking into parlor, 1948

EGV just before leaving for Japan,
September, 1946

EGV in the attic study at 333 Mt. Airy Avenue

Violet and Elizabeth in the living room at 333 Mt. Airy Avenue

* *PART* *III*.

✻✻✻✻✻✻✻✻✻✻✻✻✻✻✻✻✻✻✻✻✻✻✻✻✻

1.

The Appointment

I N THE fall of 1946 a quiet Philadelphia woman was suddenly picked up, transported halfway across the globe and dropped down again in the middle of the oldest, the most formal, the most mysterious court in the world, the court of Japan. I was that woman.

I have told the story in *Windows for the Crown Prince*, but not all of it and not as it fitted into the frame of my life, or rather, as it took apart and remade that frame. In that book I limited myself generally to what concerned the Crown Prince, whom I had gone to teach, and in *Return to Japan*, which followed eight years later, I wrote of some aspects of Japanese life which I had enjoyed and of the Crown Prince's wedding to Michiko Shoda, the exquisite girl, daughter of an industrialist, whom he loved and courted in a total break with at least a thousand years of tradition. There was not room in either book to write much about life in Tokyo under the proconsulship of General MacArthur seen, as I saw it, from the other side of the fence, or of my continuing relations with my Japanese friends in the nearly twenty years since I left there and the richness that the experience has brought into my life.

The question that immediately arises in people's minds is: How ever did it all happen in the first place? Or, in the form in which I have answered it thousands of times, How did you get the job? Sometimes, with a different emphasis, How did *you* get the job? Even many who have read *Windows* want to hear me tell the story again, hoping perhaps that some small detail, overlooked or omitted from the first telling, will cast a fresh light on this modern and international variation on the Cinderella story. I was not a teacher, not an expert on Japan, certainly not knowledgeable about royalty. Why should this extraordinary assignment have come to me?

I am going to tell it once more, and with some details that were left out of *Windows* because I did not then know them and some reflections that have come out of more than twenty years of thinking about it.

In the early spring of 1946 an Education Mission, consisting of twenty-seven American educators headed by Dr. George Stoddard, then Superintendent of Education in the State of New York, visited Japan "to advise and consult with General Headquarters and with Japanese educators on problems relating to education in Japan." Under the Occupation, the Civil Information and Education Section had already been set up and charged with the changing of the education system, which was considered to have lent itself to ultranationalistic propaganda and to have made the schools of Japan a tool of the militarists. It is not generally known, I think, that the Japanese themselves had asked for the help of such a group of experts. Mr. Tamon Maeda, who was Minister of Education following the war, told me in August, 1947, that he himself had proposed the mission, feeling that if Japan's educational system, which he considered in many respects sound and fitted to Japan's needs, was to be tampered with by outsiders, they should be directed by men of stature in the field, who would bring depth of experience and breadth of vision to the undertaking.

Mr. Maeda himself was subsequently "purged"; that is to say, dismissed from his post and forbidden to take any further part in work considered sensitive, such as education. This was a notable example of the many injustices of the purging process, which was done by the Japanese themselves under an Occupation directive, for Mr. Maeda, though he had been for a time during the 1930's head of the Japanese Information Agency in New York, stigmatized as a propaganda vehicle, was actually a distinguished scholar, a liberal, who had wide knowledge of and sympathy for Western thought; he had a great deal to give to the emerging democracy of Japan.

The Mission went to Japan on March 5 and stayed approximately a month. Among its members were George S. Counts, of Columbia University; Virginia Gildersleeve, president of Barnard; Mildred McAfee Horton, president of Wellesley; and Charles S. Johnson, president of Fisk University. They traveled to Kyoto and

Nara, to see the old Japan which had been by-passed by the war, worked with a corresponding committee of Japanese educators which included Miss Michi Kawai, headmistress and founder of Keisen School, and Miss Ai Hoshino, president of Tsuda College, as well as the president of Tokyo University and others, and on March 30 they filed a forward-looking and enlightened Report, in which there was no mention of their meeting with the Emperor.

On March 26 the Emperor gave a reception for the members of the Mission, in the middle of which he suddenly turned to Dr. Stoddard and asked him if he could find an American to tutor his son, the Crown Prince. Nobody expected this request, neither the Americans nor the Japanese men who were responsible for the education of the twelve-year-old Akihito. Although the Occupation was overhauling the Japanese system of education, it had kept its hands off the Crown Prince's affairs, which were in the care of a Council of distinguished Japanese scholars. Officially, that is to say. I have been told that earlier in the year, when it became evident that the Crown Prince would finish primary school in the spring and it was planned by his counselors to withdraw him from school and continue his education with private tutors, as had been done with his father, someone in the upper echelons of the Occupation had indicated to someone on the Japanese side that this plan was unacceptable to the Occupation, which preferred that the Crown Prince should have a more democratic education. The Middle School of the Peers' School, corresponding to grades seven, eight and nine in our terms, was then removed from the main campus in Tokyo and set up as a separate entity on the grounds of a former agricultural teachers' college in Koganei, one of Tokyo's western suburbs, and a small house was built there, with a high fence, for the Crown Prince to live in with his chamberlains while he attended school. There was also on the grounds a large and beautiful traditional Japanese building with a great thatched roof, which had been moved there after the celebration of the 2,600th anniversary of the dynasty in Tokyo some years earlier, and in which the Crown Prince was to have the special private lessons after school which would fit him for his future role in life. These included Poetry, Confucianism, and one hour a week of English conversation with Mr. Reginald H. Blyth, an Englishman long resident in Japan, a professor of English in the University of Tokyo and the Peers' School, and a well-known student of Zen Buddhism. So far as anybody knew, the Crown

Prince's educational path was well marked out for the next three years, after which it might be reviewed again.

It astonished everyone, then, when the Emperor made his unprecedented request. Dr. Stoddard, though taken by surprise, said he thought he could find such a person, and it was arranged that he should meet with the Emperor's representatives and discuss the details.

The meeting did not take place till a week later. There was a flurry of embarrassment because the Mission was billeted at the Imperial Hotel, which was "off limits" to all Japanese. Where could Dr. Stoddard receive with due honor the delegates from his Imperial Majesty? In the end, they met in his bedroom, and there they discussed the Emperor's requirements and Dr. Stoddard's ideas of the needs of the American tutor. One of the Japanese was Mr.—formerly Admiral—Katsunoshin Yamanashi, who was at that time president of the Peers' School and a key member of the Crown Prince's Council on Education. The other was Mr. Hidenari Terasaki, the former diplomat who interpreted for the Emperor in his meetings with General MacArthur.

The Emperor wished, Mr. Yamanashi reported, an American woman, aged fifty, "a Christian but not a fanatic." He did not want an old Japan hand but someone who came fresh to Japan; it was not necessary, not even desirable, that she speak Japanese; she would teach by the direct method in English. Since the Crown Prince went to school, she was to teach him in private lessons one hour a week, the same amount of time as Mr. Blyth.

Dr. Stoddard, after saying that he thought fifty too old and recommending that the age requirement be lowered, pointed out that an American woman who had only one hour a week of work would find time heavy on her hands, and it was granted, vaguely, that she might also "lecture" to the students of the Peers' School, and she could in addition do something for the Crown Prince's three sisters. Dr. Stoddard then entered into the arrangements for her living, as she would be entirely separate from the Occupation and would not be supported by it. It was agreed that she should have a house of her own, the necessary staff, a car in which to get to her teaching engagements, and a salary of two thousand dollars a year.

If the members of the Crown Prince's Council, who had not been consulted beforehand and were totally unenthusiastic about this plan, thought to stifle it at birth by the very limited opportunity they proposed for the invading American, they were markedly unsuccessful. The Emperor's request was big news. It was on the front page of *The New York Times* the next day and the subject of an editorial the following one. It caught the imagination of all Americans who heard about it because the ground had been well prepared by the best-selling book of 1943, Margaret Landon's *Anna and the King of Siam,* which had been derived from the diaries and letters of Anna Leonowens, a young English widow who went to Siam in 1862 to teach the children of the King and to whose influence were ascribed the democratic reforms of King Chulalongkorn, who had been her pupil, and of his successors. Everyone immediately entertained a vision of another Oriental despot influenced by another Western woman, happily this time an American, and the world changed for the better in consequence.

Dr. Stoddard, returning from Japan in April, told newsmen that he had been charged with the job of finding a "school marm" for the Crown Prince, and was immediately besieged by applicants.

I was not one of them. I read the brief account in the newspaper, thought casually, "How interesting! This may have a beneficial effect on the position of women in Japan," and dismissed it from my mind—until Thursday, May 23, when Samuel Marble, who as head of the Japan desk in the Service Committee was preparing a relief program for Japan, asked me if I would be willing to have my name suggested as tutor to the Crown Prince of Japan.

The idea seemed to me fantastic. I had no knowledge of Japan and little experience in teaching; I knew nothing at all about royalty. My resignation from my job with the AFSC was due to take effect on the first of June, and I had arranged to spend part of the summer at the MacDowell Colony in Peterborough, New Hampshire, working on a novel about the exiles in Virginia. My life was laid out in pleasant lines. I laughed and said no.

"Think it over," said Sam Marble, "at least over the week end."

I told Violet that evening, half jokingly, and found to my surprise that she took it seriously; indeed, that she considered it highly probable that if I did allow my name to be submitted I would get the post. She did not like the idea at all, and her solution was to put an end to it before it began, by saying no again to Sam Marble and more firmly.

Two or three days later I talked with Esther Rhoads, who was

also working for the AFSC at the time, preparing to go to Japan
as soon as the relief program got under way. Esther was a birth-
right Friend, a member of Germantown Meeting, the daughter
of a physician beloved throughout Germantown, and a great-
niece of James Rhoads, the founder of Bryn Mawr College. A
graduate of Earlham College in Indiana, she had gone to Japan
in her early twenties as a Quaker missionary, had taught for many
years in the Friends Girls School in Tokyo, where she had been
greatly loved. Brought home by the threat of war in 1941, she
had been employed by the AFSC to help the Japanese-Americans
on the West Coast who were uprooted from their homes and
thrust into concentration camps euphemistically called Relocation
Centers. It seemed to me that if any Quaker name was suggested,
it ought to be Esther's, and I said so. She replied that they did not
want an old Japan hand or a missionary, and that anyhow she
had her work laid out before her. She urged me to make myself
available.

As I thought it over, it seemed to me utterly extraordinary that
the Emperor of Japan, after a war so bitterly fought, should want
a representative of the nation that had defeated Japan for the
first time in her history to teach his son; it seemed to me something new in the world, something hopeful. I thought that here
was an unprecedented opportunity to work for reconciliation now
and for peace in the future. I had wanted to serve, had I not?
Had I not for the past fifteen months, sitting in the meeting for
worship held for the staff at 8:45 in the mornings in the old meetinghouse, said within myself, day after day, "Here I am, Lord, use
me if Thou wilt"? Was I now being taken at my word in a startling way? I decided that I could not refuse to have my name
suggested but that I would not lift a finger to get the job. It
must seek me, not I it. If sometimes, looking back, I have wondered if I was oversolemn and high-flown in thinking of myself
as thus tapped on the shoulder by destiny, I have been comforted
by Martin Buber's saying: "The free man believes in destiny and
that it has need of him."

On May 28 Clarence Pickett wrote to Dr. Stoddard:

"I am informed that you are looking for someone to serve as
tutor to the son of the Japanese Emperor. I am happy to suggest
Elizabeth Gray Vining, who is now a member of our staff."

He then listed briefly my education, travel, books, and personal
characteristics, finishing:

"I have mentioned this matter to her and she says that of course it is a complete surprise to her to think in these terms since she had in mind withdrawing from our staff to do some further writing in the near future. Also she insists that she would not lift a finger to seek the appointment, but I think she would be willing to consider it if, knowing as much as it is possible to know about her, there was a united judgment that she would be useful in that capacity. If you think she is worth considering I should hope that she might go to Albany and have a talk with you."

Dr. Stoddard replied by return mail:

"While there has been a flood of candidates there are only two or three that seem to be above all others and I am sure that Mrs. Vining would fall into this category. I had counted on interviewing two or three persons only and I should be happy to talk to Mrs. Vining."

So on June 6 I found myself sitting in his large, airy office with the light on my face, while he sat as interviewers do with his back to the window. Part of the time he looked keenly at me, part of the time he sat with his eyes closed, listening, evidently, to my voice.

He impressed me as a gentle, thoughtful man, quietly strong and without pretense, and I felt entirely at ease with him. We talked very frankly. He asked me, I remember, if I thought I could endure the drudgery of teaching English to a small boy and I answered, "I don't know. I've never tried it." I pointed out my meager experience in teaching. I remember telling him that I thought I was too tall to go among the smaller Japanese. He said, "No, they'd be impressed." I said, "More likely *de*pressed, I should think."

I asked him if there would be so much resentment against the American teacher that she would be hampered in teaching the boy, and he replied quickly that the Mission had met only kindness, openness and cooperation on the part of the Japanese. We discussed what has been generally so surprising to Americans, the Japanese lack of bitterness and their readiness to put the war behind them and enter into a new relationship. I asked him if I would be a prisoner in the Palace, imagining as I did the Palace to be a large, luxurious building where the Imperial family all lived together, with quarters in distant wings for such functionaries as tutors and the like. I had absolutely no conception of the widely scattered, small and makeshift dwellings where the members of the family who were once the world's richest were actually living.

Dr. Stoddard assured me that I would have a house of my own, and that, since supplies were still short in postwar Tokyo, I would have by courtesy PX and Commissary privileges.

I raised the point that it was a very long way to go for one hour a week with the Crown Prince, and he said he thought it would be increased after I got there, as of course it was, and that anyhow there were also the Peers' School and the princesses. He cautioned me that an American woman in this position would be in great demand for speeches and public appearances of all kinds, especially by women's groups, and that I would have to keep reminding myself that my real work was to teach English to one small boy.

Then he asked me if I could give him the names of three or four people whom he could ask about me, especially naming Rufus Jones, and I said I was sure that Rufus Jones would be willing. I gave him also the names of Howard Brinton, director of Pendle Hill, and of Stanley R. Yarnall, the former headmaster of the Germantown Friends School. Then I went home and wrote to all of them to tell what I had done, urging them if they had any doubts at all about my ability to undertake such a responsibility, please to say so entirely frankly; for if the offer came, I should consider that it was intended that I should go and I would accept it.

Two or three years later in Japan I saw the folder with the letters that my trusting friends wrote about me, but I did not copy them. Perhaps more interesting is what they wrote to me in answer to my letters to them. I have already quoted in *Windows* from Rufus Jones's letter. Howard Brinton's is notable more for what he wrote about Quakers and Japan.

Dear Elizabeth:
Your extraordinary, astonishing but most welcome letter of June 7 has been read, I need hardly say, with the greatest interest and approval. If I hear from Dr. Stoddard I shall write him the most enthusiastic and laudatory letter that I can compose. To have you molding the character of the future emperor of Japan would be a happening almost better than we have any right to hope for.

I have been feeling for some time that the Quakers have an extraordinary opportunity in Japan if they are able and willing to use it.

What I have learned of the Japanese character leads me to believe that they are unusually susceptible to our ideas. This conviction came to me long ago at Haverford College where one of my most intimate friends was the man who was to become one of the greatest Japanese novelists, Arashima. He was one of the best Quakers I have ever known. I am not suggesting that you make a Quaker out of the Crown Prince. Perhaps your adventures will be more like those of Anna of Siam.

Your letter has simply started me again to wondering how in the future in Japan we could avoid the conventional missionary emphasis which has prevailed in the past and launch out into something new and better.

Sincerely yours,

Howard

On June 19 Dr. Stoddard wrote me that he was sending my name and one other to Japan, for the Imperial Household to make the final choice. After that, silence. I canceled, without giving a reason, my reservation at the MacDowell Colony; in July Violet and I went to Burpee Hill. She was by now reconciled to the thought of my going to Japan and I had begun to hope that the opportunity might come, but still both of us would have been entirely contented if the matter had stopped right there. During those days I read *Anna and the King of Siam* for the first time, as well as *Twilight in the Forbidden City*, by Reginald F. Johnston, the Englishman who in the early 1920's tutored the Manchu prince later notorious as the Japanese puppet, Henry Pu Yi—not an encouraging book.

Years later I have been able, from the bits that people have told me, to piece together a picture of what was happening in Japan during the more than four months that elapsed between the Emperor's bombshell and the cable that finally came to Dr. Stoddard on August 4 and was telephoned by him to me saying, "The Imperial Household has decided on Vining (repeat) Vining."

In 1957, when I was in Japan for the P.E.N. Congress, Mr. Yamanashi came to see me and told me the whole story from the Japanese point of view. Many times before that he had told me parts of it, but now he was past eighty, we neither of us had any connection with the Imperial Household, and he wanted me to know it all.

He had become one of my best friends in Japan, Mr. Yamanashi—in Japan or anywhere else. He was one of the finest and most lovable men I have ever known. In *Return to Japan* I devoted a chapter to him, which I called "The Last Samurai." He had all the qualities of the ideal samurai: courage, a stern sense of duty, loyalty, truthfulness, love of beauty, an ascetic grace of living in the face of poverty, kindness, dignity. In addition he had a Navy man's experience of great spaces and broadening knowledge of other lands, other navies, other ways of life and thought, which the land-bound warrior seldom has and without which he is blind and fatally prone to hubris. Mr. Yamanashi was a man of peace, and his opposition to the militarists terminated a distinguished naval career in 1933, when he was removed from the active list. Six years later he was made president of the Peers' School, which was then under the direction of the Imperial Household, a school for the sons of peers, princes and courtiers, and a few privileged commoners. (Since the war it has been an ordinary private school, open to all who can pass the examinations and pay the fees.) It was an indication of the attitude of the Imperial Household toward the pressure of the militarists that it should have appointed as president of the Peers' School a man known to be opposed to war.

Mr. Yamanashi always prefaced his talks with me about my appointment by declaring that no one had any idea that it would turn out so well. When the plan was first broached, he and the others around the Crown Prince felt that there were too many dangers inherent in the situation. In spite of the fact that it was His Majesty's own idea, "we met it," he said, "with a gentle passivity." In his book, *The Western World and Japan*, Sir George Sansom commented that the Japanese were "masters of evasion and delay." I was fascinated to find this most devoted and loyal subject using tactics of evasion and delay even with his own Emperor. Mr. Yamanashi went on to say that His Majesty persisted; Mr. Yamanashi went to talk with Dr. Stoddard at the Imperial Hotel, and the headlines followed.

During the two months and more in which nothing came from Dr. Stoddard, they must have felt that it had all happily died away, but near the end of June the dossiers of the two candidates arrived, transmitted through the Education Section of the Occupation, because at that time no one was permitted to write more than a postcard directly to the Japanese. On Mr. Yamanashi fell the responsibility for making the final choice.

He himself decided on me from the beginning on the grounds that I had traveled in England and Scotland, countries which he himself loved, and that I had had sorrow in my life. "I said," he told me, "she knows the world, she knows life and she knows people." But he did not rely on his own judgment alone; he consulted many others: the chamberlains; the other members of the Crown Prince's Council; Mr. Blyth, whom he liked and trusted and who was of the opinion that any American woman who would seek such a job must be out for sensation and publicity; and Mr. Setsuzo Sawada, a member of the Society of Friends in Japan, who had traveled with the Emperor when as Crown Prince he made a trip to Europe. He consulted the Terasakis too.

Gwen Terasaki was an American. She had grown up in Johnson City, Tennessee, and she had met Hidenari Terasaki in Washington in 1930 when she was a young girl visiting her aunt and he was press secretary to the Japanese Embassy. They had fallen in love and had married in the teeth of opposition from both sides. Years of consular duty followed in Cuba and in Shanghai, until 1941 when they were back again in Washington with their little daughter Mariko, striving with all their heart and soul to improve Japanese-American relations. Gwen Terasaki has written in her beautiful book, *Bridge to the Sun*, about that harrowing time, and about Terry's attempt, at great personal risk, to get a letter from President Roosevelt through to the Emperor, an effort which was frustrated by Tojo in Tokyo. Pearl Harbor, coming as it did while this letter was still being held up in Tojo's office, was the most hideous shock to them, as to others in the Japanese Embassy.

When the *Gripsholm* took the Japanese diplomats caught in the United States back to Japan in June, 1942, Gwen and Mariko accompanied Terry, to spend the war with him in Japan. Stigmatized as pro-American, Terry had no post during the war. They were evacuated to the country after the bombing of Tokyo began and all but starved before at last peace came. Then all those Japanese who spoke English well and who were known to be pro-Western were called back to service. To Terry fell the responsibility and privilege of interpreting for the Emperor in his meetings with General MacArthur. The Terasakis, both unusually attractive, warm, intelligent and delightful people, had many friends among the Americans; a distant cousin of Gwen's, General Bonner Fellers, was then one of General MacArthur's aides.

Terry was ill and away from Tokyo when the material about the two candidates for tutor to the Crown Prince arrived at his house. Gwen read them and sent them on to him, with a comment in a letter of her own to him, from which she has given me permission to quote. It was dated July 8, 1946, and I saw it for the first time in May, 1968.

> About the tutor for Crown Prince. I am sure Mrs. Vining the Quaker will be the best. Her recommendations are perfect and I can almost see her character between the lines. And as you know the Quakers are people of broad vision and great tolerance and I shall be proud of her type of American for the little prince. She has travelled extensively and besides that she has known personal tragedy and I am sure she will understand in her quiet way sorrow of others. And the Quakers hate war and always have. So I am in favor of her 100%. I sincerely like the tone of Dr. Stoddard's letter. He, himself must be a man of superior judgment. As you know, this tutoring of the Crown Prince by an American woman lies very close to my heart and I am so happy to see my dream materialized.

The Emperor too saw the credentials, but he did not give an opinion. When Mr. Yamanashi went to him and in a private session told him the decision, which Mr. Yamanashi assured me was unanimous, His Magesty indicated that this was what he himself had thought but that he had not felt free to say so until after the decision had been reached—which I found very enlightening. When the Emperor delegates a decision, he does not thereafter tip the scales in any way.

Some Americans also saw the dossiers, but they too refrained from giving an opinion. Almost certainly the head of the Education Section must have seen them; two at least of General MacArthur's aides saw them, General Fellers and Colonel Laurence Bunker. I take it that General MacArthur also did or else knew the gist of them, for he had his finger on everything that went on. He, however, like Mr. Yamanashi and the chamberlains, was unenthusiastic about the whole idea. He told me, when I much later met him, that he considered it "a very dubious affair," and one of his first questions to me was whether or not I thought that my appointment was "a cynical political move" on the part of the Japanese to persuade the Occupation that they were more eager to learn democracy than they actually were. I answered, of course, that I was certain that it was not, but I found the question itself very reassuring in one way, for it offered further proof that the idea of the American tutor was not imposed by the Occupation but did indeed proceed from the Japanese themselves.

The choice of the tutor was duly reported to the Education Section, whose duty it was to transmit the information to Dr. Stoddard. Here evidently another bit of evasion and delay went on, or perhaps only genuine indifference, for one of the officers later told me that after the memorandum had been lying around the office for quite a while, someone said, "Hey, we'd better notify Dr. Stoddard." Someone sent the cable quoted above.

When he told me the news over the telephone on August 7, Dr. Stoddard cautioned me to keep silent about it until the Japanese themselves made an announcement. Three weeks later, when we and some friends were sitting around the open fire in our cottage one chilly evening, a messenger from the farmhouse arrived, saying breathlessly, "The Associated Press in Boston wants to speak to Mrs. Vining!" As I ran across the dark lawn to the telephone, I thought, "Here it comes!"

The voice at the other end of the wire asked me if it was true I had been appointed tutor to the Crown Prince of Japan. I asked cautiously what was the source of their information, and the voice replied, "The U.S. State Department." Up to this point there had been no mention of the State Department, and so far as I knew they had had no hand in it whatsoever, though no doubt they or the FBI must have been busily investigating me. On what grounds they took the announcement away from the Japanese, I do not know, but I regretted it, then and later. The fact that the appointment was announced by the State Department implied that the American tutor was imposed on the Japanese by the United States Government. Most Japanese believed this to be the case, and most Americans too, though I have done my best during the years to make it clear that it was the Emperor's own idea and that I would not have even considered the job if it had been a political device for indoctrinating the Japanese.

To the Army fell the task of getting me there, for in those days nobody went to Japan unless the Army took them. I had expected to fly, for Esther Rhoads had already been flown by the Army to Tokyo to represent the AFSC in the combined Protestant, Catholic and Quaker relief agency known as LARA (Licensed Agencies for Relief in Asia.) I was relegated, however, to the *Marine Falcon*, a former troopship which was crowded with U.S. Army dependents, missionaries returning to Japan, American and Canadian Japanese who wished to be repatriated, and a few odd characters like myself who did not fit into any of these categories. After being delayed for a week in Seattle by a strike, we embarked on October 1 and reached Japan two weeks later.

2.

My Household in Tokyo

A<small>NNA</small> L<small>EONOWENS</small> was promised a house of her own, but when she got to Bangkok she found herself quartered in one of the palaces among the ladies of the harem; a large part of her story, as Margaret Landon told it, was her struggle to hold the King to his promises and get a house where she and her son could live in privacy and freedom. My story, in this as in other ways, was entirely different. A very pleasant house was carefully and generously prepared for me and ready when I arrived there.

I say generously, because what I had was so much more spacious and more comfortable than anything that the Japanese had at that time. All of the Western-style houses that escaped destruction were commandeered for Occupation families; it had been necessary to get one of these released for me, and the responsibility of selection had fallen on Mr. Yamanashi.

Though he had been doubtful about the American tutor, characteristically he did his utmost (once the decision was made) to make his Emperor's project a success. Seeking the advice of trusted Westerners, Gwen Terasaki, Esther Rhoads and Mr. Blyth, he selected a house and had it put in order. His first consideration had been the neighborhood: it must be near the Gakushuin (the word means Institute of Learning but has been translated as Peers' School), where he was then living in the president's house, so that in case I should be attacked by a Japanese fanatic, he could come to the rescue. It was Esther Rhoads who reported this to me, and we both found it lovable and touching, for though Mr. Yamanashi had been an admiral and was brave as a lion, he was nearly seventy at that time and not much bigger than a mouse.

The house he chose for me was situated in a hilly section of

Tokyo that had formerly been the daimyo's hunting ground; it
was one of a cluster of Western-style houses, each with trees and
gardens; across the narrow lane from it was a little wooded ravine
with a small, sluggish stream at the bottom. Chinese bamboo
pheasants lived there and in the early mornings I would hear
their harsh cry, which the Japanese describe as "Chotto koi!" but
which sounded to me like "Paper weight! Paper weight!"

The slight bomb damage which the house had suffered had been
repaired, the walls inside washed with cream-colored paint, and
furniture brought from the Akasaka Palace. The living room and
dining room, which faced south, opened onto a terrace and a
garden with a bit of lawn and a pool, enclosed by shrubbery and a
bamboo fence.

The house had certain infirmities; sometimes the coal for the
furnace failed to come or the furnace itself was out of order; there
was never any hot water in the pipes and occasionally even
the cold water did not run because the pressure was insufficient or
the electric motor which ran the supplementary pump was stolen.
But at a time when electricity throughout the city was very low
and most Japanese houses were limited to a single 40-Watt bulb,
and students rode around and around Tokyo in the electric trains
to study in the dim overhead light, we always had sufficient light.

The garden was a joy. We had something for every season: plum
blossoms in late January, camellias in February, Japanese quince
in March, then daphne, cherry blossoms, azaleas, mountain kerria
through the spring, London pride and morning glories and zinnias in the summer, and in the fall sweet olive and sazanka. In the
fall of 1947 the Empress sent a gardener to plant bulbs, and the
next May we had a bed of tall, swinging tulips that brought
people from round about to stand outside the fence and peer
through the bushes, exclaiming at their beauty.

In the cold months from December to March we often had
"frost pillars," little rods of rime two inches or more high standing
like small, white organ pipes in the shady places. Ice would form
on the surface of the pool, and once an earthquake at night broke
it up and heaved it out, so that in the morning we saw it scattered like pieces of glass on the ground. Occasionally two or three
inches of snow made a fairyland there, but before the day was over
it had all melted.

When the goldfish man began to come around, as normal life
resumed after the war, I enjoyed going out to his pushcart with its

swaying tanks and picking out fish for the pool, red ones with flaring tails and fins like kimono sleeves or sooty black ones or pale silver ones. Once as we sat at lunch in the dining room with the French doors open onto the terrace, we saw a kingfisher, small, red-breasted, blue-backed, like the European kingfisher, swoop down over the pool and scoop up one after another the fish I had just bought.

Because of the little stream and wooded slope across the lane from us, birds came to our garden that you would not expect to see in a city. In March I have heard the *uguisu* singing in the shrubbery, that small, drab-colored bird with the heavenly voice that figures so largely in Japanese poetry and art. The name is sometimes translated as nightingale, but nightingale it is not; bush warbler, though less romantic, is more accurate, for it does warble in the bushes. We had great tits, like chickadees; brown-eared bulbuls, and green finches. Black and white wagtails came to teeter on the edge of the pool. In October whole flocks of brilliant blue long-tailed magpies would descend upon our few persimmons, making a dramatic contrast in color, and all year round on the lawn, probing for grubs, running under the bushes, squawking in the trees, were *mukudori*, a kind of starling rather like the myna bird of Hawaii, a clown among birds.

When I think of the garden, I think also of the roof, a flat roof with a parapet and a wide, wide view. To the west over the treetops we could see on clear days the range of the Hakone Mountains sixty miles away and above them Fuji-san. (The *San* in this case does not mean "honorable"; it means "mountain," another reading of the character for *yama*. The Japanese never say "Fuji-yama"; on the other hand, they do not say "Asama San" for the volcano near Karuizawa—they say "Asamayama." It is perhaps a matter of euphony—and perhaps also they see a pun, or double meaning, in *San* as applied to Fuji.) In the summer Fuji was not often to be seen because the air was thick with mist and dust, but in the autumn it would appear again, deep blue, then blue ribbed with white, then all white, dazzling in the sun. If it was very cold and very clear, the Chichibu Mountains to the north would come into sight, etched in white against the blue sky.

In the other direction was the swathe of burnt-over barren ground between our house and the Mejiro main street. Farther away was the sinister gray block of Sugamo Prison, where the war criminals awaited the verdict of the International Military Tribunal. At night we could often see the "flowers of Tokyo" glowing red here and there, the fires that because of the inveterate casualness of the Japanese about cigarettes and gasoline and wood shavings sprang up to devour the newly built shacks and shops.

I did not live in my house alone. I had a staff.

Besides finding the house, Mr. Yamanashi had found for me my secretary, Tane Takahashi. From the first moment when, tired and confused, I landed in the dark at Yokohama, was introduced to welcoming officials and at last sank into the waiting car to hear a soft voice beside me say, "I am Tane; I am to be your secretary and interpreter," I knew that here was someone whom I could safely trust and love. I knew too that whoever had gone to the trouble of finding her for me had wanted the venture to succeed.

Tane was twenty-nine in 1946, a Quaker who had studied at Western Maryland College and at Pendle Hill, where I might have met her if I had not been at the time much confined at home by the illness of my mother. Mr. Yamanashi had learned about Tane when he went to his old friend, the Reverend Fumio Kozaki, pastor of a Presbyterian church in Tokyo, for advice. Tane's family were members of his congregation, as Tane herself had been before she joined Friends in Washington, D.C.

Tane belonged to a liberal family of distinction. An uncle had been a well-known historian and president of a university, from which before the war he had been hounded into resigning because in one of his books he had referred to the myth of the Emperor's divine origin. Her father had studied at Princeton in Woodrow Wilson's day, and Wilson had taken especial interest in him and steered him toward a political career. He became a member of the Japanese Diet, and in 1920, when Japan was watching anxiously the forces in California beginning to press for the Oriental Exclusion Act, Mr. Takahashi was sent to the United States to plead with President Wilson to use any influence he still had to prevent the passage of the bill. He arrived in Seattle after a cold, rough crossing, was stricken with pneumonia and died in three days. Tane was then three years old.

She went to Keisen School, a private girls' school founded by Michi Kawai, a Bryn Mawr graduate and a leader in the Japanese Y.W.C.A., and from there she received a scholarship to Western Maryland College. She was at Pendle Hill at the time of Pearl Harbor and stayed there until June, 1942, when with several hundred other Japanese she was repatriated on the *Gripsholm*, the same ship that took the Terasakis back to Japan. I used to think that the *Gripsholm* must have been of limitless capacity, like the *Mayflower*, for wherever we went in Tokyo, it seemed, Tane would point out someone whom she had known on the *Gripsholm*. It was certainly a crowded ship, from the diplomats on A deck to the students jammed in the depths of the steerage.

During the next four years Tane taught English at Keisen and lived through the bombing of Tokyo. During the last years of the war when the Japanese were desperately short of manpower, the schools became factories in which students made many of the small parts needed in airplanes or munitions. Tane, who had come home from the United States imbued not only with the Quaker attitude toward war but a love for America, feared that her school too would be forced into munitions-making and wondered how she could avoid taking any part in it, but in the event she was put in charge of a class whose work was to launder soldiers' clothing This she felt she could conscientiously and compassionately do. Each day she went with her girls to the laundry; they had one hour in the morning for the study of English and she had them keep diaries in English in which they wrote freely all their thoughts and feelings.

Three days after her return from the United States she was summoned to appear before the Kempetai, the dreaded military police, for questioning. Her elder sisters felt keenly the disgrace of such a summons and would have concealed it, but Tane, incurably honest, made no secret of where she was going, even to the point of asking directions on the street to the Kempetai Building. She found the questioning, she told me, rather interesting. They could not make her say anything derogatory about the United States. "I met only kindness there," she reiterated. They told her not to teach so long as she had any "pacifist inklings" in her heart. When she asked Miss Kawai what she should do, Miss Kawai laughed and told her to ignore it. She was summoned to two more interviews by the Kempetai, and after the last one she told her interrogators that there were so many things that she did not understand in Japan that she might come back some day to ask them some questions. She must have been very disarming in her youth and honesty—and her beauty, for she was lovely to look at then and now.

Miss Kawai was aghast when Tane resigned from Keisen to work for the American tutor. She gave Mr. Yamanashi a bad time about it, and that otherwise intrepid man always spoke of Keisen's head with an awe I never saw him show toward anyone else. Many of Tane's friends warned her against the pitfalls and dangers she was letting herself in for, but she was serenely confident that it was going to be all right.

She was much more than my secretary and interpreter, or perhaps I should say that she was my interpreter in the highest sense. She did not merely translate my words to the Japanese and theirs to me, but she interpreted me to Japan—my ideas, my purposes, my hopes—and she gave me an understanding of Japan that I could not otherwise have got, not even through years of study and of travel. She guided my footsteps, especially in the early days, in the most unobtrusive way possible. I know that she forestalled many a misunderstanding on both sides, prevented me from making mistakes that I might have made through ignorance. She went with me everywhere, waiting in palace and school waiting rooms while I did my teaching, talking with chamberlains and teachers, picking up useful information for me, explaining to them what was in my mind and why I did some things that seemed to them eccentric at the least. She waited on me and took care of me in the inimitable, tactful, imaginative way of the Japanese woman. Honest as the daylight, serene, gay, intuitive and generous, she was an ideal companion, and I very soon came to love her as a younger sister. It was then that I discovered that when once you really love a person of another race, race as such ceases to raise any barrier: the people of all races become individuals, to be liked or disliked solely on the basis of character and personality. This, I have found, holds true for the black as well as the yellow race.

In our own house Tane was the liaison and interpreter between the Inoues and me. When Mr. Yamanashi had given her the task of finding a housekeeper, she had turned to Mrs. Inoue, whom she knew through Keisen. Mrs. Inoue was a woman of good family who had made—or rather, had had made for her—an unfortunate marriage. Her husband periodically deserted her, returning at intervals to father another child. When they numbered ten (of whom five were to survive, a boy and four girls), he departed permanently and subsequently died. She supported her family by cooking for missionaries, and her two youngest daughters went to Keisen School, where they had been Tane's students.

As the staff was originally set up, Mrs. Inoue was cook-housekeeper; Michiko San, the youngest daughter, nineteen, was house-maid. Yukio San, the son, who had a government job, lived in the house as male protector and furnace tender. They had two rooms on the ground floor at the back of the house. The other daughters had jobs, as kindergarten teacher, as helper in a missionary family, as seamstress. But housing in Tokyo at that time was almost incredibly difficult to find. Soon Aiko San was forced out of her lodging to make room for someone who had a greater claim on her landlord. So the northwest room on the second floor, which we did not use, a tatami-floored room with a "god-shelf," became Aiko San's bedroom and workroom. She brought her sewing machine and made dresses in that room—some of them for me. Masako San's kindergarten folded up, and she came to us. Kiyoko San, the eldest, was a frequent visitor until she developed tuberculosis and went into a hospital for an operation and long convalescence.

Mrs. Inoue must have been then only in her sixties, though she seemed older, a small, gray-haired little figure in a gray kimono, wise and good. Missionary-trained, she cooked Western food better than she did Japanese; our meals were wholesome and well-prepared; she was especially good with soups made of left-overs. She had old-fashioned high standards of behavior, and I used to think she was overstrict with pretty young Michiko San.

It was a dear family and a fragile one. Like so many Japanese of the period, they suffered from the effects of malnutrition and exposure during the war. The scourge of tuberculosis swept the country; almost every family I knew had at least one member who was "resting." Kiyoko San was the first to go down; Aiko San came next with what was called pleurisy, for which she was hospitalized for a year or so. Mrs. Inoue was ill for months with an intestinal ailment which was first feared to be cancer and later was diagnosed as tubercular. I was worried about the danger to the Imperial children who came to the house every week and I asked the advice of the Crown Prince's doctor. He examined Mrs. Inoue and assured me that he saw no danger; he was justified in the outcome.

There was one other member of our staff, who did not live in the house, our chauffeur. The first one we had proved unsatisfactory, for his real interest lay in business. After, to our mutual relief, he departed, he became proprietor of a public bath and prospered greatly. The Imperial Household then provided me with Takenaka San, a handsome young man and a skilful driver, thoughtful, cheerful and obliging. Unlike the first man, who would do nothing at all that he did not consider his work—not even open the wooden gates at the end of the driveway in the morning—Takenaka San was willing to lend a hand in the house in time of stress. When the Crown Prince visited us in Karuizawa one summer, Takenaka San was an invaluable help.

Undergirding the structure of our house was the Imperial Household. Whenever we needed anything, whenever we had a problem large or small, we telephoned the Palace.

The Imperial Household Agency, in prewar days one of the ministries of the government, occupied a large, formal building near the most generally used of the eight gates to the Palace grounds. After the burning of the Palace itself during the war, the Emperor had his study in this building and the Empress a large room in which she had her various lessons. There were also audience chambers, reception rooms, waiting rooms, and the offices of the Grand Steward and other high officials. Besides these, there were whole wings of business offices, where heads of departments directed the work of a band of clerks and secretaries. Besides the Board of Ceremonies and the Department of Poetry, there were eight or nine other departments dealing with the daily life of the Imperial Family and all that it involved: cars, furniture, houses, commissariat, and so on and on. Some of these offices had me for their responsibility as well.

When the motor was stolen, we telephoned the Palace. When we were having a dinner party involving royalty and diplomats— as occasionally we did—we telephoned the Palace for advice on the seating arrangements. When anything went wrong with car or driver, we telephoned the Palace. When the spout came off the silver teapot, we telephoned the Palace. Every summer when we went to Karuizawa, the Palace sent a truck and five men to pack up and transport our effects. Once a year I gave a thank-you party for the heads of the departments who were so kind to us. I used to wonder sometimes what I should do when I went back to the United States and there was no one to care whether my furnace ran or to do anything about it if it did not.

At the highest level, too, we had delightfully homely relations with the Palace. Over the years there was a steady stream of neighborly gifts arriving at the house on Her Majesty's thoughtful suggestion, from the orchids and roast beef that were sent to welcome me on the evening of my arrival to the traditional elaborate, rare, ceremonial meal in special lacquer boxes that was sent just before my departure in 1950. A basket of fresh vegetables, a box of trout packed in ferns and ice, a case of canned peaches, a box of ripe tomatoes, large and perfect, a basket of live lobsters: in a time of scarcity these were in every sense of the word royal gifts. Once the Emperor himself sent me a basket of *baramonjin*, an Indian vegetable that he took an interest in growing, a sort of cross between spinach and hay, quite good, and once I sent him four bananas, which a friend flying in from Hawaii had brought me and which were, I was told, the first bananas His Majesty had had since quite early in the war.

All around this house, where there was so much comfort and plenty, stretched the enormous ruined and hungry city. Tokyo had been 70 per cent destroyed by American bombs, not by a single one as Hiroshima had been, but by thousands. The greatest air raids had come in March and May of 1945, when the deadly napalm had sent sheets of fire raging through the wooden city. Everybody kept ready in their houses a small bag with valuables and a kettle with water and a towel which, dampened, they would hold before their faces as they struggled through the smoke and flames. Mrs. Tsuneo Matsudaira, the wife of the former Japanese ambassador to the United States and Britain, told me how frightened her maids had been in an air raid and how she had said to them, "Come with me. I will lead you to peace." She had meant, to the peace of death, but in a nearby park under pine trees they had huddled through the night and in the morning returned, alive, to find the house gone.

Beyond the corner of our lane, where once had been prosperous houses, there was nothing but rubble and ashes, out of which reared up here and there a part of a wall, a burned-out safe, some twisted bits of iron, a small stone storehouse. At the corner of the main street were three stores, hastily built wooden sheds with one side open to the street: a *geta* shop, which did a thriving business in wooden clogs, for leather shoes were not to be bought anywhere; a workshop where an old man made wooden bathtubs; and a food store with almost no food, only little saucers containing two or three onions and a few pickles, some piles of *daikon*, the giant white radishes, and occasionally a few eggs which sold for the equivalent of forty-five cents apiece.

Farther up the main street long lines of patient people waited for the meager ration (1,500 calories a day), which was often late. Once, outside the ration shop, where a little rice had been spilled on the muddy walk, I saw an old woman picking up the precious grains one by one with a pair of tweezers. People went out into the country in incredibly crowded trains and returned with sacks of sweet potatoes on their backs, for which they had exchanged family treasures kept through the war. They called this kind of existence "the Onion life," for as you peeled off the layers tears came to your eyes.

I watched the first new house in our neighborhood being built on a large lot on a corner that I passed each day. There were the remains of a wall around the place, and through the gaps in it we could see the lot being cleaned of its debris and then the arrival of raw, unseasoned lumber—not very much of it either, for the regulations forbade building a house larger than 15 tsubo, which meant a cabin of about 12 by 15 feet. The house was built rather quickly, an oblong box with tar-paper roof instead of the traditional black tiles. One day, coming home late on a rainy afternoon, we saw that the family had moved in. That day I had got a large food package from friends at home, and among the boxes was a tin of peanut brittle. I sent it over to the new house, with a note of welcome. The next day the woman of the house came to call, to thank me and to tell me her story. They had been evacuated from Tokyo with all their goods into the country, but had been three times burned out, losing everything and ending up in the crowded house of relatives. Her husband's company had offered to rebuild their Tokyo house if he would return to work. The wife had not seen the house in progress; she had looked forward eagerly to going home, expecting unrealistically to find something like their original lovely house. They came, on that dismal rainy day, to find this small, crude shack. She had been in despair. The arrival of the candy, she said, lifted her heart immeasurably: it was not only the sweets themselves—and they had not tasted sugar for several years—but the friendly message. She went to sleep thinking that they were fortunate to be back in Tokyo on any terms and that things would get better. With that invincible Japanese feeling that a gift must be immediately repaid, she brought me some cakes that she had made in the shape of roses out of mashed sweet potatoes.

The incident of the house and the family I used as the basis of a book that I wrote later, omitting the foreigner's gift of candy and providing the family with children, a grandfather and a dog. I called it *The Cheerful Heart*.

The daily sight of vast, indiscriminate destruction, the knowledge of great numbers of people exhausted by the war and, many of them, by grief for members of their family killed, struggling to find food for their children, to wash their clothes in cold water without soap, to get to work in jammed and dirty trains, and going to bed hungry in makeshift overcrowded lodgings, while I had a large, substantial house, plenty to eat and a car in which to ride to my appointments, gave me a constant, nagging sense of guilt at the bottom of my mind. I tried, insofar as I could, with the help of Tane and the Inoues, to share my house. Looking back, I see how little it was that I was able to give and how much more those who came to the house brought to me.

Esther Rhoads, who had reached Japan two months before I got there, had left the heated barracks to which the Army had assigned her in order to stay in the unheated Quaker Center; she came to spend every Friday night with us, to enjoy a deep, hot bath in our Japanese bathtub, the loving attentions of the Inoues and Tane, who were devoted to her, and a restful sleep in our guest room. She brought news of the relief work she was doing, of her visits to places throughout Japan where need was acute, of what was going on in the struggling city outside my daily round. She brought also for me a touch of home.

In February, 1947, Gilbert Bowles, the venerable and much loved Quaker missionary who had spent many years in Japan before the war, came to stay for three weeks with us, until with warmer weather the Friends Center could be made less rugged for him. Hosts of Japanese friends came to see him and have tea with him, and he went out sometimes to visit them, but not as much as he would have liked, both because he was suffering from an infected toe and because it was so difficult to arrange transportation for him. Most of the time my car was busy taking me to my scattered appointments. Public transportation was so crowded that people actually got broken ribs, pencils in breast pockets were splintered, and shoes were pulled off and not recovered because it was impossible to lean down and pick them up. His frustration broke through his patience one day at lunch when, looking at the sleet-bound garden, he burst out despairingly, "I feel exactly as if I were behind bars!" There is something peculiarly limiting about having to sit at home while another member of the household goes off in the only car on errands assumed to be more important than anyone else's could possibly be. Violet too found it difficult when she came to be with me two years later.

I have written elsewhere of the English Club of girls from the Joshi Gakushuin (Peeresses' School) who met twice a month to practice their English and to make garments and toys for Aisenryo, a children's home outside of Tokyo which they had adopted.

There was also the Meditation Group, which met two Sunday afternoons a month and which was a source of strength to me throughout my four years there. It was made up of about twenty Japanese and American women—the Japanese all English-speaking and the Americans a changing group who came and went from the Friends Center or the Education Section of the Occupation. We met in my big, sunny study on the second floor of the house, sitting in a circle on the Akasaka Palace's Louis Quinze chairs upholstered in crimson brocade. We would begin by reading from a book of spiritual interest—Rufus Jones's *A Call to What Is Vital* was one—passing it from hand to hand, breaking off to discuss any point that seemed important. Then we would have a period of silent meditation and then tea. The cookies and candy, sugar and sandwich spreads were supplied by the Meditation Group to which I belonged in Philadelphia; large, delectable boxes came regularly from them. I always felt that the tea was important, for most of our Japanese members were on very slim rations.

It was an interesting group of women who came. Ryu Sato Oyaizu, Bryn Mawr '17, a brilliant botanist, had for years devoted herself entirely to her invalid husband; evacuated during the war, they returned afterwards to Tokyo to find twenty-six people, all strangers, living in their house. Because their uninvited visitors had no place to go, they could not put them out, and postwar life, difficult and complicated enough at best, had an added dimension of discomfort for them. Mr. Oyaizu was reluctant to have his wife leave him even for an afternoon, but because he was a great reader and I lent him a book each time, he let her come to us. Miss Ai Hoshino, small, white-haired, lovable, with a pansy face, Bryn Mawr '12, was president of Tsuda College, the first of the Japanese women's colleges to be accredited as a four-year liberal arts college under the new education law.

With her came Taki Fujita, class of '25, then her assistant and teacher of English, a forthright, vigorous, breezy and able woman who was later to be the official Japanese observer (before Japan became a member) at the Economic and Social Council of the United Nations, and after that president of Tsuda. Yuko Chiba, a leader in the Y.W.C.A., had been in Dairen at the end of the war when the Russians came in. For a time she had had to hide from Russian soldiers, but when the first shock troops composed of men let out of common prisons were replaced by a higher type of soldier, who in due course brought their wives, she took a great interest in meeting Russians. "I thought this was an opportunity," she said, "to learn as much about them as I could. I found that if you weren't afraid of them and smiled at them, they responded." After her house was commandeered, she lived with seven other families in makeshift quarters in a church for nearly two years. "We decided that this was life and it was precious," she told me; "we were going to live each day for itself, not spend our energy looking forward to freedom." Having a gift for sewing and some prewar American fashion books, she earned money by making dresses for the Russian women. "You heard nothing from them about Marxist principles. They were just women wanting new dresses. They hadn't *anything*."

In 1949 Miss Chiba married Mr. Otsuki, and in 1950 she used to bring her baby, Izumi, meaning "spring" or "fountain," to the meetings and put her to sleep on the spare-room bed.

Others of the group were teachers, a woman member of the House of Councillors, and Miss Yamamuro, the first woman member of the Ministry of Education, the daughter of the man who wrote biographies of General Booth and George Fox and named his son Bufo after his two heroes.

The Bryn Mawr Club, also composed of Japanese and floating Americans, met once or twice a year at our house for tea or dinner. As travel gradually became easier, we had many visitors who came for a meal as they passed through Tokyo: John Haynes Holmes and his son; Roger Baldwin; Frederic Melcher, the editor of the *Publishers' Weekly*; Mrs. Sherwood Eddy; Mrs. John Sayre; John Gunther and his wife; Amos Peaslee, later ambassador to Australia, and his wife, Dorothy; Tom and Eliza Foulke, who spent a year in Tokyo for the AFSC, setting up a Neighborhood Center; and Henry and Edith Perry, who came to Japan during our last summer as Friends visiting under concern, came often to the house. In late November, 1948, Violet came to spend my last two years with me.

So over the years the house developed a patina of memories; it was the house of a family, diverse and united; it was in those days of postwar privation and hope a haven, a workshop, a trust. It was the base from which I went out each day to teach.

3.

Teaching

Three days a week during the first two years I had a forty-minute drive to Koganei, a western suburb of Tokyo, where I taught the Crown Prince both in private lessons and with his class in school. The way led through the shattered city out into a refreshing stretch of the Omeikaido, an old highway, past thatch-roofed farms, temples half-hidden among huge trees, villages where houses were open to the passer-by, and I used to see aged grandmothers sitting on the floor sewing in the winter sunshine. And in the other direction I went to the disused army barracks that had been adapted to the needs of the Joshi Gakushuin, often thought of as the Peeresses' School, whose beautiful prewar building had been entirely destroyed. Here I taught two classes of the upper school, in which were the Crown Prince's elder sisters.

They were shabby, those boys and girls. They wore thin, dark blue serge uniforms, frayed and patched, which seldom fit, having been inherited or bought at second hand—but the buttons were all carefully sewn on. Their shoes were worn and broken. They were cold, for the schools had no heat at all and the sweaters under their thin jackets could not have helped much. I have often taught in a room with a patch of ice in one corner where rain had leaked in and then frozen. They were tired. Many of them had had to leave crowded homes at six-thirty in order to get to school in crowded trains or buses. They were thin and pale, and no doubt they were hungry. The boys at Koganei had grown sweet potatoes in the school fields during the summer of 1946, and their harvest was an important part of their families' food that fall. People used to cut sweet potatoes into thin slices and dry them in the sun, to serve as cookies with tea.

I came to these boys and girls well fed, warmly dressed in a car from a heated house, and from a country which had brought defeat and military occupation to a land that had never before been defeated or occupied. In spite of all this, I found them attentive, industrious, courteous and friendly. As they developed facility in English, they told me, or wrote in their compositions or their letters, of their hatred of war, their hopes, their problems. I never left my classrooms without a lift of the heart which the contact with these young people had given me.

They had learned about war through bombs at night, through fire, flight, terror, through the loss of members of their families, through hunger and homelessness. They were thankful for peace when it came, welcoming it without bitterness or resentment. The second anniversary of the surrender brought a flood of memories to them.

"Two years ago on today," wrote one girl, "we could have peaceful joy. We will not forget today in my life." Another, a little older, wrote, "It is the second anniversary of the end of World War II. We are full of memories. My elder brother was killed in the war four years ago. He was such a nice brother that I miss him very much. Two years have passed since we renounced war and started as a peaceful nation. So many changes have been done since then. Militarism has been completely swept away and under the new constitution our country is advancing toward democracy."

The most thoughtful, the most significant, and the most moving of all was an essay which a fifteen-year-old boy in the Crown Prince's class wrote about the atomic bomb.

"Two years ago on August 6, 1945, first atomic bomb for Japan did explode above the Hiroshima City. And in this moment great numbers of people died by atomic bomb. I could not believe this cruel incident at that time. But this incident became guide of from-war-to-peace. Atomic bomb was key of the World War, but it was a devil which killed about two hundred thousand people. I hated to this atomic bomb at that time, but few days later Second World War had ended, so I did thank to this atomic bomb. And I hoped very much all countries of world will not use atomic bomb to all human race again."

The Crown Prince was two months short of thirteen when I first met him, in audience with his parents the second day after my arrival in Japan. I found a round-faced child, serious but with a sense of humor, direct, honest, friendly, shy but with an innate poise and dignity, intelligent, manfully ready to meet all his obligations squarely. He was no more eager than any other adolescent to go the second mile, but he would do whatever was asked of him right up to the exact limit. He was a child who had been made aware from his first dawning consciousness of self that he had an important part to play in the world, for which he must be daily and hourly prepared. Taken away from his parents at the age of three, he had been brought up in a house of his own, surrounded by earnest, conscientious chamberlains ranging in age from thirty to forty-five, who went with him everywhere and told him what to do at every turn, breathing out fears that he might make some mistake.

Howard Brinton, in his letter to me in June, had spoken of my "molding" the character of the Crown Prince, and the author of a newspaper article about me had used the same word. But I was not there to "mold" him and had no thought of doing so. What I wanted above all to do was to set him free to be himself.

I saw in him fine and lovable qualities, but I saw him turn constantly to his chamberlains for prompting in small matters and wait passively for them to plan all his daytime activities. "Why don't you decide?" I used to prod him. "It's *your* afternoon." It seemed to me that he was in danger of losing his initiative and the power to improvise in unexpected situations. I longed to set him free to do things he thought of for himself, to develop his own enthusiasms, to make his own mistakes and to learn from them, to have the fun that is natural to any child, no matter how placed. Once when I urged one of the chamberlains to plan some informal good times with his classmates for the Prince, he replied in honest bewilderment, "But why? He has *us*."

After the Crown Prince's private lessons, I would have tea with his Grand Chamberlain and one or two of the other chamberlains and Tane, and sometimes others who came to meet us there.

The Grand Chamberlain at that time was Mr.—formerly Baron —Shigetoku Hozumi, an elderly and distinguished lawyer and connoisseur. His wife was the sister of Marquis Kido, who was formerly Lord Keeper of the Seal and at the time one of the chief defendants in the War Crimes Tribunal. I found Mr. Hozumi charming but thoroughly frustrating. He would talk delightfully about poetry, philosophy, travel, history, but when I tried to talk with him about the education of the Crown Prince he would laugh lightly and change the subject. After about two years, when Mr. Michiji Tajima succeeded Viscount Matsudaira as the Emperor's Grand Steward, Mr. Hozumi was kicked upstairs to the Supreme Court of Japan and Dr. Shinzo Koizumi succeeded him as the man who had the most influence over the Crown Prince's affairs but, by his own choice, without the title of Grand Chamberlain. The two names, Hozumi and Koizumi, might seem confusingly similar to Westerners, but the two men were as unlike as night and day. After that everything changed. The Crown Prince came to spend a whole afternoon at my house every week; he visited me in Karuizawa in the summer vacation, staying in the house with Violet and Tane and me without a chamberlain. I was included in unprecedented and most interesting conferences about the Crown Prince's education both with the Councillors and with the Emperor and Empress themselves. Dr. Koizumi became one of my dearest and most trusted friends, and remained so until his sudden death in 1967.

The Crown Prince was not the only member of his family whom I taught. I taught also his two-years-younger brother, Prince Masahito, and his three sisters, and twice a week the Empress herself had English lessons. For short periods I also gave refresher lessons in English conversation to the Emperor's two younger brothers, Prince Takamatsu and Prince Mikasa.

Even in Mr. Hozumi's day, what I taught was entirely my own decision. Shortly after I reached Japan, the then Grand Steward, Viscount Matsudaira, said to me, "We want you to open windows onto a wider world for our Crown Prince." This I took to mean that through the medium of English I was to tell him—and his classmates—about the world outside Japan and to explain to them the ideas and principles of that democracy which the Japanese people were then adopting with a hasty and bewildered zeal. As soon as their English became fluent enough, we began to talk about a variety of things; the United Nations, the new Japanese constitution, biographies of people who had made other than military contributions to the world, exploration, art, peace, nature.

Mr. Yamanashi had told Dr. Stoddard that in the American tutor they wanted "a Christian but not a fanatic," and I understood that to mean that they did not want the Crown Prince converted to Quakerism or anything else. I never talked religion as such, though I did talk about people in whose lives it had been fundamental. I answered questions about it to the best of my ability, and when asked, as I occasionally was, to speak about Quakerism and its philosophy, I was glad to do so.

Peace I did talk about, in season and out—peace and birds. I was greatly interested in the Japanese songbirds, which had not been sufficiently protected by the laws and were often killed for food. Dr. Oliver Austin, a member of the Natural Resources Section of the Occupation and a well-known ornithologist, was working actively in this field, and that was one reason why he and his wife Elizabeth and their young sons Tony and Timothy were among my rather small number of friends, as distinguished from acquaintances, in the Occupation.

I think it does not hurt for a teacher to have one or two hobbies that she rides to the point of boredom and even caricature. The boredom protects her pupils from unthinking acceptance of her views, but some of the ideas, because of repetition and the enthusiasm behind them, stick in their minds.

In all of my teaching—and this is amazing—I had complete freedom. An editorial in *The New York Times* on March 29, 1946 (which I did not see when it appeared), said that if the American woman to be appointed "is held to a syllabus prepared by the Japanese themselves, her presence in the palace might be worse than useless because it would give a false impression." They gave me no syllabus, no books, no directions or supervision. I made up my own lessons, got my own teaching materials—Elizabeth McKie was endlessly good about sending me both the things that I asked her for and also things she thought might help—and I taught exactly as I wished. When I decided that it would be better for the Crown Prince if he had two of his classmates to share one of his private lessons each week, the two to be changed with each new term, the chamberlains agreed and asked me to select the boys. I put most of the burden of selection on the Crown Prince himself, in order to set up yet another situation where he made his own choices. He was, I found, a good judge of character, which is an inestimable advantage to a Prince or to anyone in a position of responsibility. Every now and then a delegation of the Crown Prince's Councillors in morning coats and striped trousers would come to watch a lesson, walking in silently and solemnly and sitting down in a row against the wall—an ordeal for the Crown Prince, who promptly dried up, and for me, who wanted my pupil to shine. The distinguished gentlemen never made any comments or suggestions, still less criticism, but usually it was wafted back to me afterwards that they had been pleased.

I was wholly absorbed in my work. I had accepted appointment in the first place with the hope that I might be able to make some small contribution to peace and reconciliation in the world. That hope remained always in the background of my mind, but after I got to Japan and came to know and love the Crown Prince for himself, my immediate purpose was to do the best that I could for him, to help create for him the atmosphere and support through which he could best develop his own potentialities.

I felt that I carried in my not very expert hands something fragile and precious and that it was essential for me to keep my hands absolutely clean of self-interest, both personal and national; it was clear to me that only through complete honesty and openness could the thing remain fresh and clear. I felt that I had, in a real sense, been sent to do a job and that I would be taken care of while I was doing it, but that I must live from day to day, doing my work to the best of my ability without looking toward results. It might be, I often reminded myself, that I was not destined to succeed, that all I might be asked to do was to try, and fail—but I did not want to fail out of unawareness or inadvertence on my own part.

For four years I lived under a constant sense of seeking and receiving inner guidance. It is difficult to put into accurate words what one means by that, for words mean different things to different people and even different things to the same people at different times. One of the "Queries" that Friends meetings put to themselves regularly once a year, not for the sake of the answer but for the searching effect of the Query itself, is, "Are your meetings for worship and business held in expectant waiting for divine guidance?" We do not define exactly what we mean by divine guidance. It does not imply what Rufus Jones called "visits from sociable angels"; it is not a simple directive to be taken down with a pencil on a piece of paper. I think for my own part I might say that it means putting myself deliberately in the stream of light from the Beyond that is within, by meditation in the meeting for worship and alone, in one's room, by opening the deep self to the light through an expressed willingness to obey, by carrying out what appears to be the best insight one has in a given situation. "Live up to the light that you have and more will be given you" is a familiar Quaker saying. Indifference and inattentiveness dim the light, overzealousness causes it to flicker; William Penn warned against "running before we are sent." We can seldom be absolutely sure that we are following the light: psychology has taught us that the voice of the unconscious self may take on a spurious resemblance to a divine call. We can only do the best we know at the time and trust that the Spirit, the Eternal Goodness, Reality, The Christ Within, God—the name seems to me to matter little—may be able to make use of the willingness alone, as if just wishing to be sensitive to the light removed some obstacle to the movement of the divine in human affairs.

Guidance, of course, comes through other people as well as through one's own inner leadings. I had a great deal of help from Tane, from Esther Rhoads, on whose long experience in Japan I could draw in times of puzzlement, and from the chamberlains themselves, who, though we often differed in methods, were one with me in purpose. When Dr. Koizumi took office, I had someone in authority whose wisdom and understanding I could trust.

The seriousness—perhaps the overseriousness—with which I took my work was reflected in a vivid dream. During my first winter there, I had a bad case of flu that kept me in bed for some time and made me feel guilty because of the hours and days of work that I was missing. In my dream I saw my guardian angel—rather worn and hard-pressed in appearance, as if his wings were moulting, I thought—looking down at me from above and talking to another angel. "Look at that fool," he said disgustedly, "letting herself get sick and spoiling everything. She must be an Iszard after all." (Violet used to maintain that a certain strain of sheer silliness which she discerned in the family came in through the Iszards.)

Besides my work with the Imperial family, the Gakushuin and the Joshi Gakushuin, I went once a month to lecture on literature at Tsuda College. This I did in my spare time for the love of it; I was not officially a part of the faculty.

Tsuda College had been started as a girls' school specializing in English by Miss Ume Tsuda, who had been the youngest of the first little band of five Japanese girls who came to study in the United States in 1872. Only seven when she came, she went to school in Washington, D.C., and later to Bryn Mawr College. In 1900 she established her own school in Tokyo. Through the years it has grown into one of the foremost of the women's colleges,

with a large campus and handsome buildings not far from the
Crown Prince's school at Koganei. Before the war Tsuda had always had some members of the faculty imported from the United
States or England, but in the years immediately after the war it
had to make do with lecturers like me who were in Tokyo for
other reasons. With little time to prepare my lectures, few books
and no libraries to draw on, I gave them, I fear, very thin stuff.
The talks were in simple English, slowly delivered, with a good
deal of reading of poems and explaining what they meant, filling
in the background of time and place. Beginning with two lectures
on Chaucer, I then switched to American poets: Frost, Lindsay,
Emily Dickinson, Whittier, Emerson, Thoreau, Longfellow. I enjoyed going to Tsuda, for I used to see Miss Hoshino and Miss
Fujita, who were my friends, and I liked having the contact with
the students.

Though I had taken to heart Dr. Stoddard's warning against
yielding to the constant pressure to make talks to all kinds of
groups, I did accept each year, usually in the holidays, a few invitations to speak at schools, colleges, the Y.W.C.A., Friends
groups and the like. The first of these was a large meeting of Japanese teachers of English in Yokohama on December 16, 1946.

A young American captain, the member concerned with education on the Military Government team in Yokohama, came to see
me one afternoon at my house. The English teachers, he told me,
were exhausted by the struggle to teach in burned-out and overcrowded schools and bewildered by the directives of the Occupation. He had planned a conference for them and suggested that
they ask me to speak; they had answered that there was not the
slightest chance that the Crown Prince's tutor would deign to talk
to ordinary teachers. This, of course, was a challenge I could not
refuse; I said that if the captain would provide transportation I
would go. (Gasoline was in such short supply at that time that I
did not like to use my car for anything but my regular work.) So he
came in an Army sedan one cold, raw, cloudy afternoon and took
Tane and me to a dingy hall in Yokohama, which was crowded
to the roof with some nine hundred teachers, thin, pale, shabbily
dressed, and eager, and great numbers of news photographers.
Tane interpreted for me, for though the English teachers were
strong on grammar, they had had little opportunity to hear English actually spoken. The whole time I was talking flashbulbs
kept going off in my face, a new and disconcerting experience.

My topic was "Problems in Teaching English," but I thought I should try to give them something more than that, to express, if I could, my philosophy of teaching itself. What was it, essentially, we were all trying to do for the children in our care and how should we go about it? The question was much on my mind; I had thought a good deal about it during the long hours in the deck chair on the *Marine Falcon* crossing the Pacific; after two months of actual teaching I was glad to re-examine the subject and to try to find answers as much for myself as for them.

There are, I told them, three main purposes in education for the world of the future. The first is to interpret the world truthfully to the child, to tell him about the past so that he might understand not only his own heritage but that of other nations, to explain to him the nature of the world he lived in and to open his mind to its beauties, to the laws which govern it and the ways in which its benefits can be made to serve the greatest number of people. To interpret the world, I said, calls for loyalty to the truth above all other things, including the pronouncements of official bodies; it requires a sincere and devoted search for the truth on the part of the teacher—and though we can never wholly attain truth, even the search for it is ennobling.

The second purpose of education, I thought, is to help the child to develop his full capacities of mind, body and spirit. Each child is unique, like a leaf or a flower; each child must be allowed to grow to his own best flowering in his own way. A morning-glory must be encouraged to climb, a carrot to plunge deep. We must not expect the morning-glory to give us food, or scold if its petals fold up when the sun is off them, nor must we labor over the carrot to make it produce fragile blossoms. Our aim is to develop the best morning-glories and the best carrots possible.

Much of our teaching, I thought, is unconscious; the genuineness of our respect for the dignity of each individual and his unique gifts will be revealed not by what we say but unconsciously, countless times a day, by the way in which we meet the least and the greatest of our fellow men, the most troublesome imps in our schoolroom as well as the most promising pupils. I quoted George Fox's advice to his followers, "Walk cheerfully over the earth, answering that of God in every man."

The third great purpose is to give the child the tools which he needs to do his work in the world. The gardener is helpless without spade or hoe; the carpenter must have his saw and hammer. One very useful tool in the world today, and now I came around to my advertised topic, is a working knowledge of the English language. And from there I went on to specific problems as I saw them and told how I was myself trying to solve them.

The talk had a wide audience in Japan. It was fully reported in the newspapers, was published as a pamphlet in Japanese and was printed in English, six months later, in the magazine section of the *Nippon Times*. Now, twenty-four years later, if I were asked to state my ideas on Education, they would still be substantially the same.

4.

The Emperor

THE PREJUDICE in our country against the Emperor today is intense," wrote Ambassador Joseph Grew in April, 1944, in a memo to Cordell Hull. The picture of the Emperor of Japan that almost everyone in the United States had during the war, painted in propaganda and ignorance, was that of an all-powerful Oriental despot arrogantly riding a white horse (which was somehow more arrogant than a bay would have been), worshiped as a god by his people, determined to bring the world under Japanese domination. After the end of the war, when the Emperor emerged from the wrappings in which the Japanese military party had kept him swathed for their own purposes, Western journalists produced a wholly different picture: a small, myopic figure in badly fitting clothes, inept and apologetic, saying over and over in a high-pitched voice, "*Ah so desuka?*" ("Really? You don't say?")

One extreme was as much of a caricature as the other; like all caricatures, each had some element of truth on which it was based. He did ride a white horse; he was enveloped in a myth of divinity so that idealistic young men actually did count it their highest honor to die for their Emperor; he was in himself a modest, scholarly gentleman with little small talk. He was all these, but he was very much more. These disconnected facts add up not to truth but to distortion. One of the most interesting and rewarding parts of my experience in Japan was getting to know the Emperor as I suppose no other foreigner has ever known any of Japan's 124 emperors.

When I count it up, I find that, including my visits to Japan in 1957 and 1959, I sat on the Emperor's right at luncheon, tea or dinner sixteen times. I had two long conferences with him and the Empress about the Crown Prince's education, till then an unprecedented event even for Japanese; I walked with him in the rain among the trees and wild flowers of Nasu and in a wooded part of the Fukiage garden in the palace grounds in Tokyo; I talked with him in his laboratory there. I have seen him in some of his most interesting and characteristic activities: riding his white horse with his two sons in Nasu; returning from collecting specimens at Hayama; addressing the first Diet elected under the new constitution; presiding at the New Year Poetry Party held each January at the Imperial Palace; attending Peers' School commencements when his son was graduated from the Middle School and one of his daughters from the high school. I have had special messages and thoughtful kindnesses from him.

All this could have happened only at the particular moment in history that it did, in the aftermath of war and defeat, when all Japan was looking for a different way, examining Western democracy, facing in a new direction and beginning a new life. Since it had been the Emperor's idea to bring a teacher from America for the Crown Prince, I was to some degree under his special patronage; and yet, though I was employed by the Japanese government and had no connection with the Occupation, I was also a native of the occupying country and in a small, oblique way an ambassador from it in a time when there were no normal diplomatic exchanges. All of these factors, in a rare, fortuitous and fleeting balance, made possible for me an acquaintance with the Emperor that was as happy as it was unusual.

In addition to my own meetings with the Emperor, I knew Japanese men who had been in one way or another close to him and who talked to me about him and about his part in the history of the previous years.

One day in January, 1950, Dr. Shinzo Koizumi, who had then been in charge of the Crown Prince's education for nearly a year, said to me one of the most perceptive things that I have ever heard said about the Emperor.

"The more I come to know the Emperor, the more I appreciate him. At the beginning I thought he was good, but now I have learned more and more that he is also wise. Mr. Tajima said a clever thing about His Majesty, 'He is no good at fencing but with the real sword—in a real fight—he is strong.' He is not impressive-looking, he shakes his head nervously, but he is a great man."

Dr. Koizumi had been president of Keio University, the oldest liberal university in Japan; he had represented Keio at the Harvard Tercentenary celebrations in 1936; he had been educated not only at Keio but also in Berlin and Cambridge, England. He was a man of wide learning and experience, a writer of note on economics. He had had no touch with the court until his reluctant acceptance of the responsibility for the Crown Prince early in 1949. He was often critical of its tradition-encrusted ways, especially of what he considered the excessive prostrations of ladies-in-waiting and chamberlains before the Emperor and Empress (which I never saw); he was not a man to be dazzled into suspending for the Emperor his usual kindly but acute judgments of people.

The story has been told many times how the Emperor brought the war to an end in August, 1945. My version is no different from others except that I knew personally some who were actually there when he did it.

One day in September, 1947, in the shabby little country cottage in Chiba where he was then living, Kantaro Suzuki, once baron, admiral, grand chamberlain, prime minister, told me how the end of the war came. In the spring of 1945, the grizzled, gnarled, seventy-eight-year-old Suzuki told me, he knew from the Emperor himself that His Majesty wanted to bring the war to a close. The Army, the Emperor said, had new plans, but the Army's plans never succeeded. The Emperor expressed sorrow for the loss of life, both Japanese and Allied. Mr. Suzuki did not tell me anything about the events between his appointment as Prime Minister in May and the surrender, or why he failed to carry out the Emperor's expressed wishes for immediate peace, but he did give me a vivid description of the final decision on August 14.

On the morning of that day the Supreme War Council met in extraordinary session in the presence of the Emperor in the air-raid shelter under Obunko, the small concrete library building where the Emperor and Empress were then living. The War Council did not have a unanimous decision to present to the Emperor for his approval; it was divided, three in favor of surrender, three adamant against it. It was Prime Minister Suzuki's idea that the Emperor should hear their arguments and himself make the final decision. Minister of the Army Anami, Commander-in-chief of the Army Umazu and Admiral of the Navy Toyoda argued for fighting on to the end, even if it meant committing national suicide. Admiral Yonai, the Navy Minister, Foreign Minister Togo and Prime Minister Suzuki himself were in favor of surrender.

The point on which the die-hards stuck was the position of the Emperor under surrender. The Allies had announced on August 10 that "From the moment of surrender the authority of the Emperor or the said Japanese government to rule the state shall be subject to the Supreme Commander of the Allied Powers. . . . The ultimate form of the government of Japan shall be established by the freely expressed will of the Japanese people."

Within these terms was starkly evident the possibility that the Emperor might be deposed, he might be tried as a war criminal, or the entire Emperor system might be abolished. Now at this council meeting the Emperor himself said without hesitation that he considered the terms to be "acceptable." The decision was final. Some of the men there present wept.

Late that evening the Emperor prepared a record to be broadcast next day to the Japanese people informing them that "the war situation has developed not necessarily to our advantage"—a notable understatement—and telling them to endure the unendurable and to suffer the insufferable.

Even then, even after the Imperial decision was made, some young officers, getting wind of the Emperor's record, did their utmost to prevent its actually being broadcast. They broke into the Palace, killing two guards, and made a search for the record. One of the Emperor's chamberlains, Mr. Yasuhide Toda, was wounded in the scuffle, but the record was saved. (I knew Mr. Toda well. He was transferred to the Crown Prince about a year after I got there, and I welcomed him because he was boyish and athletic, whereas most of the chamberlains were older, very sober and dignified. Mr. Toda was tall, handsome, vigorous; he would have been lord of Matsumoto if all daimyo had not been done away with at the time of the Meiji Restoration.) Some of the insurgents went on to Mr. Suzuki's house and burned it down. It was the second time that the doughty old liberal had suffered from militarist rebels; in the February, 1936, uprising he had been shot in the chest by young army officers and left for dead.

The Imperial Rescript was broadcast at noon on August 15. All over Japan the people, told ahead of time that there would be an important announcement, sat at their radios waiting, expecting to be called on to die in the streets in a suicidal last-ditch defense of Japan. An Imperial Rescript is always received with awe and veneration. Never before had one been recorded for broadcasting; never before had the Japanese people heard their Emperor's voice.

Everyone you met had some story about what they were doing and how they felt that day. It is to this Rescript and to the Japanese people's habit of obedience to their Emperor that we owe the bloodless disarming of the 2,000,000-man Japanese Army by a few thousand Allied soldiers. The United States has reason to be grateful to the Emperor of Japan.

I asked Admiral Suzuki the question that all Americans ask: Why, if the Emperor could stop the war, could he not have prevented it from starting? Why did he allow Pearl Harbor?

The Emperor, he told me, was never consulted about policies; he was only presented with the unanimous decisions of his ministers. His part was to approve. As constitutional monarch he considered himself bound by these decisions. On only two occasions did he step beyond the limits thus imposed. One was the ending of the war in 1945; the other occurred in 1936, when three cabinet ministers were assassinated by a junta of young officers, and several others, including Suzuki himself, were wounded or narrowly escaped. The remaining members of the Cabinet were afraid to oppose the young officers, who, though they were men of low rank, had powerful and dangerous supporters. The Emperor himself stepped forward decisively and gave the order declaring the insurgents rebels. In 1941, though the Emperor took no positive action, he did make his position clear. In the meeting of the Supreme War Council on September 6, when he was told the unanimous decision of his ministers to take military action if negotiations in Washington were not successful, the Emperor quoted pointedly the poem of his grandfather, the Emperor Meiji:

> Surely in this world men are brothers—all
> One family!
> Why then do winds and waves on all the seas
> Rage stormily?

Mr. Yamanashi, who also talked to me about this incident, told me that those who were present were shaken by it but that when they returned to their determined colleagues their purpose was again stiffened. At what point the Emperor was told of the Pearl Harbor plan is not clear, but certainly not until very close to the day itself. He insisted that the United States be given notice of the breaking off of diplomatic relations before the blow was struck, but this intention was disastrously bungled in the Embassy in Washington, where the note was not decoded, translated and delivered until after the bombs had fallen. Bungling, probably by Tojo's command, also prevented the delivery of President Roosevelt's letter direct to the Emperor. When the Imperial Rescript declaring war was issued in Tokyo, the Emperor insisted on having included in it the words "Against our wishes." His helplessness in the face of the determination of the militarists was recognized by Mr. Grew, who wrote in *Turbulent Era*,

"Had the Emperor opposed the military determination on war and had he refused to approve the order for the Pearl Harbor attack, there would seem in the light of the facts as we now know them little doubt that he would either have been by-passed by the armed forces or actually held in restraint so that the military could have their way."

He not only did not plan the war; he opposed it without success. That he has never quite absolved himself for not succeeding is, I think, well known.

He must have particularly hated to be at war with Britain, for it was in Britain, when he was twenty and Crown Prince, that he had some of the happiest days of his life. He made a six-month trip to Europe, the only time in all his life that he has ever been outside of Japan, and in England he found a measure of freedom and informality, a friendship with the royal family and a concept of constitutional monarchy that both released and inspired him. King George V evidently took a friendly interest in the young Japanese prince and gave him fatherly advice, so I have been told, about the duty of the monarch to accept the decisions of his ministers and not to interfere in government himself. King George probably had in his mind the Western idea of the Japanese emperor as an Oriental despot, not foreseeing a time when it might have prevented tragedy on a large scale if the Emperor had spoken out vigorously against the plans of his ministers. King George gave good advice, but like so much good advice out of context it miscarried. I used to think of that often in my own relations with the Crown Prince and wonder if through ignorance or misunderstanding I was actually preparing harm for the future. I tried never to give actual advice, only to encourage in him the development of initiative and the habit of formulating his own ideas.

The Emperor, then, was not all-powerful; neither did he consider himself divine, though it had been to the interests of the military party to foster the myth among the Japanese people and to enforce public obeisance. On New Year's Day in 1946 the Emperor issued a Rescript denying his divinity.

There has been much discussion of this action and speculation as to where the initial impulse came from. Certainly it could not have sprung up in the Emperor's own mind. He was a scientist, a man who had read widely and studied history. I cannot imagine that it would ever have occurred to him that it was necessary to deny divine origin. Someone must have suggested it.

Most people writing today, including Japanese writers, state categorically that General MacArthur ordered it, though the General in his *Reminiscences* has denied doing so. Probably it came from somewhere in the lower echelons of the Occupation, or the journalists, and worked its way up. At all events the Emperor sent for the Education Minister, Mr. Tamon Maeda, and discussed it with him.

Mr. Maeda was a member of the Tokyo Friends Meeting. Esther Rhoads rented his cottage in Karuizawa the summer of 1947, and Mr. Maeda himself was there for a time. In this cottage, on August 15, 1945, at midnight, the very day the Emperor's Rescript was read, Mr. Maeda had been awakened by four policemen pounding on the door; they had come to summon him to Tokyo to take the post of Minister of Education. I remember vividly an afternoon when we sat in the little living room looking out at the mountains through the trees, and Mr. Maeda told me of the composing of the Rescript by members of the Education Ministry, with advice on the English translation from Mr. Blyth. He gave me a piece of blue-lined paper on which was rather inexpertly typed in English what I understood him to say was an early draft of it. The text, however, is the same as that of the final document, and so it is probably an early copy rather than a draft. In any case it is an interesting souvenir.

Though the major part of it deals with postwar difficulties and encourages the nation to "face the present ordeal and to seek civilization consistently in peace," the salient paragraph is:

"We stand by the people and we wish always to share with them in their moments of joys and sorrows. The ties between us and our people have always stood upon mutual trust and affection. They do not depend upon mere legends and myths. They are not predicated on the false conception that the Emperor is divine and that the Japanese people are superior to other races and fated to rule the world."

Most Japanese intellectuals will laugh a bit uncomfortably about this Rescript and say that it was done more to reassure the Occupation than to inform the Japanese people; that the word translated as *divine* has quite a different meaning for the Japanese than for the Westerner, to whom God is not merely a superior being but Creator and source of love, and to worship is more than merely to pay respects. "Instead of thinking of the Emperor as a godlike or good person," Mr. Maeda told me, "they [i.e., the Japanese people] gave him formal lip service. They treated him like an idol." The purpose of the Rescript, according to him, was rather to prevent the use of the Emperor by the military ever again than to deny a divinity which was not seriously considered to exist.

The Rescript nevertheless gave authenticity to what was in truth a new attitude toward the Emperor. Even those who had not believed in the myth of divinity had felt an aura of fear and mystery surrounding the throne, a psychological moat far wider and deeper than the physical one. This barrier began to disappear as the mystery was removed and a picture of the "human Emperor" offered in its place. A small incident in my own home is an example of the change. Once, tying up for me a box of chocolates that I was going to give the Emperor, Tane exclaimed, "Think of me wrapping a box of candy for the Emperor! And I didn't feel awful at all! Before, I'd have shaken all over!"

An editorial in the *Yomiuri Shimbun,* one of Japan's largest newspapers, quoted in *The New York Times,* said, "General Mac-Arthur put through some foolish reforms in Japan but some of them were really fine things. Above all, stripping the Emperor of his divine status was a real historical masterpiece. The Emperor was made human and closer to the people."

What the Rescript of 1946 could not change, however, was the language in which the Emperor, or indeed any member of the Imperial Family, is referred to. It is elaborately humble in two ways: it elevates the Emperor on a structure of honorifics and it reduces the person speaking by formal terms of abasement. Tane was young, she had been educated in the United States, she was a Quaker—and Quakers in the seventeenth century would not flatter even the King of England by saying "you" instead of "thou" or taking off their hats to him. She told me with amazement and some ruefulness of the language that *grande dame* Mrs. Matsudaira used in referring to her daughter, who had married the Emperor's younger brother, Prince Chichibu. There were three kinds of language that Mrs. Matsudaira might use, Tane explained: the simple kind with which she would ordinarily refer to her own daughter—and actually did when she spoke of her other daughter; the moderate honorifics she would use in speaking of someone else's daughter; and finally the superhonorifics used for anyone in the Imperial Family, which were what she actually used for Princess Chichibu. "When you go near the Emperor everything changes," said Tane with a note of sadness in her voice.

Even Tane herself had trouble with the language when she translated an article I wrote just before I left Japan in the fall of 1950, entitled "Memories of Japan." The verbs for the Crown Prince, for example. Should she, in translating my account of his meeting with General MacArthur, use the highest honorifics for the Crown Prince and something less for General MacArthur? Or should she promote the General and use imperial verbs for both? In the end, as she was writing for me and I was the Crown Prince's teacher and therefore need not speak of him with abject respect, she demoted the Crown Prince and used the same very polite but not imperial verbs for both the Crown Prince and the General. When it came to the account of my first audience with Their Majesties, it was even more difficult. I said, in my casual American way, "We sat and chatted together informally for over half an hour." She had to give up the word *sat* altogether, not wanting to say the equivalent of "They honorably perched while I ignobly squatted." Nor could she possibly use such an informal word as *chatted* in such a connection—at least not in Japanese. She resolved the dilemma by quoting the word "chatted" in English!

That first meeting with the Emperor took place on October 17, 1946, less than forty-eight hours after I reached Japan. It was the first audience that the Emperor, the Empress and the Crown Prince had ever given together; they all three gave me their hands to shake and we sat for some forty minutes in chairs of equal height and talked informally, through, of course, an interpreter. I saw in the Emperor a slight figure of medium height in striped trousers and morning coat; he wore spectacles; his voice was rather high-pitched; he did say *"Ah so desuka?"* He was gentle, he was kind, he was concerned for my comfort, he expressed gratitude to me as an American for the food which the Occupation had made available to the Japanese people. (I did not know then that without it hundreds of thousands of Japanese would have starved the previous summer; that the Japanese when they felt outraged by some Occupation action would for years afterwards remind themselves that it was the first Occupation in history not only to bring its own food with it but to share that food with the conquered people.)

The Emperor was forty-five at that time, a year older than I was myself. From the slope where I stand now that seems rather young. He had been twenty when he became regent for his mentally ill father, twenty-two when he married, twenty-five when he became Emperor, forty at the time of Pearl Harbor.

The subsequent conversations that I had with His Majesty usually ran along the same lines. He never failed to ask about my health and comfort. On two occasions when I was in Karuizawa at a time of possible danger—when there was the worst eruption of Asama in seventeen years and several people were killed and when the notorious Typhoon Kitty struck—he had a chamberlain telephone to ask how I was. The first occasion was considered notable, for at that time he was himself away from Tokyo traveling in the north. The Emperor was not a fluent conversationalist, and he sometimes unnerved me by suddenly ejaculating "Ha!" out of a rather long silence, but he was always interested in anything that I might be able to tell him about what people—the Japanese whom I knew or Americans—were saying about public events. He read the newspapers regularly, but like the rest of us he wanted to hear at first hand about things that were happening. He always seemed to welcome my impressions of Japan itself as I went about, to take an interest in what seemed to me beautiful or unusual or significant. More than anything else, however, we talked about nature, especially birds and wild flowers.

On all but a very few of these occasions some or all of his children were present and joined in the conversation. When the children were young, there were sometimes games after dinner, and then usually the Emperor would sit and watch, smiling indulgently as little Princess Takako, blindfolded, added a beauty mark to the face of a princess, as Western children pin the tail on the donkey. Twice, however, the Emperor and Empress both joined in a game of Snap at the urging of their two youngest children. Certainly he enjoyed the increased opportunity for being with his children that came to him after the war. Before that, meetings had been occasional and formal. During the last year and a half of the war he did not see the Crown Prince even once; it was not till nearly three months after the surrender that the Crown Prince was brought back to Tokyo from Yumoto, where he had been evacuated, and the Emperor and Empress saw their son again.

The Emperor, like the rest of the Japanese people, had suffered loss and impoverishment from the war. It was not the intention of the Allies to bomb the Palace, but the War Ministry Building across the moat was an important target. After the great fire raid of May 25, 1945, the wind caught up bundles of burning papers from the War Ministry Building, carried them over moat and trees and dropped them on the vast, elaborate, wooden Palace building. The Emperor and Empress were safe in the air-raid shelter, but the Palace itself went up in flames. They lived after that in the small concrete library building, and there determinedly they stayed until a new and modern dwelling was built for them in the early 1960's. The Japanese government had wished to rebuild the palace immediately after the war but the Emperor refused, saying that he had a place to live and that while so many Japanese people were still homeless he would not have an expensive palace built for him.

In addition he lost his entire private fortune, which before the war was estimated at $400,000,000. Capital levies imposed by the Diet under the direction of SCAP (Supreme Commander of the Allied Powers) reduced it to $70,000. The Diet now appropriates money each year for imperial expenses; anything not in the budget has to be forgone. The appropriation increases each year as Japan grows more prosperous. In the early days after the war, when the Occupation was watching closely and the Communists were clamoring loudly for the abolition of the Emperor system, the Palace grounds were shabby and economies were many. I have often thought of Machiavelli's cynical observation that "A man will more easily forgive the loss of his father than of his patrimony," and I have seen it verified in families where the grief for the departed parent was pale and ephemeral compared with the intense and lasting bitterness caused by quarrels among the surviving children over the distribution of his goods. In contrast, the Emperor's dignified and unresentful acceptance of the action of SCAP that deprived him of financial independence seems to me admirable and very unusual.

The Crown Prince lived, as I have written, away from the Palace altogether, on the grounds of the school at Koganei. When his house there burned down, as it did in December, 1949, a rather modest mansion formerly used as a clubhouse for Imperial Household officials was renovated for him. The three princesses lived in a rambling Japanese house on the Palace grounds, and Prince Masahito in what had formerly been the hospital for the Imperial Household.

In the summer of 1948 the Asahi Press was preparing a book on the Palace with many photographs and a little text, as part of the effort to bring the "human Emperor" before his people. Someone else, a Japanese, had been engaged to write the main article for it, a character sketch of the Emperor, but for some reason or other it was unsatisfactory and was rejected. The official in the Imperial Household Agency who was head of the bureau of poetry and literature then came to me and asked me to write the article.

It was not an easy thing to do, and I worked on it all through my vacation in Karuizawa. For an employee to write about her boss, for a foreigner to write for the Japanese about their own Emperor, for a teacher to analyze in public her pupil's father, for a native of the occupying country to comment on the top occupied, all without breaking confidences, slipping into disrespect, condescension or breach of taste and equally without being obsequious, gushing, flattering or overimpressed, was like walking a tightrope, and I have never had a good head for high places. In the end I wrote simply as the Crown Prince's teacher seeking what was good for him, especially more contact with his father, and I strove for truth as I saw it, and tried to set aside questions of policy or desire to please. The reason I tell this incident is because of the light it sheds on the Emperor. In the article I described the Emperor's study, which I was one of the very few to have seen. I wrote:

"About a year ago the Emperor showed me his study in Obunko, the gracious, booklined room of a man of cultivated tastes. The objects that caught my attention were three busts, the same three that might have been found in the library of any western home two decades or so ago: Lincoln, Darwin and Napoleon. None was added for the benefit of American eyes; none was taken away. When I saw the bust of Lincoln there among the books I understood better a little incident that happened when I first came to Japan. I showed my class at the Peers' School a picture of Lincoln as a boy and asked them who it was. The Crown Prince was the only one who identified it immediately. Lincoln is to him a family friend."

The Chamberlain, accepting my article with thanks, suggested that as it was to be published in English as well as Japanese, they would like to delete Napoleon the dictator from the trio of busts, leaving only Lincoln and Darwin. I replied that I had actually seen all three of them; that I was perfectly willing to leave out all of them, but I did not see how I could omit one and leave the other two. After some consultation, they decided to take the article to the Emperor and let him decide. He read it, said it was *"mottai nai"* ("too good") and that nothing should be changed. All three busts were in his study. I did not know then that Napoleon was there because the Emperor had bought it in Paris on his grand tour and that it was almost the only time he had ever handled money and actually bought something with it. I would have liked to add that bit to the article.

Later I was asked to write other articles for Japanese papers, on the Empress and on the Crown Prince, and before I left Japan the Emperor and the Prime Minister both suggested that I write about their country and my experiences there. *Windows for the Crown Prince* and *Return to Japan* were the result. Neither of them was censored in any way or even seen, whole or in part, by any Japanese before it was published. They left me entirely free.

In 1949 the Emperor himself published a book on his biological researches and discoveries with an introduction in both English and Japanese by Professor Kikutara Baba. I was asked to go over the English translation and correct any mistakes, which I did. In return the Emperor gave me an autographed copy of his book, a large and handsome volume: *Opisthobranchia of the Sagami Bay,* with color plates of microscopic creatures beautiful in their enlargement. In this book, according to a review in *Nature,* fifty new species are recorded and five new genera established, a not inconsiderable scientific achievement.

This book, which was the first of several that the Emperor has published, was the fruit of twenty years of work and study and the release of a long frustration. The Emperor is a genuine scientist, his books have been received with respect by leading biologists in other countries as well as Japan, but for many years he had to pursue this interest apologetically, casually and even at times secretly. Nor could he before the war publish his discoveries under his own name.

Early in the summer of 1948, there was persistent talk about the possible abdication of the Emperor. It was the time when the judges of the military tribunal were studying the vast accumulation of evidence and argument and preparing their verdicts, which would not be made public until the fall. It was widely said that if Marquis Kido, who had been the Lord Keeper of the Seal and close to the Emperor, received the death penalty, the Emperor would abdicate. (As it turned out, the Lord Keeper was sentenced to life imprisonment and after the peace treaty was paroled by the Japanese. I met him at the Crown Prince's wedding, a slender, elegant, aristocratic man.) *The New York Times*, in an editorial the previous autumn, had called on the Emperor to abdicate "in token that all who guided Japan to her disaster have lacked in 'virtue' and must pay at least some penalty," and there were many Japanese who also advocated abdication but for a different reason. Some conversatives who considered Emperor Hirohito's image to have been tarnished by defeat thought it would strengthen the "Emperor system" if he withdrew.

There was plenty of precedent for abdication. In the Heian period, approximately 800 to 1100 A.D., a number of emperors did abdicate, retiring to temples or palaces for contemplation or the enjoyment of freedom, leaving their thrones to minor sons and regents. It would have undoubtedly been easier for the present Emperor if he had abdicated; he would have been free then to pursue his biological studies and to enjoy a much less restricted life in general.

It was Dr. Abe who on May 25, 1948, first spoke of it to me not as a possibility but as something quite certain. Dr. Abe, who had been Minister of Education at the time when Dr. Stoddard's Mission visited Japan, was in 1948 President of the Peers' School and an important member of the Crown Prince's Council on Education. I was greatly distressed. It was obvious to me that if the Crown Prince became Emperor at fourteen he would lose what little freedom he had, and I felt that it would arrest his full development. There were other signs too. One day when I went to Koganei, my lesson with the Crown Prince was delayed because a photographer for *Life* magazine was there making a color portrait of the Crown Prince for the cover of *Life*. They were getting ready, I surmised, to print it when the Emperor's abdication should be announced and the Crown Prince become Emperor. My heart sank. The head of one of the Imperial Household Departments, who hoped that the Emperor would not abdicate, said to Tane, "It is a time of crisis."

The talk went on and the weeks went by, and I was asked to do the article on the Emperor for the Asahi Press book. *Life* magazine did not use the portrait of the Crown Prince. The abdication talk died away and was forgotten. Whoever made the decision I do not know. Some say that General MacArthur spoke. I have no knowledge of this. Perhaps the will of the people prevailed. A poll conducted by the *Yomiuri Press* indicated that 90 per cent of the people wanted the Emperor to continue. At any rate the Emperor shouldered his burden and went on.

People in the United States have often asked me about the Emperor's religion. I wrote in *Windows*, echoing what I had read in books about Japan,

"In the Kashikodokoro were kept the Jewels and the Sword of the imperial regalia, the Mirror being at Ise Shrine. No regular services were held here, it was not in any sense a royal chapel, but here at different times in the year came the Emperor as head of the Shinto religion to perform certain ceremonies."

This, however, as Mr. Tajima wrote to me after the book was published, was not correct. "In the Kashikodokoro," he wrote, "is kept the replica of the Mirror of the Ise Shrine, and the Sword and the Jewel are customarily kept in the Palace or close to the person of His Majesty. The Emperor has never been considered head of the Shinto religion. What has been and is observed at the Kashikodokoro is only a system of observance of ancestor worship for the Imperial Family and has never been a religion. It is not quite the same with the so-called Shinto, of which there were two groups before the war, viz. shrine-Shinto and sect-Shinto. The former was not regarded as a religion and was under the control of the Bureau of Shrines of the Home Office, and the latter, regarded as a religion, was under the control of the Bureau of Religions of the Education Office. The Tenrikyo, Omotokyo, Kurozumikyo, etc. are some of the Shinto sects."

I was glad to have this point made clear by one whose information was beyond question. I was on firm ground, however, when I said that one of the ceremonies which the Emperor performed at the Kashikodokoro was the annual thanksgiving for the rice harvest. Though the other observances at the shrine, at New Year's and other times, were merely formalities, the thanksgiving, I have good reason to know, did have religious implications. One

November the chamberlains had planned some pleasure for the Crown Prince on the evening before the day of the ceremony, but the Emperor, who so seldom stepped in to change their arrangements, ordered the plan canceled. Thanksgiving, he said, was a solemn occasion; the evening before should be spent quietly and thoughtfully. In those years the official Japanese ration was 1,500 calories, not enough to live on, and so the Japanese people had to buy supplementary food in the black market, selling off their remaining treasures for the purpose. A good rice harvest was not to be taken lightly; it was an occasion for meditation and prayerful gratitude. Gratitude to whom? I do not know. The Outer Shrine at Ise is dedicated to Toyuke-no-Omikami, the Goddess of Farms, Crops, Food and Sericulture. But a biologist who is also an Emperor may recognize Spirit in the universe while performing ancient rituals, as biologists in other countries go to church and sing Christmas carols without compromising their scientific integrity.

A small sidelight on an ancient tradition and on the way in which the Shinto and Buddhist religions were early wedded, so that they shared rather than competed in man's life—even today most Japanese are married by Shinto ceremony and buried by Buddhist rites—was given me on a visit to Kyoto. Whenever I was there, a car from the Imperial Palace was made available to me for sight-seeing. One of the drivers, pointing out the Toji Temple (short for Kyoogokokuji, established in 823 A.D. by Kobo-Daishi) offered the information that this was one of two temples to which for five centuries the Emperor's underclothing has been —and still is—sent to be prayed over by the priests. It came to Toji on April 3; at New Year's time it was sent to a temple on Mt. Hiei. Long streamers from the past still cling around the Emperor of modern Japan—cling and sometimes bind. He is a gentle person; he does not tear with rough hands; he frees himself patiently, persistently.

On two occasions late in my stay in Japan, I had long, frank discussions with both Emperor and Empress about the education of their children, especially the Crown Prince. The first took place at Hayama. We had had lunch together, and afterwards, in the beautiful drawing room on the second floor of the palace, looking out over Sagami Bay to Mt. Fuji, perhaps the most lovely prospect in all Japan, we sat around a small table, Their Majesties and I, with Mr. Mitani, the Grand Chamberlain, who was there as interpreter.

I imagine that Mr. Mitani must have found this a somewhat nerve-wracking experience, though he appeared imperturbable. However did he put into proper imperial language the things that I was saying? For I was talking as I would talk to any other parents concerned about the welfare of their children. And I found Their Majesties, even through the interpretation, as eager, as direct, as open as one hopes parents anywhere will be.

It was always on my mind and heart that the Crown Prince should not be kept apart as much as he was from his family, especially his parents and his younger brother. It seemed to me unnatural and a great waste of opportunity for deepening his understanding and widening his heart. The compartmentalization of an intelligent, conscientious, affectionate family seemed to me an indefensible deprivation in the life of a boy who should have had and might have had the best of everything. The officials—chamberlains and the like—resisted my ideas about the Imperial Family's living together at every turn. They were embedded in the old ways and had a vested interest in them; perhaps, as they hinted to me, they knew reasons incomprehensible to a foreigner why it seemed best for the development of a growing boy to keep him apart, lonely and bored, surrounded by serious formal grown men. I never questioned their desire to do what they conceived as best for their Crown Prince, but I did think they were woefully mistaken. They all knew just where I stood—"Mrs. Vining's all right, she says the same thing to everybody," one of them was reported to me as saying—and so I was not going behind their backs when, having this unparalleled opportunity, I expressed my views to Their Majesties themselves.

That Mr. Mitani, possibly in some alarm, reported all that was said on that occasion to Mr. Tajima, the Minister of the Imperial Household, I found out the next day, when Mr. Tajima summoned me to his office to discuss it. He had complete notes on the conference, and we went over it in detail, point by point. He was not antagonistic about it; he just wanted to be sure that he knew and understood exactly what I had said.

The second such conference, which took place the following year, did not cause so much excitement, though it had an interesting sidelight. This time Mr. Tajima saw me before I talked with

Their Majesties and told me several things that he would like me to say to the Emperor that he did not feel comfortable about saying himself. Dr. Koizumi told me on another occasion that I was the only person who could express my thoughts to the Emperor as if he were an ordinary human being; the others, he said, even himself, would go very stiff with him.

Nothing much came of my efforts. The Empress was especially eager to have the two princes live together, and that seemed a possibility when the Crown Prince got his larger house in 1950. For a time, indeed, Prince Masahito spent two or three days a week with the Crown Prince, but even this came to an end after I left. A dormitory was established at the Peers' School, and both brothers spent three days a week there. By 1952 Prince Masahito had ceased to stay in the dormitory at all, and was spending only Sunday with the Crown Prince. Mr. Tajima wrote me: "Now I do not like to disappoint you too much, but I regret to say that your cherished hope for the Crown Prince and his brother to live together has not been quite realized."

Nevertheless, a beginning was made. The Crown Prince is having his own two sons and his daughter live with him and Princess Michiko.

When Mr. Tajima had something that he himself wanted to talk with me about, he would ask me to stop in at his office in the Imperial Household Building; when, however, he had, as occasionally he did, a special message directly from the Emperor, he would come all the way to my house, refuse assistance from Tane, who with Violet would retire upstairs and speculate on what was going on below, and, drawing his chair close to mine, utter the imperial message in low, pregnant tones.

In 1949 he came to tell me that Princess Kazuko, the Crown Prince's elder sister, was engaged to Mr. Toshimichi Takatsukasa, son of the Chief Priest of the Meiji Shrine. The engagement would be announced in a few days, but the Emperor had directed Mr. Tajima to inform me beforehand. I did not realize the degree of this consideration until Mr. Tajima, having fulfilled his orders, gave vent to his emotions. "His Majesty *himself* sent me!" he exclaimed. "This is much too good for you!"

I always felt perfectly comfortable with Mr. Tajima: he was ever honest and direct; I knew that he liked me; I also knew when he was displeased; I knew exactly where I stood with him. We continued our friendship after I returned to the United States, and though our correspondence fell off as the years lengthened, I had just finished a long letter to him one evening in December, 1968, when the cable came telling of his death at the age of eighty.

The Emperor never spoke explicitly to me of his friendship with General MacArthur, although it was implicit in his interest in whatever I told him about my meetings with the General. When General MacArthur was recalled, the Emperor broke tradition by going to make a farewell call on him. Though he had been to the American Embassy to call on the General some ten times during the five and a half years, he had always gone to see him in his official capacity; this last time he went to see a private citizen and a friend. It was Mr. Tajima who in a letter to me dated May 4, 1951, told me of the Japanese feelings about the dismissal of the General.

"The news of the dismissal of General MacArthur greatly shocked and grieved the Japanese people. Especially for His Majesty who had had such a personal respect and attachment to him, it was indeed a sad news. Of course we have nothing to say about the domestic matter of the United States, but I think it is natural that His Majesty should have felt sorry that the general had to go away so suddenly."

This friendship between the Emperor and the victorious general is a measure of the magnanimity of both men, but more remarkable in the case of the Emperor. Many of the qualities of his mind and spirit are of a kind unusual to find in high places. Personal courage, yes, fortitude, dignity, self-discipline, love for his people, a strong sense of duty: these one would hope for in a monarch and these he has in good measure. The sensitive concern for the comfort and welfare of those around him, the scientist's range of vision and devotion to truth, his genuine humility: these are not usually compatible with the formalities and the adulation that beset a throne. What seems to me to go beyond all these is the largeness of spirit that can enable a man to accept impoverishment and humiliation (which is quite different from humility) without bitterness, to meet the invading enemy without fear, to enter upon friendship with the triumphant General: this seems to me to partake of nobility.

5.

The General

THE STRUCTURE of the Allied Occupation of Japan was entirely different from that of Germany, where the division into four zones controlled separately by four great powers has resulted in East-West problems culminating in the Berlin Wall. In Japan General Douglas MacArthur was the Supreme Commander of the Allied Powers, known familiarly as SCAP, and he stood alone at the top. For almost five months after the surrender of Japan he had only American troops under him; then, in February, 1946, a small contingent of British, Australian, New Zealand, Indian and Canadian soldiers arrived and were based in Kure, in southern Honshu, across the bay from Hiroshima. The Soviet Union early offered to provide soldiers to occupy Hokkaido, the northern island, but the offer was promptly and firmly declined.

The windows of General MacArthur's office in the Dai-Ichi Insurance Building looked out on the outer moat of the Imperial Palace to the walls and woods of the inner Palace grounds with, on fine days, the great cone of Fuji, sixty miles away, floating in the sky above. By officials within the Palace which he overlooked, General MacArthur was known with a mixture of respect and humor, and perhaps a touch of affection as well, as Ohoribata, Honorable Across-the-Moat.

The manner of his life was well known. He lived in the American Embassy with his lovely wife and small son, Arthur. Each morning he drove to the Dai-Ichi Building, ten minutes away, with all the traffic lights turned in his favor as his long black car with the five-starred flag approached. He worked in his office till two or two-thirty, returned home for lunch and a rest, and was back in the Dai-Ichi by five-thirty, to stay until eight or nine, when he went home for dinner alone with his wife. This was his invariable routine every day in the week, including Sundays. He entertained guests at his home for lunch now and then but he never—or so it was widely said and written—attended parties anywhere else, though I was present when he went to the Dominion Day reception at the Canadian Mission in June, 1947. Each time that he went in or out of the Dai-Ichi Building followed by an aide, a little crowd of Japanese and Americans lined up on the sidewalk to watch him pass.

As a public figure he was remote, austere, awe-inspiring, all-powerful. To many Japanese he was a liberator; they respected and trusted him. An editorial in the *Nippon Times* called him "a statesman-administrator without peer." To many Americans, however, incurably egalitarian and irreverent, there was something inappropriate and even a little comic in the sight of another American enjoying so conspicuous a pedestal. A journalist dubbed him "the Star-spangled Mikado," and a G.I., watching the procession from Dai-Ichi entrance to car, said of the attendant aide, "Who's the guy walking with God?"

His purpose, often stated, in the occupation of Japan was first to disarm and demilitarize the country and to prevent starvation and disease in the aftermath of defeat, and then, using the Japanese governmental structure, to "build a future for the people of Japan based upon considerations of realism and justice," through the renunciation of war and the instruments of war, the emancipation of women, the unionization of labor, the liberalizing of education, the democratization of economic institutions and the establishment of freedom of speech, thought, religion and assembly. He wanted, moreover, to put Japan on her feet as quickly as possible, to achieve a peace treaty, to withdraw the Occupation and leave the defense of Japan to the United Nations. All this he was advocating as early as March, 1947; in 1949 he painted a picture of a peaceful neutral Japan as "the Switzerland of the Pacific." It was a noble concept; it caught the imagination and loyalty of great numbers of Japanese people; it made crusaders of many of the Occupation personnel.

I met him for the first time on the third of May, 1947, when I was invited to lunch at the American Embassy. There were seventeen other guests that day, and it was typical of my life in Tokyo that I already knew the foreigners who were present, the Dutch, the Australians and the New Zealanders, but none of the Americans except Mrs. MacArthur, whom I had met two or three times.

I had never even seen the General. He came in, like royalty, at the last, when everybody else had assembled, and there was a perceptible—almost electric—tightening of the atmosphere when he appeared.

He was sixty-seven at that time but looked more than ten years younger: handsome, tall, vigorous, magnetic, commanding, with a high forehead, deep-set, keen, seeking eyes, a clear, fresh, smooth skin, a firm, fine, sensitive mouth. His aide introduced us all, and then we went in to lunch immediately. I sat between Brigadier Quillian, the prosecuting attorney at the War Crimes Tribunal from New Zealand, and General Ferris, a Vermonter, who had come to Japan in September, 1945, with the first big landing at Atsugi airport. He had gone to Wakamatsu, far in the northeast of Honshu, in a jeep with an aide and two sergeants, to accept the surrender of 5,000 armed Japanese soldiers. The faith and the courage that made possible the disarming of Japan by a small number of American soldiers without bloodshed is something that we should remember with pride and gratitude. We should remember too that without the Emperor's word and example, it could not have been done.

After lunch I had a short talk with the General alone, for Sir William Webb, the Australian Justice for the War Crimes Tribunal, who had been talking to me, faded away at the General's approach and no one else came near until it was evident that our conversation was over. He asked me about the Crown Prince, about my life, if "they" gave me a chance, and made some reference to *Anna and the King of Siam*. When I laughed and answered, "Oh, that book!" he said with quick understanding, "I imagine that's been hard to take." He spoke of the Emperor in a tone of friendliness and sympathy, saying, "In this nation of slaves he was the number one slave, but he is being freed. He is genuinely a simple and direct man and a democratic one." He asked me to come and see him in the Dai-Ichi Building the following week. We rejoined the rest of the party, and the farewells began.

For all my encounters with the General, as for all my experiences in Japan, I have detailed journals to draw upon. These have been of immeasurable help to me in writing my books about Japan, for even "total recall" is dependable only for a few hours; after that the memory plays tricks on one.

The importance of this kind of note-taking was brought home to me by General Schilling, the Dutch General who was with General Wainwright in a Japanese prison camp. I met him at a party given by Mr. (later Sir) Arthur Comyns-Carr, the English prosecuting attorney at the War Crimes Tribunal, who was himself a very interesting man. General Schilling, in spite of all that he had been through in the war, came out of it without bitterness and with a sort of kindly, warm wisdom that was very lovable. He was a soldierly-looking man with steady blue eyes and considerable charm of manner. He asked me if I was keeping a diary, and when I told him that I was writing full letters to my sister and that she was saving them for me, he gave me a little lecture on the importance of preserving those letters. "You are writing for history," he said. "Hundreds of years from now when we are all forgotten, people will read those letters. You are the Marco Polo of your day." In spite of myself, I was impressed but also aware that Marco Polo wrote on parchment, whereas the paper on which I was typing my daily impressions had not even a rag content; it was postwar pulp of the most soluble kind.

The first of the six conversations I had with the General in his office—seven if you count the time I took the Crown Prince to see him—during my four years in Tokyo took place five days after the luncheon. All of the meetings followed the same pattern. I would arrive at the Dai-Ichi at six o'clock in the evening, when the traffic in Tokyo had died down and the shadows were long over the moat, take the elevator to the eighth floor, to be met by the aide on duty, usually Colonel Laurence Bunker, who would escort me in to the General's office, a large, paneled room furnished with an uncluttered desk, a leather-covered davenport and easy chairs, some photographs and a framed quotation from Livy on the Criticism of Generals.

He would welcome me with a rather elaborate compliment, usually the same one, and then usher me to the davenport. He would sit opposite to me in the armchair, and for forty minutes to an hour we would talk. He would ask me a few questions first, with the preface, "Tell me, Mrs. Vining, if you can and if you care to—" and always they were questions I was glad to answer. The Japanese in the Imperial Household liked to have me talk with General MacArthur; they knew I would give him a sympathetic picture of the Crown Prince, and I think they liked the indirect touch with SCAP.

It was not only a matter of question and answer. I brought up topics of my own. After I had said whatever it was I had to say, then the General took over the conversation, and for the rest of the time, he talked, and talked eloquently, about a variety of subjects, religion, India and *Kim*, the Emperor, the Philippines, Japan, China, war and peace. I sometimes felt that such a display of fireworks deserved more of an audience than one unimportant woman, but in time I realized that these fireworks were not just for me. Many other visitors too were favored with what were probably almost exactly the same words. When John Gunther wrote his book, *The Riddle of MacArthur*, the General was still in the Dai-Ichi and nobody was allowed to quote him directly, but from the topics which Mr. Gunther listed as having heard the General discuss I knew, or thought I knew, approximately what had been said. When in 1951 the General made his speech to Congress, he spoke of war in almost the same words that he had used to me. This does not make him any less sincere; it only gives a glimpse of a man who led an essentially lonely life, who thought much and liked to air his views to an attentive and receptive listener.

In that first conference he asked me if I thought the asking for an American tutor for the Crown Prince was "a cynical political move" on the part of the Japanese. "It's your first reaction I want," he said. "If there was anything of that sort it has changed now, for you have made yourself an entirely different place." I was certain that there had been no motive of the sort, that it had been a genuine—and perhaps impulsive—gesture on the part of the Emperor. Many Japanese, like some Americans, had been profoundly doubtful about the wisdom of it.

The General wanted to know about my household and whether I had ever felt spied on in any way (I had not), and he asked how long I was going to stay in Japan. I told him that my contract was for one year but that I had been told unofficially that I would be asked to stay on. He said that he hoped that I would. He asked about the school which the Crown Prince attended, and I told him that I had given the boys in the Crown Prince's class Western names, so that the Crown Prince might have for once the experience of being just one boy among others. He asked the Crown Prince's name and when I told him "Jimmy," said, "That's a good name," a comment I was glad to pass on later to the chamberlains, who had feared that the name smacked too much of informality.

He told me that when I first came to Japan, "because of the dangers involved," they could not do anything for me, but that now I had made a niche for myself I could have anything I wanted. I had already summed up this situation for myself. For the first three months I was in Japan I did not have access to the PX or the Commissary, which the newspaper men and the LARA representatives enjoyed as well as the Army and Navy civilians. The Imperial Household was supplying all the necessities of my life, but food was very scarce at that time and I did not feel free to have guests unless I could draw on American supplies; in addition there were all the thousand and one things that we buy in drugstores—tissues, shampoo, tooth paste, writing paper and the like—which were not available on the Japanese market at any price but were to be had in the PX in abundance. My loyal friends at home were indefatigable in sending me packages, but it was expensive and slow. It was thanks to the Army that they reached me, for I was permitted from the first an APO number. In January, however, I received PX and Commissary cards. There was nothing more that I needed from General MacArthur then; the following year, when I had a car of my own brought from the United States, the Army made it possible and also gave me a gas ration. In addition, when I needed a doctor, it was the General's physician to whom I went, first Colonel Kendrick and then Colonel Canada, and on two occasions I was able to get from them the sulfa drugs which probably saved the lives of two small Japanese children desperately ill with pneumonia.

To return, after this digression, to the General and that first interview in the Dai-Ichi, he asked me if I was happy. The question surprised me. I answered, after a moment's thought, that I was. I missed my friends at home; I was often deeply depressed by the hideous destruction that I saw around me and the suffering that came in the aftermath of war; I longed for the luxury of being inconspicuous; but, yes, I was happy. My horizons had been pushed back to an exhilarating degree, and I felt a new freedom in the wider scope. I loved my work. I was making friends whom I would cherish all my life.

It has been said elsewhere that General MacArthur was a religious man, and this, I believe, was true. One finds in his releases and speeches references that are not just the conventional ones of the politician but have a depth and freshness that bespeak sincerity. That first day he spoke to me of religion in the natural and simple way of a person whose thoughts run often along those lines. We had been speaking of the conviction of the value of the individual human being that lies at the heart of democracy, and he went on to say that from his childhood he had hated to read the story of the Crucifixion because of the brutality in it and the stress on physical torture, but that about three months earlier he had reread it in an entirely different light, that he felt the story was told as it was to show that in spite of physical degradation a really great idea cannot be killed. That idea, he said, must take root in Japan; he spoke of the Christian missionaries whom he was encouraging to come.

I have told of this first conversation in some detail because it was the first one and formed a pattern for the rest. I saw him three times more in 1947, in connection with the trip I made to the United States to speak at the *New York Herald Tribune* Forum, and saw him not at all in 1948. In 1949 I was again invited for lunch, and a conference at the Dai-Ichi was suggested. I took the Crown Prince to call on the General that summer, at his suggestion, and in 1950, my last year in Japan, I was twice at the Dai-Ichi for an evening talk. I kept a full account of all these meetings. Some of it is repetitious, some of it more pertinent at the moment than it would be now, but some of the things that were said then throw small gleams of light, like the pencil flashlights in a darkened theater on the programs, on a page of history that has now been turned and perhaps forgotten.

He told me, for instance, about his first meeting with the Emperor. "I pressed him rather hard," he said. "I asked him if he accepted responsibility for the war. He replied, 'Before I answer I want to say something else. You may do anything you like with me. I accept that. You may hang me. But I never wanted the war. For one thing I didn't think we could win it. But beyond that I disliked and distrusted the military party, and I did what I could to prevent the war.'"

In his *Reminiscences* the General quotes the Emperor much to the same effect but in far more formal language. I suppose the actuality, through the interpreter, was somewhere between the two.

Always the General spoke of His Majesty with liking and admiration, praising his scholarly interest in biology, his simplicity and sincerity, his innate fineness and "high character." "Whatever country it is all over the world," he said once rather naïvely, "blood tells." But a little later, as if to correct any possible imputation of snobbishness, he said of the Americans who died during the war at their country's call, "I don't know what their birth was but their death was magnificent."

He asked me about the Emperor's relationship with the Crown Prince. "The Emperor," he said, "talks to me about everything under the sun but he has never mentioned his son to me."

I was glad to be able to tell him of the deep affection between the Crown Prince and his father, of the boy's admiration for the Emperor and his happiness when His Majesty was praised.

To the General's respect for the Emperor as a man and his attitude toward the Emperor as an institution, Prime Minister Shigeru Yoshida ascribed the success of the Occupation. In his *Memoirs*, published in 1960, nine years after the signing of the Peace Treaty, he wrote: "The fact remains that the respect and understanding shown by the General toward the Throne and his decision to exculpate the Emperor from all and any relationship with war crimes, did more than anything else to lessen the fears of the majority of the Japanese people in regard to the Occupation and to reconcile them to it. I have no hesitation in saying that it was the attitude adopted by General MacArthur towards the Throne, more than any other single factor, that made the Occupation an historic success."

The General spoke to me also of the execution of General Yamashita by an American military court in the Philippines in 1945, about which a book had been written that he refused to allow into Japan. When freedom of thought comes up against military censorship, censorship wins, whatever a General may say is desirable for the Japanese.

Of Yamashita he said, "Poor man." He paused for a moment and then went on. "I suppose we did right to hang him. I think we did. But I'll never know. I remember how I felt at Bataan when Tokyo Rose was broadcasting every night. They thought they had me in a trap, and every evening for about ten minutes Tokyo Rose described how they would hang me. She described the exact spot in Hibiya Park where the scaffold would be set up and the march they would make to it and then the hanging itself. Poor Mrs. MacArthur. I kept it away from her, but she got hold of a portable radio one night and she listened to the whole thing. I thought she would collapse. But I know something of how Yamashita felt."

I murmured some comment on the hideousness of war.

He agreed and went on to give the most powerful denunciation of war that I have ever heard, for his own experience and the things he had seen, the responsibilities he had carried, had put layer upon layer of hatred of war and sorrow and disgust into his voice. He spoke of its futility ("It settles nothing; nobody can win"), its beastliness, of the contrast of modern war with the stylized game that war was in the Middle Ages, of the fact that there is no place for war in the world today.

"It's been a theological failure, Mrs. Vining," he said. "And now the whole preparedness cycle is beginning again. I've seen it happen twice, and now I see Eisenhower and the new Navy getting us ready a third time and it makes me sick to my very soul." He added that a Third World War, with the atomic bomb, would be the end of everything and that the only lucky people would be the dead.

In May, 1950, he spoke again of his hope for a peace treaty. "If it were only between Japan and the United States, it could be settled in a very short time. Unfortunately, Japan's interests have got sidetracked between the Allies and another part of the Allies [he meant Russia]. But even so, if we could get some honesty in there, the peace treaty could be made in a rather short time. We owe it to Japan. We made an agreement with her and she has lived up to her part of it, and now we are in honor bound to do ours. I think it could be done rather soon, if people don't pay too much attention to what Bob Eichelberger is saying about making Japan our military ally and getting her to fight our wars for us."

Just about six weeks later the North Koreans invaded South Korea, and the whole picture changed. That General Headquarters in Tokyo were unprepared for this movement, at any rate at the particular time that it came, is suggested by the fact that that summer for the first time the college sons and daughters of the occupying personnel were allowed to come to Japan to spend their summer vacations with their parents. The very day that the news broke, Violet and I went to a large party at the Officers' Club, at which were the children of some of our friends. Vincent and Edith Rich had both their daughter and their son, a fine, glowing young man who was later killed in the Korean War. Ellen Oppler too had just arrived. Her father, Alfred Oppler, had been the youngest judge in Berlin when Hitler came in and had had to escape both because of his liberal views and because of a Jewish grandfather. After beginning his career in the United States by raking leaves in Cambridge, Massachusettes, he found finally a place in the U.S. State Department, in an office concerned with European law, and was then in Tokyo with the Government Section of the Occupation, working with the Japanese on laws implementing the new constitution. Alfred and his vivid, warm-hearted wife, Charlotte, were both desperately distressed that night by the news from Korea, foreseeing, I thought, the beginning of another world conflagration.

The next day I received an invitation to a party to be given by some of General MacArthur's aides, who obviously were not expecting that before the party could take place, U.S. planes would be roaring over Tokyo every morning and evening as the Air Force commuted to Korea to drop bombs.

I saw the General once more in Japan, on November 29, just before Violet and I sailed for home. I had asked if I might see him to say good-by, and an appointment was made for Tuesday the 28th. On Monday, however, Colonel Bunker telephoned to say that something had come up which would make it "inconvenient" for the General to see me on Tuesday and could I come on Wednesday instead. What the inconvenience was I learned on Tuesday afternoon when the *Stars and Stripes* published the news that great numbers of Chinese soldiers, not a token army of volunteers, were breaking through in North Korea, with the UN soldiers retreating all the way along the line.

I expected to have the Wednesday appointment also called off, but it was not, and at six-thirty I saw the General for more than an hour. He looked tired and drawn but his color was good. He spoke kindly of my service in Japan, gave me advice for the future which I have not taken (that I should marry again) and advice that I have followed (that I write a book about my experiences). I think in the event, however, the book, *Windows for the Crown Prince*, was a disappointment to him, for it was centered wholly on the Crown Prince, and his suggestion to me had been that I write "a dignified and sound appraisal," presumably of the Occupation, in contrast to the "cheap and inaccurate" accounts of the journalists.

His mind that day, of course, was chiefly on the situation in Korea. He told me that there were 200,000 Chinese already there, with 300,000 more ready to pour down. He had 125,000 men and had been told he would get no more. "I can't throw these educated, carefully nurtured boys against those hordes." The suffering and death weighed heavily on him. "My losses are very heavy." He spoke with grief of one group of fine youngsters who had gone into battle, only 10 per cent of whom had come out again.

"There has been a great change in China during the last fifty years," he told me. "Up until 1900 China was divided into about five sections, each ruled by a war lord. The Chinese people themselves were peaceful. The profession of soldier was the lowest there was. But during these fifty years their whole point of view has changed."

He traced the modern attempts to unify China, through Sun Yat-sen and Generalissimo Chiang Kai-shek, to the Communists. In the process, through the years, he said, the Chinese had got used to fighting and become militarized. "Their leaders are bitten with that worst of all diseases, the only cure for which is death— the disease of power." He prophesied a Chinese conquest of Tibet, Indochina and Burma. "Japan's greatest danger," he said, "is not from Russia but from China," and he told me an anecdote about Manuel Quezon. He and Quezon, he said, had been friends since their youth, when they were gay young blades in Manila together with very little money to spend. At the time of Bataan he had persuaded Quezon to be evacuated, got a submarine for him and went down to the dock to see him off. At parting Quezon said to him, "Douglas, I haven't any doubt even in this darkest hour that we will some day defeat the Japanese. I haven't any fear of Japanese domination. What I do fear with an awful dread is—the Chinese." The General said that he did not agree with Quezon at the time but that those words had come back to him often since then.

He told me that they had had long meetings the day before in the Dai-Ichi Building, when he had recommended that Chiang Kai-shek's offer of troops be accepted and that Chinese soldiers from Taiwan be put into Korea to fight the invading Chinese. "I could get them there in ten days," he said. "I have the ships. There is disaffection among the Chinese Communists already. To find themselves fighting other Chinese would increase disaffection and confusion."

He seemed to have no fear that such an action might bring in Russia as well as China and trigger the Third World War of which he had earlier spoken with so much dread.

He spoke with feeling of the plight of Korea, whatever was done and whichever side won. "Oh, it is pitiful, pitiful. Fierce fighting men pour down from the north and then up from the south and now down from the north again. Each house has a North Korean flag and a South Korean flag and most of the time they don't know which to wave. Both sides line them up and shoot them down. The country was poor to begin with. They will be destroyed—utterly destroyed."

When I left, I said to him, "I don't suppose there is anything I can ever do for you, but if I could I would." He answered, "Yes, there is something you can do for me. Say a little prayer for me now and then."

I said I would. He took me to the outer office, told Colonel Bunker to see me to my car, and we shook hands.

Five months later *The Philadelphia Evening Bulletin* called me on the telephone to say that President Truman had dismissed General MacArthur from his post and what did I think about it. I was shocked and shaken.

It is a fundamental principle of American government that the military shall be subordinate to the political power and that the President of the United States is also Commander-in-Chief of the armed forces. He cannot tolerate insubordination on the part of even the most successful general. But I thought and still think that the way it was done was indefensible. The fact and finality of the dismissal could be neither avoided nor softened, it is true, but the blow might have been delivered in privacy, some opportunity made for him to step down with dignity, to depart with a semblance of honor.

The Japanese were stunned. They would not have dismissed the lowest menial with so little regard for his feelings and his position in the eyes of others. There was an outpouring of sorrow and gratitude when General MacArthur left Tokyo less than a week after he had heard the news of his dismissal over the radio. As I have said, the Emperor broke all precedent by going to call on him, now a private citizen. Five hundred thousand Japanese people lined the road from the American Embassy to Haneda to bow to him in farewell. There are touching stories of the efforts that they made to get there. One mountain village, for instance, raised a purse to send its most respected old woman with her grandson down to Tokyo to bow for them all. Many carried home-made signs: "We are Gratitude to General MacArthur." A Japanese friend of mine told me of a man who was ill in bed and unable to go himself, who sent his servant instead to stand in the street. He put on his formal kimono, and at the moment when he thought the General would be passing he sat up in bed and bowed low, all by himself, in tribute to the victorious enemy who had guided his country through its most difficult days.

I saw General MacArthur once more, though not for a number of years. He did not answer my notes and he made no comment on *Windows*, though Mrs. Gibbons, Arthur's governess, wrote me, "We all loved your book." He did not attend the dinner which the Japan Society of New York gave for the Crown Prince in 1953. But in 1959, after I had returned from the Crown Prince's wedding, I wrote again to General MacArthur and asked him if I might go and tell him about it. I received a prompt and cordial reply.

He welcomed me in the large living room, well stocked with Japanese treasures, of his apartment in the Waldorf Towers. Mrs. MacArthur had another engagement that day, he told me, but she had sent her regards to me. I was saddened to see how much older he seemed, but of course he *was* older, eighty instead of seventy. He was interested, briefly, in the Crown Prince, but soon began to reminisce about Japan and his experiences there. Some of the things he told me were those I had heard before in the Dai-Ichi, but now enlarged and emphasized, as if he had sat and thought about them until, like a drawing traced over and over with a soft pencil, the color deepened and the outlines blurred.

He is, still, a highly controversial figure; people are wholly admiring or wholly and often violently critical. His stock tends to be at present, following the published reminiscences of men around Mr. Truman, low. I had been dazzled when I first met him, dazzled and awed. Later I came to recognize the vanity that was his great weakness. "I did this," he would say, "I ordered that," where others might have said "we." It made him hypersensitive to criticism, unable to praise other generals, willing to withdraw into his eyrie guarded by adoring aides. But vanity is a human quality, a shadow in the picture, not the whole of it. He was a great leader, a man of brilliant mind and extraordinary courage, a man of vision. The new prosperity and peace he foresaw for Japan have come true largely because of his efforts to get them started. The United States owes him a profound debt of gratitude for what he did in our name in Japan.

6.

Diplomats in Tokyo

ONE OF the most difficult things in writing about the past is to remember—and to convey convincingly—how people thought and felt in a period that is gone. Every writer of historical fiction knows this. It is relatively simple to create the atmosphere of the physical past—the farthingale, the curtsey and the bow, the great hall with the smoke curling through a hole in the roof, the rushes on the floor and the dogs under the table, the wherry in the river—and even to do it so vividly that the modern reader feels himself there. It is altogether more difficult to cause the reader to accept the state of mind then prevailing, the ideas that people took for granted, the father's absolute control over the grown child, the rigidly stratified society, the absence of choice as to the number of children an exhausted woman must produce. That John Donne's fragile young wife died bearing her thirteenth child was in his time accepted as an act of God; modern readers, finding it incomprehensible, angrily question the depth of his love for her and even the sincerity of his religion. After my *Take Heed of Loving Me* came out, I had a number of letters from readers scolding Donne, through me, for behavior that was blameless in the mental climate of his age.

Similarly, though it is only twenty years ago, the climate of Western thought about postwar Japan is difficult to recapture. The devastation and poverty—long lines of drab people waiting for inadequate rations, pretty young girls clumping about in men's shoes inherited from fathers or brothers who perished in the war, women washing clothes beside the street in little wooden basins of cold water without soap, a family living in an air-raid shelter where the tall father could not stand upright, battered taxis running on the steam from fires of little wooden blocks, a whole city without restaurants or clothing stores: these can be grasped, even though in the present prosperity of Japan they may seem all but incredible. It is more difficult to recall the war-induced bitterness that many Westerners felt, the chasm between the Occupation and the occupied, the ban on fraternization, the stratification of the Occupation, the diplomatic life that went on circulating busily up in the air, without a foot on the ground of the country itself.

Even during the four years that I was in Japan, however, thought began to change, as events in the world outside threw their shadows into the sealed stockade that was occupied Japan. The Berlin Blockade and the allied airlift, which started in 1948 and continued through the first half of 1949, the takeover of China by the Communists and the withdrawal of the Nationalist Chinese to Taiwan in 1949, the setting off by Russia of an atomic explosion years before it was expected, the increased activity of Communists in Japan: all these factors had an effect on the purposes of the Occupation and the attitudes toward Japan. What had been at first a military occupation sent there to disarm Japan and to make it impossible for her ever again to disturb the peace of the world turned into a crusade to put her on her feet again economically, to convert her into a self-supporting democratic nation, a bastion of the free world in the East and an ally of the United States.

I had not gone there either to take part in a punitive occupation or to win the Japanese over to a political and military alliance with the United States. I went first to serve the cause of peace and reconciliation and later, when I knew the Crown Prince, to do my best for that small boy and for the other Japanese young people with whom I came in touch. I was an employee of Japan, and I wished to live my life among the Japanese with as few of the advantages of membership in the victor nation as I could manage. I was nevertheless drawn into the fringes of the Western social life that went on in Tokyo, and I found it an instructive experience to look at my own civilization from the outside, from the camp of the former enemy; to try to understand both, to watch the changes that were occurring. It was not always easy; I felt a strain in being often exposed between the two sides and under constant surveillance by both, but it was always interesting.

No one entered Japan in those days without the permission of the Occupation, which brought in all the supplies necessary for Western life—food, gasoline, cigarettes, candy, liquor, clothes— and requisitioned the remaining Japanese houses, clubs, resort hotels, and the best of the transportation for the use of Occupation personnel and their dependents. A few missionaries, who had to supply themselves as best they could, a few journalists and "traders" who had access to PX and Commissary, were allowed in; and of course diplomatic representatives of allied and neutral countries, who could not be kept out.

They returned to the embassies that were still standing or were assigned requisitioned Japanese houses. But the embassies were now called "liaison missions," and their heads, including the representative of the U.S. State Department, were posted not to the Emperor but to General MacArthur. When I first went there, Mr. George Atcheson was this representative, and I knew the Atchesons several months before I met General MacArthur.

Late in November, 1946, I was first invited to their house for dinner. Since the MacArthurs were occupying the U.S. Embassy, the Atchesons had a mansion formerly owned by one of the Zaibatsu families (the great industrial combines that controlled the economic life of Japan before the war); it was a beautiful modern Western-style house with a garden. Mrs. Atcheson, who was the niece of one of my philosophy professors at Bryn Mawr, Mrs. Frederick Delaguna, was a rather fragile, warm and charming woman. From time to time they would invite me to one of their parties, where I always met a sprinkling of journalists, some American admirals and generals, who were said to be more plentiful in Tokyo than privates, and members of the liaison missions of other countries. After one of their parties, I always got invitations to other parties from people whom I met there, and so my acquaintance widened. During the first two years, when living conditions were still difficult and many of the wives had not yet come, an unattached woman was much more in demand than she was later, and I had more invitations than for various reasons I cared to accept.

Returning hospitality was a problem, for I had a small staff, a small dining room and no liquor ration, and, in fact, I did not want one. I came to realize that in a society where people went to large formal parties seven nights a week, there was a place for the small dinner of eight, with informal conversation and simple food, and I began to invite people more freely. "If you want a drink," I would say, "get it before you come." Sometimes one of the guests would round up all the rest and they would arrive together, a little late, redolent and relaxed. During the last of my four years I was able for special occasions to borrow the Crown Prince's own cook, and then we had excellent food as well as interesting guests. I always had Japanese friends too; in the early days there were no Japanese guests at Western parties, and the diplomats were often glad to meet them on neutral ground.

There were other reasons why I did not accept all the invitations I received. My schedule soon became very full, and I was saving my strength and energy for my work. The large and formal diplomatic parties, moreover, though they had for me the charm of novelty, were not an unmixed pleasure, owing to the constant shift of acquaintances as some went home and others replaced them, the extremely cautious conversation which made them rather dull, and the screwing up of my courage which it required of me to enter upon them without an escort. Above all, the elaborate food and wines, the luxurious appointments, the throngs of Japanese servants, made too sharp a contrast with what I saw daily of the struggle of most Japanese people just to live. I did not want to be identified with this detached and unreal world; I was a teacher employed by the Japanese and, I sometimes felt, rather an expensive luxury for them at that time.

One of the early receptions that I went to, though it was one of the most interesting, crystallized my feeling in the matter. It was given by Justice Mansfield, who was then the New Zealand judge on the International Military Tribunal. He was leaving soon, to be replaced by Justice Northcroft, and this was a farewell party.

I went in my car, which was an aged and infirm Plymouth that had literally been through the war, in Singapore. On the way to the Imperial Hotel it broke down; my driver hopped out, found a piece of rusty wire in the rubble of a bomb site and mended the car within fifteen minutes. While I sat in the car waiting, I counted twenty-six men, women and children barefoot in the gray January street. True, they had wooden clogs or straw sandals, but their feet were purple with cold. Now, when I have seen affluent college students barefoot in winter on the asphalt streets of Swarthmore, I would not be so shocked, but then it seemed to me a symbol of poverty and suffering.

The cocktail party was held in the ballroom of the Imperial Hotel, that extraordinary masterpiece of Frank Lloyd Wright's, now vanished. It was a mixture of Moorish, Mexican and Adirondack lodge styles, with here and there a shy Japanese touch or two in the long, low corridors and tiled passages, shadowy nooks lit by dim lights in wrought-iron fixtures, balconies under carved stone eaves, and unexpected glimpses of gardens and trickles of water. The ballroom was vaulted and roughly cruciform, the ecclesiastical effect heightened by the refreshment table which, with its fine white cloth and branched candlesticks, suggested an altar.

Representatives of all the nations were there, except the Japanese, who could get into the hotel only as servants. General Derevyanko, head of the Russian mission and Soviet representative on the Allied Council, grasped my hand, said severely, "How do you do?" and strode on. The other top Russian, General Zaryanov, who was justice on the Military Tribunal, was more chatty. He had an interpreter with him, a small, energetic, white-haired woman as full of vitality as her chief. Somebody in the circle asked General Zaryanov how his cold was and he replied that it was better, adding that there was a Russian expression always used in such cases, "Thanks to your kind prayers." "Oh, that's like the Japanese O *kage same de*," I said, "Thanks to your honorable shadow."

"Indeed? That must be why the Russians and the Japanese get along so well."

"But you're counting," Diana Kenderdine pointed out, "on having other people's prayers."

"Certainly," he said. "That's why we're winning on every front."

That was the only time I ever actually met any Russians. They soon retired behind the iron gates of their embassy where, it was rumored, a staff of five hundred were busy grinding out Communist propaganda on printing presses in the basement, and they seldom appeared at parties.

Mr. Arthur Comyns-Carr was there, the British prosecutor on the War Crimes Tribunal. He was billeted at the Canadian Legation, where I had already met him. Later, after he returned to London, he was knighted. His mother, he told me, had written a book about Italy in the 1870's, which was illustrated by Randolph Caldecott, the much loved illustrator of children's books. He had many Quaker friends, and one of his ancestors had strayed to Philadelphia and married among the Fishers, a Quaker family of importance in the eighteenth century. Three Fisher brothers, Thomas, Miles and Samuel, were characters in my book *The Vir-*

ginia Exiles, which I had put aside when I went to Japan and which I took up again after my return and published in 1955. Mr. Comyns-Carr was tall and thin with a lock of lank brown hair that fell across his forehead and a lean, long, lined face full of kindness, intelligence and humor. I always remember him for something he said once, after he had asked me about the Crown Prince, "Brains? Oh yes, my dear. But brains are a penny a dozen. The real question is, what has he got in the way of character?"

The Gascoignes were there too that day, then Mr. and Mrs. Joseph Gascoigne; after the New Year honors of 1947 they became Sir Alvary and Lady Gascoigne. They were the epitome of the British aristocrat, just on the edge of being caricatures. Sir Alvary looked and talked like C. Aubrey Smith, the actor, and Lady Gascoigne, who was a very handsome woman, might have been Lady Tweed-Brogue of Abbey St. Ruskin, Muffins-cum-Marmalade, Haunts. She always wore dramatic clothes—that day she was swathed in a romantic black satin cloak edged with gold, with a heavy gold chain and dangling medallion—and she founded the Tokyo Society for the Prevention of Cruelty to Animals.

Justice Pal of India was there, a massive Hindu who looked more Negroid than Asian. He was to be the only one of the eleven judges on the Tribunal to dissent from the majority opinion, saying that he considered it a victors' court and not qualified to judge.

General MacArthur was not present. I saw and talked with the Atchesons and the MacMahon Balls, and Brigadier and Mrs. John O'Brien from Australia, as well as General and Mrs. Frayne Baker, General and Mrs. Mueller and others. Circulating among them all were the representatives of *Life* and *Time* and *Newsweek* with cameras and flashlights.

The chief impression I had when it was over was the unspoken but perceptible struggle for national power and advantage behind it all, and the unreality of such a gathering in the center of the huge devastated and hungry city, where people went barefoot in the cold. I said to myself, I shall go to no more Occupation parties.

But I did. Over the four years I celebrated the King of Denmark's birthday at the Danish Mission, Queen Juliana's birthday at the Netherlands Mission, Shakespeare's birthday at the British Mission in April and King George VI's birthday in June, said farewell to departing French, Indian, Dutch and Danish representatives, welcomed newcomers, and found myself again and again surrounded by American generals in a way surprising to a pacifist from Philadelphia.

The Penninks of the Netherlands Mission gave their dinners on Wednesday evenings; they always had eighteen guests. Mr. Pennink was an older man with a beautiful young wife of whom he was very proud; he combined an uproarious sense of humor with a veiled compassion that came from his very real interest in people. I missed them greatly when they left after two years. The Gascoignes entertained thirty-two at a time, and the occasion was always a formal one.

The British Embassy, which had survived the war with little damage and that quickly repaired, occupied a large site opposite the Imperial Palace on its western side. Within the white encircling wall and behind a row of some of the loveliest cherry trees in Tokyo, were the Ambassador's large house, the Chancellery, and nine or ten smaller houses for ministers, secretaries and the like. The red carpet was out over the front steps of the big house when you arrived; you were met at the door by one of the embassy young men, charming, correct, slightly nineteenth-century, and shown your place at dinner on the chart spread out on a table in the wide hall.

The dinner table was spread with glittering glass and china; at intervals down its length were silver candelabra brilliant with candles and great silver bowls of flowers. The Gascoignes, like the Emperor and Empress, sat opposite each other in the middle of the table; the ends were the chill outposts of unimportance assigned for the most part impersonally by strict protocol. (At American dinners I usually occupied whatever was the lowest seat; at foreign tables I ranked higher.) Between each two chairs stood a Japanese manservant dressed in dark crested kimono and hakama, a dignified and beautiful costume. After dinner the company broke up into little knots in the big drawing room, which had a wood fire burning on the hearth at each end. I got marooned once with an American Colonel who had been invited by telephone at his office, a frequent way of issuing invitations when mails were so uncertain. He had understood that it was to be a bachelor affair and left his indignant wife at home, insisting that she was not invited. When he arrived at the party and was asked where she was he was aghast. He spent the evening gloomily emptying every glass offered to him and reviewing over and over the way it all happened.

The Gascoignes also, of course, gave smaller parties, but I was never invited to them, just, and only occasionally, to the large dinners, and to the Saint George's Day receptions on April 23.

Each spring, when I was leaving one of the parties, Sir Alvary would walk with me all the way to the front door and see me into my car, inquiring solicitously whether I wasn't very greatly tired and burdened by my responsibilities and if I did not long to go home. Though the British had in Mr. Blyth a tutor of their own, he had slipped in through the back door, so to speak, and was not recognized by the Embassy. He had spent the war in a Japanese prison camp and, having been on the spot at the end of the war, was invited to tutor the Crown Prince by Mr. Yamanashi without consultation with the British. I always thought that Sir Alvary's concern for my great fatigue had an element of wishfulness in it. There was a certain national rivalry involved, and I was aware that I was under British inspection. At a luncheon given by Marquis Matsudaira, a prewar English friend of his, a journalist, came in late, just off the plane from London. Introduced to me, the Englishman surprised me by saying, "Oh, I know all about you, Mrs. Vining. I was reading your file in the Foreign Office in London just three days ago."

Whatever the source of their interest in me might have been, I found a number of congenial friends among the British. Diana Kenderdine, wife of the Canadian Economic Adviser, who was herself English, had been on the *Marine Falcon* with me, and I have written in *Windows* of what her friendship meant to me. Mr. R. G. H. Watts, the first secretary in the Embassy for two years, and his wife, who was a Dane born in Tokyo, gave very pleasant small parties where there was music and talk of books and plays, philosophy and history. Dorothy Britten, the sister of Benjamin Britten, the composer, was there for a time, as a visitor, I think; she was a delightful young woman with, as one might expect, a wide knowledge and love of folk songs; she came one afternoon to my house with her guitar and played and sang for my English Club girls. At the Redmans' one met a number of French people, for Mrs. Redman was French. Mr. Redman was press secretary to the Embassy; he had been there before the war and had suffered imprisonment during it.

It was at the Redmans' house one evening in July, more than a year before the final Communist success in China, that I heard for the first time discussion of the ominous spread of communism there. According to Mr. Redman the Communists were the decent, honest people in China, but we were obliged to defeat them because they were supported by Russia. It was the more difficult because the Communists were getting arms from us in two ways, by capturing those we gave the Nationalists and by buying them from them! It was a warm, moist July evening, and we sat on the terrace overlooking the garden and shivered a little at the thought of what might lie ahead. Dennis MacEvoy of the *Reader's Digest*, who was also there, was concerned about the extravagance and waste of the Americans in Tokyo and the effect it was having on the hungry Japanese. The Communists, they were saying, were the only ones who really helped people. This I had myself heard said by some of my own Japanese friends. When I asked what, specifically, they did to help, I was told that they showed the Japanese how to avoid paying their taxes: a most ingenious way of helping and doubly advantageous to the Communists in that it cost them nothing and it undermined the already shaky Japanese economy.

Though at that time one almost never met Japanese people at any of the British parties, Britain made a farsighted and generous gesture of friendship to Japan that was deeply appreciated. She brought to Tokyo for two years as a "gift" to the Japanese people the poet Edmund Blunden. His title was Education Adviser to the British Liaison Mission, but his function was to teach courses in English Literature at the University of Tokyo and to lecture in universities throughout Japan whenever he was asked to, all without charge to the Japanese.

Edmund Blunden was said to be the "ranking" English poet at the time (it seems a curiously military term to apply to a poet), although actually the world had already passed by his traditional verse and left him a poet of integrity and sensitivity but a minor poet. His prose, however, his excellent book on Shelley, his critical essays and his comprehensive knowledge of English Literature made him a gift of real worth. He had, moreover, taught English Literature at the University of Tokyo from 1924 to 1927, occupying the chair created for Lafcadio Hearn, and had been very popular.

He was a slender man of fifty-odd, with a shock of unruly

thick brown hair cut long at the back, bright, darting blue eyes and a large beak of a nose in a thin, mobile face. He reminded me of an Arthur Rackham illustration of some bright-eyed small creature peeking out from behind a gnarled tree in a not-quite-real wood, but he had a quiet, unassuming way of speaking—questioning, qualifying, understating—that revealed an impressive knowledge of his subject and complete confidence in his own views. His wife, whom he had married three years earlier, was a beautiful young woman out of one of the nicest old-fashioned English novels: golden-haired, blue-eyed, with a short, straight nose and a lovely, slightly irregular mouth, placid, quiet, somewhat dowdy, but with a mind in reserve and unexpected humor. She was a graduate of St. Hilda's College, Oxford. She had already had two little girls, and a third was born in Japan.

One of the nicest things that Edmund Blunden did was to start a poetry-reading group. Ten of us, English, American, Hindu and Italian, were invited to the inaugural meeting at the Blundens' house in the Embassy compound to plan our procedure. We met once a month to spend an evening reading poetry together, each member bringing something that appealed to him or a poem bearing on a previously assigned subject. Missing my "Poets" at home, I welcomed this eagerly. It had its ups and downs; the membership changed constantly as some went home and others came; meetings were suspended in the summer, and then the Blundens themselves went home. In addition it tended to become elocutionary rather than purely poetry-loving, the readers paying more attention to how they read than to what they read. Still, it brought something I had missed into my life again, and because of it I had the fun of taking part in my last year in the Shakespeare celebration on Saint George's Day.

That was another of Mr. Blunden's ideas, a Shakespeare program each year on April 23. He himself would lecture on Shakespeare, illustrating his points by scenes from the plays read by various people. Mr. Blunden would announce himself as the program. "I ought to be printed instead of taking up your time by speaking." In the intermission the Tokyo Madrigal Society sang madrigals. The affair was held in the ballroom of the Embassy, a spacious room with wall panels of glowing dark red silk brocade separated by white Corinthian pillars. One year General Derevyanko was there in the audience with an interpreter who poured a steady low-voiced translation into his ear. The skill that could instantaneously translate Shakespeare into Russian without apparently a pause for a word awed me, who sat behind them, dividing my attention between the two performances, the one in English on the platform and the one in Russian in the audience. At the celebration in 1950, since the Blundens had already gone, and there was no lecturer, longer portions of the plays were read. I had the part of Goneril in several scenes from *Lear*, and the three or four rehearsals beforehand were pleasant occasions also.

I used to see the Blundens in Karuizawa, where we all spent our vacations, as well as in Tokyo, and I was present at two Japanese parties in their honor, the first given by Mr. Tajima in 1949, and the second by the Crown Prince just before they left Japan in March, 1950, as a farewell and a thank-you party. It was the first time that the Crown Prince was host in his own house, and Dr. Koizumi and I were both filled with pride in his performance. In my memories of that occasion the Blundens were effaced by the Crown Prince, but in the first one they occupy the center of the stage. I remember very clearly, in fact I wrote it down in my journal afterwards, what Edmund Blunden said about World War I.

"The English people had a very simple idea about it all. Here were our old friends the Germans whom we'd always liked. Now they'd shown their true character and they were very wicked people. I can't say I could agree but that was the way most people felt. And the Germans *were* a bit abrupt, weren't they? Going through Belgium that way. It was a bad mistake."

The parallel between that and the Japanese at Pearl Harbor was clear for anyone who wanted to draw it, but it was not insisted upon. So much of Western contact with the Japanese at that time consisted of the Westerner lecturing the Japanese at length about peace, liberty, international good faith and democracy. Seldom in history, I think, can a whole people have been so lectured and scolded, or have taken it so well. I often think of them now, when Negroes in the United States are even more pointedly scolding the whites. At a session of Philadelphia Yearly Meeting a Negro said to us, "We have listened to you for a long time; now it's your turn to listen to us." I wholly agree that it is. I only hope that we can listen with as much grace as the Japanese did, sitting quietly under it, refuting none of it, taking from it what seemed pertinent and valuable and acting upon it, quietly letting the rest fall to one side.

I only once heard Mr. Blunden lecture on English Literature. He spoke in the Mingei Kan, the folk art museum, on William Blake. The Mingei Kan was one of my favorite places; originally a large farmhouse with the stone roof characteristic of the part of the country from which it came, it housed a fascinating collection of folk arts of all kinds; pottery, fabrics, iron kettles, paintings, prints, the work of the famous potters like Kawai and Hamada and of unknown craftsmen of other countries as well as Japan. When Clara Sipprell, the photographer from Vermont, visited it, she said of one vase, "Why, that looks like Bennington pottery"—and it was.

In the central stone-paved court an audience of perhaps a hundred listened to Edmund Blunden. He spoke quietly, fluently. There was a blackboard at his back on which he wrote an occasional name, but for the most part he held a piece of chalk in his fingers, passing it from one hand to another until it had almost dwindled away. Then he put it down, wiped his chalky fingers on his dark blue suit and went on talking, entirely unconscious. It was a simple, somehow lovable gesture. Obviously an erudite man, he knew a great deal about Blake, I felt, but did not like him very much.

I was sorry when the Blundens left. I missed them, until I in my turn left Japan not many months later. They went back to England for a time and then returned to the East, to teach in Hong Kong.

Poetry is, of course, one of the great contributions that Britain has made to the world; some would say the greatest. Sometimes I agree, but at other times, I believe that Britain's most characteristic gift, her real genius, lies in the theater, in the widest sense of the word. Her pageantry is superb. Her court ceremonials are not to be equaled, and many of the modern Japanese ceremonies are modeled on the British. Nobody else can march like the British, certainly not the Americans. We have never taken marching seriously enough perhaps; we like to think of ourselves still as hopping behind stone walls and taking pot shots at the Redcoats. Our Fourth of July parades in Tokyo would have been dim indeed without the Welsh Fusiliers with their two streamers down their backs to represent the pigtails they lost; the British-trained Punjabis with their beards and turbans, the kilted Gurkhas—and when Allied soldiers were still guarding the Imperial Palace, only the British soldiers had a ceremony of changing the guard on

Sunday mornings; the Americans just dropped in informally. It was English Richard Le Gallienne who wrote,

> War I abhor, but oh how sweet
> The sound along the marching street
> Of fife and drum.

British actors are probably the best in the world. British playwrights before and after Shakespeare have given the world an unsurpassed body of good plays. But it is not only the professionals that have this sense of theater, this gift of performance. It goes much deeper than that, to an inward attitude of mind. Both Shakespeare and Donne saw the world as a stage and mankind as the actors thereon. The British are aware of how every kind of role should be played; a statesman, a policeman, a public school boy, a civil servant, a diplomat, a poet, a colonial administrator, a member of Parliament; and they fill the part with style and distinction. Even muddling through is done with flair, intentionally and as it should be done. This is not in any way to suggest a lack of sincerity in the part, but only that decency, self-restraint, modesty and humor, for instance, when stylized have a much greater effect than when improvised or unconscious. I like the English, and I admire them wholeheartedly. I thoroughly like their understatement, tolerance, kindliness, decency, courage and sheer charm. On the other hand their inveterate superiority (more often justified than not) and their persistent boasting about England and the English while pretending to despise boasting, irritate me. And in all the four years that I was in Japan the thing I heard said that most deeply shocked and outraged me was said by an English businessman one New Year's Eve when a small group of us, who had been left out—or had stayed out—of the large New Year's Eve parties, sat around the open fire at the Canadian Embassy talking.

He was employed by one of the large cartels and made, he said, 10,000 pounds sterling a year, besides having an expense account and an entertainment account. He was speaking of the Japanese. "I hate them all. I'd grind them down. They're a nation of swine. There was a letter in the *Nippon Times* today signed 'An American friend of Japan.' It's astounding—an American friend of Japan! They're enemies. They're all laughing at the Americans. They know what's correct. You don't make friends with people when they're still enemies—any more than you speak to someone before you're introduced. It isn't done."

"Americans do both," I said, "and I don't know how you can stop them."

"I was born in Japan. I know these people."

A Canadian asked him how he could do business with the Japanese with such an attitude toward them. He looked astonished, as if she had asked a question almost too silly to deserve an answer.

"Why, I'm here to make money out of them! I'll be polite to them. I'll slap them on the back and drink with them and all that. They'll never know how I feel. I'm here to make money out of them and put my country back on its feet."

It may be that the role of the businessmen, in a country where business is not really respected, is not a sympathetic one.

In August, 1947, Mr. Atcheson, who had been so cordial to me during that first year, was lost with several others returning to Washington to report to the State Department when the staff plane on which they were flying ran out of fuel between Johnston Island and Honolulu and plunged into the shark-infested sea. It was a great loss to the United States of an honest, conscientious and able civil servant with a wide vision, and to me of a kind friend.

Mr. William J. Sebald took his place. I never knew the Sebalds as I knew the Atchesons, but because of my friendship with Lois Jessup, a fellow Bryn Mawrtyr, I was included in the very interesting dinner which the Sebalds gave for the Jessups on January 3, 1950. Dr. Philip Jessup, formerly professor of International Law at Columbia University, and then Ambassador-at-Large of the United States, was, with Lois, on the first leg of a two-month tour of the Far East.

All the top-ranking diplomats except the Russians were there, and no Army people at all, which made it very pointedly a State Department affair. By that time the Communists had proclaimed the People's Republic of China and had been recognized immediately by the U.S.S.R. and a little later by India. It was reported on January 3, the very day of the party, that Britain was on the point of recognizing Communist China, and everybody was agog to see how the respective diplomats would handle the situation. Lady Gascoigne's sister, Mrs. Follett, was there, but Lady Gas-

coigne herself was in bed, so it was said, with a cold. The National-
alist Chinese minister was there, but he left early, immediately
after dinner; and as soon as he was gone, as if he had been waiting around the corner for a cue, Sir Alvary Gascoigne appeared.

At dinner I was at a small table with Lois Jessup, who was still
as beautiful as she had been in college when, as a lowly freshman,
I had gazed adoringly up at her; Mr. and Mrs. Huston of the
State Department; Mr. Sebald; and Colonel W. R. Hodgson, the
Australian political adviser, who had known the Jessups in New
York. Much of the talk centered on the Russians, who had walked
—or rather run—out of the Allied Council Meeting a few days
before, in protest against the bringing up of the fact that four
years after hostilities had ended, there were still over 300,000 Japanese prisoners in Russian hands, about whom their relatives
could get no word at all. Violet had gone that day to watch the
meeting but found the room too crowded to get in. As she waited
at the door for the car, she had been startled by what seemed to be
a crowd of large Russians pelting past her and scrambling into the
cars drawn up at the curb in readiness, waiting for them.

"I've been there every time the Russians have walked out,"
said Colonel Hodgson, who was a genial man with a ripe Cockney
accent.

"You don't ascribe that to anything personal in your influence,
do you?" Lois asked with an air of innocence.

"Aow now, I had nothing to do with it," he protested seriously.

He was full of the misdeeds of his Japanese chauffeur, whom he
had just sacked, whose final crime had been parking the Colonel's
car in front of a brothel.

"A *what?*" said Mrs. Huston, affecting a pretty shriek of horror.

"A *brothel*, ma'am," said Colonel Hodgson.

Another piece of conversation that interested me—but differently—was the small bombshell that the Dutch baron who was
then head of the Netherlands Mission dropped on me. He began
by asking me about the Crown Prince and whether he was to be
sent to the United States or England when he began to travel.

"We are very much interested in him in my country," he continued. "We discuss which country he should go to first. Generally
we think it would be better for him to go to England first. In
America the pressmen would make it hard for him, but in England they are a little easier and he could be introduced to democracy by degrees. We are interested because our Queen has four

daughters and it is very hard to find princes for them to marry nowadays."

One of the ladies in the group said, "But they're very young, aren't they?"

"Oh, no. Just right. The eldest is twelve. The Crown Prince is only just sixteen."

He smiled beatifically and moved on.

I took it that this was said to me with the idea that I should pass it on, and so I did a day or two later without comment. Mr. Tajima smiled. "I think the Crown Prince will not visit Holland," he said.

What was most interesting about it was the indication of the changing currents in European thought about Japan. Two years earlier the feeling of the Dutch, who had suffered in Japanese prison camps in Indonesia, had been bitter.

After dinner, when the ladies went upstairs with Mrs. Sebald, the men gathered around a long table with Dr. Jessup at the head of it, in one of the downstairs rooms. They were still there when we came down, their heads together, looking very serious.

The diplomatic parties, I realized, were not always so unreal or frivolous as they appeared to be.

7.

Mountain Summers

IN JAPAN as elsewhere, there were summer holidays. Though the school year started in April instead of September, still, when the real heat of summer began, the schools closed down in the middle of the term for a long vacation, the Crown Prince went to Numazu on the seacoast eighty miles southwest of Tokyo, the Emperor and Empress went to Nasu in the mountains of Tochigi Prefecture, the boys of the Peers' School scattered, and I went to Karuizawa, where the Imperial Household rented for me a villa owned by the Mitsuis.

Karuizawa is a summer resort on the border between Nagano and Gumma Prefectures; it occupies a plateau at an altitude of 3,100 feet, surrounded on three sides by mountains and towered over by Mount Asama, the 8,000-foot active volcano second in size only to Mount Aso in Kyushu. On the open southwest side the plain stretches away toward the distant Japan Alps, which could be seen from high places on very clear days, far away and jagged and in late summer frosted with snow.

The resort was founded by missionaries in the late 1880's. By the 1920's rich Japanese had built large and handsome summer homes there and luxury hotels sprang up. Many of the missionaries moved on to Nojiri, where there was a lake and a simpler, less expensive life. During the war all foreigners in Japan, including Germans, who were allies of the Japanese, were evacuated there, to keep them safe from the bombing and to hold them more easily under surveillance. It was a grim time for them, for food was extremely hard to get and they had to make long bicycle trips out into the country, ranging farther and farther as time went on, to beg the farmers to sell them food in exchange for their dwindling treasures. During the first two summers that I was there, a number of German and Russian families still lingered, glum and unfriendly, but the process of repatriation was going steadily on and in time they all disappeared.

Americans were taking their places. The hotels were commandeered as rest homes for the Occupation personnel; journalists, diplomats and missionaries found houses along the streets of the village and up the sides of the hills; the golf courses came to life again. The Machi, the main street of the village, where once Tokyo's most fashionable shops had had branches, was a shabby, crowded little street, with a proliferation of curio shops, a few food stores with almost nothing in them, and a thriving photographer's shop. Once a week the U.S. Commissary train came through and people with commissary cards laid in supplies of canned goods and edible but not delicious meat. By 1949 fresh fruits and vegetables began to appear in the local shops, and there was a bakery which would take your flour and return to you loaves of firm and crusty bread considerably better than the ordinary soft and tasteless stuff that passes for bread in the United States.

Our house sat partway up the lower slope of a little mountain called Atagoyama, surrounded by great balsam trees, with a grove of larches on the hill behind it. Through the trees we could see Hanareyama, which was quite near, Mount Asama, about five miles away, and on clear days, far on the horizon, bits of the Japan Alps. Hanareyama got its name—which means "separated"—from a legend. The devil who lived in Asama had a large bowl from which he ate bean soup every day; afterwards he turned it upside down to dry—and there it is still. The air of all Karuizawa was clear and pure, but the air around our house, fragrant with balsam, was almost intoxicating after the thick and dusty atmosphere of Tokyo.

The house, which was built in the shape of a capital I, with an open terrace off the living room between the two wings, had been in its heyday very luxurious. Shabby now from war neglect, it was still comfortable and attractive and had amenities that we did not enjoy in Tokyo, such as a wood-burning fireplace and a hot-water heater.

Only a minimum amount of furniture came with the house; the rest of the things we needed the Imperial Household had sent up by truck the day before. The altitude was too high for Mrs. Inoue, who stayed at home to guard the house in Tokyo, but two of her daughters came with us. Masako San would go up with the truck the day before and Michiko San would ride in the car with Tane and me—and Violet in the last two summers. Our chauffeur would drive us up—the ninety-mile trip took almost all day to accomplish in the state of the roads as they were then and with the usual car trouble on the way—and then would leave us until time to bring us back again to Tokyo. I enjoyed driving around Karuizawa— when the car was running and when we could get the gas.

There was a great flurry as we got off: five people and a puppy packed in the car, plus suitcases, lunch basket, books, cameras, sweaters, handbags, umbrellas and the coffee percolator, which was thrust in at the last moment. We would start off with calls of *"Itte mairimasu"* from the car and *"Itte irasshai"* from the bowing figures on the front steps. Then an anguished cry from the house, and Takenaka San would put on the brake with a jerk and we would all look apprehensively back. *"Wasuremono! Genchan no omizu!"* We forgot! Master Genji's honorable cold water! A jar of water for the puppy would be rushed to the car and then we were really off.

The cities faded away behind us at last: Tokyo's wide, dingy outskirts; Omiya, where once we stopped at a garage for repairs and I saw on the rough, tool-strewn workbench an exquisite flower arrangement; Takasaki, where several railroads met and on the hill above the city a tall white statue of Kwannon loomed against the sky. Gradually the farms took over, the rice fields where kimonoed figures with huge straw hats bent over weeding, and white herons stood one-legged in the ditches or rose on slowly flapping wings; thatch-roofed farmhouses surrounded by tight, high hedges; here and there a crape myrtle in bloom (*saru-suberi* in Japanese, the monkey-slipping tree) to strike my heart with a sharp-sweet dart of memory. Then came a stretch of road with tall cryptomeria trees on both sides, for which we tried to wait so that we could eat our picnic lunch sitting on the grass in this lofty shade, looking across the fields to the jagged mountains that seemed to be cut out of crepe paper and pasted against the far horizon.

The last part of the way the road began to climb laboriously and to switch back and forth as it mounted the flank of the Miyogi range. The road was narrow and rough with ruts and potholes; wooded chasms fell away beside it, first on one side, then on the other; at the sharpest curves we met trucks hurtling down; but suddenly, perceptibly, the air would change and grow light and sweet, familiar wild flowers would blossom beside the road —wild hydrangeas, Asiatic day-flowers, wild geranium—and then suddenly we would be at the barrier between Gumma and Nagano, where an American M.P. stopped the car and examined our passes, and the gray roofs of Karuizawa lay below us, surrounded by its green mountain walls.

We drove through the village, along the Machi for a way, and then turned off into a series of narrow lanes enclosed by hedges, behind which could be seen here and there a black-tiled roof, and shadowed by tall trees, until we came to the slot in the woods where the car would be parked all summer. Here we got out, loaded ourselves with all we could carry and climbed the hill by a winding path among the great balsams, past an arum lily, a jack-in-the-pulpit in red berry and a variety of ferns and mosses, up to the terrace, the house, and Masako San rushing to meet us and take our bundles. The black and orange and white narcissus flycatcher (*kibitaki*) was nesting in the tree beside the dining-room window, the squirrel was leaping from branch to branch in the fir by the terrace, the *uguisu* was calling across the valley, the sun lay in patches on the needle-strewn earth, the air was thin and pure and spicy, the weeks lay free and endless before us: it seemed we had come to one of the suburbs of heaven.

Not that the time actually was all that free. One summer Princess Kazuko and Princess Atsuko, the Crown Prince's elder sisters, visited us; another summer the Crown Prince himself spent three days with us, staying in the house without a chamberlain in attendance, as if he were a well-loved nephew; we had a fairly steady stream of houseguests besides the Imperial ones; sometimes I had articles to write or speeches to prepare; always I had my winter's work to plan. But still it was vacation, it was freedom of a sort impossible in Tokyo, it was cool and it was beautiful.

Among the guests who came to stay with us and add to our pleasure, besides the Imperial young, were Diana Kenderdine, of the Canadian Legation; Gwen Terasaki; Miss Keiko Hani, of Jiyu Gakuen, Freedom School, which her mother had created, a school of extraordinary beauty, originality and vision; Miss Michi Kawai, the founder and headmistress of Keisen School, from which Tane had been graduated, a private school that has had great influence on generations of girls; Miss Hana Kawai, also of Keisen, and her sister Shizu, who taught in a government school;

Miss Ai Hoshino, the president of Tsuda College; Mrs. Tatsuo Takaki, the Empress's English interpreter and mistress of the robes, one of my first friends in the Court, a most beautiful, serene and able woman, a leader in the small but active Christian Science church in Tokyo; Miss Koha Taira, our beloved flower arrangement teacher, who was a pillar of the Ohara School; Henry and Edith Perry. Esther Rhoads used to rent the Maeda cottage, two and a half miles away, and we were back and forth between the two houses when she was there.

During our first summer Esther and Tane and I together held a "retreat" for some of our English-speaking Japanese friends who were teachers and who had had no vacation since before the war. It took considerable planning and manoeuvering to work out the meals, for food was still scarce and the Commissary train had not yet begun to come to Karuizawa. We pooled our resources. Esther got some LARA supplies, I had some stores brought from Tokyo, we combed the Machi, and our guests brought their rice ration. Three stayed with Esther and four with Tane and me, which made ten of us altogether in the retreat. We went back and forth between the two houses by Esther's jeep and on foot, for my car was out of commission.

There was much talk at that time of the education reforms that were being enforced by the Occupation, the decentralization, the extension of the number of free and compulsory years of school from six to nine, the rewriting of the textbooks, the abolition of the Emperor Meiji's Rescript on Education, a document that had contained some unexceptionable ethical principles but had been used by the ultranationalists to whip up emperor worship to a frenzy and to make the schools into a vehicle for militarist propaganda. So inflated had been the reverence demanded for the Rescript that school principals had resigned if they inadvertently mispronounced a syllable in reading it, and Dr. Ushimura, a well-known and greatly respected Christian university professor, was dismissed and disgraced for refusing to bow to it; that is, literally bow low before the scroll itself. Nevertheless, its removal left a vacuum that teachers did not know how to fill. I shall never forget Hana Kawai's despairing cry. "But how can we give the children a democratic education when we haven't had one ourselves?"

Gwen Terasaki was there for a week in the summer of 1948. Her daughter Mariko, a beautiful, gifted girl of seventeen, had won several prizes in adult competitions for her powerful but tragic drawings which revealed the inevitable inner conflicts and sorrows of a child of Japanese and American parents living in a Japan occupied by American soldiers. Mariko was in Karuizawa at the same time visiting some young friends in the village. In many ways Gwen was the most understanding of all my friends in Japan, for she was, as I was, halfway between the two cultures. Because of her husband's position as interpreter for the Emperor with General MacArthur, she had some touch with the court and a great deal of information about currents within it; she had both more and closer Japanese friends than I and more friends in the Occupation. She knew much more about Japanese life. I was protected from the struggle to find food and lodging and to make ends meet in occupied Tokyo as she was not; she could tell me many things that were illuminating to me and helped me to understand the problems. That summer she was facing the prospect of taking Mariko home to Johnson City, Tennessee, to start her in school there, torn by the realization that she must leave Terry behind and that he was not well.

Not all of our guests were imported from Tokyo or came to stay. We had friends spending the summer in Karuizawa with whom we exchanged meals, sat on one another's terraces, walked and picnicked together. Dr. and Mrs. Shinzo Koizumi came to stay in a nearby hot springs resort. In 1950, when the Crown Prince had the Prince Hotel in nearby Kutsukake, he and the Koizumis came to dinner with us both together and separately. Merrill and Maki Hitotsuyanagi had a cottage on the other side of the Machi. Merrill Vories was a missionary of a most unusual kind. He had come to Japan many years before, independent of any Christian Board, convinced that a missionary should work like anyone else in the country and support himself by his work. At first a teacher, later he carried on his profession of architect, designing schools, churches and dwelling houses, using the money he made to establish the Omi Brotherhood, a Christian community on Lake Biwa, whose members pooled their financial resources and devoted their lives to bringing about the kingdom of God on earth. With his deep-hearted and intelligent wife, Maki, a daimyo's daughter, and the members of the Brotherhood, Merrill founded a school, a kindergarten, a Mentholatum factory, a tuberculosis sanitarium, a church, and ran an evangelizing program as well. Foreseeing the war before it came, Merrill, to avoid being separated from what was now all of his life, became a Japanese citizen and took Maki's name. He was a poet, a musician, and a radiant person; he had the kind of humor that enables people to laugh at themselves, what Gerald Heard called the modern equivalent of the medieval virtue of humility. Maki lived for him and for their work. We enjoyed seeing them each summer in Karuizawa, and once Tane and I went to spend a week end with them in Omi Hachiman, where we were immensely impressed by the original, alive work they were doing, unhampered by convention or by directives from any denominational holder of pursestrings in far places.

Another of our Karuizawa friends was Miss Margaret Elizabeth Armstrong, a tiny Canadian missionary who, like Merrill Vories, had taken Japanese citizenship just before the war in order to stay with the people whom she had come to love. A kindergarten-training teacher, she went through the war in Niigata which, like all other large Japanese cities, was heavily bombed. She spent one night crouched under the overhanging bank of the river while the bombs fell all around and the flames of the burning city roared into the sky above her head. With her was her devoted Japanese friend, who lived with her and ran her house and interpreted for her—not in language, for Miss Armstrong spoke Japanese fluently, but in her relations with officials and neighbors. One saw it again and again, the Japanese Christian woman, selfless, able, sensitive, imaginative, who gave her life to easing the way for the foreigner who had come with a mission—as Maki did for Merrill Vories, though that was a love match as well, as many another did for the famous missionaries of the past, as Tane did for me.

Miss Armstrong was an ornithologist, and she looked like a bird herself, with her small, sprightly body, her little face with its bright eyes and prominent nose, her lilting voice. She had a tiny cottage up a steep hill, practically lodged in the trees, which she called "The Nest," and she was the author of several excellent little books, two of which she gave me, *The Rustling of Wings* and *Birds of Karuizawa*. Kotori San, we called her, "Miss Little Bird," and I continued to get chirpy little letters from her after I returned to this country, until her death in the late 1950's.

On Sunday mornings, Tane and I, missing the Meeting in Tokyo and not finding the Union church in Karuizawa a congenial substitute for it, held a little silent meeting for worship of our own in our living room. Other Friends and friends of Friends joined us. Esther Rhoads used to come with her guests when she was in her cottage; the Sekiyas came regularly. Mr. Sekiya had been at one time vice-minister of the Imperial Household, and Mrs. Sekiya, a formidable *grande dame*, was a friend of the Empress Dowager's. They had joined Friends when their son Paul, a distinguished professor, had returned after the war from Shanghai, where he had had contact with the Friends Center and had himself become a Quaker. Quite regularly we were joined by a Zen Buddhist, who felt at home with our silent meditation. Mr. Kurusu, who had been the special envoy in Washington at the time of Pearl Harbor, now lived with his American wife all year round in Karuizawa; their daughters married American army officers, their son had been killed in the war. Once when the newspapers were full of headlines about an electric company scandal featuring another Kurusu altogether, not even a distant relative, our Mr. Kurusu remarked ruefully, "Now the Americans will all say, 'There's old double-crossing Kurusu at his tricks again.' "

I have written of the Koizumis in both *Windows for the Crown Prince* and *Return to Japan*. It was one of the greatest privileges of my experience in Japan to have them for friends. Dr. Shinzo Koizumi, of magnificent physique, six feet tall and powerfully built, had been, when he was president of Keio University, a champion tennis player and so handsome that people turned to look at him in the street. During the war his only, his promising, his adored son, a young lieutenant in the Navy, was killed. He himself during one of the great fire raids had jumped out of the second-story window of his house in Tokyo when flames engulfed the stairs. After two years of hospitalization he emerged permanently lame, his face seamed with scars. At night, in order to sleep he had to tie a silk scarf over his lidless eyes. Early in 1949 he was persuaded to take the chief responsibility for the Crown Prince's education, and so began for me a friendship that was continued after I left Japan with frequent letters and occasional visits—three times he came to the United States and twice I went to Japan—until his sudden death of a heart attack in 1967. His wife, Tomi, who did not speak English, I knew less well but loved nevertheless. She is the ideal Japanese wife, "yielding on the surface but with a core of flexible steel." She has a strong individuality of her own, warmth, humor, artistic skill; she herself planned the delightful living room of their new house, she makes her own designs for her lovely kimonos, she paints in oils, she makes pottery—I cherish a ceremonial teabowl of her creation—she is a flower arranger of skill and sensitivity, she is a *sumo* fan. Their daughters Kayo and Tae, both happily married, completed a warm, united and most appealing family. Besides guiding the Crown Prince with wisdom and devotion, Dr. Koizumi was a prolific writer. He had a regular column in the *Bungei Shunju,* a monthly magazine of general interest and large circulation; he was the biographer and interpreter of Fukuzawa Yukichi, Japan's first modern thinker and the founder of Keio University; he was the author of numerous books on economics and several very pleasant books of reminiscence. He was a member of the Japan Academy, was decorated by the Emperor and was eagerly followed by the Japanese people, who looked to him for liberal and balanced leadership. His sufferings at the hands of the United States in wartime left no antagonism or bitterness in peacetime in his large and magnanimous spirit.

When the Koizumis were in Karuizawa, they would come to dinner with us, and the talk around the big coffee table afterwards was always warm and illuminating. I saw them regularly in Tokyo, of course, but away in the mountains in the holiday atmosphere the talk was more intimate, more reminiscent, more playful.

Always too we had a few of the Peers' School boys dropping in to call, especially the last year when the Crown Prince was occupying the Prince Hotel in Kutsukake, the next village after Karuizawa. They would come to see me, sitting shyly on the edge of their chairs, drinking tea or soft drinks, speaking their laborious English and sometimes falling back on Tane for help with something that was too difficult. Some of them had ambitious study projects for the summer, of which they told me with pride. They would speak haltingly of their difficulties in adjusting to the new world they found themselves in. "When I was a child," said one, the son of an admiral killed in the war, "I wanted to go into the Navy. Now I have lost my purpose."

One day Kamala Ratnam of the Indian Mission came with a photographer to take a picture of our house where—or rather in a previous house on the same site—Tagore had written *Stray Birds* and had sat in the afternoons under these same balsams philosophizing to thirty or more entranced Japanese students. Mrs. Ratnam told me that great as is the respect for a teacher in Japan, it is even greater in India, for whereas the Japanese *sensei* is purely an intellectual guide, the Indian *guru* is both intellectual and spiritual. "If an Indian child sees his father and his teacher standing together," she said, "he must pay respects to his teacher first and then to his father, for the parents produce an animal but the teacher makes a man."

Near our house at the bottom of the hill was the electric railroad that ran up through the mountains to Kusatsu, or perhaps I should say *strolled*, for it took the small engine, which was known to the missionaries as "Toddlekins," three hours to make the thirty-four-mile trip. It was a single track with turnouts at stations, and it ran so close to the bank on both sides that we could pick wild flowers as we went past: several kinds of lilies, wild pinks, spirea, jewelweed, wild clematis, St.-John's-wort, all flowers that also grow in the Appalachians.

When the day promised to be fine, which was not every day in rainy Karuizawa, Tane and I loved to take a thermos of coffee and a packet of sandwiches and go off on Toddlekins in the morning. We would alight at some station along the way and walk through the country to the next one or the one beyond that, and get the afternoon train back. Kusatsu itself we went to only once. It was a hot springs resort famous from the twelfth century on down. There was a leper colony there, too, in which the Empress Dowager took an interest, and there were many touching tales of the sacrificial devotion of doctors and nurses and the cheerful courage of the lepers. But Kusatsu was not an attractive place; the air smelled of sulphur, the inns and baths were dingy, the streets jammed with surging people. Wherever you go in Japan it is crowded. There is no place remote enough to be empty. We found Shimoda at the outermost tip of the Izu Peninsula so thronged that a car on the main street must crawl along blaring its horn constantly to force a passage among the determined hurrying masses that filled every inch of space. In Kusatsu at the end of this lonely little railway, the noise of wooden clogs clacking on the streets as people struggled to pass each other going up, going down, was restless and unending. What must be the effect of the constant rub and pressure of other bodies competing for limited space, on the mind, conscious and subconscious, which is even more vulnerable than bone and muscle?

Each summer the fifteenth of August was the time of O Bon, the feast of the Dead, when ancestors—not long-ago ones but the grandparents and great-grandparents that people remembered—

came back for a three-day visit to their families. It was a happy time, when each community in its own way provided entertainment for the unseen visitors. Karuizawa was too foreign and too sophisticated to go in for anything but the usual dance, held in the center of the village with canned music amplified to excruciating loudness that went on long after midnight, and so we liked to take the car and go in search of some smaller and more traditional village.

I remember especially one year when Michi Yamaguchi, the head of Keisen Horticultural College, was visiting us and the Matsumuras joined us. The road that led out of Karuizawa to the southwest, past Kutsukake and Oiwake, was the old Nakasendo, the inland highway through the mountains from Tokyo to Kyoto, much less well known than the Tokaido that ran along the coast, but very old and well traveled.

At a place where the road forked and the Nakasendo went off to the right was a little triangle of land with several Buddhist stone statues deep in the tall grass under big trees. Because this bit of land was higher than the road, when the Emperor Meiji came this way in the 1890's the statues were taken away temporarily lest Jizo Sama or Kwannon Sama look down upon the Emperor. Jizo Sama is the Buddha who helps little children find their way through the rocky paths in hell, and Kwannon Sama is the goddess of compassion. This Kwannon was of particular interest because she was a "Maria Kwannon" with a cross unobtrusively worked into the inscription at the base. When the Christianity brought to Japan by Saint Francis Xavier and other Jesuit fathers in the sixteenth century was brutally suppressed a century later, many Japanese put secret marks on Buddhist images and continued their Christian worship at the risk of their lives.

We reached the village of Usuda when the shadows were long and lovely. The second stories of the very old houses came out over the first stories very much in the manner of sixteenth-century English houses. In the center of the village was an enormous sycamore tree, so large and venerable that it had a tiny shrine all its own tucked at the base between its roots. Anything so old and beautiful must be sacred. We went a little beyond the village, parked the car and climbed 117 steps to the Rice God's shrine, where there was a little garden from which we could look down over the river, over the black-tiled roofs of the village, over the rice fields to the jagged mountains painted rose and gold in the sunset sky.

After we had eaten our supper, we went down into the streets of the village and walked among the crowds there, followed by a trail of a hundred or more children who found the tall American more exotic than the family ghosts. Through the gates of houses we had glimpses of old gardens with rocks and pools, pine trees and stone lanterns. As it grew dark, people began to light little fires of rice straw in front of each house, to send off the spirits of the dead on their way back to the land of the departed. They lighted incense sticks from the fires and stuck them upright in the ground, and the air became fragrant with their smoky pungence. In families where there were small children, fathers had made little lanterns on wheels, with wooden frames and paper sides decorated with pictures of flowers and birds and animals. The candles inside were lighted and then the four- and five-year-olds carefully pulled these lanterns down the streets toward the graveyard. It was a beautiful sight in the dusk and deepening shadows, all these small, wavering lights and the intent faces of the children: light and dark, youth and age, life and death bound in one living whole. Like lights bobbing on a dark stream they flowed slowly out of the side streets and on to the temple and the cemetery, where each family had its own little ceremony beside its own graves.

The temple was an old and small one, but the stone lanterns were lit under the dark trees, and in the park nearby a platform had been set up for the music of the dance, for the young men with ancient drums and the modern record player. The dancers took up their positions in concentric rings around the platform, boys with cotton towels tied around their foreheads to show that they were engaged in something important and strenuous, girls and women in their summer kimonos, blue and white, or green and white, or brown and white. The dance for this night was a simple, monotonous one with four or five basic movements, but it had rhythm and style and gaiety. As families finished their duties in the cemetery, they came and joined the dance, toddlers, adolescents, old people. Watching it had a mesmeric effect; we could have stood there for hours in the shadows outside the moving, bending, clapping rings in happy, mindless absorption, unaware of time passing, but the Matsumuras had left their baby with a neighbor. We returned to the car, still followed by about fifty faithful children, and drove home through the mild, sweet night. Whenever we came to a bridge over a stream, we saw little piles of food, vegetables and fruit, put out for the ancestors on their voyage back. As we passed through the rice fields, we smelled the unforgettable odor of ripening rice, warm, mild, not sweet but rich and nutty. When the rice is actually ripe, this odor disappears; it belongs just to a brief period of midsummer, when the strings of reflectors flash over the fields to frighten the birds in the daytime and the music of the Bon Odori throbs through the darkness from village to village.

It rains a great deal in Japan. For six weeks in June and July, the rainy season, it rains every day, steadily, gently, and very wetly. One lives in a world of damp. Clothes mildew in the closet, shoes, books, handbags, brief cases, even typewriters sprout patches of green mold. The black *"bat umbrellas"* of the West and the larger and brighter Japanese paper ones make their restless patterns on all the streets like some lugubrious flowers or peripatetic mushrooms.

But the rain is not confined to the rainy season. There is *haru-same*, the gentle, refreshing spring rain beloved of poets; there are the drenching, dogged downpours of autumn; there are devastating typhoons.

The Typhoon Kitty that hit us in Karuizawa one August was the most immoderate storm that I have ever experienced, with the possible exception of Hurricane Edna several years later in Maine, when Violet and I sat in a small cottage on Mount Desert Island and heard the voice over the radio say, "The eye of the hurricane is now over Bar Harbor"—and with that it broke off and the electric light went with it, while the howling wind was held in a breathless suspension.

The Armed Forces Radio told us of Kitty's erratic progress up the Pacific from the south and for a time promised that she would bypass Japan. Then came a day of warm, wet, restless wind; at six o'clock the sky suddenly dramatically darkened, the rain came tumultuously down and the wind rose to a screech. All that night the storm shook the house. Bedroom doors tightly closed on the inside hall were flung open and slammed shut again. Rain lashed against the windows; the trees creaked.

In the morning the house was filled with a green subaqueous light, and with the ominous sound of water trickling inside. We ran to put basins under leaks in the roof. There were leaves in the bathtub which had blown in through a hole in the screen where the window would not quite shut. Outside the windows leaves and twigs blew past horizontally on the rain. The electric lights went off; the water gurgled in the pipes and stopped. We put out a large heavy dishpan in a sheltered corner of the terrace to catch rain water, but it was immediately picked up by the wind as if it had been a piece of paper and went sailing off upside down through the bending trees.

Violet, who suffered from recurring attacks of a virus throughout her two years in Japan, was in bed with a temperature of 102. We had no water, no fruit juices, only one small bottle of Coca-Cola. Tane and I put on raincoats and galoshes and splashed down the path to the car to go to the commissary train, but the battery was dead. It would have done no good anyhow, for no trains ran that day. We made our way back again through the streams that were cutting channels in the side of the hill, and brought the sad news to Violet, who had to decide whether to drink the Coke now or save it for later.

Now and then the wind would pause and the rain drum down less heavily, as if Kitty were drawing breath or resting for a moment; then there would be a howl and a thud and the limbs of the trees would bend down under a new onslaught, the white sheets of rain sweep across the windows almost as opaque as if they had been bed sheets. There was a small earthquake in the morning, and in the afternoon an enormous bang like an explosion or a clap of thunder. Asama had erupted.

We lit a fire in the fireplace and ate our dry dinner amid clouds of stinging smoke, in the light of a cheap candle stuck in a beautiful silver candlestick from the Imperial Palace. Violet drank the second half of her Coke, which had gone flat and warm and sticky.

The next morning the wind fell, the rain stopped, the sun came out and the ground steamed. Our friend and neighbor, Mrs. Sekiya, who had a well in her garden, sent a grandson to us with a bucket of clear, cold water. Tane and I, like all the rest of Karuizawa, went out to see what damage had been done.

Our woods were a jungle of broken branches. The little stream on the other side of Toddlekins's tracks was a roaring brown torrent, which had cut away the foundations of the stone and concrete bridge. Trees were down between us and the Machi; the corn and other vegetables in the gardens were flat; dooryards were lakes. We met people carrying teakettles and rice cookers home after filling them at somebody's well. One neighbor lamented that his well had caved in altogether and would have to be rebuilt. *"Taihen, ne?"* ("Dreadful, isn't it?") everybody was saying in wondering tones. As we approached the Machi, we picked up bits of news. The reservoir had been damaged and would take several days to repair. So many wires were down that the electric power had been cut off for fear of fires. Worst hit of all were the people least able to sustain it, the poor whose small, fragile houses by the river were swept away altogether.

News from the outside world was nil, for there were no trains, no mail, no telephone, no radio. The next day someone struggled through with a newspaper from Tokyo, and the word spread that it had been the worst typhoon in eleven years, that Tokyo was the center but that Karuizawa got the heaviest rain, with 13.67 inches in less than two days. The AFSC and other welfare organizations went into action with supplies of food and clothing and medicine; the Japanese, long accustomed to the buffeting of nature in typhoons, earthquakes, tidal waves and volcanoes, picked themselves up without complaint and went about their business again. We dried out the house, cleaned up our paths and woods; Violet's temperature went down. A few days later the summer vacation ended and we went back to Tokyo.

The drive back to Tokyo was usually cloudy, hot and dusty. Against the farmhouse walls sesame-pods were drying; along the way pomegranates were turning pink, persimmons turning orange. In the heat we saw the usual variety of seminude people, small children flying about with shirts to their middles and no panties, nursing mothers bare to the waist, men in loincloths, and always at least one taking a bath in the roadside ditch without so much as a towel.

In Tokyo all the little wooden shacks huddled together on the bomb sites were shaded with loofah vines, where the flowers were still yellow, rather like squash flowers. Shopkeepers sprinkled the paths before their doors, and the acrid smell of wet dust suddenly struck the air. Takenaka San tooted the horn as we backed twice to make the sharp turn for the narrow lane through the narrow gate into the narrow driveway, and Mrs. Inoue, Aiko San and Yukio San were on the steps bowing when we reached the front door. Inside, the house was cool and ordered, flowers in all the rooms, the French doors open on the garden, where zinnias, four feet tall, still blazed. In the evening we heard the insects singing, the different kinds of crickets and the locust. It was like a September night at home, the air heavy and breathless after the mountain freshness.

During our last summer in Karuizawa I made the difficult decision not to renew my contract as I had been pressed by Mr. Tajima and Dr. Koizumi to do but to return home, as Violet wished.

I have often wondered whether I did the right thing to bring Violet to Japan. It seemed to me at the time that I was sharing with her this wonderful thing that had come into my life, that it would bring to her, without the strain of responsibility that I carried, immense color and interest, that enjoying it together we would enjoy it doubly. And this is the way I think she looked upon it in the end, when it was all over and she was safely home again, with a host of wonderful memories. This is the way her lively and delightful letters to Nanette McDonald and Beatrice Wistar painted it. But during the two years she was actually there she wished sometimes, as I know now, that she had not come.

Her journal shows that it was not what she wanted at the time. She had looked forward eagerly to retiring at sixty-five and had confidently expected that I would then come home after having had two years in Japan. When I decided to stay on and with the consent of the Imperial Household asked her to join me, she agreed, but with more reluctance than she revealed to me. She had the apartment to close and our things to put in storage; she had to make the long trip by train and plane alone.

She was delighted by the warmth with which she was welcomed by everybody from the Imperial Family down. Her Majesty had a luxurious warm silk padded kimono especially made for her to wear on cold evenings (and one like it for me); she was elated by her adventure. "Dear me!" she thought during her first dinner at the Palace; "I have flown the Pacific and I am dining *en famille* with the Emperor of Japan!" But our house was cold in winter, and the climate of Japan is a damp one. She picked up a virus that again and again knocked her out with aching and fever, until at last ten days in the Forty-Ninth General Hospital under the care of General MacArthur's doctor finally cleared it up.

I had felt that it was important that she have work of her

own to do quite apart from mine, and so she had a small class of young Japanese teachers who came to the house for English conversation once a week; she taught English Composition once a week at Tsuda College; she arranged and catalogued the little library at the new Neighborhood Center at Toyama Heights. All of these things she did successfully and enjoyed doing. We fitted her schedule into mine so that I could drop her as I went to my appointments and pick her up afterwards. She greatly enjoyed flower arrangement lessons and became proficient enough to earn a teacher's certificate. Even so she had many long hours in the house when Tane and I were away. I was absorbed in my work; Tane and I had become very close during our two years together and I was concerned that she should not feel pushed aside when Violet came. Sometimes Violet walked out to the Mejiro main street to window-shop or buy flowers; she read a great deal; but often she was bored and lonely. Retirement after years of work that was vital, useful and interesting is a difficult adjustment to make, even though there is the distraction of new and exotic scenes.

When the Korean War broke out and we were so close to it that we heard the bombers flying over our house and saw wounded soldiers being unloaded at Yokohama, Violet became desperately uneasy. She was sure that World War III was about to break over our heads. When the UN armies were pushed down into a small pocket around Pusan on the southern tip of Korea, she was convinced that the time had come for us to go home—us, for she would not go without me.

I made the decision only after much soul-searching; the work had been laid upon me; was I free to put it down? How does one know, when no clear light seems to come from within? Is one only to tell by the result, after it is all over and the decision is irretrievable?

As I thought about the problem under those great trees in Karuizawa, it seemed to me that I had given whatever it was I had to give the Crown Prince. He had grown from a little boy of twelve going on thirteen to a poised and confident youth of nearly seventeen. His horizons were beginning to widen. He was studying French now as well as English. Dr. Koizumi, with his greater stature and broader vision, had replaced Dr. Hozumi as his councillor. It was entirely possible, even likely, that if I stayed on I would be only repeating what I had done before, that the freshness might go out of it and the performance become one more ritual kept because it had become established. Esther Rhoads, who was already in Japan as AFSC representative and as principal of the Friends Girls School, could take over the hours of English conversation both with the Crown Prince and the Empress. My expensive setup, my house and staff, could be given up and the other things I did allowed to drop. I could not see that by going home I should be in any real way depriving the Crown Prince.

And what, I asked myself, was it that I wanted? Was I clothing in acceptable garments of unselfish concern for others any deep desires of my own? I was tired. I longed more even than I realized at the time for the freedom of my inconspicuous life in America. I wanted to be writing again. I had, I felt, a work of interpretation to do. There was little written at that time about postwar Japan, and I had seen an aspect of it open to so few that it might be called unique. Though I would have been happy to stay, I was in a deeper sense ready to go.

My request to retire was not accepted at once. Both Mr. Tajima and Dr. Koizumi were reluctant to put it before the Emperor. The word of release did not come until nearly the end of the summer, but when it came it was attended by quite overwhelming appreciation of my work there and warmth for both Violet and me personally. The last months were filled with farewell gifts and ceremonies, a special trip to Kyushu, parties of all kinds, and to crown it, the honor of the third Order of the Sacred Crown, an order reserved for women and usually given to princesses. We sailed for home early in December, 1950.

Looking back as the years have passed, I have felt that it was the right time to take my leave. The will of God is spoken sometimes through the voice of another person, in this case through the sister whose instinct was better than her reasons. The rightness of the decision was confirmed to me by Mr. Yamanashi, one of my oldest—in both senses of the word—friends in Japan and one of the wisest. "It showed balance," he wrote me.

✳ *PART* *IV.*

****

1.

Homecoming

WE HAD taken passage on a Danish freighter, the *Peter Maersk*, in order to avoid the curiosity and questions inevitable on a larger ship. Though the ship was tossed about a good bit in the winter swells, it moved steadily across the Pacific and reached San Francisco in eleven days. We slipped in under the Golden Gate Bridge after dark, thrilled by the beauty of the harbor and the loops of lights that spangled the city on the hills above, disembarked unnoticed at ten P.M. and went straight to the Clift, where a pile of welcoming mail awaited us. The moment when we stood together at our open window, Violet and I, and looked out on this loveliest of our cities was a moment of unclouded bliss.

There was sorrow as well as joy in the pile of letters that we opened so eagerly, the withheld bad news that so often tinges homecoming with sadness. My sister-in-law, Beatrice Hurt, was dying in a hospital in Dallas of cancer of the lungs and spine. It was not possible to go to her at once, and a week later it was too late. We had not seen each other for a dozen years, but we had written regularly once a month. Her last years had been a struggle against ill health and loneliness, but she had been capable of gaiety too; she had an affectionate nature and something of Morgan's charm. The thought of her dying in agony was grievous, and I felt a pang of regret that I had done so little for her.

National bad news greeted us too. On that very evening the President declared a state of emergency, called for a mighty effort to build the nation into "an arsenal of freedom" and named Charles E. Wilson of General Motors head of the Office of War Production. "Our homes, our nation, all the things that we believe in," he proclaimed, "are in great danger. This danger has been created by the rulers of the Soviet Union." Next day *The New York Times* declared editorially, "If we are any judge of the American people, these are the words they have been waiting for." In addition newspapers and magazines were full of the speeches of Senator Joseph McCarthy, of Congressional investigations, black lists and loyalty oaths.

It is difficult always to recapture the mental climate of a past time. When we know how a crisis actually turned out, it is hard not to find the fears of those for whom the issue was in doubt slightly ridiculous. At that time, in December, 1950, China and Russia together were an enormous, solid and threatening Communist bloc. The Korean War was going badly. Russia had discovered the atomic secrets ten years before she was expected to, and Truman had given the order to develop a hydrogen bomb. We found people depressed and fearful.

After a day in San Francisco, we continued our journey home in the "California Zephyr," sitting in a high glass "bubble" looking out at the beautiful winding canyons of the Feather and Red Rivers. Then we came out into the states of the high plains and the prairies and saw vast stretches of land with here and there a small, lonely house, mile after mile of straight, long, paved roads with only an occasional scurrying car or truck, and commonplace but solid and clean little towns. We saw almost no people: a few men working on the railroad, an occasional woman hanging out the wash, some children playing in a schoolyard. Even in the towns no one seemed to be walking on the streets. When I looked at the empty reaches of my own country and thought of the teeming cities of Japan, the never-ending stream of people trudging along remote country roads, I felt almost frightened by the contrast.

We got out of the train at Paoli at nine o'clock of the morning of December 20 and were met by Fran and Sam Fox, who took us to the Deanery at Bryn Mawr, once Miss Thomas's home, now the Alumnae House, where we had arranged to stay until we found a house. The day after we arrived the Board of Directors and Trustees met. I had early in 1949 accepted election to the Board of Trustees, expecting to be at home again that fall; now I was a year late to my first meeting. Fresh from Japan, with the newspapers hot on my trail, I came onto the Board in a burst of excitement and publicity.

My record at Bryn Mawr had been respectable—I was graduated *cum laude* in the lower ranks of the "Upper Ten"—but by no means distinguished. I had won no prizes; the *Alumnae Bulletin* had been cool about my books; on the rare occasions when I went back to the College nobody seemed to notice that I was there. Now I had, as my mother would have said, "come back in my coach and four." She had been fond of telling the story of the poor boy who left his New Jersey village declaring that he would not return until he could come back in his coach and four; he had prospered greatly but by the time he actually achieved his coach, he had lost interest in his village and no longer cared to return. But I went back to Bryn Mawr with pleasure, perhaps because my years away had taught me to recognize how much the College had given me and to be grateful for it.

Rufus Jones, who had been for so long chairman of the Board, had died in 1948, but Frank Stokes of Germantown Meeting was there and Thomas Reyburn White, whose daughter Mary Louise and I had been at school together, and Frederick Strawbridge, whose son Gordon had been in my class at school and whose yellow-wheeled carriages used to wait for him at Queen Lane Station in my childhood. Among the directors two, Nora Bury and Helen Hill Miller, the author of delightful books on Greece, were juniors at college when I was a freshman. Katharine McBride, Bryn Mawr's brilliant and much loved president since 1941, had also been graduated from Germantown Friends School and from Bryn Mawr two years after me. After dinner in the Deanery, college students in cap and gown, carrying lighted lanterns and bringing with them a breath of the frosty air from the campus outside, came in to sing Christmas carols—the old traditional carols which seemed to me lovelier than ever after the years away. I was home indeed.

There was one missing element on my return: my little dog Hamish. He was eleven years old when I went to Japan, and I had to leave him behind. First Violet and then Elizabeth McKie had tried to fit him into their working lives, but he suffered too greatly from the necessary hours of loneliness. The kennel where for years he had gone happily to visit when all of us had to be away had become his home; at thirteen, blind, he had died.

The holidays were full of gaiety. Christmas we spent with our McDonald cousins at Invercoe, their house outside of Wilmington. On New Year's Day, which was a brilliant winter day, sunny, cold and glittering, Stanley and Sue Yarnall and Janet and George

Whitney came to have dinner with us at the Deanery. The talk was lively and spontaneous; there were no pauses for interpretation or explanation, no hesitancies for fear of misunderstanding or indiscretion. Violet and I talked it over afterwards, how relaxed, how warm, how happy it was.

And yet a memory of the previous New Year's Day came back to fill me with nostalgia for Japan, not one of the striking events of a New Year's celebration but a small incident that touched the day with a flavor not to be recaptured.

The young policeman who lived with his family near us in the small wooden police-box (not much larger than a sentry-box) came with his two small daughters to wish us a Happy New Year. Dressed in his best uniform, he was redolent of sake but entirely in command of himself; the two little girls, aged five and three, wore scarlet kimonos patterned with bright flowers; they had bells tied in their hair ribbons and bells in the high hollow soles of their red and gold clogs, called onomatopoetically *pokkuri* because they made a cheerful tinkling sound as they walked.

I heard them coming, and Tane and I quickly tied up a bag of hard candies, which I offered to the older of the little girls. Her father politely demurring, she shyly refused to take it but Sachiko, the three-year-old, eagerly held out both small hands. I put the candy into them and she turned and started out for home all by herself, *pokkuri, pokkuri*, her bells tinkling. Her young father hastily said his farewells, pushed his elder daughter's head down in a bow, and off they went after Sachiko and the candy.

No more would handsome young policemen come with their children to make a New Year's call, nor, for that matter, would traffic cops salute my car respectfully. "You'll know you're home," Violet said, "when a policeman shouts at you, 'Get over to the curb, sister, where do you think you're going?' "

We had decided that we wanted a house, not an apartment, and that we would rent until we found the perfect one to buy. Houses were in short supply still, though the postwar building boom had got under way, and there were not many for rent. Fortunately Amos Peaslee had offered us one of his small houses in Mickleton, New Jersey, about twenty miles south of Camden.

I had first met Amos Peaslee in 1937 in England, when I had gone to tea at the Crossfields' house in Penn. He came across the lawn to greet me with outstretched hand, saying, "Dr. Livingstone, I presume?" I knew who he was: the Quaker lawyer who had won the Black Tom case and had used some of the money he made out of it to restore his family farms in Mickleton, creating a sophisticated and lovely estate in the midst of an old and sad and somewhat disheveled land. He had a slightly gnomelike look, short of stature with a domed forehead and pointed ears, bright, keen eyes and quick smile. His elder sister Ruth had married James Engle, a childhood friend of my mother's; the Engle farm had been not far from the Iszard farm, and a path between the two had been much trodden. Amos and his delightful wife, Dorothy, had done much for Mickleton: restored the eighteenth-century red-brick meetinghouse; made the little red schoolhouse, long disused, into a community center; and renovated some old and run-down houses which they rented to Friends and like-minded people. It was one of these houses that we moved into on January 15, a small, trim, six-room frame house with an attic, situated on the old King's Highway opposite the meetinghouse.

We had three weeks in which to get settled before we were visited by an imperial emissary, Mr. Shiro Sumikura, formerly one of the Crown Prince's chamberlains, who came with messages and a present from the Empress, and letters from the Crown Prince and the other imperial children, to see how we were getting on and to report back to the Empress. There was a thin coating of snow on the ground when he came; the village, with its old houses, big trees and rosy brick meetinghouse, looked like a village on a sampler. Already the birds had learned that sunflower seeds and suet were available on our kitchen window sill, and Mr. Sumikura was fascinated to see their numbers and their tameness. We had a pair of chickadees that reminded me of Japanese children with their dark heads, bright eyes and round, active bodies; a song sparrow whom we called the Old Man because of his bossy ways with the others; a pair of cardinals; a titmouse called Tuffy with a bold, black eye; brawling jays and starlings and a downy woodpecker or two.

We gave a dinner party for Mr. Sumikura on Saturday night in our small, crowded dining room, and the next day the Peaslees had us all for Sunday lunch, and Amos presented our Japanese guest with a copy of his own new book just published, a scholarly work on the Constitutions of the World. Apart from the sheer pleasure in seeing our friend again, it was reassuring to have Mr. Sumikura come; I was not forever cut off from Japan; visitors could come bringing and taking messages; the channels were still open.

Though the women's auxiliary of every church in the vicinity wanted me to come and tell them all about Japan over the tea-cups and though I had many invitations from larger and more distant groups, though I had not yet begun to see all of my friends, I felt that I must call a halt on going about and get down to writing my book. It seemed to me that my work in Japan was not finished until I had told the American people—or all who wished to know—about it. Out of the number of publishing houses that thought I had a story to tell and wished to publish it, I selected for various reasons the J. B. Lippincott Company. I have never regretted the decision, for to become a Lippincott author was like joining a warm, loyal, and congenial family.

It seemed natural and comfortable to go back to writing in an attic. I pushed the trunks and boxes back against the walls and set up my table, bookcases and typewriter stand beside the south window. Before long I found a capable young woman who came in the mornings to type for me, in some amazement, I think, to find herself working in an untidy and sometimes dusty garret.

The most difficult part of writing that book lay in deciding what to put in, what to leave out. I had a great deal of material, diary, letters, clippings as well as memories. The criterion that I decided upon and kept to was a simple one: I had gone to Japan to teach the Crown Prince; all that pertained to that purpose should be included in the book, whatever was peripheral or incidental should be left out. That decision made, I had the further question: How much of what I might tell was confidential and should be withheld? How much should the Crown Prince himself know —for read the book he would. Would this or that incident embarrass him?

Lying awake at night is much the same wherever you are, whether you do it in a rather battered mahogany four-poster or in an elegant bed decorated with brass garlands bought for a Prince of Wales: self-confidence is weak and apprehension strong. The sounds in Mickleton were different. Instead of the clip-clop of wooden geta on the street or the call of the man who warned people against fires, I heard the strange, grinding cry of barn owls nesting in the big trees on the meetinghouse grounds. And in the early morning, instead of the low, rich sound of the temple bell or the shrill *"Chottoi-koi, Chottoi-koi"* of Chinese bamboo pheasants in the garden, heard the rumble and clash of road machines on their way to build the New Jersey Turnpike.

While I filled the days with writing, Violet kept up her flower arranging. She visited garden clubs in Mickleton, Germantown or Doylestown to demonstrate the art and to make talks on it. But it was not the same in America. Her gracefully leaning arrangement of Japanese quince was kindly straightened up by our cleaning woman; American florists sell flowers by the dozen, all the same size with stems of the same length; it was not possible to buy a branch of flowering plum in bud or a piece of crooked pine.

Spring was lovely in Mickleton. Our rides into the country so close at hand took us past acres of peach trees in bloom and a little later of apple trees. Asparagus came in May, and the fields were full of bent figures cutting it. Along the roads and in our own village street little stands appeared with bunches of asparagus standing in a shallow tray of water, with a cup in which to drop your money. You made your own change and some time later, at her convenience, the lady of the house came out and took in her day's earnings. Asparagus grew everywhere and the seeds must have sailed on the wind, for four fat stalks came up among the tulips under our dining-room window.

Sometimes on Sundays we drove the thirty miles to Germantown Meeting, and sometimes we walked across the road to small old Mickleton Meeting, where the clock ticked aloud on the wall and the benches were narrow and straight-backed, the windows open to the trees and the fields beyond, and the silence, when it was broken at all, was broken by simple and sometimes repetitive messages. The fragile, white-haired, ninety-year-old Friend who sat "at the head of the meeting" always said the same thing: "Put your hand in the hand of God and He will lead you onward and upward to Heaven, wherever Heaven is." The open-mindedness of that last clause sweetened the repetition for me.

A killdeer nested in the driveway behind the meetinghouse— or rather, laid her eggs in a hollow in the ground without troubling to construct a nest. The word went round and everyone stopped to see it; barricades were built to keep cars from overrunning the eggs. The killdeer, flying overhead, cried "Kill-dee, kill-dee!" and I remembered my mother's talking nostalgically of this sound of her childhood.

When, years later, I came to write a novel of which the scene was laid in South Jersey, *I, Roberta*, it was not Mickleton that was the original of Ewingville in the book, or Greenwich, as some have thought, but an imaginary village bearing a family resemblance to Mickleton, to Mullica Hill of my mother's memories and to Salem which I had visited as a child.

Early in May I went to Drexel Institute, to the Library School, to ask if they had a scholarship for Tane. When she had been a student at Western Maryland College, Tane had been greatly impressed by the public libraries that she saw in every small or large town in America, and she had coveted for Japan a library movement such as ours. Now, after years of teaching in Keisen and of being my secretary and interpreter, she was free to pursue her old dream. Since Japan had only one very new and still tentative library school, she hoped to come to the United States to study. So I went to Dean MacPherson at Drexel and told Tane's story. She was interested and sympathetic but said regretfully that what foreign scholarships they had had already been assigned. "But," she added, "don't go. Stay around a little. Mr. Paul is in the building, and I think he'd like to see you."

A little later Dr. James Creese, the president of Drexel Institute, and Mr. Anthony J. Drexel Paul, the president of the Trustees, joined us in her office. After some questions about Tane, the two men exchanged glances and Dr. Creese said, "We have decided to create a special library scholarship for Miss Takahashi. We have been watching your work with interest and appreciation. We think this country owes you a debt of gratitude and we'll pay our share this way."

In June Drexel gave me my first honorary doctorate but that, though thrilling as only the first one can be, gave me nothing of the deep, warm, humble satisfaction that the scholarship for Tane gave me. I rushed home to pay my Drexel Alumni dues, even before writing the good news to Tane.

The summer heat settled down early over that flat South Jersey land like a blanket, heavy and stifling. White dust from the fields rose and sifted over everything. Asparagus turned feathery and stood shoulder-high; the miles of tomato plants exuded an acrid, dusty smell on summer evenings. Sometimes vapors from the factories on the river four miles to the west blew over the village and our newly polished silver on the sideboard was tarnished in a moment's time. We began to think about New England.

The Foxes, who had built themselves a small and charming house on Long Pond in Mount Desert Island, found a cottage for us which we rented for six weeks in August and September, where

I could work on my book in cool and quiet. The cottage was on the western side of the island, on a ledge of rocks at the edge of Blue Hill Bay. The day we arrived a thick white fog enveloped the island. Fran and Sam drove us all around it to show us the beauty that lay in store for us. "This is Otter Cliff," they said, waving enthusiastic arms at a curtain of cotton wool, and "That is Seawall—there's a beautiful view." But all we saw was a fringe of surf under a wall of gray mist.

It was like that most of the six weeks. Day after day fog rolled in over the rocks and dripped from the pointed firs above our roof. We used up all the dry firewood, and the wet logs sent stinging smoke into the living room, where I pounded away on my typewriter on a trembling card table. "It's like being in a white china vegetable dish with the lid on," said Violet.

Two months later, in Mickleton, I finished my book and sent the manuscript to Lippincott. The title was inevitable; it had been given me by the Minister of the Imperial Household, Viscount Matsudaira, when he said to me, "We want you to open windows on to a wider world for our Crown Prince." So I called it *Windows for the Crown Prince*.

That winter I spent chiefly in making speeches about my experiences in Japan, to women's clubs and colleges up and down the country, from Bradford Junior College in Massachusetts to the Mary K. Craig Class in Dallas, Texas, where an extra inducement was that I saw some of Morgan's cousins whom I had not seen for twenty years.

It was inconvenient to go forth and make speeches from Mickleton. The Walt Whitman Bridge over the Delaware was not yet built; all the New Jersey traffic funneled through Camden and over the Ben Franklin Bridge. From Mickleton to Woodbury the road ran past fields, farms and an occasional creek; but from Woodbury to the bridge there was an unbroken parade of the commercial monsters that American cities have allowed to spawn on their fringes: hot dog and soft drink stands—"Even a red-hot mama loves her ice-cold pop"—taverns, filling stations, motels, discount stores, bazaars selling pink flamingos and crystal balls, all with huge signs and garish neon lights, all, on a wet night, reflected in the black asphalt of the road mingled with the red and green of traffic lights. Whenever I went to Philadelphia to catch a train or airplane, to see my friends or just to shop, I had to struggle through this waste of vulgarity and ugliness. The Peaslees solved the problem by making an airstrip in one of their fields and coming and going by air taxi, but the rest of us had to do it by car or bus. Violet and I began to look for a house in Germantown or Chestnut Hill, a little old house with atmosphere on a quiet street.

Windows for the Crown Prince came out on May 8, was reviewed by John Gunther on the front page of the *New York Times Book Review* and got onto the best-seller list. It was promptly translated into Japanese and later into French, Spanish, German and Dutch. *The King and I*, the musical made by Rodgers and Hammerstein out of Margaret Landon's book *Anna and the King of Siam*, had opened earlier in the year and was a tremendous hit; seats were sold out for six months ahead. It was a severe trial to me that people associated and often even confused me with Anna Leonowens. It did no good at all to point out that Anna lived a hundred years ago or that Japan was a modern country with a democratic constitution, that the Emperor did not have a harem. "How *is* the dear King of Siam?" a dowager asked me at a dinner party, and after a luncheon speech to a group of Pen Women a gracious lady, shaking my hand, said kindly, "I haven't read your book but I *did* enjoy the play about you." I was nevertheless eager to see the play, and my publishers, by appealing to Gertrude Lawrence's lawyer for house tickets, got me seats in the middle of the fourth row. With them came an invitation from Gertrude Lawrence to go backstage after the play was over and meet her.

The musical was enchanting; I was captivated by the children, by Yul Brynner as the king and by Gertrude Lawrence herself, in her swaying hoopskirts, with her slight but appealing voice, her gaiety, her warmth. As in *South Pacific*, there was a note of seriousness underlying the froth. "You have to be taught," sang the young lieutenant in *South Pacific*, "to be afraid of people whose eyes are oddly made, and people whose skins are a different shade, you have to be carefully taught," and in *The King and I* the King, confused by the pressures of power politics, sings,

> "Unless somebody sometime trusts somebody
> There'll be nothing left on earth except fishes."

At the end of the play, while the audience was still applauding, an usher led us through a door and down a passage to the star's dressing room.

Richard Aldrich, her husband, was there; he explained that she had gone to take a shower. It was a warm May evening and her costumes had been intolerably hot. We had last seen her in an enormous hoop skirt encrusted with lace and flounces; when she came out from the shower, huddled in an old red dressing gown, she appeared to have shrunk to half her size. Her charm, however, was undiminished. She took the play seriously; it was, she said, the most important one she had ever been in; she felt it had a "message" that the world needed. We left after a few minutes, feeling that we had touched briefly a memorable personality. Two months later Gertrude Lawrence was dead.

That summer Violet and I, daunted by the memory of fog at Mount Desert, went to Wonalancet instead, where we rented the very house which had been such a golden place to me in my girl-hood, the Childs' cottage on the brook. It is not wise to go back and try to recapture an old magic. The Childs were gone. The garden which Mrs. Child had made a glory was now a wilderness. The floors sagged; the hearth was cold. Some friends came to visit us: Elizabeth McKie, back from two years teaching in Honolulu; Bertha and William Miller; Emma Bevan, whose chauffeur and houseman Gadson found the drive at twilight through eight miles of woods from Tamworth terrifying. Elizabeth Orton Jones, who illustrated Rachel Field's book, *Prayer for a Child*, which I had used in Japan, and Elizabeth Yates, whose fine *Amos Fortune, Free Man* had won the Newbery Medal the year before, drove up from southern New Hampshire to have lunch with us, and a friendship that was to bring me joy was then begun. But on the whole Wonalancet was dull. We went to see the Foxes on Long Pond, found Mount Desert Island this time all asparkle and full of friends. In later years a cottage became available on a slope overlooking Goose Cove with old apple trees to shade its terrace and sun to warm its living room, to which we returned summer after summer.

Back in Mickleton that September of 1952, we pulled up our roots of twenty-one months' growing, gathered together our old mahogany furniture and our Japanese treasures, the Emperor's vases, the Princesses' gold lacquer, the Crown Prince's poem, the Empress' embroidery, the Imari plates and the Nabeshima saucers, the Korean bowl, the books and the prints, and moved back to Philadelphia.

The Year of the Crown Prince's Visit

THE LITTLE house in Mount Airy between German-town and Chestnut Hill in suburban Philadelphia which I bought in 1952 was 120 years old, one of five cottages originally built for the workers in a mill on nearby Cresheim Creek. It was narrow-fronted, with a door and two windows under a pent roof, but deep, running back into a long, narrow garden with lilacs growing up to the second-story porch, old dogwood trees, a tall Douglas fir, and beds of peonies and weed-choked rosebushes along the fence. Some-one down the years had thrown the original two small front rooms and entrance hall together to make a living room twenty-six feet long, out of which a steep, straight staircase went up to the second story. On the newel post I found carved, to my sur-prise, a sixteen-petaled chrysanthemum, the symbol sacred in Japan to the Imperial Family. Who conceived this bit of decoration and whether he had any idea of the significance of it, I do not, of course, know; my guess is that this part of the modernization of the house was done soon after the Centennial Exposition of 1876, when the Japanese exhibit had attracted much attention and provided motifs for many Philadelphia lamps, sofa cushions, wood-work and the like. In any case it was an arresting coincidence, and I often found Japanese visitors quietly counting the petals.

Later modernizations had added two bathrooms and a powder room, made the old kitchen into a dining room and built on a new kitchen with a big bedroom and porch above. On the third floor there was an attic room with sloping ceilings which I could use for my study. It was just the right size for us, and our furni-ture, most of which was of the Federal period, fitted in well. The living room was marred by a hideous fireplace which dated from a modernization of 1910 or thereabouts; I bought in Mickleton a beautiful, simple mantel from a house which had been built in 1767. Fitted into place in our house, the ugly tiles replaced with good brick, it was lovely, and there were at each end of it wider places just the right size to hold the great cloisonné vases given me by the Emperor and Empress as a farewell present. It did not occur to us, as we watched over the painting and papering and had the garden put in order, that we were preparing it to receive an Imperial visitor.

In the autumn of 1952 Prince Akihito came of age at eighteen and was invested as Crown Prince in beautiful and impressive ceremonies. As usual in Japan the occasion was celebrated with an outpouring of verse. Everyone in the Court—and countless people outside it—wrote *waka*, the classic, thirty-one syllable poem on the subject which had been assigned: Chrysanthemum, the symbol for the Crown Prince. I too was asked to write a poem—in English, of course. Our language not lending itself easily to syllabic poetry, I tried to make mine as nearly as possible in the spirit of *waka* through brevity and suggestion.

> I saw in the frosty morn
>   A tender bud, tight furled.
> Now in the noon-day sun,
>   Its petals bright uncurled,
> The flower stands, straight, strong and true.
> Blow gently, wind. Fall lightly, dew.

Dr. Koizumi wrote me: "Today's papers published your poem on Chrysanthemum along with those by the Emperor and Empress, by the Imperial Princesses and a few others. The last line of your poem made me feel your motherly love to Prince Akihito and brought tears into my eyes. I am here enclosing a clipping on which the poems are printed. . . . Imagine my embarrassment when I found my poem printed beside yours. It is the very first poem of mine ever printed! I will translate it for your amusement's sake:

> The first frost of the year,
> This morning's light
> Shining in reflection,
> The chrysanthemum
> Pure in color
> Came out in bloom.

The Voice of America taped a "message" from me to the Crown Prince, on setting out on his journey of life, which was broadcast in Japan and the tape later presented to him. He sent me a cable in response: "Heartily thank you for all the thoughtful instructions tape-recorded on the eve of my embarcation, deeply appreciated and always to be borne in mind in my travels of life. All best wishes. Akihito."

Soon after this the Crown Prince's Grand Chamberlain, Mr. Nomura, wrote me that the Crown Prince would represent his father at the coronation of Queen Elizabeth II and that on the way home he would visit the United States. Early in January Mr. Moriyuki Motono, attaché at the Embassy in Washington, came to see me, bearing a beautiful leather-bound album with photographs of the Crown Prince's Coming-of-Age Ceremonies which had been sent me by Their Majesties; he came also to talk about the Crown Prince's visit to the United States and to ask me to help with the planning of it.

My first thought, when I learned that the Crown Prince was to be in Philadelphia for three days, was that he might stay in some suitably large and well-staffed house—and I had friends and acquaintances whose establishments would qualify and whose hopes I aroused prematurely—and that he might come to our little house one day for lunch. By January 22, however, word had come from Dr. Koizumi that "no house is too small for Mrs. Vining to entertain the Crown Prince," and a month later a registered, special delivery letter from the Foreign Office in Japan confirmed it: "The Crown Prince would feel more at home in your house" and the week end of September 12 was set. Mrs. Takaki wrote: "I am *very* happy to know that the Prince is going to spend a day or two in your house. What a privilege for him to sit down with you and talk quietly over many things he is confronting. I wish so much he will have much time to spend with select American young people and be acquainted with real American spirit. I hope he will be able to peep into American homes to enjoy the wholesome atmosphere rather than seeing wonderful sights and formal visits."

As Mrs. Takaki was the Empress's Mistress of the Robes and English interpreter, I took this to express the Empress's ideas as well as her own. It also accorded with my own efforts for the Crown Prince from the first beginnings of my work with him: to make as many opportunities as possible for him to see his friends informally and to meet as many Western young people as possible.

Our State Department had a ruling that visiting royalty must stay in hotels or clubs instead of private houses, which are much less easily guarded, but they made two exceptions to this rule for the Crown Prince at, I noted, the two extremes of the financial scale, our house and the Rockefeller ranch in Wyoming. It is somewhat startling for an ordinary American to contemplate entertaining for three days, in a small suburban house, the son and heir of the Emperor of Japan; but this, of course, was my own beloved pupil, who had visited me, informally, in my summer home in Karuizawa, Japan, who had been a delightful guest, thoughtful and appreciative. That however, had been a large house on a hill, in a grove of trees; the Japanese guards and policemen had assured his safety. What troubled me now was the question of protecting him in a small house on a fifty-foot lot with other houses close on either side. But the State Department promised to make special security arrangements; the Japanese seemed not in the least worried; both Ambassador Araki and Mr. Motono had been to the house and knew what we had to offer. Since they appeared satisfied, I determined not to worry, and I looked forward with real joy to his coming. Violet, pleased though she was with the prospect of seeing him again, was more apprehensive; her blood pressure, which had been normal for two years, shot up to 200 and stayed there until the visit was safely over.

Looking back, I see 1953 as the year of the Crown Prince's visit, for throughout the first ten months I was busy with preparations, the very brief visit itself, and the aftermath. Not a week passed and indeed scarcely a day without letters, telephone calls, visits from people concerned with the plans—and from many others who would have liked to be concerned with them. I went to Washington to the Embassy; Mr. Miyazaki, the counselor who had the chief responsibility for the visit, and Mr. Motono, who did the day-to-day work, came to my house. Mr. Motono developed a stomach ulcer from the pressures, and whenever he came I would first get him a glass of milk and then we would settle down to the plans.

Many Americans, some out of real kindness and interest and others out of the desire for publicity for their organizations, had plans to suggest; schools, colleges, fathers of debutante daughters, libraries, clubs and so on plied me with invitations for the Crown Prince. Even Morgan's eighty-year-old cousin, Mrs. Gazzam, telephoned to say, "Wouldn't you like me to give a little tea for the

Crown Prince and introduce him to some of my friends?" All but Cousin Nellie's I sent on to the Japanese Embassy for them to decide upon.

The Crown Prince left Japan on the S.S. *President Wilson* on March 30, seen off by members of his family, by the Prime Minister, the top diplomats and half a million ordinary Japanese who lined the road from Tokyo to Yokohama; he reached San Francisco on April 11. As the purpose of his trip was to visit England and attend the Coronation, the British government did not want the United States to skim the cream first, and so he was whisked into Canada at once, to cross the continent on the Canadian Pacific, and then brought down to New York for just long enough to embark on the *Queen Elizabeth*, which sailed at noon on April 22.

I was invited to have breakfast with him in New York and see him off for England. To make it easy and comfortable, the Embassy engaged a room for me for the night before at the Hotel Pierre. It was like old days to be waiting to see the Crown Prince, and yet it was totally different in the setting of my own country; moreover, the boy who had once been my charge was now a man and the Emperor's emissary. I lay awake late in the spring night thinking about it and savoring it; a final touch of strangeness was added when above the low, steady roar of the city I heard the short, intermittent roars of the lions in Central Park Zoo down below.

It had been arranged that I was not to go to the station but to meet the Crown Prince at the door of the hotel. Half an hour before he came the corridors were full of burly policemen, and the manager of the hotel was pacing up and down. Word came that the Prince was almost there, and I went to the door.

The next thing I knew I was engulfed and all but knocked down by the tide of photographers who were rushing ahead to get pictures of the Prince as he entered the hotel. In the midst of them was Prince Akihito himself, smiling. We shook hands, once for ourselves and many more times for the solid wall of nearly a hundred photographers surrounding us, some of them standing on chairs at the back, shouting, "Shake hands again!" "Look this way, Your Highness!" The Prince conformed smilingly but murmured to me, "It was much quieter in Canada."

Then I had a chance to speak to the men attending the Prince, whom I had known well in Japan, Mr. Takanobu Mitani, the Emperor's Grand Chamberlain; Mr. Akira Matsui, representing the Foreign Office; Mr. Shigetani Kikkawa, of the Department of Ceremonies of the Imperial Household; two of the Crown Prince's chamberlains with whom I had worked for four years, Mr. Jutatsu Kuroki and Mr. Yasuhide Toda; as well as Dr. Hishashi Sato, and Mr. Akiyoshi Sakamoto, the valet.

Plucked at length out of all the confusion, I found myself alone with the Prince having breakfast. He looked, I saw at once, well and happy; his expression was alert and interested, his eyes bright; a new assurance tempered his innate modesty and shyness. He had enjoyed his trip across the Pacific and his ten days in Canada; he told me a good bit about it and gave me the presents that he had brought from the Empress for Violet and me—dress lengths of lovely Japanese silk, the traditional imperial gift from the time of Genji on down. I had news for him of Bob Togasaki, his classmate and friend, now at Haverford College, and of Gordon, Bob's elder brother at Swarthmore, who had been active in helping with the plans for the Prince's visit. Bob was in New York that morning, and I had promised to make an opportunity for him to see the Prince at the boat. A newspaper account of the Crown Prince in New York said that "The Prince had breakfast with his former tutor Mrs. Elizabeth Gray Vining (50) of Philadelphia in rather lonesome splendor in the hotel's Teakwood Room, other members of the party being served in adjoining rooms." It may have been splendid—I was in no state to notice—but it was not lonesome.

I rode with the Crown Prince and Mr. Mitani to Pier 90, preceded, surrounded and followed by eighteen screaming motorcycles, and after his press conference on the deck I was with him in the sitting room of his suite before the ship sailed, with the Japanese ambassador, the Canadian ambassador, and Bob Togasaki. The famous captain of the *Queen Elizabeth*, a typical English sea dog, blue-eyed, ruddy-cheeked, built like Churchill, bluff and hearty, came in to welcome the Prince to his ship. When he left he said to the royal passenger, "Well, by-by," and I wondered if he would have spoken as informally to a member of his own royal family.

From an English cutting service I had a shower of clippings about the Prince's six weeks in England, and from Major-General F. S. G. Piggott, President of the Japan Society of London, letters and an article from the *Japan Society News*, so that I was able to follow his progress from London to Edinburgh, to Rothbury, Northumberland, where Lord and Lady Armstrong gave a house party for him, to Oxford and Cambridge and at last to the Coronation itself. One of the newspapers reported soon after his arrival in London, "His reception in this country has been guarded," meaning, of course, not guarded by policemen but reserved. He was met at Waterloo Station by the Earl of Selkirk representing the Queen and by the Vice-Marshal of the Diplomatic Corps representing the Foreign Secretary, and he was not received in audience by the Queen herself for more than a week. In Newcastle a visit to the Armstrong-Vickers munitions works and a civic reception by the Lady Mayoress were canceled because of angry protests by the Association of Prisoners of War and the labor unions. I was more than casually interested in these evidences of opposition to the visit of the Japanese Prince two years after the signing of the Peace Treaty, for I was wondering how he would be received in the United States, where people are on the whole less disciplined than the English. Would some crank try to do him harm when he came to New York—or to Mount Airy?

I had reports too from Dr. Koizumi, who was traveling not in the Crown Prince's suite but independently. He had at first declined to go. "A man who wears the scars of war," he wrote to me, "is not fit to be present at such an auspicious occasion as a queen's coronation, and a man who walks only with difficulty is not a right one to be a young Prince's tutor on tour." But early in May he yielded to Prime Minister Yoshida's urging and with his wife set out for England and for some of the European countries which the Crown Prince would visit, "thinking," he wrote, "that the Crown Prince's educator should have an up-to-date knowledge of the post-war Europe and America, keeping pace with the pupil-prince." In June he wrote to me from London, with understated pride, "He was perfectly all right as his father's representative at the Coronation."

While the Crown Prince spent the summer visiting kings and heads of state in Spain, France, Italy, Belgium, Holland, Germany, Denmark, Norway, Sweden and Switzerland, staying in palaces and famous hotels from the Quirinale in Rome to the Suvretta House in Saint-Moritz, Violet hemmed curtains and polished silver and I weeded the garden and painted the downstairs powder room, which we would ourselves use when we turned over our two bathrooms to the Crown Prince and Mr. Matsui, who would be the only one of his suite to stay in the house with him. We made our plans down to the last minute of every hour of the days September 13 to 16; I typed lists of the people whom the security guards were to allow into the house during that time.

We were wonderfully lucky in having Tane Takahashi near at hand. After getting her degree in Library Science from Drexel, she had taken a job as assistant cataloguer in the Bryn Mawr College Library, and so she could be with us to oil the wheels and do any necessary interpreting, as she had done in Japan when she was my right hand there. There was no room for her to stay in the house; she would sleep in the house of a friend of mine up the street and come to us early in the morning; she would cook the curry rice—the Crown Prince's favorite dish—for dinner the first night.

At that time our total "staff" consisted of a weekly cleaning woman and a colored woman named Nancy who came in three evenings a week to get dinner for us. Nancy would be available on Monday evening, but on Sunday her daughter was getting married and having a reception for four hundred people and so she would not be able to come to us the first evening that the Crown Prince would be there. Our friend Emma Bevan came to the rescue and offered us her houseman, Gadson, a wonderful old-time Negro factotum and friend. On Sunday evening Gadson would serve the dinner Tane prepared; Monday, Tuesday and Wednesday mornings he would get breakfast. On Monday evening Nancy would cook fried chicken and bring a waitress with her to serve it; we would be out for lunch both days and on Tuesday evening the Crown Prince was to have dinner at Haverford College with the students.

The plans for those three days were made in consultation with the Japanese Embassy and the State Department in Washington, the Foreign Office in Tokyo, the Mayor's Office in Philadelphia and the Crown Prince's suite in Europe, through personal visits, cables, telegrams, telephone calls and letters. Mr. Motono and I struggled hard against all the pressures to salvage for the Prince some leisure and informality and to include young people in the plans, and in the end we were reasonably successful.

In his first ten days in the United States spent in Washington, Williamsburg, Philadelphia and New York, the Crown Prince ceremonially laid four wreaths on American tombs and attended eight large, official, adult luncheons or dinners, but he also had parts of four days to himself and three evenings with young people. Besides, of course, a great deal of sight-seeing, in which he was himself the most interesting sight for most of those present.

The last few days before his arrival in Mount Airy the tempo quickened. Our telephone never stopped ringing. An enormous wooden box labeled "Glass" arrived from Tokyo, from the Crown Prince's Household, and was put on the back porch. A very much smaller package addressed to the Crown Prince was inspected by the captain of the 14th Police District of Philadelphia lest it contain a bomb, and was found to be a gift of a Stetson hat. Security officers came to look at the house and assured us that it would be guarded day and night by policemen pacing up and down, back and front, on four-hour shifts. Mr. Motono arrived in a taxi with four cases of Haig and Haig to be presented to the policemen, while I arranged to have soft drinks, thermos bottles of coffee and plates of sandwiches for them on the back porch whenever the shifts changed. One of the policemen subsequently unnerved Nancy by sticking his head into the kitchen and asking for a fried chicken leg. During the whole of the two weeks before the Prince's visit the weather was steadily, hideously hot, but the day that his plane touched down it turned cool and sparkling.

The Crown Prince reached Washington on September 8, and on the 10th Ambassador Araki gave a reception for him at the Embassy. I went down to Washington for it and watched with pride and pleasure the Crown Prince moving at ease among the guests in the midst of a gay and brilliant scene. On the 12th the Prince went to Williamsburg and the Koizumis came to Philadelphia. Violet and I asked them to have dinner with us at the Art Alliance, next door to the Barclay, where they were staying, and we had a long, deeply satisfying talk about the summer that was past and the days that lay ahead. They came to our house the next afternoon, to be there in good time for the Crown Prince's arrival, but not so early as the children of the neighborhood, who began to gather in front of the house at noon. At six I went off to the airport in a limousine provided by the City of Philadelphia to meet the Crown Prince and bring him home with me.

All of his suite came with him as well as Mr. John Farr Simmons, chief of protocol of the State Department, a delightful man who accompanied the Prince throughout his visit and was immensely helpful in a number of ways, and Mr. William Husky, the appropriately named bodyguard provided by the State Department. Outside in the street, and with difficulty prevented from entering, were photographers and reporters in great numbers. It had been agreed that pictures and interviews would take place only outside the house; no one at all was to come inside for that purpose. This was achieved only by constant watchfulness, but it meant that during those days the house was a sanctuary in which the Crown Prince could relax and be himself without any strangers to watch and comment.

After the members of the suite and the diplomats had been welcomed and had departed to the hotel in town from which they would return each day to join us in the sight-seeing program, after the Crown Prince's ten suitcases had been carried up to his room and the Crown Prince had had time for a bath and change, we sat down to dinner: the Crown Prince, Dr. and Mrs. Koizumi, Mr. Mitani, Mr. Matsui, Tane, Violet and I. The Crown Prince, who had suffered so much in the past five and a half months from Western-cooked rice, took a small, cautious spoonful of Tane's rice, tasted it—and, calling Gadson back, helped himself liberally. It was an evening of laughter and reminiscence, of easy, comfortable talk in both English and Japanese.

Mr. Matsui, whom I had known in Japan as English interpreter to the Emperor, was now counsellor to the Foreign Office. He was a slender, elegant and brilliant man, warmhearted and sensitive, who had grown up in Paris, where his father had been ambassador to France. He was to climb the diplomatic ladder swiftly as ambassador to Ceylon, ambassador to the United Nations, ambassador to France. He had my room at the front of our house, where he stayed up late each night writing endless letters of thanks on behalf of the Crown Prince; the Prince himself had Violet's big room at the back, Violet slept in the small spare room between and I went up into the attic. Tane, going up the street to go to bed, got into the wrong house by mistake.

The next day's program was full of sight-seeing in the morning: Independence Hall, Benjamin Franklin's grave (a wreath), Christ Church, the American Friends Service Committee's Self-Help Housing Project, Fairmount Park; the afternoon was taken up with a tennis tournament at the Merion Cricket Club. In the evening we had dinner at home, and after dinner the young people came in: the two Togasaki boys; Yuji Ito, a Peers' School graduate studying at Lafayette College; Koya Azumi, a classmate of Bob's at Haverford; and two Japanese girls who had been graduated from the Peeresses' School: Asako Tanaka, in her freshman year at Bryn Mawr; and Tamiko Suematsu, who was a sophomore at Swarthmore and who later, incidentally, married Gordon Togasaki. Both girls had belonged to the English Club that met twice a month at my house in Tokyo. We left the living room to the young people; the grownups went out onto the porch, where we could hear the gales of laughter from within. Mr. Matsui, later describing the evening in a speech to the America-Japan Society in Tokyo, said, "The young people were left completely to themselves. I myself was careful not to poke my graying head into the living room."

One of the things in the United States that the Crown Prince had expressed interest in seeing was a farm, and so on Tuesday he visited the farm of Robert I. Ballinger in Chester County. Mr. Ballinger was a successful architect; there was a fine eighteenth-century stone farmhouse restored by an expert, where a delicious luncheon was provided; there was a fine red tractor on which the Crown Prince perched to be photographed; there were fields and cows and an electric milker; but I fear that the Prince got a somewhat unrealistic idea of American farm life, and I doubt if anybody explained to him the workings of the income tax in regard to exemptions for losses in unprofitable ventures.

From there we went to Valley Forge, where the rolling hills with their scarves of dogwood trees, the soldiers' huts and grass-grown earthworks, the piles of small black-painted cannon balls, the sturdy stone houses of the generals evoked the memory of a long, hungry winter of icy winds and blood-stained snow. I like to take foreigners to Valley Forge; it is, I am sure, one of the few national monuments in the world dedicated not to victory but to defeat and suffering, to endurance and faith.

From Valley Forge we went to Haverford College, where the Crown Prince was turned over to his friend Bob, free for four or five hours to roam about without being watched, except for the discreet Mr. Husky trailing behind, or expected to respond to formal speeches. The college was not yet actually in session, but the football squad was there and a number of other students early back on campus for one reason or another. He saw the pond into which freshmen are sometimes thrown, the athletic fields, the dormitories and some of the laboratories; he had dinner in Founders Hall with the students and attended a seminar afterwards which was arranged by Dr. Douglas V. Steere of the Philosophy

Department so that he might see the easy relationship and informal give-and-take that exists between American students and their professors. Meanwhile I was in the president's house, taking a bath and enjoying a quiet dinner with Anne White, the president's wife.

That evening after we returned home we had a little ceremony in our living room. The secretary of the suite had come out from town and spent the whole evening opening the wooden box on the back porch and removing from the glass case inside all the strips of paper that had been pasted crisscross over its surface to keep the glass from breaking. What emerged was a case containing a silver chariot about eighteen inches long, a replica of the kind of ox-drawn carriage in which members of the Imperial Family rode in the eleventh century. This was the Crown Prince's hostess present to me, and for Violet there was a square silver jewel box etched with plum blossoms, iris, chrysanthemums and bamboo.

We sat up late that night, the Crown Prince in one corner of the davenport and I in the other, Violet in the wing chair, talking. He told us many interesting things about his travels, about the places he saw, the kings and queens whom he met, about General Franco and the Pope. His impressions of places were sharp and unconfused; though he had been briefly in ten different countries, he knew exactly what he had seen in each one, and his impressions of people were kindly, observant and youthful. It is not often that one is privileged to hear candid portraits of royal personages by another royal personage. His interests had broadened notably in the three years since I had last seen him; the little boy who cared almost exclusively about fish, horses and tennis had developed a knowledge and love of music and art; he had also acquired a considerable understanding of the history of the countries he visited. Of all the times in those days of the Crown Prince's visit, this was to me the most precious, and whenever I look back on that little house on Mt. Airy Avenue, I see the living room and Prince Akihito sitting in the corner of the davenport, smiling a little, his eyes bright, reminiscing about his experiences.

For breakfast on the third morning, I had invited my two young cousins, Louis and Elise de Branges, Louis a student at M.I.T. and Elise a senior at the Agnes Irwin School, and Mary Shaw, an attractive young girl who lived in Camden and who had met the Prince on the *President Wilson* in April and played deck tennis with him then. While we were having breakfast and later when we were in the garden taking pictures, the crowd was gathering out-side: neighbors, sight-seers, newsmen, limousines, police. The members of the Crown Prince's suite came in and joined us. The Prince's suitcases were carried out. It was time for him to leave.

The crowd of three or four hundred people applauded as the Crown Prince came out of the house and he waved to them. His farewells and mine were brief, for I had been invited to join his party in New York and Boston. The motorcycle police revved their motors; the motorcade drew away. The crowd with a few final cheers drifted off. The de Brangeses and Mary Shaw left; Tane departed for Bryn Mawr. Violet and I flopped limply onto the davenport, speechless, exhausted, unutterably thankful that all had gone so well.

A taxi drew up outside. The Koizumis appeared at the open door. They had come, most politely, all the way from town to say good-by. They took one look at our prostrate condition and burst out laughing. It was a permanent bond between us, that moment of understanding and amusement. Whenever we met in the years that followed, we reminded each other of it and laughed again. Thirteen years later, after Dr. Koizumi's death, Tomi, his wife, and I, writing to each other of the friendship that had been so precious, both recalled that September morning after the Crown Prince had gone.

We had good reason for our relief. He had come and gone; he had been, apparently, happy. No one, no one at all, had threatened him or had shown anything but friendly interest. Among all the hundreds of letters that the State Department and the City of Philadelphia and the Japanese Embassy received about his visit, not one had been antagonistic, all had been welcoming. The only criticism was that the program planned for him was too strenu-ous, not giving the young visitor enough time for rest and relaxa-tion.

From the seventeenth of September until the twenty-first, I traveled with the Crown Prince and his suite as guest of the Japanese government, in New York and Boston. A cousin of mine exclaimed when he heard about it, "Betty traveling with ten Japanese men! Who's going to chaperone her?"

A dinner was given for the Prince at the Waldorf-Astoria by the Japan Society of New York, at which John Foster Dulles in his speech described himself as "a man from the west speaking with open and hopeful heart to a young man from the east," and urged the youth of the Asian lands to "seek stable adjustment between the old and the new." Dag Hammarskjold was there, Ralph Bunche, Joseph Grew, Henry Cabot Lodge; John D. Rockefeller III presided. Mrs. Oswald B. Lord, of the UN Commission on Human Rights, and I were the only women among the forty-four men on daises A and B. Among the 1,500 guests one was conspicuously missing: General Douglas MacArthur, who lived upstairs in the Waldorf Towers. He had been invited, but had declined.

The high point of the evening for me was the moment when the Crown Prince rose to make his speech. He looked very young and slender in that large glittering assembly of the—mostly—old and solid, and very graceful in his well-fitting Western evening clothes. He was poised and modest, his voice was clear and confident as he said, in part, "During my short stay in America I have already seen many monuments of your history. I have been impressed by these monuments but I have been even more impressed by the men who made them possible, the pioneers of America, the leaders who fought for independence and most of all those unknown citizens who bore hardship and suffering to make their country great—these are to me the inspiration that America has to offer to her people and to all the world."

On one of the days in New York we went to Hyde Park, where the Crown Prince laid a wreath on the grave of President Roosevelt and we all lunched with Mrs. Roosevelt at her hospitable "cottage." In the evening of that day he went to the Music Hall to see Audrey Hepburn in *Roman Holiday* (on my recommendation) and was amused by the experiences of the princess who ran away from protocol and had a day of freedom in Rome. One of the two days in Boston we spent visiting Woods Hole, where he saw the laboratories and was presented with a rare fish, a Chimaera, to take home to the Emperor, and Naushon Island, W. Cameron Forbes's feudal estate, where he went fishing and caught a bass, a pickerel, a perch, and three turtles, and was entertained at lunch by the well-known prewar ambassador to Japan.

Late on the afternoon of the twenty-first I saw the Crown Prince off from Logan Airport for Detroit and Chicago, the Rockefeller Ranch, Los Angeles, San Francisco and Hawaii. As I watched the silver plane grow small and vanish in the vast blue of the sky, I wondered when, if ever, I would see my prince again. I thought that this moment might mark the end of my Japanese experience and I felt both sad and grateful, sad for what I was losing, immensely grateful for what I had had. In the event, it was not to end. I was to see the Prince again several times both in Tokyo and the United States, but my instinct was right: that moment there in Boston marked the crossing of a divide. My role as a teacher was finished; the boy had become a man, taking his important and unique place in the world. In essentials he had not changed; the directness, the honesty, the simplicity, the humor, the friendliness that I had loved in the boy were still there; the promise that I had seen in the child had been fulfilled in the young man.

3.

Writing

THE BOOK that I had put aside in 1945 to work for the American Friends Service Committee, in 1946 to go to Japan and in 1951 to write *Windows for the Crown Prince*, I now took up again. A book thus shelved will do one of two things: it will dry up and blow away, or it will live on quietly in the hidden regions of the mind and grow in the dark. This book grew, and in addition the events of the times changed so that the book, when it was finally written, had much more relevance—to use a word since then overworked—than it would have had earlier.

The voice of Senator Joseph McCarthy, which had been an ominous, shrill whine when we first heard it in Japan in 1950, had become by 1953 a threatening roar. The "witch hunt" which he led was tracking down people whom it labeled "security risks," confronting them with loyalty oaths, suspicion and often disgrace and ruin. Congressional investigating committees, infected with McCarthyism (the word coined by the cartoonist "Herblock") leaped back over two decades to the years of the Depression and leveled charges of communism against people who in the 30's had joined socially minded groups not until later listed as "Communist Fronts."

It was another of those cases where the climate of thought of one period is entirely alien to that of a later one and incomprehensible to it. In the 1930's, when the Depression had pointed up so bitterly the difference between those who had reserves of money to cushion their losses and those who were suddenly exposed to hunger, homelessness and despair, many thoughtful Americans began to question the validity of a system that allowed such things to be. Many looked at the communist statement of principle, "From each according to his ability, to each according to his need," and wondered if some form of this principle might not be good for the United States. What could freedom mean, some asked, to people who had nothing to eat? The real freedom was freedom to live. These questions were in the air of the time. One often heard it said that totalitarianism was inevitable and that we must choose between communism and fascism. I was shocked when I heard well-dressed, charming, benevolent ladies at a luncheon say without a blush that they would choose fascism because it would let them keep what they had. What was happening in Nazi Germany, it seemed to me, was enough to make any person of minimum compassion turn from fascism, but I could not see any reason why democracy, if it lived up to its own potential, was not still the best form of government, under which we might have both freedom from want and freedom of thought. The war came, the Russians became our allies, fascism was the enemy, democracy was worth dying for, and everybody was employed; the patterns of thought of the Depression years were laid away and forgotten. The small number—in comparison—of actual Communists and Communist agents went on with their indubitable activities probably not much affected by either the warmth of the thirties or the harsh winds of the forties.

After the war, when our ally, Russia, suddenly became our enemy, the distrust of communism revived and fear of Communists within our midst was fanned into panic. The Hiss-Chambers case, with its perjuries and stolen papers, was a lurid illustration of the whole controversy. By 1954, in the words of Senator Charles E. Potter, "a cloud of terror blanketed the United States." A Gallup Poll in January revealed that 50 per cent of the American people had "a favorable opinion" of McCarthy and thought that he was serving the country in useful ways. Only 29 per cent opposed him, and 21 per cent had no opinion.

In the spring of that year, a special Senate committee held hearings on McCarthy's charges against the U.S. Army. Week after week the harsh voice of Senator McCarthy rasped through all our living rooms. "Point of order, Mr. Chairman" became a household word. "Did or not you" do so and so? came the questions of Joseph Welch, hurled at witness after witness. Fran Fox, working a tapestry cover for a footstool while she listened to the hearings, named the finished object "Didornot." The names of Cohn and Schine became as familiar as those of breakfast foods. We all watched while McCarthy hanged himself with his own rope and a cool breeze of sanity blew over the overheated country. When the Senator was censured by the Senate in December of the same year, his own career was finished, but McCarthyism in other guises continued a bit longer and was responsible, I believe, for a generation of college and university students who wanted only security and good jobs.

In the year 1777, in the midst of our nation's struggle for freedom from Britain, the leaders of the Continental Congress and Pennsylvania's Chief Executive Council arrested a number of peaceful citizens of Philadelphia on suspicion of being "inimical to the American cause," held them without trial, and then offered them as the price of liberty an oath of allegiance, or, as it was called then, a test oath. When they refused, they were "exiled" to a frontier town in Virginia. In this little-known episode, I saw parallels with the events of the early 1950's.

There has always been in this country, it seems to me, from the very beginning of our national life, two strains: one a devotion to liberty and a regard for the individual conscience, the other a lust for conformity to prevailing modes of thought, based chiefly on fear lest our security be endangered and the precious essence of our national character be somehow lost. Two things have saved us from the second group: the willingness of individuals to stand up and resist for conscience' sake at cost to themselves, and a national gift for changing our mind and coming up with better second thoughts. In the story of the men arrested in Philadelphia, I saw both these forces at work.

Briefly, what happened in 1777 was this: On August 22 the British Army under General Howe landed at what is now Elkton on the Chesapeake and prepared to march on Philadelphia. Three days later the Continental Congress in a panic urged the Executive Council of Pennsylvania to cause all persons "notoriously disaffected to be disarmed and secured." The Philadelphia Yearly Meeting, taking the historical Quaker stand against war and fighting, had earlier issued such statements as "Let not the fear of suffering either in person or property prevail on any to join with or promote any work or preparation for war." These and other similar statements the Congress interpreted as indicating that a number of Friends were "with much rancour and bitterness disaffected to the American cause."

The Supreme Executive Council made up a list of some forty-one persons, Friends and others, and had their houses searched and themselves arrested and held in the Masonic Lodge without a hearing. Faced with the choice of subscribing to the test oath or being sent to Virginia, half of the prisoners took the oath and were released. In the end twenty men, seventeen Friends and three non-Friends started off under guard on the long journey to Winchester, Virginia, a distant frontier settlement already full of Hessian prisoners of war. The day of their departure was the day of the Battle of Brandywine, which does in some measure explain the panic of the Philadelphia leaders. The "Exiles" stayed in Winchester until the following April. They were articulate, those men. Over the months they issued a series of Remonstrances, Appeals and Addresses, powerful and well-argued expositions every one of them. Four of the wives in occupied Philadelphia got a permit to cross the lines and went to Valley Forge to plead with Washington himself. They had lunch at the headquarters with him and Martha and a number of officers, and in the end Washington gave them a letter to the President of the Council in which he wrote, "Humanity itself pleads in their behalf." It was a satisfaction to me to find my old hero behaving in so compassionate and courtly a manner.

In the end, the Exiles' arguments in their own defense, Washington's recommendation, a change for the better in the course of the war—the Battle of Saratoga was won in October and its full effect recognized during the following winter—and, I maintain, our national ability to change our minds, brought the release of the sixteen remaining exiles. Two had died and two, the apothecary and the dancing master (neither one a Quaker), had broken parole and run away. They never had had a trial, they were set free in a left-handed sort of way without examination or formal clearance; still they had suffered for a principle and a principle had been recognized.

When I first contemplated writing the story of the Exiles, I had intended to do it as a factual history of an early and dramatic example of objection to war. Now it occurred to me that it would be more interesting and would reach more people if I wrote it as fiction. This presented certain difficulties. All of the people were actual, known individuals, several of them ancestors of friends of mine. Sam Fox, indeed, claimed descent from three of them— Henry Drinker, Israel Pemberton and Samuel Pleasants. I needed, besides the dramatic action of the arrest, imprisonment and final release, a hero in whose fate the reader could feel personally involved. Should I invent a love story and other complications for one of these staid ancestors with known wives and descendants? If I did not, where was my novel? I found what I considered a satisfactory solution. I removed Owen Jones, Jr., and substituted for him an imaginary character, Caleb Middleton, Jr., to whom I gave some of the incidents of Owen Jones's experience but a wholly imaginary personality, emotions and conflicts. His parents and Loveday Parrish, with whom he fell in love, were entirely figures of my imagination. Aside from this motif, all the events in the book were exactly as they happened in history, and I went to a very great deal of effort to search out all the facts and pertinent details.

There was a wealth of material to draw on. My bible was the book *Exiles in Virginia*, which Violet had found for me so many years ago, which contained the papers they wrote, their letters and a day-to-day account of the main events. The originals of these documents—and many more besides, diaries of individuals, letters, and so on—were in the Manuscript Division of the Library of the Historical Society of Pennsylvania. From the Library of the Pennsylvania Hospital I got a medical book published in 1779 with a contemporary account of an amputation. In addition I had the Quaker collections of the Haverford and Swarthmore College Libraries to draw on. Finding the vivid significant detail or incident that revealed character had a fascination like pursuing clues in a murder mystery or fitting complicated pieces of a jigsaw puzzle together. To give one example: Owen Jones, Jr., had been arrested in place of his father, and I was eager to find out just how that had happened. For months I had no clue, and I was mulling over in my mind various inventions to account for it. I had got, I thought, everything that was to be got from the Swarthmore collection, but went back once more looking for something else. Only a day or two earlier the Library had acquired a copy of a rare pamphlet about Timothy Matlack that answered my question, and incidentally gave me one more colorful character to include in the story. Matlack was a New Jersey Friend, an ardent patriot, and assistant secretary to the Continental Congress. Because of his beautiful handwriting, he had inscribed the official copy of the Declaration of Independence, and copied the list of names of people to be sent to Virginia. When he came on the name Owen Jones, he was struck by the memory of a signal kindness that he had received from him, and knowing that

the old man was in ill health, he repaid his debt by the simple device of adding Jr. to his name. No one noticed the substitution, and
the son went to Winchester in the father's place. I had already assumed in my story a conflict between father and son, and this discovery fitted into that and gave me opportunities for some char-
acter-developing and character-revealing scenes.

I had been to Winchester in the spring of 1940 but now I wanted
to go again, to refresh my memories and also to see it in winter-
time, for it was the long cold months that the Exiles spent
there. So Violet and I set off in the car after Christmas and followed the route of the Exiles to Reading and thence to Lancaster
and to what had been Harris's Ferry over the Susquehanna, on
through Gettysburg to Martinsburg and Winchester. I had letters of introduction to Friends in Winchester, who took us in most
cordially, invited us to New Year's parties, and introduced me to
local antiquaries who could give me the sort of intimate and
convincing detail that I needed. Also we drove around the countryside, seeing the ridges where already at the time of the Revolution
they were beginning to plant apple trees, the fields threaded by
creeks embroidered at the edges with bright green water cress,
the remains of the iron works where Isaac Zane, declaring himself
"a Quaker for the times," manufactured cannon for the Revolutionary armies and also befriended the Exiles. Though it was of no
use to my book, I was fascinated to discover that this same Isaac
Zane bought up the library of William Byrd of Westover when it
was sold.

All that winter in my attic study I wrote, and in the summer
both at home and in Mount Desert, in September. This was the
first book on which I worked with George Stevens as editor, and so
was initiated a friendship and partnership which has been a continuing help and joy to me. The book was published on May 18,
1955, my first adult novel, at last, after two previous attempts had
come to nothing.

I wanted to say two things in the book: that once before in our
history freedom in our country was threatened by loyalty oaths
and the attitudes that produced them, that a conscientious stand
against them was made at some sacrifice, and that second
thoughts on the part of those in power had retrieved the situation,
so that freedom did in the end prevail. In addition, on a deeper
level, exile itself was the theme; the little band in Winchester
were the obvious exiles, but the leaders of the Congress and Penn-

sylvania were also exiles from the very principles which they were fighting to establish.

Now and again during the research and the writing I laid the book aside for one thing or another. In February, 1954, I arose out of a bed of flu, filled with shots of penicillin and vitamin C, and went to New York to receive the Constance Lindsay Skinner Award from the Women's National Book Association. In a daze of fever I went through the dinner and the ceremonies. Marguerite Higgins, back from the Korean War, made the main address; Mr. Renzo Sawada, then Japan's "observer" at the United Nations, for Japan had not yet been admitted to membership, made a most graceful short speech; and I had my sister and close friends around me to share in pleasure.

In May of the same year Columbia University, celebrating its Bicentennial, gave Dr. Koizumi an honorary doctorate of Humane Letters. He flew to New York for the ceremony and afterwards spent the night of June 6 with us. His citation read:

"A friend returned; chief administrator of Keio University . . . a scholar whose faith in mankind and whose ties with kindred colleagues survived the cruel flames of war; honored in his homeland for thoughtful and courageous leadership in the advance of his countrymen toward free and enlightened citizenship; trusted adviser today of prince and people alike; a man of peace in whose lofty mind there is an abiding hope for that future when all men will be brothers."

The Sunday he spent with us was a memorable one. I gave a dinner party for him in the evening at the Deanery in Bryn Mawr, but aside from that we had time for long and intimate talks about Japan, the Crown Prince and the Imperial Family and our other friends there. It was at this time that he asked us to call him Shinzo, without adding the formal *San* which is so universal in Japan, and he began to call us Violet and Elizabeth.

The day before had been busy. Tane, after two years in the Bryn Mawr Library, was called back to Tokyo to be head of the library of the new International Christian University there, and I had invited fifty-seven of her friends to a farewell tea party at our house. Fifty-four came, and stayed all afternoon. Fortunately it was a beautiful day, and we could have chairs and tables set out in the garden. After most of the guests had left, ten stayed on for a buffet supper.

The morning before the party had been busy too. Proofs of a little book of essays on poems and prayers, called *The World in Tune*, mostly written earlier and reprinted from two Pendle Hill Pamphlets, arrived from Harper and Brothers, to be corrected and sent back as soon as possible. Hurrying down the stairs to answer the doorbell, I had slipped on the bottom step and bumped heavily against the newel post with the famous imperial chrysanthemum. A pain in my side and back grew steadily worse as the week end progressed. It was not until I had taken Shinzo to the noon train on Monday that I had time to go to the doctor—and get a broken rib strapped.

It was still very uncomfortable on Tuesday, but I had no doubt that by Wednesday evening when I was due at a dinner party in New Brunswick and Thursday morning when I was to deliver the commencement address at Douglass College there, I should be quite restored. On Tuesday night, thanks to a sleeping pill, I had my first good rest for several days, and at 8:30 on Wednesday morning I was still sleeping when there came a frantic pounding on the front door.

Violet answered it. An unknown and distraught middle-aged lady was standing there. Why, she asked, had I not been at Dean Corwin's dinner party the night before? Was I going to get to Commencement at eleven o'clock that morning? Dean Corwin had tried to telephone me when I had not shown up at her dinner party but our number was unlisted. She had in the morning got in touch with the Douglass graduate who lived nearest to us and sent her to find out. Somehow or other I had got the dates wrong on my calendar. I was expected in New Brunswick a day earlier than I had thought.

There followed one of those harrowing times when one moves through a waking nightmare. I got out of bed with painful haste; Violet made me a cup of coffee to drink while I dressed. I opened the garage door—and found the rear right tire flat. A man came from the nearest filling station to change the wheel, and I set off without a spare, flying up the Jersey Turnpike at seventy-five miles an hour. When I reached the main entrance to Douglass College, two people were there waiting for me, one to take the car, the other to escort me to the chapel, into which the academic procession in scholarly waddle was already filing. Donning cap and gown as I went, I was led around to a back door, and reached the platform just as Rutgers President Harold Taylor and other dignitaries arrived by the main aisle and climbed the steps.

There was a violin solo, the shortest I have ever listened to, and then I rose to deliver my commencement address. Fortunately, I had a manuscript.

Later in the week, my rib still strapped, I set out for the West Coast with Tane, to see her off for Japan. We took the Zephyr train that Violet and I had so much enjoyed, and I rented a car in San Francisco. We went first to the Highland Inn south of Carmel, where we had by chance the same flower-swathed cabin that Violet and I had once had, and saw the far grander one, complete with swimming pool, which the Crown Prince had had the autumn before. From there we went to the Yosemite, where snow still covered the tops of mountains and lay in drifts beside the road in the passes. It was far more crowded than I expected or than it had been twenty-three years earlier when Morgan and I were there with the Study Tour, but there were still places where we could lose the crowd, sit on a rock beside a rushing stream, look up at El Capitan and talk about the things we had seen and done together, about our hopes and plans for the future. When I stood on the wharf in San Francisco and watched the *President Wilson* move off, I felt not quite so sad as I had when we had parted in Yokohama four years earlier. Travel between the United States and Japan had proved to be feasible—and in point of fact Tane was back the next year, to attend a National Council of Churches meeting in Indiana, and I was in Tokyo two years after that.

Before I went to Japan, however, I went back to Europe. Violet, seventy-one, said that she wanted to see Paris once more before she died; my book was finished and had gone to press. We began to talk of spring in Europe and then of following the spring north. With Emma Bevan we set forth early in March in 1955 on the *Constitution* and landed in Genoa. It had been winter when we left Philadelphia; now on the way to Portofino we saw peach and pear trees in bloom and in the grass English daisies, snowdrops and primroses. From Genoa we went to Venice and launched upon the canals in a downpour of rain.

By chance we had decided on the Gritti Palace Hotel, knowing nothing at all about it beforehand, and were delighted with its position on the Grand Canal nearly opposite Santa Maria della

Salute, its few but beautiful rooms, delicious food and superlative service. Reading one evening a brochure on a table in the drawing room, we three innocents abroad were astonished to find that we had wandered into the palace of a fifteenth-century doge, converted in 1948 into a hotel which had been enjoyed by the Duke of Edinburgh, Princess Margaret of England, Winston Churchill, Somerset Maugham and others, and declared by Ernest Hemingway to be the best inn in Europe.

The first morning we awoke in Venice the rain was pouring down and continued to pour all day; we splashed about scarcely knowing, Violet said, whether we were on the canal or in it; but the next was a glory of sun and sparkle. Early down to breakfast before the others, I sat at a window right over the Grand Canal and watched the vaporettos pass beneath with businessmen reading the morning papers as if they were in the New York subway.

No one wants to read a travelogue about places that everyone has seen; I shall speak only of the spring that we were seeking. We met it again on the way to Florence where white oxen were ploughing the brown furrows and fruit trees foamed on all the hillsides. In the flower shops in the city, branches of fruit trees in bud were sold, as they were in Japan. Through a friend of Emmie's we were introduced to a delightful Florentine, Signor Bruno de Peverelli, who came on Sunday morning with his car and took us sight-seeing. Our first stop was the Palazzo Vecchio, where he led us through the great halls full of tapestries, paintings and statues, up a stair to the rooms reserved for the Mayor and his council. He spoke of the Mayor with veneration.

"He is a saint, a real saint. Someday he will be over one of these altars. His name is Giorgio La Pira. He was a professor of Roman Law in the University before he became Mayor four years ago. Now fifty, a bachelor, he lives in a cell in one of the convents and gives away everything he possesses. If a man needs a coat, he gives him his. There is not a man in all Florence who is hungry or lacks a roof over his head. He has been opposed by the entrenched merchants and businessmen who do not wish to share their wealth and privileges, and when he comes up for re-election next year he may have difficulties."

As he was talking, the Mayor himself burst in with some young men at his heels. He and Mr. De Peverelli hugged each other and then Mr. De Peverelli introduced us to him, explaining that we spoke no Italian. The Mayor answered, and Mr. De Peverelli interpreted, "It does not matter. The eyes speak."

His face, certainly, spoke. He was a short man, slight, and shabbily dressed, with a face that glowed and shone, mobile, expressive, happy. He was gone in a moment, leaving behind a sort of electricity in the air.

As it turned out, he was re-elected the following year but only by an accident of age. He and the Socialist candidate were tied, and the City Council chose La Pira because he was one year older than his opponent. In 1961, still Mayor, he greeted Queen Elizabeth II and Prince Philip when they visited Florence, but four years later he was again Professor La Pira and it was as a private citizen seeking to serve the cause of peace that he attempted to mediate in the Vietnam War and the Arab-Israeli conflict. He may yet appear on a Florentine wall with a halo behind his head.

On the way to Rome we spent two days in Assisi, the others yielding to my interest in Saint Francis, the rich merchant's son who wedded Lady Poverty, the wandering friar who preached to his sisters the birds and made a friend of the Wolf of Gubbio, who deemed courtesy one of the attributes of God and sister to charity in quenching hatred and kindling love, who knew long nights of prayer and suffered the agonizing joy of the Stigmata, whose spiritual friendship with Saint Clare is one of the sweetest of love stories, who began by thinking that God's command to "repair my church" meant the literal rebuilding of the little ruined church of San Damiano and who ended by shoring up the whole fabric of medieval Christianity.

Spring was evident everywhere in Assisi. Flowers bloomed precariously in cracks in the old walls, and in the open niches between the tight-packed medieval houses, through which you could see the Umbrian plain spread out below and the river winding through it. Flowers bloomed too in Saint Clare's little garden in the church of San Damiano, where two years before his death in 1226 Saint Francis is believed to have composed the "Canticle to the Sun." Outside of the town, higher up on the slope of the mountain, was the little hermitage of the Carceri, crude and poor and holy, to which Saint Francis used to retreat when Assisi became too crowded and noisy for him. It clings to the side of a ravine, surrounded by dense ilex woods in which nightingales were singing their throats out that afternoon and white doves flying against the dark green of the trees.

We had planned only five days for Rome, which we had thought somehow we wouldn't like—a great mistake, for we loved it. One of the dreams that Violet and I often talked about was to go back again to Rome and spend a whole winter there, preferably in an apartment in a palazzo. We saw wild cyclamen in the grass at Hadrian's villa and smelled the sun-warmed honeysuckle; in the Forum we saw wistaria just coming into bloom. It was impossible to disentangle all the Romes, classical, early Christian, medieval, Renaissance, the Rome of Keats, of Henry James, of Victor Emmanuel, of Mussolini. We intended to return.

We spent both Easters in Athens, ours and the Greek Orthodox the following week. Easter in Greece is as immediate as today's news. On Good Friday the newspapers came out with pictures of the Crucifixion on the front page, as if it had just happened, and in every parish throughout the country the women decorated a bier which was carried in procession through the streets that evening to the accompaniment of ancient Byzantine chants and followed by crowds that were silent, reverent and expectant. All day church bells rang, and high in one belfry we saw two small choirboys in red gowns swinging on the ropes. The next day men walked the streets with the Paschal Lamb held by the feet over their shoulders just as in the Bible pictures of my youth. The shops were full of red Easter eggs and candles, and little girls in red dresses seemed to be eternally bustling about on important errands. On Easter Eve at midnight in the cathedral the archbishop announced "Christ is risen!" and lit the King's taper from his own. "He is risen indeed!" was the answer, and the King touched his taper to another. All over Athens people crowding the churches and lining the streets lit one long, slender, white taper from another and cried joyously, "Christ is risen!" "He is risen indeed!"

On Easter Day itself no one was to be seen. We went to Phaleron and walked along the deserted boardwalk looking out over the brilliant blue water to the islands. All the Greeks were indoors feasting on lamb after the long week of really severe fasting.

We saw the Parthenon by moonlight, and we saw Delphi with the spring sun on snow-crowned Parnassus, and wild flowers—daisies, scabiosa, mustard, wild pinks and many others—thick in the grass about our feet. Around the remains of the basin of the Castalian spring a great number of French tourists, very exuberant, had congregated to watch the clown they all called Réné climb the wall that surrounded the spring and make faces over the top of it, while the Americans looked on, aloof and dignified.

Whenever I think of the trip in 1955, it is Delphi that I think of first, of the towering snow-topped mountains, the three white columns of the Athene Pronaic, the charioteer, grave and exalted, the hillsides covered with olive trees that fall away to the brilliant blue Gulf of Corinth below, and the incredible light of Greece, so clear and so brilliant yet never harsh, touching everything with a luminous tenderness. I remember too the young girls who served as guides at Delphi, at Sunion, at Eleusis and Daphne—their charm, their remarkable knowledge of the history and archeology and art of their country, and their passionate love of freedom. I remember too the desperate poverty of the country, the old women muffled in black riding slow donkeys on narrow country roads with a few vegetables in their panniers, the porters in the hotel dividing each bag-carrying into five stages so that five men might each get a small coin.

From Greece we went to Lucerne and saw sheets of wild white crocuses, violets, blue and white, and a little rosy flower whose name I did not know in the fields high on the side of the Rigi, and walked in the Engelberg Valley under the great mountains along a swift-flowing brook. Suddenly I remembered that Rufus Jones had been here many years before and that he had written of it in words that I had to wait till I got home to read again:

"I came once up the Engelberg Valley in Switzerland to a place which the natives call the End of the World—das Ende der Welt. A huge mountain closes the pass, the road stops abruptly and no one can go on there. It is a terminus. I stayed there in a little inn at the End of the World. How often in life the gateway shuts, a semiphore drops in front of us, the way closes. We have come to a terminus. The next day, however, I found a zigzag path farther down the valley that went up the side of the mountain. I climbed up and up and went on over the End of the World. There is always, if one can find it, a way higher up that goes over these closed ways which confront us."

I had known the truth of that in my own life; I saw with interest the place that had inspired Rufus Jones's thought.

We spent a week end in Geneva, where I stayed with Chesley and H. G. Baity of Chapel Hill, while Violet and Emmie lodged in a nearby hotel. Here we met spring again in its early stages, with trees in tiny leaf and gentians bright blue and small in the grass, saw the top of Mont Blanc floating apparently detached from earth above the clouds, and walked on the Salive with English Friends who knew birds and wild flowers. We watched a kestrel hovering high in space over a valley, and I thought of "The Windhover," the poem that Gerard Manley Hopkins dedicated "To Christ our Lord" and, like his, "My heart in hiding/Stirred for a bird."

In Paris the famous horse chestnuts were in bloom and apple blossoms were pink and white all along the way to Chartres. We met Douglas and Dorothy Steere at the Friends Center, and at lunch at the Japanese Embassy I found Mr. Matsui, who had stayed in our house with the Crown Prince, just arrived the day before to be first Secretary, and for the first time met his charming wife. In England the primroses were over, but bluebells made lakes of sky under beech trees in bright green bud and the hedges were white with hawthorn. I have not even yet got over my first disappointment when I found that the much looked-forward-to hawthorn could not hold a candle to our dogwood, but the bluebells fill me with delight and surprise every time I see them.

Almost immediately after we reached home, *The Virginia Exiles* was published to the accompaniment of a luncheon, orchids, radio interviews and press conferences, all very exciting to me. It is remarkable how different one feels about the press at different times and in different circumstances. When in Japan I was engaged in work of a delicate nature that I was trying to protect, I looked on reporters with fear and dread and fled from them whenever I could. When I had a new book out, I welcomed them with pleasure. Unfortunately, their eagerness to see you is usually in inverse proportion to your eagerness to see them.

Less than a week later, Mary Hoxie Jones asked me if I would write the biography of her father, Rufus Jones.

✳✳✳✳✳✳✳✳✳✳✳✳✳✳✳✳✳✳✳✳✳✳✳✳✳✳✳✳✳

4.

Friend of Life

Rᴜғᴜs Jᴏɴᴇs had long been one of my heroes. I counted him as one of the four men whom I had been privileged to know that I would call great, the other three being Shinzo Koizumi, the Emperor of Japan, and General Douglas MacArthur. It is difficult to think of four men more diverse. Rufus Jones, Friend, humanitarian, historian, teacher and often termed saint, though he himself would have repudiated the term vigorously, was a large, sandy-haired, homely man alight with love for mankind, both individually and collectively; his impressive qualities of mind and spirit were tempered by spontaneous and homely humor. Head of the Philosophy Department of Haverford College for many years, a founder and for most of twenty-six years the chairman of the American Friends Service Committee, author of fifty-four books and innumerable articles, a traveling Friend, a compelling speaker, he was known and loved in Japan, China, India and South Africa as well as the United States and parts of Europe. English Quakers cherished him as one of their own; he had guided the work of the AFSC in France during World War I and had been a leading force in the feeding of a million German children after the war. In 1939 he had been the leader of the three Friends who went to Germany to plead with the Gestapo on behalf of the persecuted Jews. He was also a welcome sight in Philadelphia, where he was known as "our Rufus" and his presence at Sunday dinner was much in demand. He had taken a great interest in my appointment in Japan, and when I returned in 1947 for two months one of the things I took most pleasure in doing was going to see Rufus Jones, sitting in a rocking chair on his front porch on the Haverford campus, and telling him all about it. That had been the last time I saw him, for the following June he had died.

During the years since his death his daughter Mary Hoxie Jones and his wife Elizabeth had examined and sorted the immense accumulation of papers in the study and attic of their home at 2 College Circle. A trunk containing bundles of letters belonging to the period of his youth and first marriage had turned up under the eaves in the attic; desk drawers were crammed with such mementoes as menus of transatlantic voyages—useful for pinpointing dates of trips—programs and invitations; there were boxes full of manuscripts of speeches, articles, reviews, and of course masses of letters. After Elizabeth Jones's death, Ruth Smith, author of *The Tree of Life*, had helped Mary with the organizing and arranging of these papers. In addition Mary had asked for, and received, letters or copies of letters from Rufus Jones which had been kept by friends and relatives, and she had talked to many who had known him well, both in England and America, and written down their accounts of him. As some were old and had since died, these records were invaluable. She had herself, moreover, written a brief, perceptive biography of her father, which had been published as a pamphlet in England. All of this wealth of material which had been given to Haverford College was in beautiful order in steel filing cases on the balcony of the Treasure Room in the Library, waiting for someone—me?—to use it as the basis for a biography of Rufus Jones.

It seemed to me a great responsibility to write a biography of a man of such caliber. My first thought was to consult Henry Cadbury about it. Well known as Hollis Professor of the New Testament at Harvard, now retired, one of the translators of the Revised Standard Version of the New Testament, author of a number of books, chairman of the AFSC succeeding Rufus Jones, Henry Cadbury was also Rufus Jones's much younger brother-in-law and Mary's uncle on her mother's side. He encouraged me to go ahead with it, and I knew that I should have him to turn to in difficulties. He lived in Haverford and was in and out of the library many times a week; he was besides a person as selfless as he was learned, of great sweetness of nature and a delightful, puckish humor all his own. Violet had some reservations about the project; she thought it a great deal of work, and she had a perennial fear that I would become too serious and religious. George Stevens at Lippincott was enthusiastic. After a week or so of rumination

I gave Mary the answer that was to add so much richness to my life.

For the next three years I lived very close to the mind and spirit of Rufus Jones and in constant communication with Mary. We already knew each other well, for besides the ordinary Quaker associations and our having both worked for the AFSC at the same time, we were members of a group of twenty delightful women, known as "Poets Walk In," who met regularly twice a month to read and write poetry together. Mary was a happy combination of her father's humor and outgoing friendliness, her mother's deep sweetness and serenity, with a beauty beyond any physical assortment of features and a poetic quality entirely her own, to which her two published volumes of verse as well as the many poems she has read in "Poets" meetings bear witness. She was an ideal person to work with.

On the face of it, it is far from ideal for a writer to compose a biography of a man with his daughter right at hand, but Mary was unusual. She was utterly candid, she was objective, I could ask her anything without embarrassment, she opened all the material to me without reserve and she left me free to use it in my own way. But then, there was nothing in Rufus Jones's life that anyone would wish to conceal or gloss over.

For more than a year I did nothing but read. Every morning I drove the ten miles to Haverford and late in the afternoon I came back again; I remember especially the frosty winter twilights with an apple-green sky or a silver eyelash of a moon and the mixture of fatigue and exhilaration that I felt as I followed the dark curves of the road that ran along Mill Creek. A table was reserved for me on the balcony of the Treasure Room, which contains, besides the Rufus Jones files, a valuable collection of Quaker manuscripts and books, Rufus Jones's own great collection of mystical writings from Plato and Plotinus to Evelyn Underhill, Baron von Hugel and Thomas Kelly. It is presided over by a portrait by Sir Peter Lely entitled "George Fox in an Ecstasy," for which the best word might be *fanciful*. Quite lovely in its colors of soft greens and browns, it portrays the founder of Quakerism not in the traditional leather breeches but in a romantic Robin Hood hat with his eyes rolled heavenward. I had been present when it was unveiled in a ceremony to which the weightiest of weighty Friends were invited, along with the young convinced like myself. We got there a little late, Violet and I, and so had to take the last seats in the gallery right above the draped portrait. When the unveiling took place we could not see what was disclosed—but the expression upon the faces of the elders below us told us much.

By the time I came to work on Rufus Jones, I was quite accustomed to Sir Peter Lely's masterpiece and scarcely saw it. I shared the end of the balcony during those months with William Bacon Evans, an ancient and most lovable Friend out of a past century. Wearing a broad-brimmed hat and a gray coat without lapels, he still used the *Thou* as well as the less grammatical *Thee* into which most modern Friends have slipped. At that time he was eighty years old; an English Friend, meeting him in his lively ninetieth year, described him in these words:

"He is a Quaker institution. His sayings are written down, his jokes are passed from one Quarterly Meeting to another, his home-made puzzles are unravelled by children, his mathematical conundrums are worked out at the back of Monthly Meetings and his bird pictures sold for the benefit of the American Friends Service Committee. He visits every Yearly Meeting in the country, believes in the brotherhood of man, the fatherhood of God and the neighborhood of Philadelphia." He was also a poet, and his little book called *Seven Score Bird Songs* was full of the actual, recognizable sounds of birds' voices.

His last years were devoted to a monumental labor of love, his biographical dictionary of Quakers from 1652 on, who were "distinguished in Religion, Education, Art, Science or Industry." His table on the balcony of the Treasure Room was at right angles to mine, and after the morning greetings we worked in silence, back to back. Usually during the morning there would be a brief exchange. He would come to stand in front of my table, and say, "Elizabeth Gray Vining, I hope I do not interrupt?" To which I replied cordially, "No, indeed, William Bacon Evans." He would then offer some bit of information or comment on his reading. One day, after the usual formalities, he surprised me by saying,

"Hast thou ever thought of wearing the Quaker dress?"

The feminine costume corresponding to what he wore would have been a full-skirted drab gown with a white fichu and a plain bonnet. I replied that no, I really hadn't considered it.

He said with a little sigh of regret, "If thou are called I hope thou wilt be faithful."

I said that I hoped that I would but that I thought it ex-

tremely unlikely that I should be called, to which he magnani-
mously replied,

"I wish thee well anyhow."

A few days later I was working away as usual and because I
was going out to a luncheon afterwards I was wearing my best hat,
a little affair of dark blue felt leaves which I considered very modish.

"Elizabeth Gray Vining, I hope I do not interrupt?"

"No, indeed, William Bacon Evans."

"I like thy Quaker bonnet."

In the files I came on many letters over a long stretch of years
from Herbert Hoover, first as head of the American Relief Commission, then as Secretary of Commerce, as President of the
United States and as private citizen. As I read through them and
saw the ups and downs of negotiation between government as
represented by Mr. Hoover and the American Friends Service
Committee, headed by Rufus Jones, the evidences of stress, the
growth of understanding and friendship, it seemed to me that the
relationship between Herbert Hoover and Rufus Jones might make
a very interesting chapter in itself. I had often heard it whispered
about in Service Committee circles and elsewhere that Mr. Hoover
was sometimes an explosive and formidable person to deal with,
and I was interested to see what form this temperamental difficulty
took and how Rufus Jones met it.

I found that one could trace the course of the relationship in
brief from the salutations of Mr. Hoover's letters. The very first
one, in 1919, when Mr. Hoover wrote to ask the AFSC to undertake the child feeding in Germany, began with an old-fashioned
Quaker usage: "Friend Jones." This was soon succeeded by the
more conventional, "My dear Mr. Jones," which continued for
two years. Then some stress arose over the program of feeding in
famine-stricken Russia, and Mr. Hoover wrote, evidently in annoy-
ance, "My dear Jones." In the 1930's, however, when all of the
struggles were memories, Mr. Hoover began his letters, "My dear
Friend," and finally, "My dear Rufus."

In regard to the Russian feeding, there was one main point of
tension between Mr. Hoover and the AFSC. The AFSC, in
hope of keeping its skirts entirely clear of politics, wished to deal
directly with the Russian government in regard to the conditions
of its relief operations there. Mr. Hoover, then Secretary of Commerce, insisted that all the relief organizations, Red Cross, Jewish

Joint Distribution Committee, Federal Council of Churches, and so on, should be affiliated with the American Relief Organization and be bound by the conditions which it laid down with the Russians. Radical groups in the United States, believing Mr. Hoover to be rigidly anti-Communist, made many loud criticisms of him, comparing his methods unfavorably with those of the AFSC, which they thought more open. A letter from Wilbur Thomas, then executive secretary of the Committee, to Rufus Jones, chairman, describes an interview with Mr. Hoover, which reveals what it was that Mr. Hoover did to frighten people.

"He got so angry that he literally pounded the table and swore like a trooper."

There is no doubt that Mr. Hoover was in many ways right and that he was under considerable provocation, and Rufus Jones throughout the correspondence and the negotiations was unequivocal in declaring his friendship for Mr. Hoover as well as his determination to keep the AFSC free of any sort of political coloration.

As I pondered over this material, I realized that it would be necessary to see Mr. Hoover himself and get his point of view if possible. Accordingly, in February, 1957, I wrote to him, told him what I was doing, and asked for an interview. I got a prompt and cordial response. He would be glad to see me, he wrote, but first he would like to send to Palo Alto for his files on Rufus Jones, so that he could have all the material that was pertinent. After a fortnight I received the file itself, a whole bundle of letters and copies of letters between Herbert Hoover and Rufus Jones. There were more of the later letters in the 1930's than the early ones, and there were no copies of the peppery letters from Mr. Hoover. There were, however, some interesting letters from Rufus Jones which I had not seen. I then wrote again to Mr. Hoover, but he had gone off on a trip. While he was away I wrote my chapter, which I called *Herbert Hoover and Friend Jones*, drawing on the Hoover file, the Haverford files, the AFSC files, and the second volume of Mr. Hoover's own *Memoirs*.

About the middle of April a note came from Mr. Hoover saying that he was back in New York and that if I would call his secretary she would "fix up a time." So I put in a person-to-person call to Mr. Hoover's secretary. I heard the telephone operator inquiring of the Waldorf-Astoria switchboard if they had "a Mr. Herbert Hoover" registered there, and I indulged in some reflections on the ephemeral nature of fame while I waited for the connection to be made.

On the 25th of April I found myself on the thirty-first floor of the Waldorf-Astoria Towers. Mr. Hoover was sitting at his desk in a corner of the big drawing room in the apartment in which he had lived since 1934. As he came forward to greet me, I saw that he was tall, immaculate in a well-pressed light gray suit, white-haired, gray-eyed, pink-skinned, with a mouth pursed like a baby's. He was eighty-three, a little hard of hearing. He waved me into a chair that had been drawn up close to his desk and opened the conversation with, "So you're going to write a book about Rufus Jones."

When he went on to talk, there was little about Rufus Jones but much that was interesting about Herbert Hoover. Of the period when Mr. Hoover worked with the AFSC on feeding the children of the unemployed miners in West Virginia, and Clarence E. Pickett, radiant, gentle, selfless and tireless, was the Executive Secretary of the Committee, Mr. Hoover said:

"I had a grudge against the Friends Service Committee later. When I was in the White House I raised $250,000 for them to feed the miners' children, but they went over to Eleanor Roosevelt and they never gave me one word of credit about that money or the organizations I got it from. . . . Who was that fellow that was the head of the Friends Service Committee?"

"Clarence Pickett?"

"Yes, that's the one. . . . That Pickett fellow was too much of a politician, more of a politician than a Quaker ought to be unless he's in the business."

For a Quaker to be President of the United States, I gathered, was to be "in the business."

I felt a good deal of sympathy for Mr. Hoover, for I thought, and still do, that he was through those years deprived—though not by the AFSC—of the "credit" that he deserved for his conduct of the Presidency, and for his great achievements in relief in Europe and Russia.

He tried again in World War II, when the Low Countries were invaded by the Nazis, to establish a program of relief for the Belgian and Dutch children, but he was prevented from doing so, he told me, by Roosevelt and Churchill.

"I got agreements from Hitler. I had a plan set up for Belgium. I would supply the fats and Hitler would supply the grain. He would have kept his word, too. I could get things from Hitler that other people couldn't. As a result when the war was over conditions were terrible. A whole generation of children was undernourished."

He went back to the time of the famine in Russia and the Riga Agreement. "The old Bolsheviks were a different set of people from the fellows Stalin brought in. They were a decent lot by comparison. They had fantastic minds but they were intellectuals. They did their best to keep all the promises and agreements."

He asked me a little about my experience in Japan, and then I gave him a copy of my chapter. I told him that I had put into it everything I found in the files that seemed to me relevant or interesting but that of course no part of any of his letters would be used in the book without his permission, that I would be grateful if he would read the manuscript and return it to me with any comments he might care to make. Then I said good-by and went to the Commodore where I was spending the night, and wrote the whole interview down before I should forget it. The next week I departed for England.

My chapter was waiting for me when I got back a month later, with a letter from Mr. Hoover's devoted, and somewhat defensive, secretary, who wrote in part:

"I have made extensive suggestions in certain paragraphs to give a more accurate picture of the association of Mr. Hoover and Mr. Jones. These suggestions, corrections and additions have met with Mr. Hoover's approval."

Somewhat apprehensively I looked at my manuscript. It had been cut apart and pasted together again with inserts and there were blue pencil marks on many of the pages, which had increased in number from twenty-two to thirty-four. When I examined it more carefully, however, I felt better. There were no corrections in the actual facts: much had been added about Mr. Hoover; very little had been cut out. "Dear Jones" must be omitted altogether; the passage now went from "My dear Mr. Jones" to "My dear Friend." In Wilbur Thomas's letter, "he literally pounded the table" was permitted to remain but not "he swore like a trooper." A paragraph which I had quoted verbatim from Mr. Hoover's *Memoirs* was cut out entirely.

In the interest of space and for the sake of consistency in style, I condensed and rewrote the material that had been added, omitting long letters of praise of Mr. Hoover by Maxim Gorki and the Soviet Government and a sentence of the secretary's: "Here again the background of Mr. Hoover's activities must be made clear." I did indeed wish them to be clear, but I was after all writing a book about Rufus Jones.

When I sent the revised chapter back to Mr. Hoover, he replied, "That is a most interesting chapter to me—and in your usual fine style of writing. I have asked one of my assistants in European relief activities to read it over. He makes a few minor suggestions and explanations. But there is no demand to adopt his ideas."

When the book was published I sent Mr. Hoover a copy, and he wrote that he was looking forward to reading it. Whether he did or not, I have no way of knowing, but I imagine not. But he had been courteous and kind to me, giving me of his time, and I felt that the chapter was an interesting record of significant contacts between two distinguished Americans whose backgrounds were so similar and whose careers were so different.

The need to talk with the English Friends who had so much loved Rufus Jones and among whom he had spent so much of his life sent me in May, 1957, to England, to Woodbrooke, the Quaker college in Selly Oak, Birmingham, which he had helped his friend John Wilhelm Rountree to conceive and found and where he had lectured many times, to York and Oxford to talk with members of the Rountree family, to London to talk with Alfred Braithwaite, whose father, William Charles, had written the first two of the five-volumed Quaker history edited and in part written by Rufus Jones.

In the train on the way to York I met a refugee from the Hungarian Rebellion which had been so brutally suppressed the previous autumn. At Euston Station a hasty and rather harried-looking woman deposited in my third-class compartment a girl probably in her twenties with a grief-stricken face and frightened eyes. She had no English, and she huddled in her corner silent and unsmiling; the only thing along the way that attracted her attention was a field where behind a high wire fence stood rank upon rank of tanks. As if shot through by an electric charge, she leaned forward and watched intently until we had passed the last of them, when she sighed and leaned back again.

When the attendant came through the train with tickets for lunch, she shook her head and said, "No money." I engaged two seats and managed to make her understand that she was to be my guest. The lunch was ample if not exciting and she ate ravenously. Color came into her face, her eyes brightened and for the rest of the way every time she caught my eye she smiled. In York we were both met at different ends of the platform, and I did not see her again. I have often wondered what became of her. It had been so brief an encounter, so infinitesimal a drop of help in an ocean of need, and yet this small personal contact made me aware of the Hungarian tragedy as no amount of reading reports could do.

While I was in York, I took a week end off for the Schools Pilgrimage. This was an annual excursion to Quaker shrines made by older students from the three northern Quaker schools, Bootham, the Mount and Ackworth. Thirty-three boys and girls, six teachers and three foreign guests set out in buses to visit Pendle Hill, Firbank Fell, Preston Patrick, Brigflats Meeting, where a pen was provided for the sheep dogs that accompanied their masters, and other spots famous in the early history of the Quaker movement. The three foreign guests were Benjamin Ngaio, clerk of the largest Quaker body in the world, the Kenya Yearly Meeting; Tom Bodine, an attractive young businessman and member of the Hartford, Connecticut, Meeting; and I. Tom had a British driver's license, which empowered him to drive cars, locomotives and reversible tricycles. Our merriment over this was boring to the British young, for everyone knows that a locomotive is a tractor and a reversible tricycle one of those tiny cars with two wheels in front and one behind.

The weather was perfect, that May week end, with great clouds rolling across the sky and piling up in masses and towers, trailing their shadows over the bare hills and the fields marked out by tall, thin stone walls. Old farmhouses huddled in the folds of the hills, and streams wound tree-bordered through the valleys. In each of the Quaker shrines the group was met by Elfride Vipont Foulds, the author of a number of well-known and well-loved books for children, who herself lived in a seventeenth-century house called Greengarth in the village of Yealand Conyers. She was a small, brown-haired, brown-eyed, rather Arthur-Rackhamy-looking person with an unexpectedly deep and vibrant voice and an eloquence that was arresting. As she told the story of George Fox on Pendle Hill or of Margaret Fell of Swarthmore Hall, there was not a soul there, not the most indifferent adolescent, who was not stirred.

During this month I went also to Germany for four vivid days. I flew from London to Frankfurt am Main and took the train to Heidelberg, where Marjorie Stewart, who had spent the winter in Munich and Vienna, met me at the station. When he was a young man of twenty-five, Rufus Jones had taken a year off from teaching in Friends' Schools and had spent it in England, France and Germany, studying French and German Quakerism and mystical religion in general. The four spring months of 1887 he had spent in Heidelberg, studying under the famous Kuno Fischer, reading Goethe and enjoying the beauty of the old town and its surrounding countryside.

In two golden spring days foaming with fruit trees in bloom, I found the places he had known, visited the old university, the castle, the Philosopher's Walk and had a boat ride up the Neckar, that lovely river said to be more beautiful than the Rhine. From Heidelberg we went to Marburg an der Lahn, where in 1911 Rufus Jones, with Elizabeth, his wife, and Mary, then a very small girl, had spent the summer months working on the German mystics in consultation with Pfarrer Theodor Sippell, who was an authority on the Brethren of the Common Life. The book on the fourteenth-century mystics that came out of this year's research, titled *The Flowering of Mysticism*, was my favorite of all Rufus Jones's books, except *Finding the Trail of Life*.

The Joneses had had rooms in an old stone house high on the hill under the Castle beside the Marienkirche. The house had belonged to Pfarrer Hapich, who had long since died, but his daughter Hanna still lived in Marburg and Mary had written her that I was coming and why. I had a cordial letter from Fraulein Hapich, promising to meet my train at the station, "standing on the outlet with a little red dictionary."

She was a great help, taking us to the house which the Joneses had had, showing us the University and the Castle, introducing me to Pfarrer Sippell, now very old and frail, who welcomed me warmly and talked a little about Rufus Jones but a little more about himself. In Marburg too I met Carl and Eva Hermann, who lived in a small modern house overflowing with cats of all ages and colors, perched high on a hill looking across a deep valley to the Castle. Both of the Hermanns had survived two years of Nazi prisons to which they had been sentenced for helping Jewish friends, and from which they were freed by the arrival of American troops in 1945. Eva Hermann, still youthful-looking, with a round, cheerful face, golden hair and an enthusiastic way of talking, gave me a copy of the booklet which she had written about her experiences called *In Prison—Yet Free*. In it she made the almost incredible statement that she "would not have missed those two years for anything." Almost incredible—yet I have heard survivors of Japanese prison camps say the same thing. The wife of the correspondent Russell Brines told me that she would not for anything go through Santo Tomas again but that she would not like to have missed it. "I got an entirely new set of values," she said. "I learned what was important and what was not." To Eva Hermann the power of prayer, the sharing of love and the wellsprings of joy became real under conditions of suffering and fear of which the mere thought is terrifying to me who have always been safe and free.

All of the people who talked to me about Rufus Jones during those two years said approximately the same thing, though in varying words, as an English Friend at Woodbrooke: "Of course his books and sermons were wonderful, but that was not the main thing about him. It was the way he went out to each person he met. No matter how young and obscure you were, he made you feel that you really mattered and that it was important what you did with your life." Douglas Steere, Harry Emerson Fosdick, Ernest Hocking and others who were not young or obscure spoke also of his intellectual achievements and his influence on modern religious thought.

Much of the actual writing was done in two successive summers in Arlington, Vermont, in two different rented cottages neither spacious nor very comfortable. I wrote steadily with only a little time off to enjoy the friends who were in the neighborhood: Elizabeth McKie, visiting her cousin in Cambridge, New York, just over the mountains to the west; Clara Sipprell and Phyllis Fenner in their charming little house in Manchester; Dorothy Canfield Fisher, small and white-haired, vivacious and elegant, who lived on the northern edge of Arlington. Elizabeth Yates McGreal, who was at the time writing a biography of Mrs. Fisher, later published under the title, *Pebble in a Pool: Widening Circles in the Life of Dorothy Canfield Fisher*, fairly often drove over from Peterborough, sometimes with Bill, her huband, who was so radiant and so aware of all that went on around him that one would never guess that the eyes behind the dark glasses were sightless. John and Margaret Farrar were in the region too; John was president of the American P.E.N. which was going to send me as a delegate to the Congress in Tokyo in September.

It was an absorbing, a stimulating, a demanding and a rewarding book to write, but it was not an easy one. I rewrote the chapter on the mysticism of Rufus Jones six times. But still even with six weeks out for Japan, I finished the book and got the manuscript to George Stevens early in February, 1958. The question of a title arose. I had intended to call it *Rufus M. Jones: A Biography*, which seemed to me accurate, forthright and Quakerish. That year, however, fashion in biography decreed that there should be a colorful or provocative phrase, with the subject's name in the subtitle. The sales department of Lippincott came up with a bright idea which struck me as hilariously funny: *Mystic from Maine*. When I hastened to report this suggestion to Mary, she replied, "Well, he actually spent more of his life in Pennsylvania than he did in Maine. Why don't you call it *Hick from Haverford?*" A few days later my subconscious mind produced *Friend of Life* and everybody was satisfied.

It was published on September 28, 1958, and in October Haverford College, celebrating its 125th anniversary, gave me the first honorary doctorate of letters that they had given a woman.

The year of the publication of *Friend of Life* and the two following ones brought sorrow in the form of the death of several people who had been dear. It seems sometimes that such things do not happen at reasonable intervals but in clusters. "When sorrows come, they come not single spies, But in battalions."

In January Sam Fox, who had come to seem to Violet and me almost like a brother, died after nearly a year's illness, during which Fran had nursed him with selfless heroism. Fran was with us for part of the winter and then with great courage returned alone to Mount Desert Island and the beloved little house which she and Sam had built on a point in Long Pond. Fran occupied herself the first summer alone with building a guest cabin for her son and his family and for friends. In September Violet and I visited her there, staying in the cabin (rustic but provided with an electric dishwasher) looking down the lake to Western Mountain, hearing loons calling at night, going on lobster picnics, talking late before the open fire and all the other things one does on such a holiday.

It was while we were there that word came of the death of our cousin, Ann Heebner McDonald, the daughter of Mother's elder sister Emily. She and Violet, both only children, had grown up together like sisters; they had gone abroad with both mothers when Violet was seventeen, and Nan had stayed on in Paris to study painting. She had some success with portraits until her marriage to Dr. Edward Ellice McDonald and the birth of two children, Diane and Ellice, diverted her energy for many years. Ted, her husband, was a Canadian, descended from the Mc-Donalds of Glencoe; he was a distinguished physician and, during the latter part of his life, head of the Biochemical Research Laboratory of the Franklin Institute. Ted had died the previous year. They were a colorful, original and somewhat eccentric pair, and a measure of warmth and interest went out of our life with them.

Our two indomitable and inimitable Scottish aunts had come back into our orbit after a rather long hiatus when they moved in the 1940's into an apartment in Germantown. Aunt Christine had been born in Aberdeen shortly before the family sailed for America in 1865; Aunt George came into the world in Philadelphia four or five years later.

There were two distinct physical types among the Grays: some were tall and slender, with deep-set gray eyes, strong noses and chiseled chins, like my father and Aunt George; others, like Aunt Christine and Uncle Tom, short and square, with blunt noses, wide mouths and rugged jaws. The two aunts were different in temperament as in appearance: Aunt Christine was outgoing, expansive, articulate and confident, Aunt George reserved and shy—but gifted with a wry and salty humor. Both, like all the other Grays, were inveterate readers.

Both were dedicated Presbyterians, but whereas Aunt George said little about her beliefs, Aunt Christine carried aloft the banner of her fundamentalism. It was not faith alone with her, however; it was also works. In her younger days she had been, without any previous training, a social worker of a courageous and adventurous sort. Someone encountering her at a prayer meeting had discerned her crusading spirit and got her interested in a mission to rescue prostitutes. A refuge called The Door of Hope was just being established for those who wished to change their way of life, and Aunt Christine at thirty-two was put in charge of it. She not only ran the place but went out into the streets to recruit guests. Convinced that many of those poor girls had got into prostitution through ignorance, bad luck and weakness and would willingly be rescued, she looked for them on the streets of Philadelphia's red-light district, followed them into their shabby rooms in unsavory lodginghouses and set before them an alternative life of respectability and faith. Many of them, she admitted freely, were not interested and she recognized the fact with a surprising tolerance and understanding, but those who were receptive she was eager to help. For a number of years she led a steady stream into the Door of Hope. As soon as her girls were morally on their feet and ready to face the world, she found jobs for them. The available openings were meager, mostly third-rate shops and housework. Her friends were pressured into employing ex-prostitutes as waitresses, chambermaids and cooks. Some married and came back to see her, bringing their children. One, tutored by Aunt Georgina, entered a commercial school and graduated to a successful career in business.

When she was forty-two, Aunt Christine met an equally devoted Presbyterian, W. Lehman Yerkes, who was superintendent of the Sunday School in her church, and they were married. It was an extremely happy marriage that lasted until Uncle Lehman's death thirty years later. They had no children, but a huge black cat named Caruso for his vocal gifts supplied their place; he lived to be seventeen years old, owing no doubt to being supplied with a quarter of a pound of fresh calves' liver every day. Uncle Lehman had an unctuously pious manner that set my teeth on edge, but Morgan looked upon him as a delightful example of a rare species and always referred to him as Uncle Billy Sunday.

Aunt George, tall and thin and unswervingly erect, had light red hair of the shade called, in her girlhood, carroty, and not admired. Once, as a young girl out walking, she heard one urchin in the street behind her call to another, "Did you ever see an angel with a ramrod down its back?" There was something of the ramrod about her and something too of the angel. Naturally keen and independent of mind, she had determined on a business career and desired of her elder brothers that they stake her to a commercial course. My father, who had the most commanding voice in the family, considered business infra dig for a lady; she should teach, he said. He would pay for a normal school but not for a commercial course. Aunt George went through a time of crisis, searched her soul, and came up with the decision that if she was to teach, it must be God's will for her. She would purge herself of selfish motives and embrace teaching as a way not to seek success for herself but to help humanity. She would teach only in schools where there was the greatest need—in, therefore, the slums of Philadelphia. She became an excellent teacher of small children, gentle, firm and thorough; her pupils loved and perhaps feared her, her principals respected and depended on her. More than once she was offered a principalship, but she always refused—she was not seeking power or status or even a higher salary; she was there to serve children who needed help.

She bought a little house on a country road in South Jersey where her brother Tom, whom she adored, and his family lived with her. Every day she came to Philadelphia on the bus, and she stayed overnight with Aunt Christine when the weather was bad. After Uncle Lehman died and Aunt George reached retiring age and the nieces Katherine and Ruth were married, my two aunts joined forces and rented an apartment in Germantown. Even after they moved there, they returned each Sunday morning to their old church on North Broad Street, Aunt Christine with enthusiasm, Aunt George dutifully following. When the neighborhood surrounding the church became predominantly Negro, the white members of the church decided to sell it and build a new church in the suburbs. Aunt Christine elected to stay with the old church and its Negro congregation. The minister was devoted to both my aunts, but especially to Aunt Christine—"Christine makes a holy cause of Negroes," Aunt George said once to me; "I like them but I can take them or leave them"—and was most wonderfully kind and generous to her. When at the end of her life she was no longer able to go to church, he came to see her often, bringing not only Communion but gifts of food and flowers.

After Aunt George died at eighty-seven in March, 1958, Aunt Christine stayed on alone in their apartment. Five nieces who lived within a radius of thirty miles kept an eye on her, the two youngest, who lived in New Jersey, taking most of the responsibility, and she had devoted friends ever at hand. At ninety-three she was more than half-blind, a little deaf, and she had a blood pressure so high that it went out the top of the sphygmomanometer. When I was so rash as to murmur something about a retirement home, she replied tartly, "This way I can do exactly what I like and there is no one to tell me what to do. Of course," she added pointedly, "they come in *from outside* and tell me what to do, but I don't have to pay any attention to that." The next day she went to see a friend who was ill and got lunch for her.

During the fifteen months that she lived alone I was often with her. She liked to be read to; she liked to talk about religion, for she considered Quakerism next door to heathenism and had hopes of rescuing me from its clutches; sometimes she could be led to talking about the Door of Hope or telling family stories about the Grays. The last few months of her ninety-four years she was ill and had to have nurses; it was a race between her expenses and her money, but she managed that as competently as she managed everything else, dying just in time to take care of all her bills and conscious to the end.

They were the last, Aunt George and Aunt Christine, of that family of eleven children; long-lived, independent, steadfast, redeemed, of the breed of the Covenanters. None of the next generation can touch them; we are flabby and frivolous in comparison. I am glad to have known them.

5.

Japan Again

I INTERRUPTED the writing of *Friend of Life* in September, 1957, to go to Tokyo to attend the P.E.N. Congress (the international club of Poets, Editors, Novelists and others concerned with writing) and to stay on afterwards to renew my friendships and to enjoy the experience, novel to me, of being a tourist and a visitor in a newly prosperous Japan.

It was the first time I had been to a large international gathering of writers, and I found it illuminating, stimulating and confusing. The announced theme of the Congress was "Reciprocal Influences of the Literatures of the East and West on Writers of the Present Day and of the Future," and the flags of fourteen countries were displayed on the platform at the opening session.

The Japanese P.E.N., our hosts, had made preparations and organized it all in the most efficient, generous and imaginative way possible. New small buses took the members twice a day from their hotels to the Sankei Kaikan, an admirable new building belonging to one of the big newspapers, where morning and afternoon sessions were held in an auditorium equipped, like the UN, with earphones and simultaneous translations of speeches into Japanese, French and English. Lavish and colorful luncheons, teas, dinners and evening entertainments filled the hours not scheduled for addresses and discussions.

Among the more than 140 non-Japanese present—honor guests, delegates and attenders—only a few were really well known either in their own countries or in the world outside. Alberto Moravia, Stephen Spender, Angus Wilson, André Chamson, John Steinbeck were the outstanding honor guests. The American delegation was further strengthened by John Hersey, Elmer Rice, John Dos Passos, Ralph Ellison and Elizabeth Janeway. The largest delegation of all was the French, who brought forty in a chartered plane and, according to the British, took entirely too much of the limelight. The Korean delegation, also one of the largest, emerging from years of domination by the Japanese and the agonies of the Korean War, was perhaps naturally defensive, and was considered aggressive by most others. There was a scattering of delegates from Communist countries, Czechoslovakia, Poland, East Germany, though none from the U.S.S.R. or Communist China, and a number of strongly anti-Communist "Writers in Exile." The large Japanese group was itself divided in its sympathies, for most Japanese intellectuals have a leaning toward communism. These currents were evident below the surface, emerging most clearly when resolutions were introduced protesting the imprisonment of certain writers in the Soviet Union.

My own sole contribution to the Congress was faithful attendance at all the morning and afternoon sessions, listening to all the addresses and taking notes on many of them. To my surprise this modest contribution was noticed at the highest level. Dr. Koizumi later sent me a translation of an article by Yasunari Kawabata in which he said, "Thinking of Mrs. Vining's relation to the Crown Prince we were pleased to invite her as one of our guests of honor. She, having many good friends here (not to speak of the Imperial Family) could have enjoyed generous entertainments apart from the other delegates, but she never failed to attend the sessions and otherwise strictly observed the schedules as a dutiful participant of the conference." I was not actually so virtuous as I seemed: I had five weeks more in Japan ahead of me. Much of the time there were large empty areas where the foreign members had their places, and I used to wonder whether they were off sightseeing or visiting with personal friends or engaged in important, high-level caucuses. I never quite decided whether more was going on than I was party to, or less.

The President of the Japanese P.E.N. was the novelist Yasunari Kawabata. The year before I had read with interest his novel *Snow Country*, a book of haunting beauty of which the scene is laid in the western part of Honshu, where snow falls deep in winter, so deep that people go to and fro in tunnels through it. It is the story of a well-to-do dilettante from Tokyo, a visitor to a hot springs resort in the snow country, of a geisha's love for him and his inability to love anyone. Mr. Kawabata, who was fifty-eight at the time of the Congress, was a slight, intense man with a lion's mane of gray hair, large, luminous eyes and a wide, sensitive mouth. Reportedly very shy, he chaired the meetings with poise and skill. Later the Japanese government declared him to be a "national treasure," a delightful and unique form of recognition to a living person, and still later he won the Nobel Prize for Literature.

One of the most interesting of the many addresses made at the Congress was made by Mr. Suekichi Aono, a critic and the vice-president of the Japan P.E.N., who said among other things that Japan was an assimilating country in all fields but that she had chosen what she wanted.

This was a subject that had interested me from my first days in Japan, because I had heard so often the Western cliché that Japan had no originality but existed by making copies of things developed by other countries. This of course is untrue. Japan has been influenced greatly by other civilizations at different periods, notably by China from the sixth through the ninth centuries, by Europe in the latter half of the nineteenth century, by the United States in the post-World-War-II years, but always she has taken what fed her own genius. Each time there has been a reaction afterwards and what remained after the reaction was a certain essence, impregnated with Japan's own color. Moreover, numerous aspects of her civilization are entirely her own. Arthur Waley, writing in 1941, pointed to the complete originality of Japan's poetry, her Noh plays, costume, sculpture, woodblock prints, tea ceremony, architecture. The first psychological novel in world literature, *The Tale of Genji*, still one of the great novels of all time, perhaps the greatest, was written by a Japanese woman in the early eleventh century. In Japan's adoption of Western technology, there may be an element of "Anything you can do, I can do better." It will be interesting to see what, in the end, Japan makes of Western democracy. In her modern literature she has unquestionably been influenced by Western writers, especially the Russians and the French, but Kawabata's novels not only are distinctively Japanese but are, according to Donald Keene, having an influence of their own upon Western novels. In a world increasingly one, reciprocal influences are not only inevitable but fructifying.

By the time that the Congress was over the Imperial Family had returned to Tokyo from their summer places in Nasu, Karuizawa and Numazu, and over the next five weeks I had the immensely happy experience of being warmly welcomed and entertained, twice at dinner at the Crown Prince's house, twice at the Imperial Palace, invited to lunch by Princess Chichibu, to dinner by Prince and Princess Takamatsu and Prince and Princess Mikasa; the Crown Prince also gave a wonderful picnic for me on an island offshore from Hayama and a reception to which all of his classmates at Gakushuin were invited. My old friends Mr. Yamanashi and Dr. Abe entertained for me, and the Koizumis, besides having me to meals at their home, took Tane and me on a motor trip to the Izu Peninsula and Hakone. We saw the sea through leaning pines, the "equinox lilies" brilliant in the rice-field ditches, the amazing view from Jugoku (ten counties) Pass, the barrier at Hakone famous in poem and story and Hiroshige's print, saw Fuji floating pale blue in the sky above Hakone Lake, and on the way back to Tokyo stopped for lunch at Oiso with Prime Minister Yoshida, who turned on his waterfall for us. We saw it as we sat in the dining room, a slender stream of bright water cascading down from high rocks into the garden below as if it flowed naturally day and night.

The Imperial Household had put at my disposal a new Mercedes sedan and one of their best drivers, Sato San, an able and likable young man who took his work so seriously that he never—on duty —smiled. Throughout the time that I was there Tane was satisfyingly able to free herself to be often with me, and was constantly doing the sort of imaginative, thoughtful little acts so characteristic of her. When I reached my room in the Imperial Hotel the first night, I found on the desk a Japanese-English pocket dictionary, a calendar of the engagements already made for me and a list of telephone numbers of friends. After I left the hotel I went to stay with Tane in her apartment at the International Christian University before spending the last few days at the Friends Center with Esther Rhoads.

Late in September Tane and I went off in "my" car to revisit Karuizawa. The crape myrtle was in bloom and white herons rose from the rice fields as we drove north through warm rain toward the distant, jagged mountains. As the road was being repaired, there was a more than usually strenuous struggle up the last steep slope and more than usual relief to come into the cool, wet purity of the balsam-sweet Karuizawa air. After checking in at our room at the Mampei Hotel, which had been an Occupation stronghold when I was in Karuizawa before, we put on raincoats and went out to walk in the narrow lanes between stone walls green with wet ferns and lichen and overhung with dripping trees, all shimmering in a green underwater light.

Our old cottage was boarded up and looked forlorn, but monkshood was in bloom beside the path that wound up the hill to its neglected door. The little Catholic church which had been a favorite stopping place on the way home from the Machi was unchanged: a small, simple and beautiful building created by the architect Antonin Raymond out of the local materials, gray stone, natural wood and bamboo. We visited too the little flower shop on a side lane where we used to buy flowers almost daily for the house.

The next day the sun came out, and every leaf and blade of grass sparkled. Two writers came to call on us, Mrs. Yokoyama, who wrote books for children, and Mrs. Kiyoko Tanaka, who had translated *Sandy* into Japanese. She was a graduate of Tsuda College and I had seen her first, during my first autumn in Japan, in a performance of *Quality Street* put on by Tsuda graduates in English, in which she had played the part of Phoebe. Since the publication of *Sandy* we had kept in touch, and it was good to see her again. We saw too Miss Armstrong, our friend Kotori San, in her hillside cottage; past eighty, she was more like a bird than ever, her nose sharpening to a beak, her eyes sweet and merry, her voice a chirp. We went to call on Sato San, who had been our faithful stand-by when we had the cottage. He used to bring us trout when he went fishing, gave us advice and could be counted on in any emergency. Rather a delicate-looking man with thick hair splashed with white, he and his wife lived in a house with a lovely garden, next to the Tokugawa cottage, of which he was caretaker. All through Karuizawa under the pines and in sunny, open spaces we saw wild flowers and counted once again the seven grasses of autumn.

One afternoon after our return from Karuizawa we went to see the Inoues. After a long search for a place to live, they had been offered at last a house belonging to the minister of their church, who was none other than the great Toyohiko Kagawa. It was a tiny house in a tiny garden on the very edge of Tokyo; across the narrow lane were rice fields. In this small wooden house, two rooms up and two rooms down, lived in dignity, in the miraculous Japanese way, seven people: Mrs. Inoue, her son Yukio, his tall, pretty wife and nine-month-old baby Katsumi, and Mrs. Inoue's three daughters, Keiko, Masako and Aiko. Michiko, who had worked in a publishing house and married a man whom she met there, lived nearby in an apartment house, just she and her husband without the mother-in-law. Now we were all together, the family who had lived for four years in the Western-style house in Mejiro. We had lunch with my favorite *chawan mushi* (literally "steamed teacup," a sort of custard soup) and talked. The only missing one was Genji, our white Spitz, who had loved Aiko best of all and became her dog when Violet and I left. Only a few days before I got there, Genji had died of some mysterious ailment and had been buried under the tree in the garden. He had been famous in the neighborhood, and while we were there two or three neighbors came to pay their respects to him by bowing in front of his grave.

Tane's mother and two sisters celebrated her birthday by inviting me to a performance of the motion picture, *Around the World in Eighty Days*, in a new and modern theater, followed by dinner at a *tempura* restaurant, where we sat at a counter of pale, new wood and ate bits of crab, chicken, fish, fresh ginger, spinach and other things deep fried in batter right before our eyes. It was a happy occasion and made arresting to me by the fact that Tane's mother, then in her early seventies, had just seen the first motion picture of her life.

The food that I ate during those weeks was a revelation to me. For most of my four years in Japan, so soon after the war, food had been a problem to almost everyone. The ration had been small; fruit and fresh vegetables had come slowly back into production; the things I got from the U.S. Commissary had been canned or cold storage. There had been no restaurants at all. In inns and in Japanese homes I had eaten delicious Japanese food, but those were rare and special occasions. Now food stores were filled with all kinds of good things; Tane took me to a bakery on the Ginza, for instance, which had an amazing array of breads and buns and rolls. Tokyo was full of fascinating restaurants of all kinds. One night we went to a Hungarian restaurant, another to a French restaurant run by Mr. Yoshida's former chef. Miss Taira, our flower arrangement teacher, gave a luncheon party for me at a Buddhist temple, where we were waited on by grave and elegant young women in mauve kimonos, trained in the tea ceremony, who moved as if in a slow, graceful dance. The food was entirely vegetarian, but not what I usually think of when I hear that

dreary word. Invention and skill had been lavished upon a succession of exotic and improbable delicacies of varied textures and
flavors, set forth artistically on handmade pottery: minute bamboo sprouts no more than an inch long, served whole, a fig deep-
fried in a batter of *omochi* rice, the seeds of some rare tree fried
in a batter of powdered green tea, and so on and on, all of it
beautiful to look at. One evening Mrs. Takaki took Tane and
me to a tiny restaurant where the first course was a seacoast
scene: on a sand-colored plate decorated with a branch of pine
were some tiny cones made of ground and broiled octopus and
two miniature scarlet crabs boiled in oil and deliciously crunchy.

One evening Tane and I and several of the young faculty from
the International Christian University went to a restaurant in a
pine forest, which specialized in international cookery, each
course representing a different country. Japan provided a very
good fish with a delicate sauce. Halfway through it, one of the
guests raised her head and said hesitantly, "This is *fugu* we are
eating." Consternation. *Fugu* is blowfish, which has a gland in it
that is literally deadly poison if a trace of it is left in the fish;
I well remember seeing headlines in the *Nippon Times* about two
men who had died of eating *fugu*. The proprietor, when questioned, admitted freely that it was *fugu* but assured us that his chef
was a famous expert in its preparation and that we had not the
slightest cause for alarm. As I had already eaten half of it, I
thought I might as well finish my portion and I did. Later when I
told Shinzo Koizumi about it, he shook his head in disapproval.

Interspersed with all these events were telephone calls, visits
from old friends, acquaintances and strangers, and stacks of letters, many of which came from people who had odd and interesting ideas of what I might do for them. One was from a Japanese
student who had some questions that he wanted me to answer:

1. What is the prospective destination of American and English
literature?

2. What is literature?

3. What is the reason why literature is existing?

I kept it because it was typical of the sort of large, vague question
to which Japanese students so often address themselves.

The third question was the one to which, I have read, Soseki
Natsume, Japan's first great modern novelist, devoted a "ten-year-
plan" of the study of philosophy, psychology, sociology and ethics
as well as literature itself in hopes of finding an answer. I did not

feel that I could tackle it between telephone calls and appointments.

When on October 15 I left Tokyo, I had a great send-off at the airport. The farewell is an essential part of Japanese hospitality and friendship; Japanese visitors to the United States find it difficult—and often very hurting—to understand why we make such a fuss about welcoming visitors but let them depart with only a handful of closest friends to say good-by at the end. At the last moment a great sheaf of roses and cosmos picked by Her Majesty herself was thrust into one of my arms and twelve giant chrysanthemums from Miss Taira into the other. There was no place to put them on the crowded plane, and so I shared my seat with them and sat all the way to Honolulu up to my knees in flowers. It was a good thing that I enjoyed them in that way, for at Honolulu the plant quarantine forced me to abandon them.

During the nearly eighteen months between trips to Japan, I finished *Friend of Life* and delivered it to the publisher and wrote a book for children, *The Cheerful Heart*, the scene of which was my own neighborhood in Tokyo and its rebuilding. The episodes in it were those I had seen happening among people whom I knew: the single egg that a family could buy, the small child who insisted upon carrying it home, and dropped it; the preparations for the New Year; the theft of a bicycle; "Sports Day" at school; the stray puppy that adopted the family; the moon-viewing party; the building of a new and better house with the longed-for room for the little heroine; the recovery of the bicycle; the return of Honorable Elder Brother from Siberia, where he had been a prisoner of war.

May Massee was enthusiastic about the book and eager to find just the right illustrator for it. With her especial gift for seeing the potentialities in untried artists, she came up with a young Japanese artist who had recently arrived in New York. Kazue Mizumura, out of rare skill and, I suspect, her homesickness, produced pictures for my book so full of authentic Japanese atmosphere and detail, so faithful to the story and the characters, so beautiful in themselves and with such delicious touches of humor that *The Cheerful Heart* became the third of my books whose illustrations seemed to me perfect. The other two are Marguerite de Angeli's pictures for *Meggy MacIntosh* and Robert Lawson's for *Adam of the Road*.

During the fall of 1958 speculations about the Crown Prince's engagement, a subject that had excited interest for at least six years, began to appear in newspapers and magazines. On November 14, two weeks before the engagement was actually announced in the United States as well as Japan, Shinzo Koizumi wrote to me:

"I hasten to write this letter to fulfill the promise I made years ago that the name of the Crown Prince's bride shall not be made known to the newspaper people before to you.

"Her name is Michiko Shoda (24) the eldest daughter of Mr. Hidesaburo Shoda, an industrialist very well known among the business world. Last night I went to see the Shodas at their home, less than ten minutes drive from here and had their final 'yes'. Then I saw the girl (we were acquaintances) and talked with her alone for some time, mostly about the Crown Prince. Then I had tea with the whole family (two brothers and one sister) and then departed.

"This morning I saw Mr. Usami [The Emperor's grand steward] and have conveyed the Shodas' 'yes' to him. The engagement will probably be officially announced towards the end of this month.

"Miss Shoda enjoys the highest reputation among those who know her for her good looks, fine character and her intelligence. Her non-aristocratic birth (although of an old family of good name) has of course made us hesitate to decide the choice. But after possiblest considerations we have decided. It is not only his but our choice too (We rather chose first.) The wedding will take place probably late next year."

A little less than five months later I was on my way to Japan to the wedding, carrying in my hands the whole distance the box containing a Steuben glass ornament in the shape of a rooster. I had chosen it for the Crown Prince's wedding present because he had been born in the Year of the Rooster and because in the room at Koganei where I had had my first lessons with him, there had hung a dramatic painting of a rooster by the great modern artist, Kawai Gyokudo.

At Haneda Airport I was met by the Koizumis, Tane, Esther Rhoads, the Inoues, a number of my former students, and a hundred reporters, in a downpour of rain and wind.

During the fifteen days that I was there, I saw the Crown Prince six times, aside from the wedding and wedding luncheon, and the girl who became Princess Michiko three times. The generosity with which those two very important young people, in the midst of the busiest and most breathless days of their lives up to that point, made time for me still amazes and touches me.

On March 10 Dr. Koizumi had written me, "During the wedding weeks the Kunaicho officials will unmistakably be busy. But not I. I shall have few things to do in those days. So my time will be entirely at your service during your stay here. We, at least on my side, shall have plenty of time to talk and go round together. Do just tell me what you want to see and where to go."

To his thoughtfulness, his kindness, his wise advice and frequent presence I owe much of the seamless happiness of that fortnight.

Miss Shoda, on the day when her household effects were being ceremonially and formally transferred from her parents' house to her future home, came to a luncheon given by the Koizumis so that we might meet before the wedding. Even before that she had taken the time and thought to have waiting for me in my room at the International House a basket of deep purple pansies and a note of welcome.

A beautiful young woman, intelligent, graceful, warm, charming, endowed with dignity and underlying strength and the sense of humor which the Crown Prince had earlier declared to be one of his requirements in his bride, Michiko Shoda had been the outstanding graduate in her year at the College of the Sacred Heart, in her studies, in athletics, in her relationships with students and faculty. She had been in no hurry to marry, enjoying after college her home, her family, her friends, tennis, music, and the other things that fill young girls' lives. At the Tennis Club in Karuizawa one August day she was roped into making the fourth in a doubles match in which the Crown Prince was playing. He was not in form that day, and Miss Shoda and the American boy who was her partner defeated the royal adversary. The romance which developed from there had to overcome formidable obstacles—of tradition, for the brides of previous crown princes had come from one of five noble families, and of the parent Shodas' reluctance to see their daughter disappear behind the clouds above which from time immemorial the Imperial Family has been considered to dwell. Dr. Koizumi, on whose list of possible brides Miss Shoda had had a place even before the tennis match, and Mother Britt of the College of the Sacred Heart gave counsel and support, until at length, as Dr. Koizumi said to me, "The ice began to melt." The engagement was announced on November 28, 1958, and the wedding date set for April 10, 1959.

In the past the brides of crown princes had had at least two years to be prepared for their exalted positions; Miss Shoda had less than five months for fittings for her trousseau, for cere-monies, for lessons in English and French, in court etiquette, in the Japanese Constitution—and in the writing of poetry. It seemed to me so right, so truly Japanese, that when so much had to be curtailed, the poetry lessons were considered essential. Her teacher was Mrs. Goto, whom I had enjoyed meeting at the P.E.N., and it developed that in this as in all else Miss Shoda had a natural and unerring instinct for the right word, the essential nuance of sound.

The Crown Prince had saved an evening for me, in which we had dinner alone together, a dinner composed of the dishes that his chef remembered to have been my favorites. The talk that we had that evening remains in my heart as the most deeply rewarding experience of all that richly happy time. He had grown into his full stature, a young man with new confidence, deeply in love, comfortable with himself and his world. That the Japanese people had responded with universal enthusiasm to his choice of a bride must have been immensely encouraging to him.

Three days later on April 10, on a morning of sparkling sun-shine and blossoming cherry trees, the wedding took place in the Imperial Shrine deep within the Palace grounds. About a thou-sand people were there, sitting under the great trees in the courtyard of the Shrine, high government officials on one side and on the other members of the court and relatives of the bride. Only a few women were among all the morning-coated and striped-trousered men, for wives were not included; you had to be there in your own right as a Diet member, a princess, the mother of the bride, a member of the Crown Prince's council, like Mrs. Matsudaira, or a former teacher, like me.

It was a beautiful, very simple ceremony, made colorful by the eleventh-century costumes of the bride and groom and their attendants, who were chamberlains and ladies in waiting, and made solemn by the deep quiet, broken only by the twittering of birds, and by the serious voice of the young prince as he spoke the vows for himself and his wife.

Between the ceremony in the morning and the departure of

the Crown Prince and Princess in the afternoon, Dr. Koizumi and I spent the time in one of the waiting rooms of the Imperial Household Building, eating a picnic lunch and talking. He described it in his diary (which was later published) and sent me a translation:

"Mrs. V and I stayed at Kunaicho. We were especially permitted to see the Crown Prince and Princess off on their departure from the Palace. I took my chauffeur's advice to stay here, since it would be impossible to get through today's traffic jam and get back by 2:30.

"Going into the waiting room where we had been before, we sat down on chairs by the window in that wide room and while we talked the time of waiting drifted by. During the time noon came; I had brought sandwiches from home and without tea or water we ate them. Three hours passed.

"Only one window was open, looking out on an inner court of the government office building; from this came a cool breeze which stirred the door. Outside the window the green of ginkgo leaves was pleasant to our eyes; though in the sky there was the incessant roar of a helicopter and an airplane and from somewhere came the sound of band practice, the room inside was quiet and our conversation was not disturbed. I continued my conversation saying that on such a gay day of celebration as this I did not think it was possible to have such a relaxed talk."

He went on to tell what we had talked about, writing, Shakespeare, his experiences in England, Kabuki. One bit he quoted directly:

"She said, 'I don't like to read my own things. Right after I have written them I read them, but afterwards I don't want to. How is it with you?'

"Generally it's the same with me, but I think from time to time, reading my own articles, oya! unexpectedly I read something delicious.' As I said this, she nodded."

Later the Shodas came in, and for the first time I met Princess Michiko's parents. Her father was a well-set-up, substantial-looking businessman, her mother slender, gray-haired, poetic-looking; she seemed to be moving in a cloud of wonderment.

A Japanese Crown Prince and his bride do not enjoy the luxury of an untrameled honeymoon. They had to call on the Imperial relatives, present themselves at a ceremony to receive the congratulations of the Governor of Tokyo, make a trip to Ise to inform the Crown Prince's ancestors of their marriage and spend three days giving luncheon-receptions to high-ranking members of the government, to the diplomats and to all the rest of those who might expect to be invited, the Shoda family, the cousins of the Crown Prince, former chamberlains and ladies in waiting, former tutors. Esther Rhoads was also invited to this, and we went together.

Meanwhile, I had a trip with the Koizumis, two days of Kabuki, a second wedding—that of my former student and the Crown Prince's friend, Bob Togasaki, which was held at the International Christian University—and several other delightful parties. I also saw a great deal of the press, radio and television people.

Dr. Koizumi had written me, "I hope you will be lenient to them in so far as your time and humor permit. I know very well of your disinclination to publicity. But you must also know that whatever you say about the Crown Prince will be unmistakably appreciated by the Japanese public more particularly on such an occasion as his marriage."

He himself accompanied me to a press conference in the International House on the first morning I was there and sat with me behind a table with six microphones facing a roomful of reporters and photographers. I had a statement which I had prepared beforehand in which I begged the press to give the Crown Prince and his bride freedom and privacy. When I uttered the last word, I heard Shinzo saying *sotto voce* to a Japanese reporter, "Don't translate *that*," and I realized that I had in good will and ignorance committed a solecism. Privacy is not a nice word in a crowded country where people live out their lives in public and do not seek to be alone. But times change, and several years later I read an interview in which Dr. Koizumi himself pled for privacy for the young couple.

I was sorry that I had made an error but not deeply disturbed as I once would have been. A brief exchange on the way into the conference had pointed up the difference in my present and my early relations with the press. An American reporter whom I was not aware of having seen before said to me,

"I am one of the reporters who were so rude to you when you first came to Japan in 1946."

I replied, "Oh, you frightened me dreadfully, but I have long since forgiven you."

"He was very meek, wasn't he?" observed Dr. Koizumi.

They were different, but also I was free. I no longer had a very sensitive job which I was trying to preserve from misquotations and misunderstandings. If I said anything foolish now, it reflected only on me; it would not imperil the course of my work. I had also learned better how to handle myself with reporters, learned to play the instrument a little. It was no longer like picking up a tuba and wondering which end the noise comes out of.

The last thing that I did on the afternoon of the 15th was to go to the Palace to say good-by to the Empress, who gave me kind messages for Violet and a beautiful flower basket to be sent home after me via the diplomatic pouch, and to the Crown Prince's house to say my farewells to him and to Princess Michiko. Dr. Koizumi went with me on this latter errand. We found them relaxed and smiling, apparently not tired by their strenuous week. The Princess was wearing a suit of Black Watch plaid, and on the lapel with characteristic thoughtfulness she had fastened a silver pin which I had brought her.

Afterwards Shinzo told me that he had dropped in to see the Crown Prince the day before and, finding him alone, had asked to see the Princess. Instead of ringing the bell and sending a servant for her, the Crown Prince went out of the room himself and fetched her. Dr. Koizumi was delighted with the informality and naturalness of it, and he asked me if I could remember the first time that he had sat in on one of the Crown Prince's private lessons with me. He went on to tell me about it. The Prince and I sat at a table in the center of the room, he himself on a chair against the wall. I asked the Crown Prince to take the book we were using to him and show him what we were working on.

"That must have been the first time he was asked to be a messenger! It must have been a very new thing for him. Oh, many good things started from that time!"

I was always interested to get Shinzo's comments on my relations with the Crown Prince because some of the things that I did that seemed to me so natural were to him new and even daring. He spoke many times of the day when I had invited two American boys and an Australian to spend the afternoon with the Crown Prince at my house and Shinzo had come in to watch one of the games that I had planned. I gave each boy a famous historical incident to act out for the others to guess. The Crown

Prince complained that his was too difficult. "Oh, well, do the best you can with it," I said. Shinzo repeated my words and added seriously, "I felt your authority." Even to him, scholar and educator and man of the world that he was, it was a little startling to see me speak to the Japanese Crown Prince exactly as I did to other boys.

In the long hours in the sky on the way home and the three days resting on a beach in Honolulu, I thought about Japan and what my experience there, the four years and the two visits, had given me, not only in the great enlargement of my personal life, the deep friendships, the new opportunities, the opening up of a hitherto unknown country, with all its beauty, its history, its poetry, its art, but also in deeper and less tangible ways, in new modes of thinking and feeling.

The difference between Western and Eastern thinking that struck me most forcibly was the difference in attitudes toward nature. The beauty of nature had long been of fundamental importance in my life, as a joy and a source of comfort and strength in time of sorrow or perplexity, but I had accepted without examination the Western assumption that man dominates nature, conquers it, uses it.

The indigenous religion of Japan, before Buddhism, was a nature worship of a gentle and appreciative kind, based not on fear but on thankfulness. In a country where natural disaster may strike in many ways—earthquake, tidal wave, volcanic eruption, typhoon, fire, flood—it is surprising that man does not fear or propitiate nature but feels gratitude for her bounty and beauty. A majestic tree, a towering rock, often bears a little shrine before which a prayer may be said or flowers or food offered. Buddhism too brought with it a doctrine of harmlessness toward nature and of unity with it, an attitude that pervades the East and indeed is held by tribes of American Indians, themselves probably Eastern in origin.

This attitude shows itself in daily life in small ways. Food, for instance, is enjoyed seasonally in Japan. Each season brings its own fruits and each is savored in its time; the grapes, the pears, the bamboo sprouts of spring, the mushrooms, the persimmons of autumn. Decorations in a house reflect the time of year. In the ancient black iron kettles in which water is boiled for the tea ceremony, iron filings are placed to make a tinkling sound with the boiling water, heavy ones for winter, lighter ones for summer. One lives to a rhythm not of one's own making. The brilliant sun of winter, the softness of spring rain, the mists of summer mornings, the cool sound of insects on summer evenings, the fragrance of autumn, the cold brilliance of winter moonlight—all are savored in their turn.

In his important book, *Design of Cities*, Edmund Bacon noted the effect on architecture of the different attitudes toward nature that prevail in different parts of the world. "By defining the point of juncture between mass and space," he wrote, "the architect is making a statement about the relationship of man and his universe. . . . Chinese architecture is a powerful expression of a state of harmony with nature, not dominance over it. The concavity of a roof is an expression of the modesty of man, of the receptivity of his structures to universal space which these roofs gracefully receive and which becomes the core of his architectural composition in the courtyards."

On our visit to Eleusis in 1955 we were told by our young Greek guide that whereas the Romans paved the ground, the Greeks did not, having too much love for Mother Earth to so imprison her. Arnold Toynbee, seeing in Afghanistan the immense modern attacks on the problem of irrigation, the bulldozers preparing the ground for great dams, suggested that the ancient people who also had harnessed the Indus in order to water the land had with their more gentle and primitive methods been fully as effective without inflicting the harsh scars that result from modern tools and attitudes.

G. K. Chesterton once said that when renting a lodging we should ask the landlady not about the southern exposure or the price of the room but what would be her answer to the question, "Is the universe friendly?" In the long run, he thought, our comfort in the room would depend upon her answer to that. But perhaps we should phrase the question in the opposite way. "Are we friendly to the universe, or are we aggressive, dominating, exploitative?"

When I first came home from Japan and talked about living in harmony with nature, my friends looked at me uncomprehendingly. "But we must conquer nature," they said. "That is how our civilization has advanced." Now, however, the acute problems resulting from our rape of the land and pollution of the air are forcing us to re-examine our attitudes. It is probable that we shall have to meet the problems in a rational and scientific way, since that is fundamentally our character, but it may be nevertheless that East and West will move closer to mutual understanding in this area.

In my first autumn in Japan I encountered Zen, which came upon me as something absolutely new, and I became interested in it largely through my admiration for the great and gentle Zen Buddhist scholar, Dr. Taisetz Suzuki, whom I first met at a tea ceremony at Enkakuji in Kamakura. He gave me a copy of his illuminating book, *The Influence of Zen on Japanese Culture*, and, the greater gift, his friendship. I read more about Zen in others of Dr. Suzuki's books and later in those of the Americans, Alan Watts and Thomas Merton. I was privileged to meditate one evening in May with the monks at Enkakuji. I recognized the presence of Zen in much of Japanese life, in the tea ceremony, in flower arrangement, in poetry, in art. I saw too similarities to Quakerism, in the use of meditation and the rejection of theology—and also in the way that both religions, having declared that experience, not words or "notions," is fundamental, then proceed to write books upon books of explanation.

I am convinced that only the very rare Westerner can really penetrate the depths of Zen and practice it. "Instant Zen" is a travesty. We have no understanding of the rigors of mental and physical discipline that are necessary before enlightenment can be achieved. But even while we fail so completely to enter into its meaning that we often don't even know we are missing anything, there are treasures to be picked up in the outer precincts. Japanese swordmakers, archers, businessmen—and professors of English too—study Zen as a way of deepening and sharpening their powers of concentration. I was greatly drawn by its simplicity, its closeness to nature, its emphasis upon the "suchness" of things, things as they are in their own essence and reality without man's interpretations and abstractions. Dr. Suzuki gives an example of this difference in his comment on two similar poems from East and West, Tennyson's "Flower in the Crannied Wall" and a haiku by Basho:

> Carefully seen
> Nazuma in bloom
> In the hedge!

"When Tennyson noticed the flower in a crannied wall he 'plucked' it and held it in his hand and went on reflecting about it, pursuing his abstract thought about God and man, about the totality of things and the unfathomability of life. . . . Compare all this with Basho and we see how differently the Oriental poet handles his experience. Above all he does not 'pluck' the flower, he does not mutilate it, he leaves it where he has found it. He does not detach it from the totality of its surroundings, he contemplates it in its *sono-mama* state [suchness], not only in itself but in the situation as it finds itself—the situation in its broadest and deepest sense." *

There is a similar contrast between Bryant's "To a Waterfowl" and a poem by the thirteenth-century Japanese poet Dogen. Bryant writes:

> There is a Power whose care
> Teaches thy way along that pathless coast—
> The desert and illimitable air—
> Lone wandering but not lost.

Dogen states only:

> Though coming and going
> Its track does not stay
> The waterfowl never
> Loses its way.

I think also of another poet, and I wish that I could ask Dr. Suzuki about him. In one of his sermons John Donne wrote: "God is an angel in an angel, a stone in a stone, a straw in a straw." Perhaps he would think this was dualistic. But this sentence of Donne's seems to me to compress into seventeen simple words the essence of the Christian doctrine that God is both immanent and transcendent. What I miss in Zen is that after it has made of man a most sensitive instrument, it finds no Hand to pick him up and use him. So, substituting a name in the lines that Yeats wrote to Von Hugel, I would say to my Zen friend,

> "So get you gone, Suzuki,
> But with blessings on your head."

---

* Suzuki: *Mysticism: Christian and Buddhist*, pp. 101–102.

6.

Wallingford

IN THE spring of 1960, just after *Return to Japan* was published, we moved away from the little house in Mount Airy. The house that I bought in Wallingford, southwest of Philadelphia between Swarthmore and Media, was really for Violet, though I too was charmed with it. She had not liked the house in Mount Airy, as she had not liked any house in which she had lived since the one on Wayne Avenue in which I was born. She was by then seventy-seven; if ever again she was to live in a house that she really liked, there was no time to lose.

The house on Plush Mill Road (named for an actual plush mill on Crum Creek which had once made plush for Pullman cars) was of gray stone and white clapboards, built in 1936 for Homer and Edna Morris by the architect Pope Barney, who had received for it second prize in a small house competition. It was in the Pennsylvania farmhouse style so popular at that time, with an open stone terrace, and a study on the second floor already provided with bookshelves, the first study I ever had that was not an attic. The big bedroom over the living room, which was to be Violet's, had a door opening onto a southern balcony overlooking the back garden and the campus of Pendle Hill beyond.

The garden itself was small, a little less than half an acre, and shady, with seven dogwoods, two tall white pines, some bordering hemlocks, and over the terrace a big red maple, but from the earliest spring on through the May tulips, there was a succession of blossoming bulbs, crocuses, daffodils, narcissi of many kinds, scylla, both early and late, and tulips. Against the north side of the house pink and white rhododendrons rose to the second-story window sills. A rosebush or two under the southern window of the living room struggled through weeds, and the lawn contained more chickweed, plantains, wild onion, false strawberry, dandelions and prunella than it did grass. It had great appeal for an amateur gardener, and I flung myself into it fervently, fighting weeds and trustfully planting annuals and perennials that required two or three times the amount of sunshine that I could offer them.

Catbirds, thrashers and robins nested in the shrubbery, and a pair of wrens raised their second family in the wrenhouse that I hung from the dogwood by the terrace. All through the winter birds flocked to the feeder: titmice, chickadees, downy woodpeckers, cardinals, purple finches, goldfinches, towhees and occasionally a visitation of evening grosbeaks. Early in the mornings the ring-necked pheasants that lived in the wooded valley across the road promenaded across our lawn, uttering an occasional deep-throated squawk; raccoons discovered ways to get into our sunken garbage can at night, young rabbits scampered over the terrace, squirrels lived high in the red maple, and a chipmunk in the low stone wall between us and Waysmeet next door, and unseen moles made looping tunnels under the false strawberry in the back lawn.

To the east and south we were bounded by Pendle Hill; our neighbor on the west, who had a really old Pennsylvania farmhouse, was a garden club prize winner who made us each year a most beautiful della Robbia wreath for Christmas.

It was a dear house and we both loved it, in spite of the fact that during the seven years we lived there we suffered more accidents and serious illness than at any other similar period of years in our lives. The house had, I discovered, a history of broken hips and broken marriages, as if some bad fairy had presided over its christening.

On the second morning after we moved in, with boxes of books, china and bedding still standing about and the new kitchen range still not working, I tripped on the stone front step and broke a bone in my foot—"creamed it" was the expression the doctor used after seeing the X ray. With a cast and a crutch I was about again at once, but it slowed down the process of settling in. Yuki Takahashi, Tane's elder sister, who was studying at Pendle Hill, ran in whenever she had free time and quietly and persistently unpacked and shelved our books.

We were fortunate, in moving into a house which needed a good deal in the way of painting, refinishing of floors and small repairs, to come under the aegis of Roy Wood, a carpenter and contractor who took care of the houses of most of our friends and acquaintances in the neighborhood. A short, slender, sandy-haired man of the kindly, protective type who took the sort of personal interest that belongs to another age, he could do anything from putting on a new roof to mending a catch on a cupboard door, and though he had to portion out his time over many houses, so that now you saw him and now you didn't, he was always on hand at once in an emergency. A leak in the roof, a flood in the cellar, trouble with the septic tank, termites in the bay window—whatever it was, Roy Wood was there, calm, comforting and capable.

"You must be terribly busy," Violet said to him once.

"Oh, I am," he answered, shaking his head. "I have thirty widows on my hands and they're all helpless."

In Wallingford we found ourselves seeing more often than before our friends who lived in Wayne or Haverford, Wilmington or Mickleton, as well as, naturally, nearby Swarthmore, where Elizabeth McKie had a house with her friend Genevieve Buck. My cousin Diane de Branges, Nanette McDonald's sensitive and poetic daughter, whose marriage to an American-born French vicomte had broken up in the stress following the war, lived in Wayne with her son Louis, a young mathematical genius who was technically in residence at the Institute for Advanced Studies in Princeton. When Henry Cadbury gave a series of lectures on the Epistles of Paul on Monday evenings at Pendle Hill, Diane and Louis would drive over. Louis would spend the evenings in my study ostensibly pursing his mathematical specialty, Hilbert Space, but actually, I found, reading the detective fiction he discovered there, while Diane, Violet and I walked through the back gate to the lectures. Outside of Wilmington Diane's brother Ellice McDonald, and his wife, Rosa, had moved into Invergarry, their new house across the creek from Granogue, where Rosa's uncle lived in feudal state. Invergarry was now only half an hour away, and Broad Reach, Ellice's house on the Chester River, with its guest cottage, named Buster's Bungalow in honor of the dean of their seventeen or more cats, also moved appreciably nearer to us.

The house in Wallingford had two more features that enriched our life, its proximity to Pendle Hill and also to the beautiful rolling country that lay just beyond Media. My association with Pendle Hill had been a long one, as student, sojourner, summer school head resident, member and then chairman of the Publications Committee, board member; now I became next-door neighbor and I taught in the spring a writing workshop. Howard and Anna Brinton were no longer the heads of Pendle Hill as they had been when I first knew it, but they had a small house on the campus still and Howard taught courses in Quakerism that were luminous and absorbingly interesting. Howard's book, *Friends for Three Hundred Years*, which was published in 1952, remains, I think, the best single book on Quakerism; he has written also numerous pamphlets on aspects of Quakerism and of mysticism that are distinguished for insight, lucidity and learning. His slight figure with the aureole of white hair and radiant countenance was a beloved and revered sight on the campus, and his presence drew to Pendle Hill leaders of religious thought from far places over the years. U Nu, prime minister of Burma, Hu Shih of China, Gurdial Malik of India, Taisetz Suzuki of Japan were four who made special trips to Pendle Hill for the privilege of talking with Howard Brinton. His wife, Anna, was herself a scholar; her knowledge of the classics and of Eastern art was impressive; she had besides a rare gift for speaking and especially for the fitting and graceful word at weddings, funerals and other occasions; everything she did she did with style and grace; her sense of what is wise, what is appropriate and what is possible were of the greatest help in the counsels of Friends everywhere; both she and Howard were greatly in demand for Quaker Yearly Meetings, conferences, and occasions of all sorts. Both had, in addition, a warm sense of home; their four children and sixteen grandchildren often came back to Pendle Hill to be with them. Both had a keen sense of humor; both had open hearts. Howard had grown up in West Chester and Anna in California, and they had met in postwar Germany; though they had taught, before they came to Pendle Hill, at Earlham College in Indiana and Mills College in California, they both had their roots deep in the soil of eastern Pennsylvania. They took pleasure in finding ancestors on both sides established in the Pendle Hill neighborhood on Holmes's 1718 "Map of the Province of Pennsylvania with the names of the original purchasers from William Penn." It pleased us too, after we settled in at Wallingford, to find on the same map, on the Chester Creek, our own ancestor, Michael Iszard, though his name there was misspelled Mitchell.

When we moved to Wallingford, Dan Wilson was Director, and

had been for several years, a gentle, slow-spoken, wise counselor to the students. Douglas Steere, known all over the world for his books, his visits to Friends in other countries, his contribution to the ecumenical movement, his gift of vivid and persuasive speech, and his work as head of the Philosophy Department at Haverford College, was Chairman of the Board. He too attracted to Pendle Hill people of stature and color. The student body, which was made up of Friends and non-Friends of all ages and many countries, was small at any one time, but sojourners came and went for a night, a week end, a fortnight; some to speak, some just to be there; one never knew whom one would find talking to an entranced group in the Barn, sitting at dinner on the terrace in the spring sunset, silent in the morning meeting for worship, perched on a stool at the kitchen table late at night over a snack and a discussion of anything from the state of the public hospital in Houston, Texas, to the tales of the Hassidim and the ideas of Martin Buber.

A ten-minute ride in the car to the south and west, and we were free of the suburbs, out into the farming country of Delaware and Chester Counties, a land of rolling hills and the valleys of creeks that like fingers pointed toward the Delaware; old stone farmhouses, large stone barns, pastures fenced in whitewashed wood and dotted with horses or herds of Black Angus cattle, a network of narrow, winding roads between the two old pikes, the Baltimore and the Lancaster; it was a rich, beautiful land, laced with dogwood in spring, brilliant with maples, ash, sweet gum, tupelo in fall. It lay open to us for the little rambling rides we loved to take, restful and refreshing in and out on the old roads with the old names; Providence Road, Street Road, Sycamore Mills Road, Paxon Hollow Road, Doe Run Road, Sugartown Road, Goshen Road, and all the others. Few of the farms now were working farms; most were the sophisticated country places of rich city men, to whom I am forever grateful for maintaining at great expense the lovely unspoiled country for me to enjoy. There were two hunt clubs, the Rose Tree and the Radnor, and on Thanksgiving we sometimes liked to follow the hunt in our car from road to road as it streamed across the landscape. During the few years that we lived there we saw many of the old farms near Media succumb to high taxes and high prices; one after another they were taken over by developers and cut up into two- or three-acre lots, that spawned large and handsome but depressingly similar "new homes."

By the end of July, that first summer of 1960, I was out of my cast and we set off for Mount Desert Island and Cove Ledge, the cottage in West Tremont, on the western, unfashionable side of the island, which for a number of summers we rented from a friend. It had been a fisherman's cottage, much run down, when Dorothy Durling, a teacher at the Germantown Friends School, had bought it and renovated it. Surrounded by old apple trees, it stood in a sunny field that sloped down to a cove of Goose Cove in Blue Hill Bay. Behind us was a wood with the tall, pointed firs for which the Maine coast is famous; before us the waters of the cove, dotted with lobster boats at anchor and far away against the sky the horizon islands. There are two schools of thought among owners of summer cottages; those who like to live in the woods, and those who like to live right on the shore. I like trees, but my early life spent on a small lot with eleven large trees conditioned me to want them far enough away not to cut off the sunshine. Violet liked the ocean but she wanted it far enough from the house not to breathe at her through the windows and make her sheets damp when she went to bed. So we both were delighted with this sunshiny cottage with its trees behind and the bay below. We liked the terrace, the big screened porch, the tiny living room with its fireplace, the big, warm red-and-white kitchen, and the two small bedrooms above.

Fran was eight miles away on Long Pond, outside of Somesville, and when we left Cove Ledge we stayed a while with her in The Bubble, her guest cabin. We had friends in Southwest Harbor, eight miles or so in the other direction, and there was a constant mild whirl of social life, of picnics on the rocks and tea and supper parties—and luncheons too, but I wrote in the morning and generally avoided them—in which the same people met each other again and again and never lacked for something to talk about. One of the nicest picnics that I remember was one at Seawall, given by Fran's friends, the Weimers, and memorable not only for happy companionship but for food. Paul Weimer was the minister of three churches in Tremont and West Tremont; he had a boat and he had gone out and caught the lobsters himself. Unlike the commercial lobstermen, he had not plugged their claws with little bits of wood, so that there should be no nervousness or resentment to spoil the flavor. Trudy, his wife, had cooked them just before we left for Seawall and they were still warm. They were unquestionably the best lobsters that I have ever eaten, but a little nagging discomfort stays in my mind: the thought that lobsters might be mentally aware enough to feel nervousness and resentment. What then of the pot of boiling water?

One of the joys of our new house, as of the old, was our Japanese visitors. When we had heard that our beloved flower arrangement teacher, Miss Koha Taira, was coming to the United States, we had hoped to have her with us for a week, but then her arrival coincided with our moving and with my broken foot, and so her visit was cut down to a luncheon on the terrace, with friends who brought her up from Baltimore for the day. Another day Miss Hoshino and Miss Fujita, who were among those to be honored on the celebration of Bryn Mawr's seventy-fifth anniversary, came, Miss Hoshino still pansy-faced, a little whiter, a little slower in her movements, Miss Fujita easily combining the deferential care of Miss Hoshino with her own increased stature as one of the important women leaders of the new Japan. Bob Togasaki, now a doctoral student at Cornell, came with his lovely wife Fumiko, and in the fall, after our return from Mount Desert, the Crown Prince and Princess Michiko made a visit to the United States, on the invitation of President Eisenhower, to mark the hundredth anniversary of the first America-Japan treaty, the one negotiated by Townsend Harris, following Perry's opening of Japan.

This time Philadelphia was not included in the imperial itinerary, but I was invited to meet them both in Washington and New York. It was an added joy that Dr. Koizumi was to accompany them. He wrote me on August 17, "I shall be with the Prince and Princess all the way as a regular member of their suite. As a lazy, retired old man I was at first reluctant to go abroad or to be away from home for weeks but thinking that I may be of some use for Their Highnesses' relaxations during the trip, I accepted Mr. Usami's invitation to join their suite. But it is an unexpected fortune for me that I should see you again so soon." Mrs. Takaki, one of my very first and one of my dearest friends in Japan, was also of the suite, as well as two of the chamberlains whom I knew, Mr. Suzuki and Mr. Toda, once the youngest and most boyish of them all, now a substantial middle-aged figure, and Dr. Yumoto, the Crown Prince's physician.

I saw them first at the state dinner which President and Mrs. Eisenhower gave for them on September 27. The occasion was doubly happy for me, primarily because I was seeing again that radiant and beloved young couple, and then because, though I had dined many times in the Imperial Palace, this was my only time to dine at the White House.

It was a cloudy, warm September evening; my taxi driver, who was a Jehovah's Witness, scolded me about my godlessness as we approached the brightly lit White House looming out of its surrounding dark. Guests emerging from the steady stream of cars were taken care of by young aides in dress uniform with fouragères, escorted to the stately East Room and disposed in a large circle. When the President and the Princess, Mrs. Eisenhower and the Crown Prince came in, the circle began to move and each of us had a brief moment in which to shake hands, to exchange a word or two with them.

Princess Michiko looked even more beautiful than she had at her wedding; motherhood—a son had been born the previous February—had made her slimmer and had deepened her look of tenderness and wonder; more than a year of the kind of grooming and dressing that a princess receives had brought her to a perfection of physical exquisiteness. She wore a long, full gown of white brocade with some sort of brilliants that caught the light, and a tiara on her dark, graceful head. The Crown Prince, in white tie and tails, with his bright orders, was handsome, confident and gracious. The President and Mrs. Eisenhower I felt to be two very simple, sincere, honest and good people. The moment in which we clasped hands and spoke was quickly over; for the rest of the evening I was one of a large and interested group of spectators; I think my eyes seldom moved from the Crown Prince, though in the course of the evening I did have a chance to exchange a few brief, mutually congratulatory words with Dr. Koizumi.

At dinner the President made a fatherly speech of welcome to the Crown Prince, who replied with grace and deference, a young man to a distinguished older man. After dinner there was "An evening with Gershwin," thanks to the U.S. Marine Band, in the East Room, before the party broke up at ten-thirty or thereabouts.

To Marjorie Stewart, with whom for more than thirty years I have carried on a lighthearted correspondence, I sent a postcard: "I have the honor to inform you that I dined at the White House with the aid of 5 gold forks, 3 gold knives and 2 gold spoons."

Three days later I was in New York at the airport meeting the plane that brought the Crown Prince and Princess Michiko from Washington. During the four days they spent in New York, I was to see them several times, in both formal and informal circumstances and once, for half an hour on the morning before they left, alone. The Japan Society dinner was much like the one that had been given for the Crown Prince seven years earlier. This time the royal guests stayed in the Waldorf Towers instead of at the Pierre, and though General MacArthur did not come down to the dinner, at some time during the four days the Crown Prince went to make a call upon him.

Their program in New York was filled with the engagements that visiting royalty is subject to, a mixture of things that they really enjoy—such as the Crown Prince's visit to the Bronx Zoo and Princess Michiko's to a famous toy store to buy a present to take home to the baby—and of the things that must be done because they are always done or because someone's image would be damaged if they were not. They went through them smilingly with apparent pleasure. On Sunday evening the Crown Prince and Princess Michiko gave an "informal dinner" in their suite at which there were just six guests, most of whom knew each other well: Princess Michiko's brother, who was then a student at Yale, Shinzo Koizumi, Tatsuo Takaki, Esther Rhoads and I. It was a time of easy, intimate talk and laughter, of anecdotes of their trip, and of the showing of a number of photographs of the baby, Prince Naruhito, which the proud parents had brought with them. He was a beautiful child, and I was happy to see that their new palace was built so that their children could be brought up close to them. All through the time of their visit, there had been other visitors also in New York; Khrushchev and Castro had come to the meeting of the United Nations Assembly, and New York's police had been busy guarding the roped-off street in which Khrushchev's hotel was, and in the newspapers the presence of the Crown Prince and Princess Michiko had to share headlines with the antics of the Communist leaders. This was the time that Khrushchev took off his shoe and banged his desk with it, and Castro cooked his own meals in his hotel in Harlem. This too we talked about.

That night I stayed in the Waldorf Towers as the guest of the Crown Prince, and the next morning, before we all went to the airport to see them off, I had leisurely talks with Shinzo Koizumi and with Tatsuo Takaki as well as with the Crown Prince and Princess themselves.

From New York they went to Seattle, where they stopped for a day or two before they flew back to Japan and their son. Virginia Barnett, a friend of mine who lived there, wrote me of the impression that the Crown Prince made on her husband. "There was a public meeting in the University Plaza and the Prince gave a brief address, met the consular corps, etc. Arthur was really very much moved by the young man's appearance and demeanor—he tried to put it into words and said, 'There's a fineness and a sweetness about him that is very unusual. He seems so young, so direct, so artless.' Arthur said that the Prince read his brief address and then in a very quiet, gracious way simply looked at the throng as if to wish it well, without any self-consciousness or false dignity. And if you realize that Arthur has all the feeling of the Irish for royalty in general you can see what a truly deep and unusual response and reaction his was."

Early in 1961 I decided to write the biographical novel about John Donne that had lain in the back of my mind ever since the early 1940's. I had put it aside then, feeling that I was not yet ready, not mature enough, to write it. If I am not mature enough now, I said to myself at fifty-eight, I will never be. And so I got out my old notes and plunged into research again, fortunate in having, five minutes away by car, the library of Swarthmore College to draw upon. It was an ambitious project and often I quailed, but I found the research utterly absorbing and fascinating, and the writing a stretching experience.

On the twenty-third of March, 1961, a week after Violet's seventy-eighth birthday, we went to Yearly Meeting, which was held in the big old meetinghouse at Fourth and Arch Streets. It was a dark day with rain pouring down in sheets, driven by the wind, the kind of weather that Philadelphia traditionally endures during "Quaker Week." After the morning session we found the lunchroom in the meetinghouse overcrowded, so we splashed up the street a little way to an old restaurant famous for excellent steaks and sea food. At the end of the meal, getting up to go out, Violet tripped over an unlighted little step beside our table and fell.

There followed a nightmare hour of which every detail is as clear in my memory as if it happened yesterday. It was obvious from the first that she was badly injured; entirely conscious, she lay there unmoving, self-contained, quiet, trusting me to manage. The restaurant's only contribution was to urge that she be hoisted up into a chair so as to facilitate the serving of lunches; I was determined that she should not be moved until I could get a doctor. The telephone was in the basement. At this point Mary Hoxie Jones appeared from another room and stood guard while I telephoned the hospital where I thought our friend and physician, Emma Bevan, was likely to be at that hour. At the moment that I was connected, the switchboard operator saw her walking in at the door. She came at once.

After Violet had reached the hospital and the X rays were taken, we knew that she had fractured her pelvis and the femur close to the hip joint. The next two weeks were anxious ones. The usual operation and insertion of a pin were impossible because of the fragmented bones and the condition of her heart; a cast was impractical: the doctors decided that sandbags and traction with a prospect of six months in bed were the only means open to them. Violet's will to live, her acceptance of the situation, her uncomplaining endurance of pain, her fortitude, her unquenchable humor were beyond praise. The first thing she said when she realized what had happened to her was, "Now I won't see spring come in the garden." The first two months of her sentence she spent in the hospital. Late in May I brought her home.

The preparations had taken most of two weeks. Her big sleigh bed was taken down and stored away, a hospital bed with an overhead structure of pulleys and bars set up in its place, nurses, after many false hopes and disappointments, lined up. Our McDonald cousins, with imaginative generosity, brought an air conditioner and a television set with remote control. Eshin Nishimura, the young Japanese Zen Buddhist priest who was studying at Pendle Hill, came in and made a welcoming flower arrangement for her bureau, where she could see it from the bed. On one of the most dazzling of May mornings, when roses were out in the garden and tall blue squills and the late tulips, the ambulance backed into the drive and Violet was carried up the narrow, twisting stairs strapped to a tilted stretcher.

The nurse whom I had finally got for the most important shift, seven to three, was a handsome, slender young woman, taut as a fine wire, half Cherokee Indian, half Negro. For the next three months, through one of the hottest and most humid of Philadelphia summers, Elode Gregory was our strength. Under Emma Bevan's watchful direction, Mrs. Gregory's indefatigable care and skill brought Violet through. She had grown up in an Indian settlement on Chincoteague Island, off the coast of Virginia, where the wild ponies are rounded up and sold each year, and her stories of her childhood and of her Indian heritage carried Violet over many a weary stretch.

After the first shock and anxiety were over, I went on with my life in a necessarily withdrawn and restricted way. For several weeks we lost the nurse between Mrs. Gregory and the night nurse, and could not find another who could get herself to our house, a mile from public transportation. I perforce filled in, which was not easy either for Violet or for me. Nursing is not one of my gifts, but I learned to wind the ace bandages and adjust the traction.

Friends were indefatigably kind. Elizabeth and Genevieve came constantly to visit the patient and do things for me; I had a standing invitation to drop in for a meal at their house without notice whenever I could slip away. Visitors came from Germantown, from Wayne, Wilmington, and from Pendle Hill. There was a steady flow of letters, cards and presents. Eshin Nishimura came in often to make his flower arrangements in Violet's room where she could watch him do it; he brought his own materials with him, grasses, wild flowers, branches of shrubbery that he picked around the edges of Pendle Hill. Books, as always, were a lifesaver. Looking as pretty as ever she had looked, with her white hair, her blue eyes, pink cheeks and pink bed jacket, Violet lay propped against the pillows and read a book a day. I went to the local library once a week and brought home a market basket full.

Helen Campbell, from Northern Ireland, who had retired from her teaching at the Training College in Belfast, where she was a pioneer in nursery school education, and come to Pendle Hill as a Fellow, was a frequent visitor, and during those months a lasting friendship developed between us. She was an amateur ornithologist of note, knowing more about American birds than ninety-nine out of a hundred Americans do; often in the early mornings we went birding in the Swarthmore Woods or—if we had more time—in the Tinicum Nature Sanctuary near the Delaware.

For the time I found the Donne book too arduous and demanding, but in my research I had come on ideas for a book for children in the same period. So I turned to this, and in the mornings, while Mrs. Gregory was in the house, I worked on a story about a harum-scarum, theater-mad boy named Andrew who met Shakespeare and acquired a direction to his life. Andrew was a great source of solace to me that summer, and when in the fall I wrote the last words I called the book *I Will Adventure*.

By the end of August Violet's courage and patience and the good care she had had bore fruit; first she sat up and dangled her legs over the end of the bed; then she stood on one foot and gently swung the other. She was ready now to go to a Rehabilitation Center for extensive therapy.

Yuki Takahashi had been for two years at Pendle Hill, which is as long as students are encouraged to remain there; she was eager however for another year, for she was engaged in translating Howard Brinton's *Friends for Three Hundred Years* into Japanese. So I asked her if she would live with us, as a member of the family, attending what courses she wished to at Pendle Hill, working on her translation and, especially, being with Violet at times when I needed to be out. She agreed, and for the next ten months was a helpful and cheerful presence in our house. With a Taiwanese student to keep her company, she stayed there while Violet was in the Rehabilitation Center and I went off to Mount Desert to visit Fran Fox for three weeks, to rest and drink deep of beauty and peace and the joys of friendship.

When I returned I brought Violet back from the hospital, where she had endured a rigorous time, hating every moment of it, but achieving what she went for, the ability to move about again freely. In a few months she was able to discard her cane and to walk with only a slight limp. So it was that after a second winter of intensive research on Donne, I was able to go to England in the spring, to glean what more I could in the British Museum and the Public Record Office and to visit the places where he lived and worked.

Late in March, leaving Yuki with Violet, I embarked on the *Sylvania*, seen off by Marjorie Stewart, and met in London by

Fran, who had preceded me by a month. London, after rather a gray, rough crossing, was gay and sparkling, with daffodils bright in the window boxes, the streets full of cars and hurrying people, the women in stovepipe hats with their eyelids painted blue or green or purple. I was surprised to see a glass and chrome skyscraper towering over Westminster Abbey and new roads with "fly-overs" bursting out all over.

Throughout April I worked in London, while Fran flew off visiting friends and going on cruises put on by the National Trust for Scotland, now and then returning for a week end with me—the most satisfactory way for two people of similar but diverging interests to travel together.

Most weekday mornings I walked down Berkeley Street to Piccadilly and took a bus to the British Museum, where I mingled with rabbis and beatniks and less colorful scholarly folk waiting for books to arrive from the vast recesses behind the reading room. One day as I waited I took down one of the volumes of *Notes and Queries* from a nearby wall and riffled idly through the pages; a call slip fluttered out, signed several years before with the name of a girl whom I had known in college and not seen since, though I had heard that she came to England regularly to do research in her field. It was an unusual name, and there was no doubt that it was the same person, improbable though it was that in this vast dune of learning two infinitesimal grains of sand should meet in this way, and I felt a reminiscent flash of youth and laughter.

Soon I caught on to the trick of putting in my requests for books when I left in the afternoon at five; presumably someone scurried about all night finding them, for when I arrived at the opening of the doors next morning, my books were there waiting for me.

From the British Museum I went to the Public Record Office in Chancery Lane, a very much smaller place with quicker service. The material there is limited to public records and I found little about Donne, but I realized that I had hit a gold mine for Flora MacDonald, whose biography I was planning to write next. The Loyalty Papers, of which I had seen photostat copies in North Carolina, were all there, and more. There were also many documents having to do with the Rising of '45, including letters from "Butcher" Cumberland saying what he thought of the Scots and also, most interesting of all, his account of the capture and questioning of Flora. I realized that when I was actually ready to work on her biography I should have to come back again, and I found the necessity pleasing.

Nearly across from the Public Record Office was Lincoln's Inn, where Donne had been a student in his youth, and where in his religious maturity he had been elected Divinity Reader, charged with the duty of preaching fifty sermons a year to a highly critical body of students. I walked through the fine early Tudor gatehouse and applied to the porter for admission to the Old Hall. He put on his top hat, took a large iron key and opened it for me. First built in 1492, it still had the hole in the roof for the smoke from the center fire to escape; it was large, dim and ancient. Here Donne, a nineteen-year-old student, had written his first *Epithalamium*, a poem that is now conceded by scholars to have been a spoof for a mock wedding staged as part of the Winter Revels, yet still a poem with some beautiful lines and a freshness and zest that promised much for his future work. The Chapel, which was designed by Inigo Jones to replace an older one, was known to Donne in his later, soberer years; indeed, Donne had taken a leading part in raising money for it, had laid the cornerstone and preached the dedication sermon.

On the days when the sun was out and the April wind not too knifelike, I went out to see places that had some connection with Donne, to Waltham Cross, to look at the gateway that was all that was left of Theobalds, the place that had been one of James I's favorite houses, where Donne had been often in attendance and where the King had at last told him that he would help him to become a preacher but not to any of the positions of state that he wanted. It was not easy to reconstruct in imagination the seventeenth-century scene of royalty and nobles and hangers-on all in brilliant silks and velvets, of guards with pikes, of horses and carts and ladies in litters, in the midst of the commonplace modern scene of trams and shops and neat little semidetached houses with pansies and lobelias in their small lawns. Serene in the midst of the traffic stood the beautiful 1291 Eleanor's Cross, one of the only three left of the thirteen that Edward I put up to mark the funeral procession of his wife Eleanor of Castile from Northampton to Westminster Abbey. Equally difficult to reconstruct was Whitehall Palace, which for 230 years spread along the Thames from Charing Cross to Westminster. Now all that is left of it is the banqueting hall from a window of which Charles I stepped out to the scaffold, eighteen years after Donne's death.

What I wanted especially to see was Loseley Park, a few miles out of London, where Donne's lovely young wife, Anne, had been born and brought up, but it was not open to the public until June. A friend of Fran's, Sir Eric Machtig, came to my rescue; he wrote to the owner and asked if it might be opened especially for me. On a beautiful April morning Sir Eric came for me in his car and drove me down to see it. Situated in the open country three miles southwest of Guildford, it is an Elizabethan mansion that has been lived in continuously by descendants of the man who first built it out of stone from Waverley Abbey, which had been destroyed in Henry VIII's Reformation. The grandson of the builder was Sir George More, the irate father of Anne; he had his presumptuous son-in-law, John Donne, imprisoned in the Fleet and dismissed from his post of secretary of Sir Thomas Egerton, Lord Keeper of the Privy Seal. Anne was brought home in disgrace and kept there until John, ruined but determined to have his wife, won his lawsuit and took her away from Loseley. We approached the long, low, handsome building, oriel-windowed, by a driveway across the fields past the brick buildings of the "home farm" and the company, "Cedar Homes Limited," by which the present owner, Mr. James More-Molyneux, is enabled to keep up his expensive ancestral home, in one wing of which he lives with his young family.

Over the front door were the More arms, with the punning moor hens and the sober motto, *Vinca sat vincere*. We were met by Mrs. More-Molyneux, attractive, modern and young, with three small children at her heels who took a look at us and vanished. She led us through the entrance hall with its "screens" and stairs to the minstrel's gallery above, to the great hall, which had paneling brought from Henry VIII's palace, Nonesuch, and portraits of Mary Queen of Scots, James I and Anne of Denmark, Anne Boleyn, Edward VI, and Queen Elizabeth I, by Zucchero, looking very stern. She had visited Loseley three times, leaving behind her cushions for two maid of honor chairs (very low and wide) which she had embroidered herself with colored silks still bright and fresh. Even more interesting to me than the royal portraits were those of Anne's father, narrow of face with a pointed beard, and her red-haired, red-bearded brother, Robert. I had hoped to find one of Anne herself, but there was none. There was beautiful and rare furniture in the rooms that we saw and much of historical interest, but the portrait of Anne's father was for me the high point. "By nature passionate," wrote one of his sons-in-law of him, "yet in his wisdom he conquered that passion so much that you would think him to be of a mild disposition. He was little of stature but of great abilities. . . . He was little and good." Certainly he was not mild in his dealings with John Donne, but perhaps, like other fathers before and since, he learned something from sad experience. He and John were reconciled before Anne's death, at thirty-two, of her thirteenth pregnancy several years before Sir George's own death.

The house was built facing north in order to avoid the prevailing breezes in case they should bring plague with them. Bubonic plague has been so nearly conquered by modern medicine and sanitation that we forget what a menace it was at one time. Between the famous Great Plagues of 1349 and 1665, there were other serious outbreaks; it was in Donne's time one of the everyday threats to life, along with famine and battle, murder and sudden death, as airplane crashes and traffic accidents and bombing incidents are today.

As always since my years in Japan, I found wherever I went Japanese friends or people who became friends because they too had had some close connection with that country. I spent a happy week end in Cheltenham with George and Edith Braithwaite, Quakers who had lived many years in Japan before the war and had had a cottage at Hayama near the Imperial Villa where they had often seen the princesses as little girls playing on the beach. I found Dr. Koizumi's daughter and son-in-law, Kayo and Tadashi Akiyama, who had been posted for two years to the London branch of the Mitsui Bank, ensconced in a house made out of an eighteenth-century chapel just off Belgrave Square. They gave a dinner party for me, to which came other Japanese friends, Chise Mita, who was Dr. Koizumi's niece, and her husband, and Mrs. Matsudaira's son and daughter-in-law. With Major-General F. S. G. Piggott, who was president of the Japan Society of London, I had had a lively correspondence about *Windows for the Crown Prince* and the visit of the Crown Prince to England in 1953; his daughter Juliet was my London literary agent. Now I met them both for the first time. General Piggott, who had been for many years the very popular military attaché at the British Embassy in

Tokyo, was now retired; old and frail and very gentle, he was one of the slight, round-faced, clipped-moustached English officers of the old school. They knew many of the same people as I did, and we had most happy and satisfying talks together.

Twice Fran returned and we went off for a weekend together, to Canterbury for Easter, where we had sunny skies and a temperature of 63, which the newspapers headlined as "hot." The Easter service in the cathedral was headed by the Archbishop in his robes bearing his golden crook and followed by a great procession not only of churchmen but the Lord Mayor of Canterbury and all his aldermen in somewhat moth-eaten eighteenth-century costumes. The Red Dean, who seemed to enjoy being seen, managed, by doubling back along the side aisles, to march past four times. On Easter afternoon, having heard that Godmersham Park was open, we took a bus to that lovely Georgian brick house belonging to Jane Austen's brother Edward which Jane used to visit. The grounds were at their springtime loveliest, and we wandered all afternoon through acres of daffodils, narcissi, hyacinths and primroses under the great trees in the park and in the intimate walled gardens just beginning to awaken. Violet and I were both "Janeites" and I think that of all my adventures on this trip, this visit to the place which had meant so much to Jane Austen was the one that she envied me the most.

The last weekend in April Fran and I spent in Cornwall with a rented car, a Ford Anglia which we named Angela, and which Fran drove because I was suffering, as I did for nearly a year, from tendonitis in my wrist, a new name for old-fashioned writer's cramp. I had taken too many notes with a ball-point pen. It is a painful ailment, and it took me the better part of a year and treatments of many kinds to get over it. We went to see George and Janet Whitney at Saint Mawes, where they were living in "South Cottage," a tiny old house on the "front" with a most lovely view across the harbor. Janet had published a novel, *Not for Ransom*, the year before, and George was painting portraits and landscapes.

After Cornwall I went to Ireland, to spend ten days with Helen Campbell roaming about in her little car, from Belfast to Dunfanaghy in Donegal, to Columcille, where St. Patrick was born, to Sligo for Yeats, to Clonmacnoise for the ruined twelfth-century churches along the River Shannon, and to Dublin for Yearly Meeting. Ireland was a revelation to me; I had had no idea of its almost mystical beauty, its variety, its birds, its moors and flocks of sheep with the vivacious lambs, or of the bitterness of the history that lies so close beneath the surface. We walked on the walls of Derry, said to be the only unspoiled medieval city walls in Europe, and looked down into the Bogside, where, Helen told me, the Roman Catholic minority lived crowded together in poverty and bitterness. Since then the word *Bogside* has exploded into headlines all over the world. We lay on the rocks on the edge of a cliff looking over at the immense bulk of Slieve League, with the breakers white against his feet far down below, and Helen told me that it was here that the legendary lovers, Grania and Diarmuid, rested in their flight.

We stayed one night at a hotel in Athlone, intending to be off early the next morning so as to stop at Clonmacnoise on the way to lunch in Dublin and the opening of Yearly Meeting. The hotel advertised breakfast from eight to ten, and so that night before we went to bed we "booked" ours for eight. But when we came down in the morning, there was no one at all to be seen—no hall porter, no one at the desk, nobody in the large, empty kitchen where the huge stove was covered with a metal hood. Wandering about disconsolately looking for help, we found a small room where two men sat drinking whisky and talking. They were not up early, it developed, they were up late. They had not been to bed. They were actors who had come to Athlone to judge a drama contest the night before, and they were still hashing it all over. Springing up from their easy chairs, they gallantly volunteered to get breakfast for us. The hooded stove defeated them, but in a surprisingly short time they had routed out a maid and we were seated at a table in the dining room, with a pot of coffee before us and plates of bacon and eggs. At least that was what Helen and I had. The more vocal of our rescuers—the other one had disappeared—was breakfasting on whisky and fried bread. His name, it developed, was Ray McAnally, and he was on the board of the Abbey Theatre in Dublin and an actor of note.

"And why," he inquired, "do you have to be up so early?"

We wanted to be in Dublin in time for lunch and hoped to see Clonmacnoise on the way.

"My God," he cried, thumping the table, "why do you care about lunch if you can see Clonmacnoise?"

This led to an interesting discussion about time. Different people, I had discovered—it had, indeed, been brought forcefully to my attention in Japan—approach time in very different ways from the tense, time-ridden, time-is-money attitude of the Americans. The Irish, who look on nine-thirty as a sensible hour for arising in the morning, have a relaxed way with time, Mr. McAnally told me, because they are Catholics; they know they will all go to heaven in the end, and so there is no hurry about anything. From there we went on to Quakerism and the Inner Light and other religious and philosophical topics, and at nine-thirty, when the dining-room had begun to fill up, we were still sitting there, talking. We did get to Clonmacnoise and to the opening of Yearly Meeting and we had enough lunch to keep the breath of life going. The next afternoon I flew to Scotland to meet Fran for a National Trust Castles and Islands cruise of a week among the Hebrides and the lochs of the west coast.

Two weeks later Helen joined us in Edinburgh, we rented another Ford, which we named Angela II, and went back to the western Highlands and to Skye. By now I knew definitely that my next book after the Donne would be the biography of Flora which I had first determined to write in Chapel Hill in 1930, and though I had been twice to Skye, I wanted to go again and this time to get to the north of the island, to see the home where she lived for several years after her marriage to the son of MacDonald of Kingsburgh.

We covered a lot of very beautiful ground. We drove through Glencoe, that narrow pass enclosed with towering mist-swathed mountains, and saw beside the rushing stream here and there a small whitewashed stone croft of the type in which Campbell guests stayed with trusting MacDonalds and at a prearranged signal rose up and murdered their hosts. (I did not realize quite how pointedly Fran and I commented on the dark deeds associated with the name of Campbell until several years later Helen told me that she wished she had known then, as she was at pains to find out subsequently, some of the things that MacDonalds had done to Campbells.) We had a picnic lunch on a grass-grown rocky point overlooking Loch Duich, with the Five Sisters of Kintail in the background. Every day, in fact, we took a picnic lunch, and Helen, who was both skilful and indefatigable in such things, built a fire of whins and other bits of wood that she could find and boiled a kettle both for lunch and tea. We went as far north as Kinlochbervie and came back to Edinburgh by Garve and Inverness, spending a night each at Muchalls and at Kellie Castles, with friends of Fran's, whom I too had known on the cruise, but in the middle we had three days on Skye.

We made our headquarters at the Sligachan Inn, from which we drove south to Armadale, where Flora's mother and stepfather had lived and she had spent part of her girlhood, and where also Violet and I had started our long ride to Portree that summer evening nearly thirty years earlier; west to Dunvegan Castle, my third visit there, but this time I was especially aware of the Flora MacDonald relics and interested to see the brooch made out of a lock of Prince Charles's hair; and north beyond Portree to Floddigarry, where behind a Victorian hotel is the low, white stone cottage where the first five of her seven children were born, and from which she had a glorious view of the waters of the Minch, of Floddigarry Isle and the blue mountains on the mainland in the distance. We saw too her monument on the other side of the island, near the place where she brought Prince Charles ashore disguised as her maid after their perilous night crossing from Uist and hid him in a cave while she went to Mugstodt House and diverted the suspicions of the soldiers who were there to hunt for him. Kingsburgh House, where she and her husband, Allan, were living when they were visited by Dr. Johnson and Boswell, is no longer standing, but we saw where it had been, and more important, got the lay of the land, the feel of the surroundings.

Less than a month later I was at home again at Wallingford, greatly refreshed and stimulated, and eager to be writing. I found the house serene and ordered and welcoming, the cool of its stone walls swathed in June. Violet and Yuki were well. Violet was moving about almost as easily as she had done before her fall. We went to Cove Ledge for August and part of September, where every morning I wrote away on my novel about John Donne.

Soon after our return to Wallingford, I had my sixtieth birthday.

7.

Sixty and Beyond

SIX DECADES are a good round number. At sixty one has reached a sort of continental divide, or at least some little knoll from which one can survey the path over which one has come, ask oneself what has been the meaning of it all, look at the several people one has been. It seems to be a good point at which to tie up the threads of this book. Not that I had any intention on my sixtieth birthday to stop writing; I hoped not to stop growing; I considered nothing finished except perhaps middle age. Violet and I were to have more trips together: another summer in Maine, a trip to North Carolina in June, 1964, to visit the Brookses in their eyrie west of Asheville, to return to Chapel Hill, to follow the trail of Flora MacDonald among the sand-hill pines and to Moore's Creek Bridge, where the fatal battle was fought in 1776, and another trip, later the same summer, to London and Edinburgh for the Public Record Office and the National Library of Scotland, and to Belfast to see Helen Campbell and a little more of Ireland. But I do not want to write about Violet's second broken hip and first stroke or about the years of suffering and utter weariness that closed down over her until her death in December, 1969. Sixty seems to me a good place to stop.

This book is not, and has not been intended to be, a comprehensive account of my life. I have not told all. I have tried to avoid confession, gossip, historical fiction and homiletics. Much is omitted. Some friends whom I have loved are not mentioned here. I have said nothing about men whom I might have married and did not. There are institutions which I have watched with great interest and with which I have had a more than casual touch: Bryn Mawr College, of which I have been a trustee for twenty years; the International Christian University in Tokyo, on whose

Foundation Board in New York I sit and of whose Women's Committee I was for five years national chairman. Of the places to which I have gone to speak and the people I have encountered there, I have said nothing. Nor am I going to write about the selling of the Wallingford House to Pendle Hill and my return to Germantown to live in a large apartment complex built on the old Strawbridge place, from which used to come the yellow-wheeled carriages that waited at Queen Lane Station when I was a child. I have come full circle; I am living three blocks west of the house (now vanished) where I was born, two blocks north of the house in which I grew up. This book has been concerned with the four main threads of which the fabric of my life has been woven, with my writing, my marriage, my contacts with Japan, my sister. The one that still remains is the writing thread. Having written that, I stop to qualify it. One cannot push an analogy too far. I shall go again to Japan. The past lives on; the person that one was once and is no longer still lives in some other slice of time, not recoverable but not lost.

In any case, I am a writer still. The novel about John Donne, *Take Heed of Loving Me*, was published in January, 1964; *Flora, A Biography*, in early 1966, and *I, Roberta*, a novel that welled up out of my New Jersey background and the things that as a child I used to overhear my mother and big sister talking about, in 1967. I have ideas for more books after I finish this one. A writer, like a painter, a photographer, a musician, does not retire.

That I have never been the writer that I wanted to be has not greatly diminished my satisfaction in the work of writing. Every book has fallen short of my vision for it, with the possible exceptions of *Adam of the Road* and *I, Roberta*, both of which were escape books. With Adam I escaped from the dark shadow of modern war into the thirteenth century, and with Roberta I slipped out of a household of illness and anxiety into a milieu of family memories in which the problems had nothing at all to do with my own, except as the rather painful process of examining one's own life is everybody's problem. In both Adam and Roberta I had characters who seemed to have lives of their own that unfolded before my interested eyes and whom I knew as if they had been living people. Their books were theirs, not mine, and I was on the whole content with the way they managed them. But all my other books have sooner or later come to a stage where I have groaned and anguished, thinking it was never going to be right. "It isn't any good," I would mourn to Violet three quarters of the way through; "I'm simply not up to this book." And she would answer comfortingly or wearily or briskly as the case might be, "You always say that and it always turns out all right." But when it was finished, in spite of her assurances I have felt disappointed because it was not what I had seen in my mind beforehand.

I always, up until *Flora*, read my books aloud to Violet as I went along. A writer needs one listener whose literary discernment he can trust, to whom he can read his work in progress. It is not criticism as such that is needed, though a pointed question is often useful, not even praise, though a spontaneous exclamation of pleasure is uplifting; it is the quality of the attention, receptive, alert, entire, that makes the perfect listener. Reading aloud to such an audience, one hears one's ineptitudes and clumsinesses without being told of them and marks them for correction; following the listener's expression, one sees when a passage is not clear; or perhaps one simply realizes that something has gone flat. But the expectancy, the implied interest and respect give one heart to go on struggling to find ways to get the inner vision somehow onto paper. All of my life, from my earliest efforts up until *Flora*, Violet had given me this sort of listening.

In spite of the anguish and the disappointment, I have never contemplated not writing. There must be many people like me, who are not first-rate writers but who are born writers, who write because we would rather write than do anything else, because we are fulfilled while writing, because in some obscure way we feel guilty when we are not writing, as if this were the task set before us and we must be about it. I could not believe James Boyd when he told me that he liked everything about being a writer but the writing itself, and I thought he must be joking. I like the actual writing, and the times when it goes well, when everything else fades away and one feels as if one were taking dictation or simply describing a scene that unfolds before one's inner eye, are pure heaven.

I have found that these times are most likely to develop when I have managed to get into touch with a deeper level of my mind, the writing self down below the top layer. I do not want to be whimsical about it, and I do not mean exactly what Barrie called M'Connachie and I. A. R. Wylie, George. It is not another person down in the cellar. Nor is it simply dropping a bucket into a well, as E. M. Forster described it, and pulling it up full of water. It is more like Faulkner's walking around after his characters and watching what they do. It is, or so it seems to me, a getting access to another dimension of one's psyche, where one dwells in another world among the people of one's imagination simultaneously with the present ordinary active life, or attending to the play of moving images across the screen of one's mind. Then when I sit down at my desk, if the immersion has been adequate, the writing that day is simply the describing of what I have inwardly seen and heard.

Similarly, but more narrowly and directly, the unconscious, the deep mind, can be drawn on for help in the solution of a particular problem, the resolution of a dilemma. To give a very simple example: I was dissatisfied with the working out of a chapter in *I Will Adventure*. I rewrote it three or four times, and still it was static. At length I realized that this was a matter for my deep self. I expressed in words, not written but articulated in my mind, my need for an incident that should forward both the character of the boy and the action of the story, and then I put my papers away and dismissed the book from my mind. The next morning I began to write a little behind the passage where the trouble had begun; I kept on writing, the solution unfolded itself in a bit of action that I had not till then conceived of at all. It seemed to me, when finished, exactly what I wanted at that juncture in the story.

This is, I am quite aware, nothing new, nothing that I invented. It is the creative process, about which so much has been learnedly written. The mind meets a problem, analyzes, examines, assembles all the pertinent and available knowledge—and leaves it; at some later and perhaps unexpected moment—Archimedes in the bathtub—the mind throws out the solution. I am not claiming to have discovered anything unusual; it is common knowledge; but I did find it out for myself in the days when I wrote in my end of our attic in Chapel Hill and Morgan was working at his end. I put it tentatively into practice, and when I read Mary Austin's *Everyman's Genius* I knew with the joy of recognition what she was talking about.

Like other writers I have had "blocks," arid stretches when even though I had ideas that seemed to me valid and worth developing I was not able to write, when the streams refused to flow, the pictures in my mind would not unroll; when everything stopped and I would sit paralyzed and miserable before my desk, or would write sentences and paragraphs so pedestrian, so wooden, so altogether without juice, that I could only tear them up in despair. Sometimes these periods have been of short duration; sometimes they would last for a year or more. Although theoretically I knew that this was a necessary part of the whole process, that I must give the springs time to fill up, that I needed rest and refreshment in the deepest places within me, still I felt also the stultifying fear that perhaps the block would never end, perhaps I was not going to be able ever to write again, perhaps I was written out. And the fear itself reinforced and prolonged the paralysis. But always, ultimately, the time has come when some chance sight, some new idea, some conversation with an understanding person, has brought a feeling of lightness, a sense of something stirring, and I have grasped my pen and made a start; cautiously at first and then with a rush I have known it was going to be all right, I could do it. Like George Herbert, I could have cried out, "Who would have thought my shrivelled heart/Could have recovered greenness? . . . After so many deaths I live and write. . . ."

Though I have had to recognize that I am not the writer I hoped to be, I have always written as well as I could; I have never given it less than my best, thinking to spare the effort or that something else might sell better. I have not written to order. What I have written has been written because an idea, an incident, or more often a character, real or imagined, has taken hold of my imagination, lingered in my mind, nudged me, until I have discharged it by means of a book.

I have had modest successes, occasionally a book for a time on the best-seller list; other books have sold moderately but steadily; a small but faithful public has read the newest book because they have liked previous ones. I have never needed a great deal of money, so that it has been possible for me to be one of the comparatively small number of writers in this country who make their living by their writing. And for this I have been profoundly grateful. The most fortunate people in this world, I am convinced, are those who can make their living by doing something that they enjoy doing, whatever it may be; teaching, art, business, the professions, gardening, carpentry, driving a truck, whatever it is that they really like to do.

I still look forward as well as back. In fact, I am quite sure that whatever the years may indicate, one never really feels old inside, perhaps never even really sure and experienced but always liable to be taken by surprise, still gauche and inadequate in areas where one has been so before. And like Ulysses one is sailing still into new waters, into the paths of all the western stars. . . .

I know great changes lie ahead. I am not afraid of change. I do not, as I once did, believe that every change must be for the good; such openness is an irrecoverable attribute of youth. On the other hand, I do not want to put things back the way they were. I should like to discriminate between bad change, necessary change, and desirable change. I know that I am on the far side of the generation gap and that the gap is real and wide and deep between those who can remember the Depression and the World Wars and those who have been born in the nuclear age. I do not think the young can hear me cheer them on as they crusade against war, against racial injustice, against poverty, and offer them, more faintly, my approval of their scorn of security. I am sure they do not wish to hear me murmur a question as to whether they are not perhaps sometimes a little volatile or wonder if they have the staying power necessary to unseat the well-mounted forces of greed and arrogance and inertia, or add my voice to theirs when they cry that through our exploiting of the natural world we are threatening its very life and the future of men on our planet. I know it is of no interest to them for me to say that sex without love seems to me pitiable, or that patience and perseverance work more lasting improvements than violence, or that there are better ways to mystical experience than blowing one's mind with drugs.

The long hair of the young does not disturb me in the least. There is nothing sacred about short hair, not even anything very time-honored. It is only about a hundred years that men have been cropping their hair. A photograph of my grandfather at twenty shows him with a bob that would have been much too long for a shingled girl of the twenties. Some of today's young men have beautiful hair, thick and wavy and shining. And long hair, of course, has the advantage of being an immediately visible symbol of an attitude, a rejection of today's culture, authority, values and shibboleths, and this is exactly why it is so disturbing to the generation which invented the crew cut—a hideous style if ever there was one. There is much to be said for having such an immediately apprehensible signal to show where one stands; it warns and repels the opposition, it informs and attracts the like-minded. It must have been equally disturbing to elderly Cavaliers with ringlets when the radical young Puritans began cutting their hair and wore with pride the scornful label Roundheads.

I am less cordial about beards, but that is because of my grandfather.

Even if I were seriously disturbed about long hair and beards, I should still forgive them because of two things that the young are saying. One is that love is the most important thing, and the other is tied up with it, that the goods of this earth can—and must—be shared with all. It is a long time since I heard my father say, "That kind of people all think they can have cars," and asked myself, "Why shouldn't they, if they can pay for them?" Now the young are saying, that kind of people should have all the good things, food, shelter, education, and also respect and consideration, whether they can pay for them or not. This is an idea that has a fiercely surging life within it, a volcanic life that is causing the earth to heave and tremble, that sooner or later will burst through the crust and change the face of the world. I am glad to be living in a time when such an idea takes hold.

As I look forward to the personal changes which inevitably lie ahead of me, I am not disturbed by them either. I know that there are compensations in growing old. Violet, as long as she was well, rejoiced in the sunny slopes of her old age, saying not once but many times, "I never realized how much I should enjoy it." It is not age itself one dreads so much as illness and pain, but even these do not last beyond what can be endured. I have loved—I love—life, but when the greatest change of all comes, the change we call death, I shall be ready. Or so I think now.

❋ Index